Lecture Notes in Artificial Intelligence   6789

Subseries of Lecture Notes

LNAI Series Editors

Randy Goebel
  University of Alberta, Edmonton, Canada
Yuzuru Tanaka
  Hokkaido University, Sapporo, Japan
Wolfgang Wahlster
  DFKI and Saarland University, Saarbrücken, Germany

LNAI Founding Series Editor

Joerg Siekmann
  DFKI and Saarland University, Saarbrücken, Germany

Argiro Vatakis   Anna Esposito
Maria Giagkou   Fred Cummins
Georgios Papadelis (Eds.)

Multidisciplinary Aspects of Time and Time Perception

COST TD0904 International Workshop
Athens, Greece, October 7-8, 2010
Revised Selected Papers

 Springer

Series Editors

Randy Goebel, University of Alberta, Edmonton, Canada
Jörg Siekmann, University of Saarland, Saarbrücken, Germany
Wolfgang Wahlster, DFKI and University of Saarland, Saarbrücken, Germany

Volume Editors

Argiro Vatakis
Cognitive Systems Research Institute, Athens, Greece
E-mail: argiro.vatakis@gmail.com

Anna Esposito
Second University of Naples and IIASS, Vietri sul Mare, Italy
E-mail: iiass.annaesp@tin.it

Maria Giagkou
Institute for Language and Speech Processing, Athens, Greece
E-mail: mgiagkou@ilsp.athena-innovation.gr

Fred Cummins
UCD School of Computer Science and Informatics, Dublin, Ireland
E-mail: fred.cummins@ucd.ie

Georgios Papadelis
Aristotle University of Thessaloniki, Greece
E-mail: papadeli@mus.auth.gr

ISSN 0302-9743   e-ISSN 1611-3349
ISBN 978-3-642-21477-6   e-ISBN 978-3-642-21478-3
DOI 10.1007/978-3-642-21478-3
Springer Heidelberg Dordrecht London New York

Library of Congress Control Number: 2011941859

CR Subject Classification (1998): I.2, J.4, F.4.1

LNCS Sublibrary: SL 7 – Artificial Intelligence

Typesetting: Camera-ready by author, data conversion by Scientific Publishing Services, Chennai, India

Printed on acid-free paper

Springer is part of Springer Science+Business Media (www.springer.com)

Preface

The idea of creating a multidisciplinary network of scientists working on time and time perception was entertained in 2007, was formulated as a proposal in 2008, and was realized in 2009, when funded by the European COST (European Cooperation in Science and Technology; www.cost.eu) agency under the title "TD0904: *Time In MEntaL activitY: theoretical, behavioral, bioimaging, and clinical perspectives (TIMELY)*" (www.timely-cost.eu). TIMELY just completed its first year of existence bringing together over 150 junior and senior scientists from 20 different countries.

This volume is the product of the first meeting of the TIMELY network that took place in Athens, Greece, during October 7–8, 2010. This 2-day international workshop on the "Multidisciplinary Aspects of Time and Time Perception" brought together scientists from different disciplines to present their work on time and its percept with the ultimate goal of setting the stage for communication among the different laboratories and foster future collaborations.

The reader of this volume will get a taste of some of the major research areas of time perception, different views on temporal experiences, different methodologies used for measuring one's time percept, and the interaction/relationship of time with other cognitive processes. The collection of papers in this volume covers topics under the four main themes of TIMELY: (Note that papers in this volume fall under two or more of the themes below, thus no theme categorization is adopted.)

A. *Conceptual analysis and measurement of time*: Currently, there is no common code of communication as to the different aspects of time perception. A debatable definition also leads to problematic measurement methodologies. Reaching an agreement regarding the conceptual analysis of time will also lead to more efficient and accurate measures of the human and animal time perception.

B. *Exploring factors associated with time perception variability*: High variability in time perception has been reported within and between individuals. This variability represents a barrier in understanding time perception. Thus, a close examination of various cognitive/biological processes in relation to time is needed.

C. *Extending time research to ecologically valid stimuli and real-world applications*: The majority of time perception research has focused on simple stimuli, necessitating the use of more informationally rich stimuli (e.g., music, action) for advancing time perception research and, thus, extending the results to real-world applications.

D. *Uncovering the neural correlates of time perception*: Advances in neuroimaging allow observation of the brain-in-action. It is necessary to identify the techniques appropriate for studying time perception in both animals and humans and for examining time distortions in specific neurological/psychiatric conditions and other impairments.

The TIMELY network and the volume you are now holding was funded and supported by COST and the people working for the ISCH (Individuals, Societies, Cultures, and Health) domain. I would like to thank Anna Esposito for initiating contact with publishers and Alfred Hofmann for giving us the opportunity to publish this volume with Springer. I am grateful to the co-editors of this volume (Anna Esposito, Maria Giagkou, Fred Cummins, and Georgios Papadelis) for their patience and detailed work with all the author contributions. I also thank all the authors that contributed to this volume and all the members of the TD0904 International Scientific Committee who provided insight and helpful recommendations as to the improvement of the papers that are now printed in this volume. Additionally, I am thankful to the School of Architecture for hosting the TIMELY meeting in Athens and G. Papadelis, F. Cummins, and M. Giagkou for assisting me with all the organizational details. My special thanks goes to Thanos Fouloulis for the technical support and his willingness to realize all my visions (TIMELY website, live broadcasting of talks, video recording etc.) and my students for always being there (Eliza Bakou, Konstantina Margiotoudi, Stamatis Paraskevas, and Ifigenia Pasiou). Finally, a warm thank you goes to all the members of TIMELY that were willing to support this network and that responded to all my calls with excitement and encouragement.

July 2011   Argiro Vatakis

Organization

International Advisory and Organizing Committee

Argiro Vatakis   Cognitive Systems Research Institute, Greece
Anna Esposito   Second University of Naples and IIASS,
    International Institute for Advanced
    Scientific Studies, Italy
Maria Giagkou   Institute for Language and Speech Processing,
    Research Centers "Athena", Greece
Fred Cummins   University College Dublin, Ireland
George Papadelis   Aristotle University of Thessaloniki, Greece

International Scientific Committee

Rossana Actis   University of Milano-Bicocca, Italy
David Alais   University of Sydney, Australia
Stanislava Antonijevic   National University of Ireland, Galway, Ireland
Valtteri Arstila   University of Turku, Finland
Fuat Balci   Koç University, Turkey
Lera Borodisky   Stanford University, USA
Bruce L. Brown   Queens College, USA
Domenica Bueti   University College London, UK
David Burr   University of Florence, Italy
Niko Busch   Centre de Recherche Cerveau & Cognition,
    France
Daniel Casasanto   Max Planck Institute for Psycholinguistics,
    The Netherlands
Nicola S. Clayton   University of Cambridge, UK
Sara Cordes   Boston College, USA
Fred Cummins   University College Dublin, Ireland
Barry Dainton   University of Liverpool, UK
Beatrice de Gelder   Tilburg University, The Netherlands
Yvonne Delevoye-Turrell   Laboratoire URECA, Univiversity of Lille Nord
    de France, France
George Dellatolas   INSERM, Université Paris Descartes, France
Valérie Doyère   Neurobiologie de l'Apprentissage, de la
    Mémoire et de la Communication,
    CNRS, France
Sylvie Droit-Volet   CNRS, UMR 6024, France
Anna Eisler   Stockholm University, Sweden

Anne Reboul	CNRS, UMR 6024, France
Leah Roberts	MPI for Human Cognitive and Brain Sciences, Germany
Katya Rubia	King's College London, UK
Maren Schmidt-Kassow	Johann Wolfgang Goethe University, Germany
Daniele Schön	CNRS, France
Charles Spence	Oxford University, UK
Catherine Stevens	University of Western Sydney, Australia
Elżbieta Szelag	Polish Academy of Sciences, Poland
Niels Taatgen	University of Groningen, The Netherlands
Barbara Tillmann	Université Claude Bernard-Lyon I, CNRS UMR 5020, France
Rolf Ulrich	University of Tübingen, Germany
Leon Van Noorden	IPEM, Belgium
Hedderik Van Rijn	University of Groningen, The Netherlands
Argiro Vatakis	Cognitive Systems Research Institute, Greece
Jiri Wackermann	Institute for Frontier Areas of Psychology and Mental Health, Germany
Petra Wagner	University of Bielefeld, Germany
Vincent Walsh	University College London, UK
John Wearden	Keele University, UK
David Whitaker	University of Bradford, UK
Marc Wittmann	University of Munich, Germany
Agnieszka Wykowska	University of Munich, Germany
Dan Zakay	Tel Aviv University, Israel

Sponsors

The following organizations supported the international workshop:

- European COST Action TD0904 "Time In MEntaL activitY: theoretical, behavioral, bioimaging and clinical perspectives (TIMELY)" (www.timely-cost.eu)
- School of Architecture, National Technical University of Athens, Greece
- Institute for Language and Speech Processing, Athens, Greece

Table of Contents

Further Steps in the Science of Temporal Consciousness?

Valtteri Arstila

Department of Behavioral Sciences and Philosophy,
University of Turku, Finland
valtteri.arstila@utu.fi

Abstract. Temporal consciousness, the field that focuses on how time figures in our conscious states, is essentially interdisciplinary and has received attention from philosophers and psychologists alike. Nevertheless, there has been little cross-talk between these two disciplines. In this paper, I argue that the reason for this resides in crucially different interests: whereas philosophers have been preoccupied by phenomenology, psychologists have approached the field by downplaying the phenomenology and emphasizing their subjects' performance in various experiments. Despite this difference, existing research already suggests that there are fruitful grounds for interdisciplinary collaboration, should philosophers and psychologists aspire for it.

Keywords: Temporal consciousness, Husserl, James, Phenomenology.

1 Introduction

Our conscious states, in so far as they are brought about by neural processes, do not occur instantly. Furthermore, our experiences and perceptions themselves are not always only of instant events in the world. Quite contrary, sometimes the crucial features of stimuli that we perceive are temporal in nature. Examples of these include perceived temporal order, pace, and duration.

Investigation of our awareness of the previous temporal phenomena belongs to the field of temporal consciousness (I am following Barry Dainton's [1] terminology here), which is sometimes also called time consciousness. It can be defined as a field that focuses on how time and temporal properties figure both in consciousness and as contents of conscious states. This is a rather broad characterization, yet such is needed to address the multifaceted and interrelated issues in temporal consciousness.[1]

Although the topic is interdisciplinary in nature, interaction between philosophers and psychologists of temporal consciousness has remained scarce. This is somewhat surprising, given the state of affairs in similar issues. In consciousness studies, for example, philosophers make explicit use of many empirical research results and theories, and scientists have begun addressing the questions philosophers have posed

---

[1] Indeed, researchers from many different disciplines have tackled the topic and the field appears to be at the center of the interdisciplinary TD0904 (TIMELY) COST Action (www.timely-cost.eu).

A. Vatakis et al. (Eds.): Time and Time Perception 2010, LNAI 6789, pp. 1–10, 2011.

to them. In the topics of self, agency, and ownership, such interdisciplinary discussion is even more prominent, and this applies also to discussions related to social cognition. Regardless of these encouraging examples of cross-disciplinary influence, it is yet to occur in the topic of temporal consciousness (with late Francisco Varela's research [2,3] being a notable exception).

The overarching objective of this paper is to take steps toward bridging the gap between philosophers and psychologists of temporal consciousness. I will begin by explicating what I take to be the central reason why philosophers have not paid much attention to empirical research on temporal consciousness. Given that my background is in philosophy, I will not speculate on the reasons why scientists have not found the philosophy of temporal consciousness significant for their studies. It is nevertheless worth reminding oneself that one obvious reason for the lack of cross-talk between philosophy and psychology is that the research questions in one of the disciplines are not often relevant in the other. Instead of elaborating on the issue of crucially different research questions in the two disciplines, I will end this article by providing a brief discussion on the detailed topics where a common theme already exists. I hope that these few examples will illustrate why engaging in interdisciplinary discussion would in some cases be useful.

2   Two Approaches to Temporal Consciousness

Prima facie it appears that the issues in temporal consciousness can be approached in two different ways. On the one hand, one can ask what the relationship is between the temporal properties of a stimulus and our experiences and judgments about it. For example, how asynchronous do two stimuli need to be for us to perceive them as asynchronous? How do we estimate that certain duration time has passed? Given that these questions need to be approached through subjects' performance in various experiments, I call this a *performance-based approach*.

On the other hand, the issue of temporal properties as experienced can also be raised without any reference to the external world and the properties of stimuli. In this case the questions that one aims to address are whether we really experience phenomena with temporal properties and, if we do, then what is the nature of consciousness and conscious states that makes it possible? This approach can be called a *phenomenology-based approach*, as here the emphasis is on the question of whether temporal properties figure in contents of experiences in the same way as colors, tastes, and sounds do. That is, can we really experience temporal properties such as simultaneity, temporal order, and duration?

Although nothing prevents one from investigating the issues in temporal consciousness by combining both approaches (and in fact Paul Fraisse [4] and William James [5] did so), they can also be investigated independently. More importantly, as will be discussed below, it appears that this has happened and in accordance with the distinction between the disciplines: psychologists have focused on the performance-based approach and philosophers have adopted the phenomenology-based approach (with very little regard to the psychological mechanisms underlying the phenomenology).[2] As each line of research can be conducted without the other, cross-talk between these disciplines has been lacking.

Philosophers' preference for the phenomenology-based approach is understandable—after all, the other approach would require experimentation, which is not their forte! As a result, in their own research on the field of time consciousness, philosophers have instead focused on two interrelated questions concerning phenomenology.[3] The *first one* is whether we really experience temporal properties such as simultaneity, temporal order, and duration. Thomas Reid famously argued that this does not happen. He writes:

> It may be here observed, that, if we speak strictly and philosophically, no kind of succession can be an object either of the senses, or of consciousness; because the operations of both are confined to the present point of time, and there can be no succession in a point of time; and on that account the motion of a body, which is a successive change of place, could not be observed by the senses alone without the aid of memory. [6, p.235]

Reid argues thus that our consciousness, and the things we can be conscious of, are confined to momentary points in time—neither of them have any temporal width. Our experiences are static, motion-free snapshots that do not have any duration. Accordingly, Reid claims that we do not really experience succession, change, persistence, melody, or any other temporally extended phenomena. This also includes motion, which for Reid is merely a matter of succeeding snapshots. In fact, for Reid the stream of consciousness is mere continuous stream of momentary states of consciousness.

Although Reid's view of consciousness provides us with *the succession of experiences*, whether they are related to, say, visual stimuli or tones, it does not provide us with *experiences of succession* or melody. Our phenomenology suggests however that we can experience also succession and melodies.[4] Hence, those philosophers who draw their intuitions from such phenomenology (which includes

---

[2] It should be noted that the claim how philosophers prefer the phenomenology-based approach over the performance-based approach concerns only on how philosophers approach the topic of temporal consciousness. Accordingly, it makes no claims as regards to how philosophers approach the study of time. Indeed, on this latter topic conceptually-oriented and even logic-oriented approaches are commonly used, while there is little use for the phenomenology-based approach.

[3] Although it is safe to say that the topics philosophers have engaged with belong to this approach, no philosopher has been as explicit about the importance of temporal consciousness as Edmund Husserl, who is one of the most influential philosophers on temporal consciousness. He writes that "[the key themes in the phenomenology of time consciousness are] extremely important matters, perhaps the most important in the whole of phenomenology" [7, p.346]. That is, those philosophers who aim to understand our experiences better should give proper attention to issues such as how temporal phenomena can be experienced in the first place when considered from the point of view of a subject.

[4] Here we are reminded by Husserl's remark that the "duration of sensation and the sensation of duration are two very different things. And this equally true of succession. The succession of sensations and the sensation of succession are not the same." [7, p.12].

almost everyone) have disagreed with Reid's view. Thus, they maintain that our awareness and/or its contents are not confined to durationless moments. For example, William James writes in his much cited passage that

> the practically cognized present is no knife-edge, but a saddle-back, with a certain breadth of its own on which we sit perched, and from which we look in two directions into time. ... we seem to feel the interval of time as a whole, with its two ends embedded in it. [5, p.609-610]

In the light of our phenomenology, James suggests that we need to distinguish two notions of 'present'. On the one hand, there is the strict mathematical notion that is durationless, and on the other hand, there is the "cognized present" that possesses a brief duration. Since this latter notion refers to the phenomenon that is not really present in the mathematical sense but comprises a short temporal width, James calls it "specious present" (others have sometimes called it "subjective now"). Because our subjectively experienced present has a short temporal width, we can *experience* change, persistence, and other temporal phenomena.

It is important to note that accepting the idea that subjectively experienced *now* is not a durationless moment does not yet provide a proper explanation for the specious present nor for the experiences that this notion is supposed to help us explain. Consider the experience of succession for instance: those who disagree with Reid and endorse some notion of specious present maintain that our experiences can really have succession as their content. Accordingly, they argue that in one episode of experiencing or awareness, we can experience one stimulus succeeding the other because in such episodes both stimuli are somehow present (and thus their temporal relation itself can be experienced). But this sounds paradoxical: if we have one episode of an experience, and this is what we experience as *now*, then how can our experiences related to two stimuli not be experienced as simultaneous (and yet they cannot be, because otherwise we could not experience one succeeding the other)?

We are therefore led to *the second question* that the philosophers of temporal consciousness focus on: assuming that we do have temporally extended experiences (such as experiences of succession, melody, and persistence), then what must consciousness be like to provide us with them? Given that most philosophers do disagree with Reid, the debate over the philosophical issues in temporal consciousness has mainly centered on the best way to resolve the paradox resulting from specious present.[5]

It should be noted that one aspect of this debate is the apparently seamless flow of our consciousness, which James called the stream of consciousness. This is, of course, apparent in the sense that this is how the stream appears to us; the phenomenology of how one conscious state transforms to another. Its neural or metaphysical background

---

[5] Essentially, two different views have been proposed to resolve this paradox. The first one is the Extensionalist view that is often related to James's theory. According to this alternative, it is the episodes of experiencing that are temporally extended. The alternative is Husserl's Retentionalist view, where the episodes of experiencing are momentary but their contents are temporally spread.

does not need to be seamless. The stream of consciousness implies the passage of time because specious present describes what is experienced as now, whereas the stream of consciousness describes how these states, specious presents, follow each other. One specious present concerns the contents of our consciousness in one subjective now, whereas the stream of consciousness concerns the phenomenology of how one specious present changes to another. Philosophers, especially those in the Husserlian tradition, refer to this by the term 'temporality'—the continual background awareness of passing time.[6]

Despite the fact that the performance-based approach requires experimentation, and is thus not something that philosophers do themselves, one might think that results achieved through it would be useful in philosophers' endeavors. Yet, a brief look at the philosophical papers shows that empirical results are rarely (if ever) cited in them. In fact, it appears as if they silently agree with Husserl, who wrote:

> It might also make an interesting investigation to ascertain how the time that is posited as objective in an episode of time-consciousness is related to actual objective time, whether the estimations of temporal intervals correspond to the objectively real temporal intervals or how they deviate from them. But these are not tasks for phenomenology. [7, p.4]

The above may at first appear surprising but on closer inspection Husserl's indifference to the performance-based approach is actually quite understandable. As discussed above, the disagreement with Reid's view, and the resulting paradox, are at the crux of philosophical debates. This is significant for the topic at hand because most of the research done by psychologists is compatible both with Reid's and with his opponents' view. Accordingly, this research does not touch on the issues in which philosophers are interested in and, hence, the lack of philosophers' interest in the performance-based approach to temporal consciousness.

To see this more clearly, consider the temporal order tasks (where one of the two stimuli appears first). Arguably, to account for our performance in them does not require us to address the issue of whether we really experience succession or not. For example, what happens in the cases of succession could be explained with the help of memory: when the second stimulus is perceived, we still have a lingering memory of the stimulus that preceded it. Another possible way to account for the performance in temporal order tasks is simply by reference to some automatic, unconscious mechanisms.[7] Yet another possibility is that the performance mirrors our experiences of succession. In the first two cases, we would have succeeding experiences, whereas

---

[6] Two key issues concerning temporality can be used to separate the philosophical theories of time consciousness. The first one asks how much continuity there really is between two episodes of experiencing. The second one is: what establishes the continuity? Is it memory, contents of experience, self? What this means in practice is that philosophers tend to combine the issues at hand with the broader context of consciousness (and in many cases self-awareness too). Accordingly, the question they want to address is the general question of what the conditions for conscious experiences are.

[7] Much like the visual guidance of our actions is done by unconscious, dorsal processing and not by the conscious experiences that we base our reports on.

only in the latter case would we have an experience of succession.[8] The first two are thus compatible with Reid's view whereas the latter is compatible with his opponent's views. In so far as we only know the performance in these tasks, little is revealed about the possible mechanisms underlying them and nothing is revealed about the nature of conscious states.

This conclusion is supported also by the fact that psychologists themselves write about temporal order *judgments* instead of *experiences*, despite early remarks by Fraisse, who emphasized the phenomenology related to them.[9] Obviously this does not mean that psychologists deny the possibility that these judgments are accompanied or even based on related phenomenology. Instead, it only suggests that psychologist consider phenomenology unhelpful in their pursuit of understanding the mechanisms underlying the role of timing in human behavior. Nonetheless, it is exactly because of such a noncommittal approach to the phenomenology that psychological results have only a little direct bearing on the matters that philosophers are interested in.

A similar consideration holds for duration perception. Fittingly, psychologists emphasize that we do not experience durations. (It has been argued, for example, that there is no sense organ for time perception in a sense there are sensory organs, say, for vision and hearing.) The fact that we do not experience durations *per se* does not however mean that we could not have some accompanied phenomenology. Correspondingly, although philosophers agree with psychologists on the experiences of durations themselves, many of them argue that we can experience something related: persistence—that something has lasted, been present, for some time. In fact, the phenomenology of persistence is one of the reasons to postulate the notion of specious present (see for example [1,9]).

Here again appears the gap between performance-based and phenomenology-based approaches to temporal consciousness: Given that psychologists explicitly deny the existence of the experienced durations, they pay no attention to the possibility of related phenomenology and write about duration estimation (rather than duration perception), thus emphasizing the cognitive side contra phenomenology. Hence, their research is largely restricted to the performance-based approach. From the philosophers' side, on the other hand, it is not obvious how the experience of persistence relates to the duration of stimuli—even though it appears likely that one cannot have a feeling of persistence without some way of tracking the passage of time. Thus, for philosophers, it appears likely that merely focusing on performance for example in duration estimation, duration generalization, and temporal bisection tasks does not provide new insights into this phenomenology because it does not address the issue of what causes the feeling of persistence.

In short, I have been arguing the following. Philosophical investigations are by their nature mostly limited to the phenomenology-based approach to temporal

---

[8] Here is a useful analogy to think about: Based on the footprints on the beach one can infer that someone has walked there, but one only sees the footprints not the person who made them. Likewise here, maybe we can infer that two stimuli were presented in succession based on two separate experiences and with the help of some unconscious processes (or memory) or maybe we can indeed experience the succession itself and our performance is based on them. It could be either case, but if we look only the results in the task and never ask the questions concerning the phenomenology, we do not know which case it is.

[9] Needless to say, there are also exceptions [e.g., 8].

consciousness. More importantly, however, the research done on the performance-based approach is such that it largely has no (direct) relevance to the issues philosophers are interested in. For example, the mechanisms for something can be researched without taking a stand whether the research results indicate that the temporal properties are experienced or that they are simply judgments that the subjects make. Thus, there is little need or interest from philosophers' side regarding the performance-based approach.

Both performance-based and phenomenology-based approaches are viable options for psychologists, unlike for philosophers. Yet they tend to emphasize the performance at the expense of phenomenology. From psychologists' point of view, it does not appear to matter much whether the results mirror the experienced phenomenon or mere judgments.[10] Of course the latter are based on experiences too (except possibly in the forced choice tasks—think of blindsight) but not on the way that something is really a content of an experience instead of being merely inferred from the contents of experiences. The above does not mean, obviously, that psychologists could not also incorporate the phenomenology-based approach in their research.

3　Bridging the Disciplines

Although philosophers and psychologists have kept the performance-based and phenomenology-based approaches to temporal consciousness largely separate, there are issues where these two disciplines have much to offer to each other. For instance, there is no reason why properly planned experiments that put emphasis on phenomenology in addition to performance should not benefit both philosophers' and psychologists' endeavors. One could, for example, incorporate subjective confidence ratings in experiments and their analysis—as is done nowadays in some experiments concerning consciousness (see for example [10,11]). Instead of elaborating on this option, in this section I want briefly to mention more specific topics that have a bearing on philosophers' interests and in which some empirical research has been done. These serve as examples where collaboration between the disciplines is most likely to bring about advancements in both.

To begin with, philosophers' discussion on specious present means in practice that they are interested in issues that could shed light on the nature of specious present. For example, empirical issues that philosophers find interesting in relation to the notion of *specious present* are those that either motivate the endorsement of the specious present itself (perception of succession, change, etc.) or particular features of it (such as the notions of persistence for retended content and temporal orienting for protention in Husserlian tradition).

Another take on this matter concerns the minimal duration of experiences; if some notion of specious present is empirically sound, then each episode of sensing has some (kind of) temporal extension. Accordingly, it is reasonable to ask how long this temporal extension is (what the duration of one episode of experiencing is) and

---

[10] This should not be taken as a criticism against the way research is done (and in fact, the author himself has been involved in few studies of this kind), but merely as an indication that psychologists' interest in the issues of temporal consciousness does not reside on the related phenomenology.

whether its duration is fixed. James, for example, thought that specious present could last up to twelve seconds, whereas more recently Dainton has argued that it lasts around half a second. Both of these questions, at least *prima facie*, are close to, although not identical, with Robert Efron's [12,13] research on the minimal duration of perception, whereby he explicitly separated the duration of stimulus, processing epoch, and conscious perception. Furthermore, he argued that the minimal duration of experience differs for visual and auditory sensory systems, which in turn suggests that the duration of specious present is not fixed. This, in turn, fits nicely with some philosophical theories of time consciousness but not necessarily with others.

Empirical investigations have a bearing on the issues concerning *temporality* too. One obvious example of this is the quantification of experiences and mental processes. Is our conscious perception discrete as is sometimes argued or is it continuous [14]? Or maybe merely some mechanisms leading to perceptions function in a discrete manner [15]? That is, some discontinuity in our stream of consciousness could happen either in the level of how one specious present follows the other or in the contents of succeeding specious presents. Whether there is some discontinuity or not, it is obvious that the experiments that psychologists have conducted and the theories they have subsequently put forward (especially concerning the notion of psychological moment [16]) appear to have a close connection with the philosophers' debate on how much continuity there is in the stream of consciousness.

Imagine, for example, that we find that our conscious episodes are in fact discrete. Although philosophers can still maintain that this is not how it appears to us—our phenomenology is a continuous stream—this would mean that philosophers only need to explain the appearance of continuity. On the other hand, if there are no grounds to argue for discontinuity, then philosophers need not only to explain the appearance of continuity but also to do it in such a way that the underlying process itself could be continuous. Currently, very few philosophical theories incorporate such continuity.

Another, previously mentioned, issue concerning temporality where empirical research could have a direct impact is the question concerning the interrelation between the experienced passage of time and performance in the duration tasks. Can they vary independently of each other or is one's judgment on the passed duration dependent on the experience of the passage of time?

One can also begin bridging the gap between philosophy and the psychology of temporal consciousness by pondering what philosophers can offer psychologists. Despite my modest knowledge of psychology, I think that here too are grounds for possible cross-talk. The most obvious contribution that philosophers can make to psychological undertakings derives from their interest in the phenomenology of temporal consciousness.

For instance, phenomenologically-oriented philosophers have put forward some notions that psychologists have later (often independently of philosophers) begun researching themselves. One example of this that relates to specious present comes from Husserl, who appeared to regard retention as separate from mere (visual) persistence. Here, Max Coltheart's [17] notion of informal persistence, formulated 70 years after Husserl, is rather similar

Another example of the inspiration that phenomenology of temporal consciousness can bring about concerns the Husserlian notion of temporality: the idea of a continuous stream of consciousness and the general emphasis on the temporal structure of consciousness have been successfully used in developing new methods of fMRI analysis, which in turn has resulted in new perspectives on schizophrenia [18].

It may be worth adding that most philosophers focusing on temporal consciousness link their discussion to the broader context. Thus, Husserl (and other phenomenologists) as well as Dainton [19], for example, link the discussion on temporality to the discussion on the notion of (pre-reflective) self-consciousness. Julian Kiverstein [20], in turn, approaches these issues from the perspective of embodiment. As regards specious present, Rick Grush's [21] trajectory estimation model puts emphasis on spatiotemporal illusions such as flash-lag effect and representational momentum. This opens up new frameworks on how to approach temporal consciousness in general and hence philosophers working with abstract theories can also suggest frameworks that might be useful to explain certain empirical results within more psychologically-oriented theories. Philosophers have used, for instance, results in the timing of experiences in short timescales to propose a view where the experienced time can differ from the time of representing and then contextualized this research in temporal illusions on a broader framework of consciousness studies [22,23]. More recently, Shin'ya Nishida and Alan Johnston [24] postulated a time-marker view that makes explicit use of this framework that was first put forward merely as a theoretical possibility.

4 Summary

Temporal consciousness, the field that focuses on how time figures in our conscious states, has been a keen interest of both philosophers and psychologists. Although one could assume that these two disciplines have had some influence on each other while tackling related issues, such cross-talk has yet to occur. The objective of this paper was to begin amending this situation.

One possible reason why philosophers and psychologist have had so little interaction on these matters is that their approaches are so far apart that they have little relevance to each other. It was argued that this is indeed how things currently stand, as philosophers focus on phenomenology and psychologists on subjects' performance in various experiments.

Another, equally valid, reason is that cross-talk between disciplines is difficult, if not even impossible, when researchers in one discipline do not know what researchers in the other disciplines work with. Hopefully, this latter reason has lost some of its force with the explication above on where philosophers' interests lie in the topic of temporal consciousness, because some of the research that has been done suggests that there are fruitful grounds for interdisciplinary collaboration for those philosophers and psychologists who wish for it.

References

[1] Dainton, B.: Temporal Consciousness. The Stanford Encyclopedia of Philosophy (2010), http://plato.stanford.edu/archives/fall2010/entries/consciousness-temporal/

[2] Varela, F.J.L.: The specious present: A neurophenomenology of time consciousness. In: Petitot, J., Varela, F.J., Pachoud, B., Roy, J.-M. (eds.) Naturalizing Phenomenology: Issues in Contemporary Phenomenology and Cognitive Science, pp. 266–329. Stanford University Press, Stanford (1999)

[3] Varela, F.J.: Present-time consciousness. Journal of Consciousness Studies 6, 111–140 (1999)

[4] Fraisse, P.: The psychology of time. Harper & Row, New York (1963)

[5] James, W.: The principles of psychology. Dover, New York (1890)

[6] Reid, T.: Essays on the intellectual powers of man. In: Walker, J. (ed.). Derby, Boston (1855)

[7] Husserl, E.: On the phenomenology of the consciousness of internal time (1893-1917). In: Brough, J.B. (ed.). Kluwer Academic, Dordrecht (1991)

[8] Bschor, T., Ising, M., Bauer, M., Lewitzka, U., Skerstupeit, M., Müller-Oerlinghausen, B., et al.: Time experience and time judgment in major depression, mania and healthy subjects. A Controlled Study of 93 Subjects. Acta Psychiatrica Scandinavica 109, 222–229 (2004)

[9] Kelly, S.D.: The puzzle of temporal experience. In: Brook, A., Akins, K. (eds.) Cognition and the Brain: The Philosophy and Neuroscience Movement, pp. 1–26. Cambridge University Press, Cambridge (2005)

[10] Overgaard, M., Overgaard, R.: Neural Correlates of Contents and Levels of Consciousness. Frontiers in Psychology 1, 2008–2010 (2010)

[11] Overgaard, M., Rote, J., Mouridsen, K., Ramsøy, T.Z.: Is conscious perception gradual or dichotomous? A comparison of report methodologies during a visual task. Consciousness and Cognition 15, 700–708 (2006)

[12] Efron, R.: The relationship between the duration of a stimulus and the duration of a perception. Neuropsychologia 8, 37–55 (1970)

[13] Efron, R.: The minimum duration of a perception. Neuropsychologia 8, 57–63 (1970)

[14] VanRullen, R., Koch, C.: Is perception discrete or continuous? Trends in Cognitive Sciences 7, 207–213 (2003)

[15] Stroud, J.: The fine structure of psychological time. In: Quastler, H. (ed.) Information Theory in Psychology. Free Press, Glencoe (1955)

[16] Allport, D.A.: Phenomenal simultaneity and the perceptual moment hypothesis. British Journal of Psychology 59, 395–406 (1968)

[17] Coltheart, M.: Iconic memory and visible persistence. Perception & Psychophysics 27, 183–228 (1980)

[18] Lloyd, D.: Functional MRI and the study of human consciousness. Journal of Cognitive Neuroscience 14, 818–831 (2002)

[19] Dainton, B.: Stream of consciousness. Routledge, London (2000)

[20] Kiverstein, J.: The minimal sense of self, temporality and the brain. Psyche: An Interdisciplinary Journal of Research on Consciousness 15 (2009)

[21] Grush, R.: Brain time and phenomenological time. In: Brook, A., Akins, K. (eds.) Cognition and the Brain: The Philosophy and Neuroscience Movement, pp. 160–207. Cambridge University Press, Cambridge (2005)

[22] Dennett, D.: Consciousness Explained. Little, Brown, Boston (1991)

[23] Dennett, D., Kinsbourne, M.: Time and the observer. Behavioral and Brain Sciences 15, 183–247 (1992)

[24] Nishida, S., Johnston, A.: Marker correspondence, not processing latency, determines temporal binding of visual attributes. Current Biology 12, 359–368 (2002)

Temporal Illusions — Philosophical Considerations

Sean Enda Power

Department of Philosophy, School of Sociology and Philosophy,
University College Cork, Cork, Ireland
http://www.ucc.ie/en/philosophy

Abstract. Does the status of certain temporal experiences as illusory depend on one's conception of time? Our concept of time in part determines our concept of what we hold to be real and unreal; what we hold to be real and unreal partially determines what we hold to be illusory; thus, our concept of time in part determines what we hold to be illusory.

This paper argues that this dependency of illusions on the concept of time is applicable to illusions of time. Two possible temporal illusions given the evidence are examined, simultaneity and the experience of the past; it is argued that the evidence points at temporal illusions depending on which conception of time is true.

Keywords: illusions, temporal illusions, theories of perception, philosophy of time, simultaneity, experiencing the past, temporal order

1 Introduction

The evidence seems overwhelming that we experience illusions, e.g., the Müller-Lyer illusion (e.g., McCauley & Henrich 2006), the waterfall illusion and the rubber hand illusion (MacKnik & Martinez-Conde 2010, p.102). However we interpret the appearances in these cases, we have to hold that something is not as it seems. Not being as it seems, I assume, is what it is for our experience of something to be an illusory experience or perception.

Yet, although there may be an illusory experience, there is still the question of what it is that is illusory. Answering that may seem trivial: if we are motivated to posit an illusion at all, what motivates us should be that there is some discrepancy between appearances and reality. By judging that some object I see does not have the shape or colour it seems to have, then I also judge that the shape or colour is illusory.

I think that this is right: once we establish that there is a difference between what appears to be the case and what is the case, how we establish that requires our recognition of what is different. Thus, looking at what seems to be a yellow apple, in the very act of establishing that the yellow is not the actual colour of the apple, we also establish at least one thing that is illusory here, the yellowness of the apple.

A. Vatakis et al. (Eds.): Time and Time Perception 2010, LNAI 6789, pp. 11–35, 2011.

However, one's conception of time is relevant to establishing just this illusory status. Given we have different conceptions of time, there is this question: can we assume that certain perceptual or experiential illusions are the illusions that we take them to be? I argue that we should not assume this: because our thinking about time alters how we think about what is real and unreal, then it also alters what exactly it is that we can say is illusory, even where we are forced into thinking that *something* must be illusory. I do this by considering a category of illusion relevant to one's conception of time, that is, *temporal* illusions.

This paper proceeds through the following discussions:

(a) The difference between an experience and a perception, and why it is important in discussing temporal illusions. The issue here is that, if we wish to be consistent with views from philosophers of time, we ought to talk about a more general class of illusions, *experiential* illusions, as opposed to just *perceptual* illusions.

(b) The conditions under which an experience is a perceptual or experiential illusion. It is asserted that, although we may hold that a particular experience is of certain illusory properties or relations, this does not mean that this particular experience is of only illusory properties and relations.

(c) A brief description of different temporal features and different concepts of time.

(d) These sections prepare us finally for an examination of whether or not some alleged examples of temporal illusions are best understood that way, i.e., as temporal illusions. The examples are (i) simultaneity and (ii) memory-experience. It is argued that, combined with one's concepts of experience and perception, the answer depends on one's concept of time.

2   Time-Experience and Time-Perception

This section considers the relationship between experience, perception and illusion, a relationship which is both important to how we talk about temporal illusions and is also affected by how we think about time.

Throughout this paper, I attempt to use terms in their most common English senses. However, some terms have taken on specific meanings in various traditions. Because the study of time and perception is of interest in a wide variety of disciplines, there is the risk of terminological confusion in its discussion.

The relationship between two terms, I think, raise particular difficulty in this discussion. These are *experience* and *perception*. As such, I wish to briefly indicate and explain how these are used.

'Experience' in philosophy seems to be used in a number of slightly different, but not necessarily incompatible, ways, e.g., experience is:

- the *subjective aspect* or properties of conscious perception (most typically sensory perception), also sometimes referred to as the phenomenal character or properties of consciousness, the 'what it is like' to see, hear, touch, taste, etc. When we see, we *experience* visual sensations (e.g., Chalmers 2004, p.618).

- an intrinsic (and, to some, questionable) effect common to perceptions and/or hallucinations which 'happen to a subject [...they] must happen within the subject [...their] intrinsic natures are independent of anything that happens outside the subject' (e.g., Snowden 1990, p.123).
- a *representation* of things in the world, even in cases where there's nothing there (such as in illusion or hallucination), e.g., I have an experience *as of* a red squirrel; my experience visually represents a red squirrel (e.g., Lycan, 1996, p.82).
- inclusive of conscious episodes that are not easily considered sensory in the temporal, empirical or mundane sense, e.g., mystical and religious experiences (e.g., Yandell 1999, pp.213-232).

I use experience here with these various descriptions in mind. However, I also need to extend its use in order to talk about *temporal* experience – and of temporal illusion. This comes from issues with (a) referring to the *perception* of time and (b) the need to talk about experience and illusion that is not just of present things.

It is generally agreed by all sides in the philosophy of time that what we seem to perceive seems to be present: when seeing a bouncing ball, the ball appears to be bouncing now (for discussion, see, e.g., Callender 2008). I could be hallucinating or under an illusion, and not seeing the bouncing ball at all (thus, I only seem to see it); or I could be having a particularly overwhelming and vivid memory, as is sometimes alleged of trauma victims, and the bouncing ball is actually in the past (thus, it only seems to be present). But still, the sides agree, if I seem to see it, hear it, feel it, and so on, it seems to be present.[1]

If this is so, then the perception of time can only refer to one understanding of time as it appears: time that appears to be present. Time-perception is present-perception. We cannot, in this view, perceive time that is past or future. Now, there may be no issue here with perceiving the future – this is not something I assume here needs to be explained. But with the past, there is a more difficult issue. For whatever we mean by the awareness of the past, as we might say of remembering particular episodes in one's life, this assumption in the metaphysics of time means that such past remembering cannot even seem to be a kind of perception.

This has the following effect on talk about temporal illusion: if the temporal illusion is a *perceptual* illusion, it can only be an illusion of something which seems *present*, e.g., something appears to be present but it is not.

Yet, as will be discussed, temporal experience and illusion do not seem to be only of present things. Discussions about temporal illusion include duration, temporal order, and the past. If philosophers of time are right about perception, can we refer to such temporal illusions? We seem to have two options:

- Either we have perceptions of temporal features other than those which belong to (apparently) present things. Or:
- Illusions need not be perceptual illusions.

---

[1] Instead, the disagreement concerns what is required for something to seem present (e.g., Callender, *ibid*, and later in this paper.)

Some argue that, in order to make sense of our perception, we ought to agree that we perceive temporal features such as duration and temporal order (e.g., Hoerl 2009; Power 2011).[2] Dainton considers a notion of compound presentism, in which reality is constrained to a subset of all times. In that case, given we identify the present with the real, we might then say this subset of times, which is a duration, is the present; thus, we have a somewhat presentist concept of a present with duration (2001, p.95). Also, given B-theory, in which the present is analogous to 'here', any arbitrary duration can be ascribed presentness, just as any spatial extent can be ascribed 'here'-ness. But with A-theory, I cannot see how this can work: the fundamental distinctions between moments in time are supposed to be the positions in the A-series, a series in which there is only one present; but if there is only one present, how can several moments be distinguished in this A-series as present? Pending a clear answer on this, I leave it aside. However, such claims are not so easily found with discussions about the past. Putting aside reasons from analytical philosophers of time, there are no obvious claims in the philosophical literature that we genuinely see past summers when remembering our childhood, or hear past notes when listening to a tune. In fact, one finds quite the reverse, e.g., Husserl claims that our awareness of past notes is nothing like hearing a continuing echo of such a note; this motivates his particular analysis of time-consciousness (e.g., Husserl, 1991, p.33).

Yet, there is talk about the *phenomenology* of remembering, of things appearing in memory. And it has been argued that what appears in memory is, or at least includes, past things (not present things). For example, Husserl writes:

> I now remember vividly the terrain of a military exercise. I have the color of the sky, the varying tints of the green of the meadows [...] These colors are past colors; namely, colors of objects that I am remembering but that certainly do not stand before me as objects that are now present along with all their determinations. Are there (I am now remembering) other colors in the memory phenomenon? No, the colors that are experienced there are ascribed to the past [...]
>
> In actual perception, the sensed colors are taken as belonging to the same temporal position as the perceived colors. The situation is analogous in the case of memory. The memorial appearance together with its body of sensuous contents (which themselves fall into the appearance) is taken to be the re-presentation of the earlier perceptual appearance; consequently, the sensed color, just like the remembered color, is taken as having been.

(Husserl 2005, Appendix XVI, pp.243-244)

And, as we will see, at least one author quoted here discusses the necessary illusion of memory. In order to respect that way of thinking, I suggest the following:

---

[2] This assumes that, given any number of moments in time, if any moment is present, only one moment can be present, while all other moments must be either past or future. As such, only a single moment in any duration can be present; no duration in its entirety can be present. An anonymous reviewer suggests that there may be formulations of tense compatible with presentism and the A-theory that allow the present to have a duration.

Consider the use of experience above. Experience seems to correspond to appearances, to occasions in which something is apparent; there is *phenomenal character* when we have an experience. However, although what we experience might be present, it does not necessarily require that what we experience *appears* to be present. With this in mind, I use experience here for conscious episodes where something is apparent but does not (necessarily) appear to be present. And thus we can extend illusion to such cases as well: although it is not present, as something is apparent here, this appearance may be mistaken; thus, we may even have illusory experiences of things that are not present.

For this reason, I sometimes distinguish between (i) what we experience and (ii) what we *seem* to experience. An anonymous referee holds that this distinction is unfounded. However, when considering the previous understanding of experience, I think it is important to allow the possibility of a separation between appearances and actual experience; it allows us to have illusions of non-present events, e.g., memory-illusions. If there are to be temporal illusions, and this illusion involves experience rather than just perception, one still needs to distinguish appearances and reality here. What I do experience is what is actually the case; what I seem to experience need not be. This is analogous to what I perceive and what I seem to perceive, except without the commitment to an appearance of presentness.

This, however, leads to one final issue in my use of 'experience': if x is what we experience, this does not necessarily mean that x is real. That is, we might experience something unreal. Again, we could have an illusion here, due to the discrepancy in appearances, for we may in these cases seem to experience something *real*. This is relevant to both positing something as an illusion generally, as will be discussed in the next section (where illusions of the imagination are discussed) and with temporal illusions in particular, as will be discussed under memory-illusions.[3]

To summarise: my use here of 'experience' can be thought of as referring to the larger or more general set of conscious episodes than those described as perceptions. In doing so, I still distinguish the appearance of what we experience from what we experience itself, and thus allow for experiential illusions; but, in order to allow that certain experiences can appear and may even be of unreal things, I also include the possibility here that we experience unreal things. I believe these distinctions are necessary to discuss temporal experience and temporal illusions.[4]

---

[3] My own intuition here is that we can only experience real things, e.g., Power 2009, and thus any apparent experience of things that are actually unreal is an illusory experience (see, later, concerning memory). However, this is currently only an undeveloped intuition so I will not argue for it here (the issue comes up again later, when discussing experiencing in imagination).

[4] One might still want to hold that perception extends to all such cases of what I consider here to be experience; thus, one insists that we have perceptions of the past perhaps, we even see, hear, etc. things in the past or we have perceptions of unreal things; indeed, Husserl seems to talk this way when discussing time-consciousness (although he also has difficulties, e.g., Husserl 1991, §16). Due to the debate about time from which this discussion comes, I will not follow such usage but hopefully my terminology is clear enough to translate into these other terms should they be preferred.

3   Illusion

The relation between there being a distinction between appearance and reality does not necessarily lead to there being an illusion. Initially, there are two ways there one might think that there is such a difference:

(a) Something (x) appears to have some real property or relation but x does not have that property or relation.
(b) x does not appear to have some real property or relation but x does have that property or relation.

I take it that cases of (a) are acceptable as illusions: if we seem to see a red squirrel, but it is not a red squirrel, then we are under some kind of illusion; if the moon looks to be tangled amongst the branches of the trees, but it is not tangled there, then we are under some kind of illusion.

However, not all cases of (b) are necessarily illusions. It may be that there is no appearance of anything related to the relevant properties or relations. It may simply not be apparent to me in any way at all that x has such properties or relations, e.g., looking at the red squirrel, it many not appear that it is more red than another red squirrel two copses over (although it is); nor may it appear that it is smaller than a grey squirrel I saw this morning (although it is). I can even fail to experience properties or relations that the object has intrinsically or even requires, and yet not be under an illusion, e.g., while looking at the squirrel, I can fail to experience the weight of the squirrel, yet this is not an illusory experience of its weight; similarly, if I feel the the squirrel on my shoulder, but do so in a dark room, I do not see it; but this does not mean that I am under a visual illusion. That something does not seem to be red because we do not see it at all because we have our eyes closed or are in a dark room – this is not an illusion.

So, to make cases of (b) illusions, we need for the object to seem to lack a property – and not just that we do not seem to experience the object having it. The question of whether or not something can be illusory by seeming to lack a property which it actually has is relevant to questions about temporal illusions because, in some cases, one might want to say of our temporal experience that we seem to experience unreal things. That is, some of what we at least seem to (temporally) experience lacks reality. If it is, in fact, real, then I think that our experience will be illusory (as will be discussed).

3.1   Illusion in Imagination

Are there any cases of (b) which are not just the failure to detect something? In some cases, we might hold that something we experience appears as if it lacks properties or relations that it actually possesses. A significantly relevant example for this paper is if something appears to exist separate to our experiences or thought. Following Nudds, call this property an *NR*-property, a 'naive realism'-property; it is so-called because of what is said to be the naive theory of perception, *naive realism*: the position that we directly or immediately experience mind-independent (and external and public) things (Nudds 2009; see later for more discussion on this position and one important alternative).

The possession of an NR-property is possessed by the vast number of the things that we seem to experience, e.g., the distant mountains, our clothes, a red squirrel. However, some of what we experience seems to lack the NR-property. We can easily *imagine* something which in no way appears to us to be real separate to such imagining, e.g., the imaginary mansion made of solid gold does not involve a gold mansion that is in some way exists beyond imagination. However, evidence suggests that the imaginary or mind-dependent appearance of what we experience may, in some cases, disagree with what we are actually experiencing.

In the *Perky Effect*, subjects were placed in front of a screen and asked to imagine seeing something, e.g., a banana. The subjects then believed that they were only imagining seeing a banana on the screen, not that they actually saw something on the screen, i.e., whatever it was they were experiencing, it was not something independent of them out in the world.

However, the evidence suggests otherwise. While subjects imagined seeing the banana, a projection of a banana was displayed on the screen, the illuminated strength of which was higher than the visual threshold (MacPherson (forthcoming)). When asked to describe what they were imagining, and not seeing, subjects' descriptions were of this projection, often to their surprise, e.g., when an upright half-peeled banana was projected, many subjects stated that, although they originally intended imagining an un-peeled banana on its side, they found themselves imagining one half-peeled and upright. Yet, it did not seem to them that were really *seeing* anything; it still seemed to them that were just imagining the half-peeled banana. That is, although it seemed that way to them, these features of what they were imagining were not, in fact, mind-dependent; they were dependent on an actual projection on the screen (Perky 1910, MacPherson (forthcoming)).[5]

There is an issue with this analysis that might raise concern. The analysis of the experience of imagining assumes that, when we are imagining seeing something, we seem to experience something unreal (the imagined banana). But is it right that when we imagine, or indeed have any other sort of experience, that what we experience ever seems to be unreal?

If some philosophers are right in their analysis of appearances, then yes: we should hold that we, at least, seem to experience unreal or merely imaginary things. Sartre holds that to think otherwise is to fall for the *illusion of immanence*, the error that what *appears* in imagining must be a surrogate or stand-in image rather than the imagined thing. The mistake is that we 'depicted consciousness as a place peopled with small imitations and these imitations were the images.' (Sartre 1986, p.5) But instead, 'in the mental image we are in the *presence* of a horse. Only, that horse has, at the same time, a kind of nothingness.[...] One should not suppose that 'the mental image is a horse in miniature [...it is] the horse itself that appears to consciousness.' (*ibid*, p.83). This is not

---

[5] Given *naive realism* (see below), at least, where subjects directly experience (indeed see) the image on the screen; otherwise, what they experience is not so obviously mind-independent.

to say that what we experience *is* the imagined thing (that is a different issue) only that it seems that way – and that is all that we seem to experience.

But what we seem to experience also seems to not be real, present or spatially related to us: whatever we imagine seems in the imagining to be unreal, or *absent* (or spatially unrelated to us, at least, e.g., McGinn 2004, p.29). That is, an imagined unicorn does not seem to be real; the imagined Eiffel tower does not seem present or near us. But they are in some way apparent to us; we seem to have some kind of experience of them. Discussing the sensible qualities of imagining, Sartre writes that 'these qualities are perfectly externalized but imaginary' (e.g., Sartre 1986, p.87).

Given these are correct descriptions of what imagining is like, then we may still have cases where we are under an experiential illusion: as with the Perky effect, with the projection on the screen, if what we experience in our imagining is real and present e.g., if we are actually seeing it, then that it seems only to be imagined is the illusion. Again, this is relevant to discussion about temporal illusions.

3.2   Illusions Could Have Alternative Interpretations

The next issue is this: we need to pick out what in particular is illusory in an experience. In the case of temporal illusions, it is the temporal features, the temporal properties and relations, that are illusory. Similar focus is applied when we talk about illusory colours or spatial illusions: something that we experience does not have the colours, hues, spatial distance, size, shape, etc. that it seems to have – and whatever that is, that is what makes it a colour or spatial illusion.

However, it is just as important to highlight the other side of saying something is illusory: if something apparent but not actually the case is not a particular property or relation, then neither is it an example of illusions of that property or relation. If I seem to see a red squirrel, but in fact I see a red statue of a squirrel, I may be under an illusion of there being a squirrel but I am not under the illusion of seeing the colour red (given this evidence, anyhow).

This can be true even of different members of the same class of properties, e.g., different kinds of spatial properties may be illusory while others are not. Sitting in a Bed and Breakfast in some tourist resort, I seem to see a giant castle off in the distance, but it turns out to be a house-sized castle just down the road. The size is illusory – it's not as big as it seems – and the distance is illusory – it's rather nearer than it appears. However, it would be a mistake to think that, just because I am under an illusion of size and distance, then I am also under an illusion of spatial properties generally, e.g., however distant it is, it is indeed castle-shaped; the apparently gigantic (but actually cat-flap sized) portcullis is indeed to my left, the pennant is to my right; pending other reasons to think so, these spatial features are how they seem.

As will be discussed, in the philosophy of time, and indeed normal conversation, 'time' or 'temporal' can refer to many different temporal features. It is not necessarily the case that illusions of some such temporal features are illusions of others. As such, just because some kinds of temporal experiences may be illusory, this does not mean that all kinds of temporal experience are or can be illusory.

It is also relevant here that, although one may have a case where there is definitely an illusion, what it is that is illusory needs to be made clear, e.g., that it is an illusion of colour rather than one of space, or space rather than colour. But I also think this is part of the issue: we hold an experience to be illusory not from what is apparent in the experience itself. One believes there are illusions because of beliefs we have otherwise, beliefs we hold to override whatever we seem to experience. (Someone who believes in magic does not believe a disappearing assistant is actually an illusory disappearance).

That we draw on beliefs outside the experience itself leads to the following possibility: different subjects may give different interpretations of an illusion; each may assert that different members of the same range of apparent properties and relations are illusory or real. This is because each may have different beliefs when presented with the illusion itself.[6]

Consider one of the most commonly discussed visual illusions, the Müller-Lyer illusion.[7] One demonstrates that there is an illusion here by showing that, when it comes to measuring the apparently differently extended lines, they then seem to be the same length. The question is: what properties are illusory here?

The usual, possibly universal, interpretation is that the lines are the same length and the difference in lengths is illusory. However, here are two other ways one *might* interpret the illusion:

- The lines are different lengths. The equal lengths demonstrated afterwards are illusory.
- There is no illusion of length at all: the lines before measurement are different lengths and the lines during measurement are the same length.

So why not advance these alternative interpretations for the Müller-Lyer illusion? One assumes that the first is not considered because the experiment is set up so that the length of the lines are as equal as discernibly possible; we should not be able to tell any actual difference (though no doubt there is some in most examples, at least on the microscopic scale). I assume that the second is not popular because we assume that the lines persist unchanged throughout the measuring.

These seem to be reasonable assumptions. But it should be noted that they are not given in the perception of the lines themselves. They come from assumptions held by the observers.

This leads to a final point on illusion generally, a point which is relevant to the discussion of temporal illusions. Whichever interpretation one might give of the Müller-Lyer illusion, one is committed to the general charge that there is some kind of perceptual illusion here: either (i) the appearance of a difference in the lines' lengths, (ii) the appearance of equality in the lines' lengths or (iii) the persistence of the same length in the lines. Yet, even though there is always a

---

[6] That one can interpret an illusion in different ways is discussed in classical Indian epistemological, in particular concerning the standard example known as 'the snake-rope' illusion (see Mohanty 2000).

[7] Depictions of this illusion are common. From the references here, see, e.g. MacPherson (forthcoming).

perceptual illusion here, however we interpret it, establishing that one feature is illusory seems based on an assumption that others are not illusory, e.g., having it that the earlier lengths are merely apparent, one assumes later lengths are real.

Something similar may apply to temporal illusions: to establish that one temporal feature is illusory, we need to assume that other temporal features are real.

3.3   Two Theories of Perception and Experience

Finally, before moving on to talk specifically about time, we need to briefly introduce two different theories of perception and experience in the philosophy of mind.

Consider the following broad theories of perception:[8]

- *Naive realism*:[9] (Most of) what we (directly) perceive is what it seems to be: something out in the world beyond our bodies or brains (naive or direct realism, e.g., Nudds 2009).
- *Indirect realism*: What we (directly) perceive is internal to us, e.g., to our brains or our minds. However, we do indirectly perceive the outside world, usually through the outside world causing what we perceive internally (e.g., Lowe 1981).

These two theories are not the only theories of perception. But they are introduced here because the particular distinction between them is relevant to

---

[8] Some philosophers describe experiences as follows: Our experiences are representations (internal to our bodies, brains or minds). There is not necessarily any object that we experience, despite how it appears (thus, unlike indirect realism, nothing *through* which we experience what we seem to experience). There are only representations of such objects (Lycan 1996; Crane 2006). Similarly, illusions are sometimes discussed as cases where perceptions (and experiences generally) misrepresent or are inaccurate representations of things in the world; alternatively, illusory perceptions are one class of *non*-veridical perceptions; the content represented in the perception does not match how things are in the world. This way of speaking may have its merits but it often seems to be another way of saying that what we appear to perceive is different to how things actually are. For example, Batty writes:

> We can think of the representational content of an experience as the way the world appears to a perceiver when she has that experience. If the world is that way –if the representational content matches world, we might say – then the experience is *accurate* or *veridical*. Otherwise – if the content doesn't match the world – it is *inaccurate* or *non-veridical*.

(Batty, 2011, p.164) It might be that perceptions can misrepresent or be inaccurate or non-veridical without reference to appearances at all. However, even if one might call such a state a *perception* I cannot see how one can call such a case an illusion if either nothing is apparent to us or the appearances are irrelevant. As such, I will keep the description of illusion in terms of appearances and reality.

[9] 'Naive realism' is sometimes identified with 'direct realism', in contrast to 'indirect realism'. However, I want to use the term naive here to highlight its claim that we perceive something outside of us in the world as being the naive claim in the discussion on perception (this does not necessarily make it false).

this paper. Taking a side on this concerns what commitments one has toward illusory perception and experience in its turn, this affects one's commitment to temporal illusions.

The common accusation leveled at indirect realists from naive realists is that indirect realism requires a fundamental discrepancy between, at least in some cases, appearances and reality. For we do seem to experience, and to directly experience, the properties of external things (e.g. Hacker 1987). Indeed, some philosophers argue that even when we attempt to introspect the properties of our perceptions themselves, we still only seem to be aware of external entities (see Nudds 2009 for discussion) – entities which, for the indirect realist, can only be indirectly experienced. As this is not how it seems, this position requires a discrepancy between appearances and reality, i.e., they make our experience or perception illusory.

The accusation of commitment to illusion may be right; but, in the position's defence, it is also motivated by cases of illusion or hallucination. A general charge against naive realism is that it cannot deal with illusion and hallucination. Even if one is committed to some kind of illusion with indirect realism, one is lead there away from naive realism because naive realism cannot account for illusions and hallucinations. This has lead to further theories of perception such as representationalism (Lycan 1996) and disjunctivism (e.g., Smith 2010).

This debate is important for considerations about temporal illusions. As will be discussed, such a commitment by indirect realists to something fundamentally illusory is relevant to claiming that some illusions are specifically temporal illusions.

4   Time

We can talk about time as independent of other things, e.g., as time without changing or persisting entities. This kind of time is not the focus of interest here; it is not clear that such a time could enter into our experience (e.g., Shoemaker 1991); arguing that it can is a further step than what is required for this discussion (though see Dainton 2003 for some interesting thoughts). Instead, the time of concern here is the time that structures entities in the world, the time that determines how they exist or are related to one another (or, at least, might seem to do so).

4.1   Temporal Features

The entities we encounter in the world, including those that we both do and seem to experience, can be said to have different (what I will call) *temporal features*: temporal properties and relations. Such temporal features include (but may not be exhausted by):

(i) Simultaneity, as in 'A is simultaneous with B'.
(ii) Pastness, presentness, futurity (and their degrees), as in 'A is past when B is present'; 'A is more past than B'; 'B is in the far future, A is in the near future.'

(iii) Temporal order, succession, earlier-than/later-than, as in 'A before B'; 'B succeeds A'.

(iv) Duration, as in 'A lasts a very long time'; 'B has no duration - it happens in an instant.'

 (v) Change, including movement, e.g., a ball rolls from here to there; a grey hob heats until it is glowing red.

4.2   Metaphysical Conceptions of Time

By a 'metaphysical' conception of time, I mean a conception of time as it is independent of what we believe or how the world appears to us; it is not just time as we think it or as it seems to us; it is time as it is were there no-one around to think about it or feel it at all.

There are several conceptions of time like this, many of which are held by their advocates to be incompatible. Space precludes detailing the reasons for holding these conceptions in any detail here. However, it is important to give a brief description of these positions because they make different assertions about:

(a) What is real and unreal in time.

(b) What temporal properties things in time really possess.

Both issues are relevant to illusion in this way: if we seem to experience or perceive things occurring in time in ways that a particular theory denies can be the way things are, then it seems right to say that this experience or perception is illusory.

The four main positions are *presentism*, *eternalism*, the *A-theory* and the *B-theory*. They come from two main debates:

1. The reality of times and things (objects, events) at those times.
    (a) *Presentism*: The presentist conception of time is that there is only one real or existing time; past or future times are not real or do not exist. Markosian writes:

    > Presentism is the view that only present objects exist. More precisely, it is the view that, necessarily, it is always true that only present objects exist. [...] According to Presentism, if we were to make an accurate list of all the things that exist i.e., a list of all the things that our most unrestricted quantifiers range over there would be not a single non-present object on the list. Thus, you and the Taj Mahal would be on the list, but neither Socrates nor any future Martian outposts would be included.

    (Markosian, 2010, online)
    (b) *Eternalism*: The Eternalist conception of time is the opposite position to presentism: all times are as real or existent as each other, whether they are past, present or future (e.g., Mellor 1008, Le Poidevin 2003).
    Presentism is typically considered to be more intuitive than eternalism. Considering the question 'what is the temporal extent of reality', Caplan and Sason write:

In answer to this question, it is fairly natural to think that reality is limited to the present and that the past and future are, in some sense, unreal. This view is known as *Presentism*. *Presentism:* Reality is limited to the present. It is especially tempting to accept Presentism if one already thinks that reality is dynamic. For it is natural to think, as the future becomes present, it comes to be: it becomes a part of reality. And conversely, it is natural to think that, as the present slips into the past, it ceases to be: it ceases to be a part of reality. Presentism is often contrasted with *Eternalism*, according to which reality includes the past and future as well as the present.'
(Caplan and Sason, 2011, p.196)

2. The reality of the past, present and future, and *temporal passage* (the 'tense' debate).

   (a) The *A-theory*: The A-theory conception of time is that events are ordered by the *A-series*: the series of moments running from the future, through the present, into the past (the series of 'tenses'; 'A-properties'). Only one of these moments is present, only one is a week past; only one is a year in the future, etc. A further claim of A-theory is that events really change their positions in this series; they really change in being past, present and future. This concept of a real change in events by their changing from being in the future, to the present, to the past, is usually what is referred to in this tradition as *temporal passage*. A-theorists hold that the reality of this temporal passage is necessary for the reality of time (e.g., Schlesinger 1982, Lowe 2003; for extensive discussion, see Smith & Oaklander 1995, and Markosian, *op.cit.*).[10]

   (b) The *B-theory*: The B-theory conception of time is that events are ordered by the *B-series*: the series of events ordered by 'earlier than' and simultaneity ('B-relations'). The various moments in the past, present and future, i.e., moments in the A-series, are indexed to the times of these events; e.g., 'two weeks past' just refers to events two weeks earlier than a particular event; what is 'one year in the future' refers only to an event one year after the event. As such, there is no unique present, or past, or future, i.e., no unique A-series. And there is no real temporal passage of events through *the* A-series (e.g., Mellor 1998; Le Poidevin 2003).

The four positions are not fully independent of each other. Many A-theorists are presentists, though there are exceptions (e.g., Lowe, *op.cit.*). However, eternalism seems almost universally accepted by B-theorists.

4.3   Temporal Illusions given only the Metaphysics

Even without further discussion, the two metaphysical debates here already assert that certain temporal features are illusory. It is not always obvious in the

---

[10] Presentism is often considered to be a dominant version of the A-theory, but there are also eternalist versions (e.g., Lowe 2003).

discussion, by saying such features are just illusions, that they mean experiential or perceptual illusions, i.e., as something apparent which is not actually the case. So a first question is: do we seem to experience certain temporal properties and features?

Some in the debates on time do make this claim that our experience seems to be of various temporal features, indeed that such features are fundamental to what we experience. As such, they also resist certain conceptions of time because these conceptions make these features illusory.

Of particular significance is the question of whether or not temporal passage, conceived here as the change in event's locations in the A-series, is really such a change or only seems to be such a change (i.e., is illusory). B-theorists deny that there can really be such a change – and thus any appearance of it must be illusory. If it is illusory, it is clearly a case of temporal illusion.

This is an issue A-theorists consider deeply problematic for B-theorists, as they argue that this passage is fundamental to our general experience. Consider this statement from Craig:

> We do not experience a world of things and events related merely by the tenseless relations earlier than, simultaneous with, and later than, but a world of events and things which are past, present, or future. In fact, the reality of temporal becoming is even more obvious to us than the existence of the external world. For in the inner life of the mind we experience a continual change in the contents of consciousness, even in the absence of any apprehension of an external world, and this stream of consciousness alone constitutes for us a temporal series of tensed events. Some of our thoughts are now past, we are aware of our present mental experience, and we anticipate that we shall think new thoughts in the future. And there is no arresting of this flux of experience; there is constant and ineluctable becoming.

(Craig 2001, p.159) (For further discussion, see, e.g., Smart 1955, Schlesinger 1982, Le Poidevin 2003, Lowe 2003, Prosser (forthcoming)).

Also, B-theorists do not hold that there is a unique present; the present, along with the past, future, and other tenses – these are just properties indexed to a point on the B-series. Such A-properties are similar to egocentric spatial locations. Events are as much 'past', 'present' or 'future' as objects are 'here', 'there' or *spatially* present (e.g., Mellor 1998).[11] However, A-theorists insist that our perceptions themselves show that the presentness of perceived objects is not merely like spatial presence, not merely like 'here' rather than 'there'; perceived

---

[11] Thus, according to the B-theorist, the appearance of events as being uniquely present, or indeed past or future, is something that has to be illusory. Such A-properties are more like the way different objects seem to be different sizes due to their spatial distance from us, i.e., such A-properties are more like the perspectival properties of objects than the actual shapes of objects; they are due to our own temporal location, to our own temporal point of view (e.g., Hoerl 1998, Le Poidevin 2007), rather than anything belonging to the events themselves.

events seem to be present in a particularly vivid and unique way. And this, for the B-theorist, must be illusory: there is no so unique present.

As discussed earlier, that what we perceive is present seems acceptable to all sides of this debate. However, recently some B-theorist philosophers have argued against a unique present. They have made two claims against it:

(i) There is no need to explain our perception in terms of a unique present, i.e., a unique or special 'present' is not something apparent in our perception; instead, the appearance of 'presentness' is just the appearance of something being perceived (e.g., Mellor 1998; Callender, *op.cit.*; Le Poidevin 2007).

(ii) We can describe some difficult features of what we seem to perceive better in B-theory terms than A-theory terms. E.g., if, as all sides agree, whatever we seem to perceive also seems to be present, then if we seem to perceive change, this will seem to be *present change*. And we do seem to perceive change (this is one current interpretation of the specious present; see Power 2011). However, change is something that happens over more than a single time; if we seem to perceive it, it will seem present. But this means we will seem to perceive the duration of the change, i.e., more than one time, and this duration will seem present to us. This is particularly problematic for the A-theory for the A-theory requires there only to be one time which is present. However, some B-theorists argue that it is not so problematic for the B-theory (e.g., Oaklander in Smith & Oaklander 1995, Hoerl 2009; Power 2011).[12]

Given the undermining of the appearance of A-properties in claim '(i)', and the difficulties for A-theory from claim '(ii)', these arguments suggest both that the B-theory need not explain the appearance of certain temporal features in terms of the A-theory. Thus, for the B-theorist, these are not cases of temporal illusions; A-properties need not be features, at least, of what we seem to experience, so their absence in reality is not a difference between appearance and reality.

As such, within the metaphysical debates themselves, there are questions of whether or not certain experiences involve temporal illusions. These questions

---

[12] This assumes that, given any number of moments in time, if any moment is present, only *one* moment can be present, while all other moments must be either past or future. As such, only a single moment in any duration can be present; no duration in its entirety can be present. An anonymous reviewer suggests that there may be formulations of tense compatible with presentism and the A-theory that allow the present to have a duration. Dainton considers a notion of *compound presentism*, in which reality is constrained to a subset of all times. In that case, given we identify the present with the real, we might then say this subset of times, which is a duration, is the present; thus, we have a somewhat presentist concept of a present with duration (2001, p.95). Also, given B-theory, in which the present is analogous to 'here', any arbitrary duration can be ascribed presentness, just as any spatial extent can be ascribed 'here'-ness. But with A-theory, I cannot see how this can work: the fundamental distinctions between moments in time are supposed to be the positions in the A-series, a series in which there is only one present; but if there is only one present, how can *several* moments be distinguished in this A-series as present? Pending a clear answer on this, I leave it aside.

rest on the issue of whether or not certain temporal features are apparent and, also, if they are, whether or not they *must* be illusory. Different conceptions seem to force them to be, as can be seen. However, we might also ask if we are forced to hold that there are temporal illusions in any case, i.e., independent of our metaphysical conceptions of time. Let us consider two possible candidates for temporal illusion, and see if they remain temporal illusions whatever concept of time we hold.

5   Two Possible Temporal Illusions

I consider here some examples of what might be temporal illusions from evidence of psychological research. The intent here is to consider what it takes for them to be temporal illusions given one's theory of perception (and experience generally) coupled with one's metaphysical conception of time. This is meant as an illustration of how such an analysis might go, in the hope that it might serve as a guide for understanding other alleged temporal illusions (of which there may be many). For reasons of space, this discussion will also be confined to the debate about the reality of things in time, i.e., the debate between presentism and eternalism.

The two examples are these: the perception of simultaneity and memory-experience.

5.1   Simultaneity

A and B appear to be simultaneous if they seem to happen at the same time. So, there will be an illusion of simultaneity if two perceived events seem to be happening at the same time but are *not* happening at the same time.

Some philosophers and scientists consider it obvious that there is evidence of illusory simultaneity, e.g., Eagleman 2008 lists it as one example of temporal illusion.[13] The following cases have been presented as examples of illusory simultaneity:

1. A television picture appears to be a single simultaneous image spread out over the screen; however, at each moment, only one point of that screen is being illuminated; thus, the image is composed of *successive* illuminations of the screen, not *simultaneous* illuminations (e.g., Gombrich, cited in Le Poidevin 2000).

   Generally, we (allegedly) experience a similar illusory simultaneity with any motion blur: the translucent flickering that is seen when seeing a whirring fan seems to fill a volume about the axis of the fan, i.e., to simultaneously occupy

---

[13] Eagleman's work includes temporal illusions such as the sense of time dilation, that events can seem to take more time than they actually do, e.g., under stressful circumstances such as a car crash or being dropped from a great height (which is a component of Eagleman's experiments). Such illusions are illusions of duration, an interesting topic but one unfortunately not discussed here.

different regions of that volume. Yet, this is due to a successive occupancy of the fans' blades through that volume. Both of these are likely to be related to the *simultaneity threshold* of visual perception (e.g., Dainton 2000).

2. As with vision, there is also a simultaneity threshold of auditory perception; successive sounds can seem to be simultaneous when they occur close enough to each other (e.g., Deutsch 1987; Dainton 2000).

3. Certain experiences seem to be of cross-modal simultaneity, e.g., bangs and flashes that are not simultaneous can seem to be simultaneous, as in when we seem to simultaneously hear and see a film's out-of-sync, i.e., non-simultaneous, soundtracks and pictures.

So what does our concept of time have to say about these alleged examples of illusory simultaneity? This depends on what it is that we actually experience rather than just what we seem to experience. This involves considering the answer from the two theories of perception above.

The evidence suggests that there is a temporal illusion of simultaneity if naive realism is true. Given naive realism, we perceive the two mind-independent events that we seem to perceive, e.g., the successive positions of the dot on the television screen, the bang and flash, etc. Such events are not simultaneous, contrary to their appearances. Whatever apparent simultaneity there is here, it is not simultaneity between the experienced events themselves.

However, we do not need to assume this given indirect realism. Certainly, the elements of what we indirectly perceive or what are represented are not simultaneous. However, this does not mean that what we *directly* perceive in perception is not simultaneous. The illusion need not be of simultaneity but only of *what* is simultaneous. This is an illusion to which indirect realism is committed in any case (this is just the accusation levied at this position by the naive realist). This is because, for indirect realism, we seem to directly perceive external things but we do not – we only directly perceive internal things; the externality of what we directly perceive, given indirect realism, is illusory. Yet, this is not a temporal illusion. It is a further question if what we directly perceive is simultaneous or not. Thus, for indirect realism, the evidence, although it may demonstrate *some* kind of illusion, does not demonstrate temporal illusion.

Recall the possible re-interpretations of the Müller-Lyer illusion and the example of the merely apparent giant and distant castle. Certainly, the Castle's portcullis is not forty feet high; that is an illusion. But that does not make it an illusion that it is portcullis-shaped (or to the left of me). Similarly, we ought not to assume that if, in a particular experience, certain properties or relations that we seem to experience are illusory then, because these properties are illusory, *all* properties and relations that we seem to experience are illusory.

Next, consider the metaphysics.

Given a further assumption about what we can perceive, we may be committed to the idea that what we directly perceive *must* be simultaneous. This further assumption is similar to one discussed but suspended for experience in general. However, it seems far more plausible with perception. It is that, whatever it is that we directly perceive (given naive or indirect realism), it must be real.

Given presentism, anything real must be present. It is generally accepted by A-theorists, including presentists, that whatever is in the present is at the same time as whatever else is in the present; if it were at a different time, it would be past or future. If so, then, if all of these different things are at the same time, then there will be no duration between them. Thus, all of them, being real, will be simultaneous. Thus, if presentism is true, we cannot only indirectly perceive simultaneity; the various things that we directly perceive must be simultaneous themselves. We cannot have an illusion of simultaneity, given presentism; we can only have an illusion of what is simultaneous.

However, an eternalist cannot assume simultaneity between what they directly perceive. Thus, they may very well have examples of illusory simultaneity.

In fact, given one motivation for eternalism, eternalists might need to hold that, in most cases, the appearance of simultaneity is illusory. The theory of relativity holds that the simultaneity of spatially separated events is relative – relative to arbitrary and conventional inertial reference frames. Considered from a different inertial reference frame, the exact same events will not be simultaneous. Many eternalists are motivated to be eternalists by this theory (e.g., Mellor 1998). Yet, Power argues that, given one accepts such relative simultaneity, simultaneity is illusory in nearly all cases of perception, for what we actually perceive cannot be so relative; as a result, if we do seem to perceive simultaneity between spatially separated things, this is an illusion (for details of this argument, see Power 2010a).

This difference between the commitments of presentists and eternalists highlights an implication for the relationship between one's conception of time and one's theory of perception. If naive realists need illusions of simultaneity in order that we can directly perceive the external things that we seem to perceive then, since eternalists can (or perhaps usually must) have illusions of simultaneity, they could, perhaps, be naive realists. However, assuming that we can only directly perceive what is real, then since presentists deny that anything that we directly perceive can be non-simultaneous, it seems that, as the apparently perceived external objects are *not* simultaneous, presentism and naive realism are incompatible.[14]

5.2   Experience of the Past

As discussed, most philosophers in the debate about time accept that the appearance of what we perceive is of it being present; they just deny the importance of that being so (e.g., A-theorists think this is an additional property to what

---

[14] A related issue concerns the *time-lag argument* for indirect realism, the argument that, because there is a delay between external events, which we seem to perceive, and effects of those events within us, e.g., the stimulation of our retina or neural activity as a result of light from such external events, then we cannot directly perceive external things, despite how it appears to us. This might be another example of a temporal illusion, this time one of presentness, though I think this will depend again on one's conception of time. For a recent discussion considering this from the perspective of the presentist/eternalist debate, see Power 2010b.

we seem to perceive; B-theorists think it is only the appearance of having a perception). If this is so, then when talking about experiencing what seems to be the *past*, we are talking about experiencing something that does not seem to be present. As a result, it will not seem to be perceived. We might, however, have some other kind of experience of the past. What kind, and how we are to understand it given different conceptions of time, is part of what might it the case that there are illusory experiences of the past.

The most immediate example of experiencing the past is through memory, in particular episodic memory. Arguably, with some episodic memories, there is a phenomenological component – visual, auditory, tactile – to our recollection. Thus, one might hold that some episodic memories could be illusory. In addition, that what we experience appears to be past seems to be a condition of such memory-experience; if what we experience seems to be happening now, or to be about to happen, whatever else it seems to be, it does not seem to be a kind of memory.

Given our memories are about the past, and have a phenomenological component that seems related to the past, do we have illusions of pastness? Two reasons to think so will be discussed here: the evidence for false memory and the idea that memory is like imagination.

There is a great deal of evidence for illusory cases of memory, of *false* memories, where subjects fail to distinguish episodes that actually happened from episodes that they have imagined (e.g., Brainerd & Reyna 2005; Sabbagh 2009). However, does the evidence establish that such experiences involve an appearance of something past that is not actually past, i.e., a temporal illusion?

According to one model (discussed in Brainerd & Reyna 2005), the evidence for false memories is due to a failure in what is referred to as *source monitoring*: the subjects mis-attributed imagining an episode with having actually lived through it (see also, Lindsay & Johnson 2000). Given just that description, one might argue for a temporal illusion in this way:

1. What the subject experiences in false memory is what they experience in imagining.
2. What the subject seems to experience is what is experienced in remembering.
3. What is experienced in imagining is what is present.
4. What is experienced in remembering is what is past.
5. Thus, (from 1 and 3) the subject is experiencing what is present but (from 2 and 4) seems to be experiencing what is past.
6. Thus, the subject is under an illusion of pastness, i.e., a temporal illusion.

However, it is not clear from the evidence for false memory that the subject misidentifies an act of remembering with an act of imagining. Tests of memory are carried out after both imagining and the original recollection have occurred (e.g., Brainerd & Reyna 2005). That is, the subjects are not confusing imagining *now* with remembering *now*; they are confusing an occasion where they were imagining *before* now with an occasion of remembering *before* now. The illusion is that a past experience, an imagining, is remembered as having been another kind of experience, a remembering. The illusion is between two kinds of past episodes, not between the past and present. Confusing the memory of one of these with memory of the other is not an illusory experience of the past.

Another reason to suppose that an apparent experience of the past, e.g., in memory, is illusory is that what is past is not around us; the past cake is not on the table beside me. It seems intuitive to hold that we cannot experience what is not around us. Yet, in memory, this is just what we appear to do. Thus, we might argue that what we appear to experience – the past, a temporal property – is different to what we can experience; thus, we have a temporal illusion.

MacKay refers to this kind of experience in memory as illusory, in particular because of the immediacy of such past events when we recall them:

> The illusion of which I speak is the direct awareness of past objects or events that seem to be involved in the process of memory. It is the apparent existence of that which has not only ceased to exist, but is known at the moment of remembering to be non-existent. That we should seem to be aware of objects which, as we know, are not there to be perceived, is of the sort that Kant may have had in mind when he spoke of necessary illusions. This is an illusion that arises in the nature of the experience.[...] [The illusion is that memory] should seem to be an acquaintance with the past [...that it] pertains only to the quality or immediacy of the memory experience. In remembering, it is as if things past were nevertheless present, or as if there were a consciousness, a direct awareness, of the presence of remembered events, known to have occurred in the past. Memory [is a] "presence of things past", to use Augustine's paradoxical phrase.

(MacKay 1945, p.297)

Like Husserl, MacKay thinks memory-experience is like this: we are not aware of an intermediary present entity, such as an image, which we experience directly and *through* which we experience the past event. But does this mean we are under an illusion if we experience past things? If other philosophers are correct, then this is not so obvious. For consider the quote earlier from Husserl: all that seems to be apparent to us in memory-experience are the features of the remembered past episode – in remembering red things, only past sensations of red are apparent, not present sensations. However, not only are these past sensations only what is apparent but, according to Husserl, they also appear to be past in our memory-experience. Thus, as these events are themselves past, then this appearance in memory does not disagree with how things are. Thus, there is no illusion here.

But how can we experience something that also seems past without some kind of intermediary entity through which we experience them? This is a problem similar to one already discussed earlier in this paper: the 'appearances' in imagined events. Recall that the difficulty there is one wants to say that one is aware of something, something is apparent, yet one also wants to deny that there is anything being presented. When I seem to be visually imagining a unicorn, it does not seem to be presented. But even if I imagine something real like a donkey far away in the field near my family home, although it seems to be of something real, it still does not seem to be present in any way; it seems to be absent. This absence, this non-presence, whether because it is unreal or because it just is not around me in any way, is precisely why such an experience seems to be an act of imagination.

With memory, there is something similar. However, there is a significant difference: what is remembered always appears to have *happened*. As such, there may be the following two options for a basic description of how the past appears in memory:

1. Past events do not seem to be present, or to be around us, because they do not seem to be real. They seem to be unreal, as imaginary things seem unreal. This is possibly part of the motivation for presentism: only the present seems real; the past and future do not.
2. Past events do not seem to be present, or to be around us, because they seem to be at another time. They do not seem to be happening now; however, they do appear to be real – they just appear to be real at another time.

Both of these options makes remembering episodes very like imagining episodes – the events and things are not happening here and now – and the same question applies. If, just like we imagine, the appearance of the past is of something that is absent, how can its *being* absent make that appearance an illusion?

As stated, one (very plausible, in my view) response is that any appearance of absence must itself be illusory, e.g., we can never experience something that is absent. In that case, we do have an illusion here: our memory-experience seems to be of something absent from this time; but we cannot experience something absent from this time; thus, we are under an illusion.

However, as with false memory syndrome, even if there is an illusion, there is still the question about whether or not the illusion is a *temporal* illusion. The inability to experience something which is absent applies to imagining in general, not just remembering; what is imagined also appears to be absent. If just absence is what makes the experience an illusion, then this is not a temporal illusion.

However, perhaps this is a temporal illusion because there is a special kind of *temporal* absence; not only is it mistaken that we seem to experience a non-present thing but, particularly, in memory it is non-present because it is specifically past. But again: if what we experience is in fact present and here, what does adding 'temporal' to its absence do here that makes it that particular kind of illusion? If some positive answer can be given for this, then we may have here an illusion of time.

It should be clear from the foregoing discussion that the issue of whether or not *memory* illusions are *temporal* illusions require a decision on whether or not either of the following is true of experience:

1. What we can experience must be present.
2. In memory, what we seem to experience is past.

Deciding both of these, I think, involves engaging with one's concept of time. We can say that there are temporal illusions given either of the following scenarios obtain:

1. Presentism and an apparently real past:
   (a) What we experience seems past and real (just absent now) when we remember.
   (b) Presentism is true: only what is present is real.
2. Eternalism and an apparently unreal past:
   (a) What we experience seems past and unreal (and not just absent now) when we remember.
   (b) Eternalism: anything at any time, including the past, present, or future, is real.

In these cases, if we experience what appears to be past, we have cases of temporal illusions. For, given how the past seems in memory: - '1.' implies that we could not be experiencing the past as it seems to be; the past is unreal, contrary to appearances. - '2.' implies that we could not be experiencing the past as it seems to be; the past is real, contrary to appearances.

Thus, if this is how we think things seem when we remember, then to avoid temporal illusion we need to engage with the metaphysics of time.

Finally, perhaps there is another way to deal with this issue. This is to resist the interpretation given so far of what memory-experience is like or how it *seems*. We deny that this is an experience which seems to be of the *past* - or at least directly of the past. Instead, we always seem to experience only present things. With memory, these present things are like images which *stand* for past things. This alternative view may allow one to withdraw from engaging with the metaphysical debate on time and memory. One assumes that, where something present *is* thought to be unreal, its unreality is not related to its temporal properties. The image seems to be present and it is present. However attractive this interpretation may seem, one must first establish it; one must show that this is what our memory-experience is like (again, not how it *actually* is). This is not a metaphysical question, perhaps. Although still a philosophical question, it looks to be one within the domain of phenomenology (for more on the memory-image, see e.g., Locke 1971, Le Poidevin 2003).

6   Conclusion

In conclusion, to summarise, this paper has:

(a) Briefly considered what it is for something to be a perceptual (or experiential) illusion.
(b) Briefly described different temporal features and different concepts of time.
(c) Argued – and attempted to show through two examples – that whether or not some evidence could be interpreted as evidence of temporal illusions partly depends on one's concept of time.

If the general argument here is right, I suggest that it is because of the following chain of reason:

(i) One's concept of time partially determines one's concept of what is real.
(ii) One's concept of what is real partially determines one's concept of what is illusory.
(iii) One's concept of what is illusory partially determines one's concept of what is a temporal illusion.

Linked in this chain is a more general conclusion, one which may be significant to the study of illusion in general: *one's concept of time partially determines one's concept of what is illusory.* Such conclusions suggest that thinking about time has interesting consequences for how one interprets experience in general.

Given the concern of this paper, however, the next step is to examine whether or not other possible temporal illusions can be interpreted differently given different concepts of time. One significant example which could not be examined in sufficient detail here is the phi phenomenon, in particular colour phi (e.g., Kölers 1972, p.171; Dennett 1991, p.115). Dennett uses this example to argue that temporal order need only be represented in perception, i.e., perceptions need not have the temporal order that they appear to possess. Where they do not, as they seem not to in the phi phenomenon, we have an example of temporal illusion (at least according to the naive realist).

However, before deciding that temporal order is what is illusory here, we might ask this: perhaps this interpretation of the phi phenomenon is dependent only on some conceptions of time? And so: could it be interpreted differently given other conceptions? This is something for future work.

Acknowledgements. This research was carried out during a Postdoctoral Fellowship at University College Cork, support for which was provided by the Irish Research Fellowship of the Humanities and the Social Sciences. An early talk on this work was presented at the Centre for the Study of Perceptual Experience at the University of Glasgow. I am grateful for comments from contributors there, and for personal correspondence from Fiona MacPherson, particularly on the concept of illusion. I am also grateful to Julia Jansen, Joel Walmsley and Andrew Whitehead at UCC for their suggestions. And, last but by no means least, for detailed and thought-provoking commentary from three anonymous referees of this paper.

References

1. Alston, W.: Perception and Representation. Phenomenological and Philosophical Research 102(2), 253–289 (2005)
2. Batty, C.: Smelling Lessons. Philosophical Studies 153 (2011)
3. Brainerd, C.J., Reyna, V.F.: The Science of False Memory. Oxford University Press, Oxford (2005)
4. Callender, C.: The Common Now. Philosophical Issues 18, 339–361 (2008)
5. Caplan, B., Sanson, D.: Presentism and Truthmaking. Philosophy Compass 6/3 (2011)
6. Chalmers, D.: The Problem of Consciousness. In: Heil, J. (ed.) Philosophy of Mind: a Guide and Anthology. Oxford University Press, Oxford (2004)

7. Craig, W.L.: Wishing It Were Now Some Other Time. Philosophy and Phenomenological Research 62(1) (2001)
8. Crane, T.: Is There a Perceptual Relation? In: Gendler, T.S., Hawthorne, J. (eds.) Perceptual Experience. Oxford University Press, Oxford (2006)
9. Dainton, B.: Stream of Consciousness: Unity and Continuity in Conscious Experience. Routledge, London (2000)
10. Dainton, B.: Time in Experience: Reply to Gallagher. Psyche 9, 12 (2003), http://psyche.cs.monash.edu.au/symposia/dainton/gallagher-r.pdf
11. Dainton, B.: Temporal Consciousness. In: Zalta, E.N. (ed.) The Stanford Encyclopedia of Philosophy (2010), http://plato.stanford.edu/archives/fall2010/entries/consciousness-temporal
12. Dennett, D.: Consciousness Explained. St.Ives, Penguin (1991)
13. Deutsch, D.: Auditory Illusions. In: Gregory, R.L. (ed.) The Oxford Companion to the Mind. Oxford University Press, Oxford (1987)
14. Durgin, F.H.: The Time of Consciousness and Vice Versa. Consciousness and Cognition 11, 284–290 (2002)
15. Eagleman, D.M.: Human time perception and its illusions. Current Opinion in Neurobiology 18(2), 131–136 (2008)
16. Gallagher, S.: Sync-Ing in the Stream of Experience: Time-Consciousness in Broad, Husserl, and Dainton. Psyche 9(10) (2003)
17. Hacker, P.M.S.: Appearances and Reality. Basil Blackwell, Oxford (1987)
18. Hoerl, C.: The Perception of Time and the Notion of a Point of View. European Journal of Philosophy 6(2), 156–177 (1998)
19. Hoerl, C.: Time and Tense in Perceptual Experience. Philosophers' Imprint 9(12), 1–18 (2009)
20. Husserl, E.: On the Phenomenology of the Consciousness of Internal Time (1893-1917). In: Brough, J.B. (trans. and ed.). Kluwer Academic Publishers, Dordrecht (1991)
21. Husserl, E.: Phantasy, Image Consciousness, and Memory (1898-1925). In: Brough, J.B.(trans. and ed.). Springer, Dordrecht (2005)
22. Kölers, P.A.: Aspects of Motion Perception. Pergamon, Oxford (1972)
23. Le Poidevin, R.: The Experience and Perception of Time. In: Zalta, E.N. (ed.) The Stanford Encyclopedia of Philosophy (Winter 2000), http://plato.stanford.edu/archives/win2000/entries/time-experience/
24. Le Poidevin, R.: Travels in Four Dimensions, London, Oxford (2003)
25. Le Poidevin, R.: Images of Time. Oxford University Press, Oxford (2007)
26. Lindsay, D.S., Johnson, M.K.: False memories and the source monitoring framework: Reply to Reyna and Lloyd(1997). Learning and Individual Differences 12(2), 145–161 (2000)
27. Locke, D.: Memory. Macmillan, London (1971)
28. Lowe, E.J.: Indirect Perception and Sense Data. The Philosophical Quarterly 31(125), 330–342 (1981)
29. Lowe, E.J.: A Survey of Metaphysics. Oxford University Press, Oxford (2003)
30. Lycan, W.: Layered Perceptual Representation. Philosophical Issues 7, Perception, 81–100 (1996)
31. McCauley, R.N., Henrich, J.: Susceptibility to the Müller-Lyer Illusion, Theory-Neutral Observation and the Diachronic Penetrability of the Visual Input System. Philosophical Psychology 19(1), 79–101 (2006)
32. McGinn, C.: Mindsight: Image, Dream, Meaning. Harvard University Press, London (2004)

33. MacKnik, S.L., Martinez-Conde, S.: Sleights of Mind: What the Neuroscience of Magic Reveals about our Everyday Deceptions. Henry Holt, New York (2010)
34. MacPherson, F.: Cognitive Penetration of Colour Experience: Rethinking the Issue in Light of an Indirect Mechanism. Philosophical and Phenomenological Research (forthcoming)
35. Markosian, N.: Time. In: Zalta, E.N. (ed.) The Stanford Encyclopedia of Philosophy (Fall 2010), http://plato.stanford.edu/archives/win2010/entries/time/
36. Mellor, D.H.: Real Time II. Routledge, London (1998)
37. Mohanty, J.H.: Theories of False Cognition (Khyativada). Classical Indian Philosophy. Lanham, Rowman & Littlefield (2000)
38. Nudds, M.: Recent Work in Perception: Naive Realism and its Opponents. Analysis 69(2), 334–346 (2009)
39. Overgaard, S.: On the Looks of Things. Pacific Philosophical Quarterly 91, 260–284 (2010)
40. Perky, C.W.: An Experimental Study of Imagination. American Journal of Psychology 21, 422–452 (1910)
41. Power, S.E.: Complex Experience, Relativity and Abandoning Simultaneity. Journal of Consciousness Studies 17(3-4) (2010a)
42. Power, S.E.: Perceiving External Things and the Time-Lag Argument. European Journal of Philosophy (2010b), http://dx.doi.org/10.1111/j.1468-0378.2010.00436.x
43. Power, S.E.: The Metaphysics of the Specious Present. Erkenntnis (2011), http://dx.doi.org/10.1007/s10670-011-9287-x
44. Prosser, S.: Passage and Perception. Nos (forthcoming)
45. Sabbagh, K.: Remembering Childhood. Oxford University Press, Oxford (2009)
46. Sartre, J.-P.: The Imaginary: A Phenomenological Psychology of the Imagination. In: Webber, J. (trans.). Routledge, Oxon (1986)
47. Schlesinger, G.N.: How Time Flies. Mind 91(364), 501–523 (1982)
48. Shoemaker, S.: Time without Change. In: Le Poidevin, R., MacBeath, M. (eds.) The Philosophy of Time. Oxford University Press, Oxford (1991)
49. Smart, J.J.C.: Spatialising Time. Mind 64(254), 239–241 (1955)
50. Smith, A.D.: Disjunctivism and Illusion. Philosophy and Phenomenological Research 80(2), 384–410 (2010)
51. Smith, Q., Oaklander, N. (eds.): Time, Change and Freedom: An Introduction to Metaphysics. Routledge, London (1995)
52. Snowden, P., Robinson, H.: The Objects of Perceptual Experience. Proceedings of the Aristotelian Society 64, 121–166 (1990)
53. Yandell, K.: Philosophy of Religion: a Contemporary Introduction. Routledge, London (1999)

A.N. Prior's Notion of the Present

David Jakobsen

Department of Communication and Psychology, Aalborg University
Kroghstraede 3, 9220 Aalborg East, Denmark
davker@hum.aau.dk

Abstract. This paper presents a fresh look at A.N. Prior's *Notion of The Present* (1970), in order to cast light on the article through Prior's own notes from the Bodleian library. This will be done in order to evaluate two critiques of Prior's notion of the present: That is self-contradictory (see [17]), and that it is unable to account for change (see [6]). This article will argue that a revisit to Prior's notes will provide clarity at places where confusion gives ground to criticism of Prior's definition as self-contradictory. The notes will also underline how radical Prior's notion of the present is, and that he was aware of it. They thus help us to see more clearly what Prior actually meant by saying that the present is the real considered in relation to two realms of unreality, namely the past and the future.

Keywords: Ontology, A.N. Prior, Time and existence, Tense-logic, Presentism.

1 The Notion of the Present

When A.N. Prior is credited for playing a role in bringing metaphysics out from the heydays of logical positivism (see [20]), it is in large part due to his development of temporal logic that gives pre-eminence to the present together with his commitment to temporal realism.

Prior developed temporal logic as a modal logic with four operators. Two for the future: the weak operator F for "it will be the case", and the strong operator G for "it will always be the case", defined as ⌐F⌐. And two for the past: The weak P for "it has been the case", and the strong H for "it has always been the case", defined as ⌐P⌐. The essential metaphysical commitment behind this logic is the idea that propositions have changing truth-value.

This development of temporal logic, not only sparked the birth of a new kind of logic, it also gave new life to metaphysical discussions on the nature of time, between those who defend a view of time in which propositions have changing truth-value, and those who defends a perspective of time, in which propositions have eternal, or static truth-value. The former is typically defended as part of the larger paradigm, called presentism, in which the central motivating intuition is the idea of becoming, which only seems to be defensible if reality is denied to that which isn't yet the case, or no longer is the case. The latter, called eternalism, is typically defending a larger paradigm of time against what is perceived to be problematic, unscientific or even contradictory results of presentism.

A. Vatakis et al. (Eds.): Time and Time Perception 2010, LNAI 6789, pp. 36–45, 2011.
© Springer-Verlag Berlin Heidelberg 2011

One of the central problems in this debate has been the definition of the present given by Prior in *The Notion of The Present* (1970), which has become the go-to article for a definition of presentism, and, for this reason, arguably one of the most influential works by Prior on the metaphysics of time. Due to his early death, though, in 1969, at the age of 55, it has largely been up to his inheritors to continue the defence of presentism. This defence has been taken up by quite a large group of philosophers who have produced book-length defences of a tensed view on time, in which presentism typically is an essential element (see [15,4,1]). Others could be mentioned who treat the metaphysical questions surrounding the notion of the present, but the general picture is the same in all of these, and is brought out by Nathan Oaklander in his critique of Prior's presentism when he says that:

> Each of the philosophers I shall discuss, William Lane Craig, John Bigelow and Robert Ludlow, all avowed presentists acknowledge their debt to Prior, but for one reason or another find his particular explication of presentism wanting. Prior's views have recently received critical discussion by other A theorists such as Craig Smith and Tooley" [8:76-77].[1]

The Notion of the Present (1970) was written in 1969 for a conference on time he attended in Austria at the launching of *The International Society for the Study of Time*. It was published the year after, but not by Prior himself. The central, and controversial part, of the paper is Prior's view that the concept of the present and the concept of the real are the same, with the radical consequence that the past and the future should be treated as having the same ontological status as stories and imaginations of centaurs and possible worlds. They are just as equally unreal.

The critique of such a definition of the present, summed up in the name Solipsistic Presentism is that it is self-contradictory, and that it cannot account for the central intuition behind Presentism, namely the idea of becoming.

Even though we do not have Prior's reply to these critiques of his notion, we are very fortunate that we, at the Bodleian Library in Oxford, have his notes to *The Notion of the Present*. This is interesting, since we in these can see Prior struggling to get the definition right, producing two discernable variations of the definition. It is furthermore clear from the notes that Prior was aware of the radical nature of his notion of the present. While there is little hope that the notes can settle the philosophical dispute surrounding the Priorian notion of the present, (could anything?) a revisit to the notes might bring clarity to how he meant his definition of the present to be understood.

2 The Definition of Presentism

In general, presentism is the view that to exist, or to be real, is to be present. This means that a presentist denies reality to the past and the future. While this sounds short and lucid, what meaning is there in saying that to exist is to be *present* when *being present* isn't explained in relation to some extension that gives a meaning to the

---

[1] Oaklander's reference here is to [3,13,15-16,18] To these could also be added criticism from Bourne (see [1]) who joins the camp of the B theorists concerning the need of truthmakers for tensed facts, but none the less finds room for such within a presentist framework.

word? The presentist seems to need the past and the future to do that. Just as up and down are needed in order to explain what *in between* is, so the presentist has to relate the present to the past and future. But at the same time such relations are controversial to say the least. Prior's definition of the notion of the present looks like an attempt to navigate these waters:

> they [the present and the real] are one and the same concept, and the present simply *is* the real considered in relation to two particular species of unreality, namely the past and the future [12:245].

Presentism exists in many variants, several of which are critical towards Prior's own version. Several versions of presentism are of course to be expected when one joins together two difficult metaphysical issues in a single concept. However the more specific reason is the above-mentioned problem. If only the present is real, then what does it mean to relate the present to the past and the future? A common assumption is that relations between two entities entail the reality of both.

If it does, then presentism is self-contradictory, when it claims that only the present is real, but also related to the unreal past and future. Prior's definition of the present and the real has been criticised by Smith (see [17]) for being just that.

If the present, on the other hand, isn't related to the past and the future, then how can presentism account for the notion of becoming? David Lewis (see [6]) argues that presentism, in virtue of treating other times as abstract constructions is unable to account for change. If Lewis's charge is right, then it is a hard blow to presentism, since one of the primary motivations for accepting it is, according to Zimmerman:

> The desire to do justice to the feeling that what's in the past is over and done with, and what's in the future only matters because it will eventually be present [19:212].

2.1   Is Prior's Notion of the Present a Contradiction?

Smith's criticism of Prior notion of the present turns on the temporal relations Prior talks about between the past/future and the present:

> I believe solipsistic presentism is logically self-contradictory. The main founder of solipsistic presentism, Prior, tellingly defines it in an implicitly self-contradictory way … 'the present simply is the real considered in relation to two particular species of unreality, namely the past and the future.' If the real stands in relation to the unreal, the unreal is real, since only something real can stand in relation to something. Unreality can no more stand in relations than it can possess monadic properties [17:123]

Smith's argument assumes that

1) If x is related to y, then both x and y are real

He also assumes a reading of Prior's definition to the effect that "considered in relation" should be understood as affirming a relation between the present and the past and the future. If this reading is correct, and given the assumption that the present is the real, then it follows that

2) If the present stands in relation to the past and the future, then the real is related to the unreal

From these Smith concludes that

3) If the real is related to the unreal, the unreal is real.

Smith's argument is not just directed against Prior's notion of the present, but also other versions of presentism, which follow Prior in claiming that the past and future are unreal.[2] Whether or not Smith is correct in his reading of Prior is actually solvable with the notes we have from the Bodleian archive. He isn't, and this will be clear later, but it doesn't settle the problem for Prior's notion of the present. The contradiction is namely deducible, not only from relations between the present and the past and future, but from quantification over non-present objects. This means that whether or not Prior, in his definition, only speaks about a *considered* relation, a new argument could be made if Prior takes this to imply that we in such a *considered* relation between something in the past and future actually quantify over *something* in the past and future. Since the logic of relations typically presupposes quantification theory, this is a more serious problem. The core of the matter is not just that a relation between x and y commit us to the reality of both x and y, as Smith assumes, and which Prior can dodge in talking about a mere consideration. With regard to relations, in order for xRy to mean anything we have to bind the variables by an existential or universal quantifier. But then, already in speaking about relations *as considered* between the past and the future, Prior assumes that we can quantify over *something* in the past or the future. The issue of quantifying over non-present objects is therefore more fundamental than temporal relations between the past and the future. Prior actually seems to affirm this in *Past, Present and Future*, when he with regard to tensed fact about past or future individuals says:

> One argument in favour of the view that if we are to use individual name-variables at all, we should let them cover non-existents, is that we often want to express *relations* between what now exists and what does not [11:169].

If the presentist therefore believes that he in his *considerations* quantifies over something in the past and the future, then a new argument can be mounted against him with the conclusion that presentism is contradictory. The B theorist Robin Le Poidevin has spelled out an assumption for his criticism of presentism's quantification over non-present objects that can be used in such an argument. I will refer to this as Le Poidevin's principle:

> a theory which involves ineliminable quantification over F's is committed to a realist position over F's [5:38].

With this assumption or *dictum de omni et nullo,* the charge against Prior's self-contradictory definition of presentism can be outlined in a syllogistic form

---

[2] The charge of solipsism with regard to the present covers a wider range of philosophical issues. (See [5], and [4] for a response)

4) Any theory that involves ineliminable quantification over non-present objects is committed to a realist position over non-present objects

5) Presentism involves ineliminable quantification over non-present objects

From 4 and 5 it follows that

6) Presentism is committed to a realist position over non-present objects

This conclusion is in clear contradiction with Prior's definition of presentism, and not only Prior's, but any version of what Smith calls Solipsistic presentism. Furthermore we have very good reason to believe that Prior was committed to something like Le Poidevin's principle. It is an underlying principle of Prior's rejection of tensed facts about that, which doesn't exist. (see 11:137-174]). This is already seen in *Time and Modality* from 1957:

> Where x stands for a proper name, it seems to me that the form 'x exists' must be logically equivalent to, and definable as, 'There are facts about x', ... If there *are* facts about *x*, I cannot see what *further* fact about *x* would consist in its existing [9:31].

The crucial point is that Prior did not allow *ineliminable* quantification over non-present objects. This is also already clear in Time and Modality:

> In other words, in the form 'There will be an *x* tomorrow which Φ's, the bound variable *x* has as yet no range of values at all, and its truth-value depends, so far as it depends on a range of values, on the range of values which the bound variable in 'There *is* an x which Φ's will acquire tomorrow. And what it now states is not a fact *about* any of tomorrow's objects, though if the statement is true there will be an *x* tomorrow with a fact about it of the form 'x Φ's' [9:32].

This remained a clear core conviction of Prior's tensed logic, and part of his argument in *The Notion of The Present*, which we will return to later. For now it is enough to point out that Prior's presentism is not guilty of self-contradiction on any reading of his definition. A Priorian presentist can still maintain that he isn't committed to a realist position over non-present objects, by avoiding *ineliminable* quantification over non-present objects. In syllogistic form he could maintain

4) Any theory that involves ineliminable quantification over non-present objects is committed to a realist position over non-present objects

7) Presentism is not committed to a realist position over non-present objects

8) Therefore: Presentism does not involve ineliminable quantification over non-present objects

It is evident from Prior's reasoning in *The Notion of The Present (1970)* that Prior affirms 4, 7 and 8. For Prior *what will be*, and *what has been*, fall under the same category as *what could have been*, *what might have been* or for that matter *what Greek mythmakers have imagined*. Accordingly, just as any quantifier that extends over modal statements or imagined objects has to be understood as not only picking out certain objects, but as also eliminating those entities, so must the quantifiers in connection with the temporal operators. This has the consequence of drastically reducing tensed facts about the past and future to facts of a logical kind only. The past is, thus, treated by Prior as the *now-unpreventable*[3]. It is not treated as a set of facts that are somehow a past truth, but rather something that is a present truth:

> Moreover, just as a real thought of a centaur, and a thought of a real centaur, are both of them just a thought of a centaur, so the present pastness of Dr. Whitrow's lecture, and its past presentness, are both just its pastness. And conversely, its pastness is its present pastness, so that although Whitrow's lecture isn't now present as so isn't real, isn't a fact, nevertheless its pastness, its *having* taken place, *is* a present fact, *is* a reality, and will be one as long as time shall last [12:247]

Prior's presentism leads him therefore to deny that there are any facts about the past, because *what was the case*, is a prefix, just as *what would have been the case,* and as such entail that whatever it connects to isn't real.

Smith is therefore wrong in arguing that Prior's notion of the present is contradictory. He is also wrong though in his wider argument that any theory that only affirms reality for the present is in contradiction. The final syllogistic form with relation to the *dictum de omni et nullo,* is to argue that there is an exception to Le Poidevin's principle. It is logically valid to affirm 5, that presentism is involved in ineliminable quantification over non-present objects, but also affirms 7, that presentism isn't committed to a realist's position over non-present objects. This of course can only be done by denying principle 4, that any theory, which involves ineliminable quantification over non-present objects, is committed to a realist position over non-present objects. Thus the final position, the *dictum de excepto* is

5) Presentism involves ineliminable quantification over non-present objects
7) Presentism is not committed to a realist position over non-present objects
9) Therefore: It is not the case that, any theory that involves ineliminable quantification over non-present objects is committed to a realist position over non-present objects.

5 and 7 characterises the position of a presentist like Craig [4]. The consequence of affirming both that the past and the future aren't real is that one cannot adhere to the *dictum de omni et nullo,* but so much the worse for that principle one could say.

It is therefore possible for the presentist to give two answers to Smith's criticism of the definition of presentism. First of all it is possible to deny the principle behind Smith's criticism, following the cue of Craig. A reason for doing so is that it isn't just quantification over future and past objects that give us problems with 4. Should we also be committed to the existence of non-hobbits, when we affirm that there are no hobbits?

The second answer, which Prior would give, is that he isn't committed to relations between the past, present and future, even though these terms are part of his definition of the present. He would seem to affirm that if he was guilty of ineliminable quantification over non-present objects, then he would end up in a contradiction, but he isn't since his temporal operators of his tensed logic, in virtue of being a prefix, come with no ontological commitments.

---

[3] As in his treatment of Time and Determinism, in [11].

3   Revisiting "The Notion of the Present"

Two interesting places relate to the present discussion in Prior's notes to The Notion of The Present. The first is directly related to Smith's criticism and the second shows Prior's awareness of a weakness in his version of presentism.

It turns out that Prior was struggling with getting his definition just right, and we find two alternative phrases in his notes. The first phrasing Prior was attempting was

1. Attempt: "the present simply is the real considered in relation to a particular" [13]

The word included here, which didn't make it to the final version, is the word "a" before "particular". The second attempt perhaps shows us why Prior first wrote "a particular" in the first attempt

2. Attempt: "the present simply is the real considered with a particular kind of contrasting unreality in mind, namely the pa" [13]

Prior clearly tried to describe the notion of the present as *a consideration* of the present as the real, a consideration of *a particular* kind: a kind that involves a contrasting between the past and future as unreal, and the present as real. The phrase he ended up with dropped the singular term 'a' with regard to 'particular consideration,' leaving it ambiguous whether the relation Prior speaks about between the real and the unreal has to do with something *merely* under consideration, or a particular relation between the unreal past and future and the real present. From the notes it seems clear that Prior is struggling with defining the present without affirming to much about the past and the future. On one hand, he wants to affirm that the present and the real are one and the same concept. On the other hand, he also needs the past and the future in order to denote what it is that he is claiming to be the same concept as the real. This is problematic since if the past and the future are needed in order to denote what *being present* means, then one has to describe in what way the past and the future are related to the present. He therefore has to speak about the past and the future as being on the ontological level *of considerations*, while at the same time describing how such considerations are relevant in speaking about the relation between past, present and future.

Thus the words *considered in relation* in Prior's definition of the present are to be understood as just that. The present is the real, simply. The temporal prefixes for past and future, which is needed to describe 'the present', and give meaning to the concept has the ontological status of a *consideration,* and just as prefixes like *could have been* and *is imagined that*, according to Prior, do not denote some relation between the real and the unreal, neither do temporal prefixes.

Smith seems to be aware that Prior's use of the phrase "considered in relation" should not be taken literally as involving temporal relations between the real and the unreal, and anticipates the reply that Prior merely talks about a thinker's consideration of the present in relation to the past. He doesn't find this helpful either though, since "I cannot consistently consider the unreal to stand in a relation to the real" [17:123]. Smith's charge of inconsistency is off the mark with regard to Prior's definition though. The reason is that since Prior categorizes temporal prefixes together with characters of fiction, the only kind of inconsistency possible is of a logical kind. Should we take Smith charge to question the logical validity, as such, of temporal logic?

While Prior's notion of the present isn't inconsistent, it is, as Butterfield notices a radical position [2]. Firstly, Prior's lucid definition of presentism, is achieved by lumping, not just past and future objects, but any non-present tensed proposition, together with Zeus and unicorns. Secondly, clarity seems achieved at the expense of intelligibility when Prior defines what reality consists in as "the absence of a qualifying prefix" [12:247]. As Craig points out, it is hard to see what the existence of my lamp has got to do with the fact that it lacks a prefix [4].

It is rather interesting that Prior's notes to *The Notion of The Present* show that he was aware of how radical this view on tensed facts was. In direct connection to his past tensed facts, he immediately began a consideration on the difference between tensed and modal facts. In the crossed out section he wrote:

> There is, indeed, a great deal more law and regularity about the logical behavior of the prefixes "it has been that" and "it will be that" than there is about the logical behavior of "it is imagined that" [13].

After having crossed the section out Prior didn't return to the topic of how the logical behaviour of temporal prefixes differs from other prefixes, and more importantly, what he believed we should attach of importance to this with regard to tensed facts. Had Prior himself finished up the article for publication, he might have done something more about this than what we have before us now.

4 Presentism and Becoming

Based upon this analysis of Prior's notion of the present, and the notes we have at the Bodleian library, the question arises whether such a notion, doesn't lay itself open to Lewis's criticism (see [6:202–204]) that presentism is unable to account for change. Lewis rejects presentism's ability to account for change since it treats other times as "false stories" or "abstract representations composed out of the material of the present." And he seems to have a point with regard to versions of presentism that treats other temporal prefixes as *merely* fictional prefixes. If only what is present is real, and all quantification over future or past objects are to be eliminable like quantification over objects of fiction, then what is it that changes? What is it that can be said to endure through time? As Merricks comments on Lewis's argument, (see [7]) such a version of presentism would be a theory of everything as instantaneous. At each successive moment a set of statements would be true and say something about reality. Others would have prefixes like "it is imagined that", and still others would have a prefix like "it will be the case that", but the only things that would be real, would be facts, are statements without a prefix. It would seem in such a view on time that reality is reduced to what is a present tense truth at an instant, with no enduring objects.

Since becoming arguably is the primary intuition behind an A-theory, defining presentism in this way would be bordering on self-defeat.

A presentist should, in order to avoid Lewis's charge, minimally affirm that every *truth* about the future and the past are primitively present at each successive instant. This is done by presentists who affirm that we can make ineliminable quantification over non-present object. If we can't, then while temporal prefixes might contribute to a psychology of temporal reasoning, it appears to accounts just as much for becoming, as fictional prefixes ascribes properties to characters of fiction.

The problem for the Priorian notion of the present arises from its solution to the problem of temporal relations. Prior's notion of the present is able to give an account for temporal relations in terms of prefixes under a thinker's consideration. But by drastically reducing the ontological import of these temporal prefixes about the past and future, it makes the notion of the present vulnerable to Lewis's attack. The question is: If there are no facts about the past and the future, then how can there be a fact about becoming?

Prior has actually argued against the idea of *being brought into being* (see [11]) and seems satisfied with affirming a notion of *starting to be* instead. While this seems defensible, it is only because it doesn't require a thicker ontology than what his notion of the present allows. But, given this definition, the problem doesn't only arise with regard to becoming, but also with regard to *having past*. While a presentist easily can agree that *having past* shouldn't be parsed as stating a property about a none existing object, wouldn't a Priorian presentist need to parse it as not even involving a fact about a none existing object, and instead affirm a notion of *ceasing to be*?

With this said, it must be kept in mind that Prior *doesn't* argue against the notion of *having past*. On the contrary, he says that while the pastness of Dr Whitrow's lecture isn't a fact, "its *having* taken place, *is* a present fact, *is* a reality, and will be one as long as time shall last." [12:247]

5 Conclusion

Prior's notes to *The Notion of The Present* gives us valuable insight into the reflections he made while working on his speech, which only after his death was published. The criticism Prior's definition of the present as the real has received by Smith [17], can be shown to be not only false, but also based upon a misreading of the definition, with help from the notes. The notes make it clear that when Prior relates the present to the past and the future, it is with an emphasis upon a *considered relation*. The notes also reveal that Prior was aware of how radical his view was, when he categorizes temporal prefixes together with fictional prefixes as regard ontological import. While a Priorian notion of the present is therefore able to save itself from Smith's charge of contradiction, it isn't so clear that it can save itself from Lewis's charge of being incapable of accounting for change. It is unclear to me, and worth investigating whether other versions of presentism that follow Prior in only allowing eliminable quantification over non-present facts are able to avoid Lewis argument. One way to avoid both problems as a presentist is to deny that quantification over non-present objects entails the existence of non-present objects.

Acknowledgments. I am grateful to Dr. Mary Prior and to The Bodleian Library for giving me access to the Prior collection in Oxford.

References

1. Bourne, C.: A Future for Presentism. Oxford University Press, Oxford (2006)
2. Butterfield, J.: Prior's Conception of Time. In: Proceedings of the Aristotelian Society, pp. 193–209 (1983-1984)
3. Craig, W.L.: Is Presentness a Property? American Philosophical Quarterly (1), 27–40 (1997)
4. Craig, W.L.: The Tensed Theory of Time: A Critical Examination. Kluwer Academic Press, Dordrecht (2000)
5. Le Poidevin, R.: Change, Cause, and Contradiction: A Defence of the Tenseless Theory of Time. Macmillan, London (1991)
6. Lewis, D.: On the Plurality of Worlds. Blackwell, Oxford (1986)
7. Merricks, T.: Truth and Ontology. Oxford University Press, Oxford (2007)
8. Oaklander, L.N.: Presentism, Ontology and Temporal Experience. Cambridge University Press, Cambridge (2002)
9. Prior, A.N.: Time and Modality. Clarendon Press, Oxford (1957)
10. Prior, A.N.: Formal Logic. Clarendon Press, Oxford (1962)
11. Prior, A.N.: Past, Present and Future. Clarendon Press, Oxford (1967)
12. Prior, A.N.: The Notion of The Present. Studium Generale (23), 245–248 (1970)
13. Prior, A.N.: Notes to The Notion of the Present. The Prior Collection, Bodleian Library, Box 7, Oxford
14. Smith, Q.: The Infinite Regress of Temporal Attributions. The Southern Journal of Philosophy (3), 383–396 (1986)
15. Smith, Q.: Language and Time. Oxford University Press, New York (1993)
16. Smith, Q.: The 'Sentence-Type Version' of the Tenseless Theory of Time. Synthese (3), 233–251 (1999)
17. Smith, Q.: Time and Degrees of Existence: A Theory of 'Degree Presentism'. In: Callender, C. (ed.) Time, Reality and Experience, pp. 119–136. Cambridge University Press, Cambridge (2002)
18. Tooley, M.: Time, Tense and Causation. Oxford University Press, USA (1997)
19. Zimmerman, D.: Temporary Intrinsics and Presentism. In: Zimmerman, D., van Inwagen, P. (eds.) Metaphysics: The Big Questions, pp. 206–220. Basil Blackwell, Cambridge (1998)
20. Zimmerman, W.D., Loux, J.M.: Introduction. In: Zimmerman, W.D., Loux, J.M. (eds.) Oxford Handbook of Metaphysics, pp. 1–7. Oxford University Press, Oxford (2003)

Towards a Common Language for the Discussion of Time Based on Prior's Tense Logic

Peter Øhrstrøm

Department of Communication and Psychology, Aalborg University
Kroghstræde 3, 9220 Aalborg East, Denmark
poe@hum.aau.dk

Abstract. Time is not definable in terms of other concepts. On the other hand, it is generally accepted that Augustine was right in claiming that we as human beings have a tacit knowledge of what time is. But how can this tacit knowledge be explored and discussed, if time as such cannot be defined? This paper suggests that temporal logic, and in particular the hybrid logic corresponding to A.N. Prior's 3rd grade of tense-logical involvement, may be useful as a precise conceptual basis of a common language for the formal discussion of time. The paper offers a general investigation of this suggestion illuminating the conceptual potential and also some of the open questions within the study of temporal logic. It is argued that the endeavour of the logic of time can be seen as the study of some important manifestations and structures of our tacit knowledge of time.

1 The Conceptual Challenge in the Study of Time

According to St. Augustine (354-430) time cannot be satisfactorily described using just one single definition or explanation. In his own words: "What, then, is time? If no one asks me, I know: if I wish to explain it to one that asketh, I know not" [18:1]. Time is not definable in terms of other concepts. Every attempt to tell what time is will be an accentuation of some aspects of time at the expense of others. Therefore, it will not present time in its fullness. It may even be misleading. Time is unique and sui generis. On the other hand, this does not mean that precise studies of temporal matters and of time as such will be impossible. On the contrary, according to the Augustinian insight we all have a tacit knowledge of what time is, even though we cannot define time as such. However, if such studies are to lead to a deeper understanding of time itself, various disciplines have to be brought together in the hope that their findings may form a new synthesis, even though we should not expect any ultimate answer regarding the question of the nature of time itself. If such a synthesis is to be formed, a certain degree of homogeneity in the conceptual structure will be needed. For instance, if we have to design a computer system to handle discussions of time in general, it must be possible to state in a rather precise manner what is meant by words like 'during', 'since', 'until', 'past', 'future', 'before', 'after', 'what must be', 'what might be', 'what could have been', etc. The possibility of describing the logical relations between such notions is essential, if we want to be able to reason about the

A. Vatakis et al. (Eds.): Time and Time Perception 2010, LNAI 6789, pp. 46–57, 2011.
© Springer-Verlag Berlin Heidelberg 2011

temporal aspects of reality. This means that we need a common formal language, which is relevant at least for the kind of discussion of time that we have in mind.

It is important to emphasise that the question concerning a common language for the discussion of time is not psychological, but rather conceptual and systematic. When looking for such a common language the main question is not how the human mind actually works, but rather what notions will be needed in various kinds of scientific discourse dealing with the temporal aspects of reality. In particular, this question has recently turned out to be very important in computer science (see [6], [22], and [23]). The common language we a looking for in this context should not only allow for the precise specification of all notions relevant in scientific discussion of temporal matters, but it should also make it clear how these various notions are conceptually related. Such a common language may be useful within specific sciences like psychology and the physical sciences that are dealing with issues related to time. And even more important, if such a common language can be established and accepted as the common conceptual background, it may significantly support interdisciplinary research concerning the temporal aspects of reality. This means that there are very good reasons for looking for a common and precise language for the formal discussion of time.

The 20th century has seen a very important development within the philosophical study of time. One of the most important contributions to the modern philosophy of time was made in the 1950s and 1960s by A.N. Prior (1914-69), who became the founder of modern temporal logic. Prior presented his ideas and theories in a number of books and papers. He was very much inspired by his studies of the long history of science and philosophy. In particular, he found important inspiration in ancient and medieval thought. In fact, Prior considered several logical systems. We shall suggest the use of the conceptually richest temporal logic suggested by him. This may facilitate the practical use of temporal ideas and formal relations in all relevant ways. In a sense the endeavour of such a logical language of time makes it possible to study important manifestations and structures of our tacit knowledge of what time is. The system in question, which was originally invented by Prior, belongs to the family of systems which has later been characterised as so-called hybrid logic (see [3]). A logical system belonging to this family includes a special class of propositions (in the present case the so-called instant-propositions). Recently, hybrid logic has been demonstrated to be very useful within various kinds of computer science (see [3]).

2   The Two Classical Languages on Time

In his famous paper 'The Unreality of Time' [7] the philosopher John Ellis McTaggart (1866-1925) suggested a distinction between the so-called A- and B-series, which in fact corresponds to a distinction between the following two sets of fundamental concepts concerning the temporal aspects of reality:

A-concepts: past, present, future
B-concepts: before, after, 'simultaneous with'

The A-concepts are well suited for describing the flow of time, since the future will become present and the present time will become past, i.e., flow into past. The B-concepts seem especially apt for describing the permanent and temporal order of events. Clearly, the two kinds of temporal notions can give rise to two different approaches to time.

Firstly, there is the dynamical approach (the A-theory) according to which the essential notions are past, present and future. In this view, time is seen "from the inside". Secondly, there is the static view of time (the B-theory) according which time is understood as a set of instants (or durations) ordered by the before-after relation. Here time is seen "from the outside". It may be said to be a God's eye perspective on time.

There is an ontological difference between the two theories. According to the A-theory the tenses are real whereas the B-theorists consider them to be secondary and unreal. According to the A-theory the 'Now' is real and objective, whereas the B-theories consider the Now to be purely subjective.

Formally, the A-language is tense-logical, i.e., it includes operators, P, F, and $\lozenge$, which can be used to form new propositions. If q is a proposition, Pq, Fq and $\lozenge q$ stand for the propositions "it has been the case that q", "it will be the case that q", and "it is possible that q", respectively. It is assumed that the truth-values of the propositions in question can vary from time to time. Using these three operators we may define the dual operators: $H \equiv_{def} \sim P \sim$ ("it has always been that ..."), $G \equiv_{def} \sim F \sim$ ("it will always be that ..."), and $\square \equiv_{def} \sim \lozenge \sim$ ("it is necessary that ..."). In addition, it is possible to introduce temporal units, e.g. days, using $P(n)$ for "it has been the case n days ago that ...", and $F(n)$ for "it will be the case in n days that ...". The basic formalisms of temporal logic have been discussed in details in [18].

Formally, the B-language is based on the idea that time is a set of instants with an ordering relation, i.e. (TIME,$\leq$). In addition, there is a truth-function, T. If t stands for an instant of time, and q stands for a proposition, then $T(t,q)$ stands for "q is true at t". In working with the B-language one major question will be how the basic structure (TIME,$\leq$) should be described. In particular, there is a focus on the properties of the relation, $\leq$.

The debate between the two theories has received a fresh impetus due to Prior's formal analysis of the problem. (See [18: 216 ff]). It turns out that in addition to the A- and the B-theories it would in fact be possible to define a position between the two theories according to which the B-notions are just as fundamental that the A-notions. On this view the A-notions cannot be defined in terms of the B-notions or vice versa, but the two sets of notions have to be treated on a par. (See [15: 117 ff].) Calling the traditional B-theory the first grade of tense-logical involvement, Prior has termed this intermediate position the second grade of the tense-logical involvement. However, it does not seem that anybody since Prior's first analysis has wanted to defend this second grade.

It should be mentioned that in Prior's analysis there are in fact two different versions of the classical A-theory. This distinction has to do with the modal operator. In what Prior has called the 3rd grade of the tense-logical involvement there is a primitive notion of temporal possibility (or necessity), i.e. the operator, $\lozenge$ (as well as its dual operator, $\square$). In the so-called 4th grade of the tense-logical involvement this modal operator is defined in terms of the tense-logical operators, *P* and *F*. Obviously, the latter theory is simpler from a systematic point of view. On the other hand, it is also evident that a lot of the expressive power is lost, if we drop a primitive modal operator. Among other things, it would be very difficult to express the idea of a true future (as opposed to 'the possible future' and 'the necessary future') without the use of a primitive modal operator.

3 The Importance of the Dynamic Aspects of Reality

The most common theory dealing with the relation between the A- and B-language is the B-theory according to which the B-notions are more fundamental that the A-notions. Following this theory the A-notions have to be defined in terms of the B-notions. The tense operators, *P* and *F*, may be defined in the following way:

(1) $T(t,Fq) \equiv_{def} \exists t_1 : t<t_1 \wedge T(t_1,q)$

(2) $T(t,Pq) \equiv_{def} \exists t_1 : t_1<t \wedge T(t_1,q)$

According to the B-theory tense-logical statements will have to be evaluated as the B-logical expressions, which occur when these definitions (1-2) are used. If for instance the structure (TIME, $\leq$) is supposed to be linear, then tense-logical theorems like the following may easily be proved to be valid at all times in the structure:

(3) $FFp \supset Fp$

(4) $FPp \supset (Pp \vee p \vee Fp)$

(5) $PFp \supset (Pp \vee p \vee Fp)$

However, it should be emphasized that on the B-logical account such theorems are only abbreviations of complex properties regarding the structure (TIME, $\leq$).

Prior pointed out that there are obvious weaknesses of the B-logical approach. The most important problem is that this theory does not include any idea of 'Now'. From a B-logical point of view, the present time can only be represented as an arbitrary instant. This is of course quite acceptable, if we take the view which Albert Einstein expressed in a letter to Michele Besso: "There is no irreversibility in the basic laws of physics. You have to accept the idea that subjective time with its emphasis on the now has no objective meaning." [12: 203] If the 'Now' and consequently also the other A-concepts are purely subjective, all we have to bother with when dealing with the temporal aspects of the objective world are the B-concepts. Viewed in this way reality is just a four-dimensional co-ordinate system, and time is nothing but clock-readings and dates. However, according to Prior even Einstein was a bit uncertain regarding the status of the 'Now'. He referred to the fact that Einstein once "explained that the experience of the Now means something special for men, something different from the past and the future, but that this important difference does not and cannot occur within physics." [15: 136-7] Prior found that this observation is very important. In his opinion, the distinction between the tenses is essential for the understanding of reality. For this reason Prior argued that it would be misleading to base the description of reality on "a language in which the difference between being, having been, and being about to be becomes inexpressible." [16: 323]

In Prior's opinion it would be mistaken to assume that the 'Now' and the tenses can be derived from the logic of earlier and later. For this reason he rejected the B-theory, and instead he argued in favour of the A-theory. Prior insisted that 'the Now' is real, and consequently that the distinction between the tenses is real (see [4: 47]). His main idea regarding the importance of temporal logic was philosophical. He wanted first of all to emphasize that we have to focus on the role of the tenses if we want to grasp the reality of the passage of time.

Prior pointed out: "Time is not an object, but whatever is real exists and acts in time." [4: 45] In his view, time is not just a structured set of instants, and "this earlier-later calculus is only a convenient but indirect way of expressing truths that are not really about 'events' but about *things*, and about what these things are doing, have done and will do." [4: 45]

The distinction between past, present, and future is in fact essential for the proper understanding of Prior's philosophy and logic. His central ontological tenet was that the distinction between past, present, and future is essential for a correct understanding of the objective world. In his own words: "So far, then, as I have anything that you could call a philosophical creed, its first article is this: I believe in the reality of the distinction between past, present, and future. I believe that what we see as a progress of events *is* a progress of events, a *coming to pass* of one thing after another, and not just a timeless tapestry with everything stuck there for good and all." [4: 47]

Prior criticized the common approach to logic according to which only unchanging (eternal) truths are studied: "Certainly there are unchanging truths, but there are changing truths also, and it is a pity if logic ignores these, and leaves it to existentialists and contemporary informal 'dialecticians' to study the more 'dynamic' aspects of reality. There are clear, hard structures for formal logicians to discover in the world of change and temporal succession. There are practical gains to be had from this study too, for example in the representation of time-delay in computer circuits, but the greatest gain that a logic of tenses brings is the accurate philosophical description of the reality of the passage of time." [4: 46] In this way, Prior maintained that the changes in the world should be analyzed in terms of tense-logical notions.

To some extent, Prior conceived his work as a continuation of Peirce's philosophy and logic. In fact Prior sometimes even called himself a Peircean. Prior clearly found some inspiration in the following statement made by Peirce in 1903: "Time has usually been considered by logicians to be what is called 'extra-logical' matter. I have never shared this opinion. But I have thought that logic had not yet reached the state of development at which the introduction of temporal modifications of its forms would not result in great confusion; and I am much of that way of thinking yet." [10: 4.523]

Prior wanted to take up this Peircean challenge and to carry out the task by integrating tenses in logic. He argued that we should in fact accept "tense distinctions as a proper subject of logical reflection" and that we should accept that "what is true at one time is in many cases false at another time, and vice versa" [13: 104].

4 The Origin of the Idea of Branching Time

Prior's main argument in favour of the A-theory was based on his strong belief in indeterminism. He wrote: "... I do not see how indeterminism can be expressed in a tenseless language at all. For indeterminism asserts a certain difference between the future and the past..., which is not at all the same thing as a difference between the earlier and the later." [21]

In addition to the fundamental creed regarding the role of the tenses in a proper understanding of reality, Prior held that freedom of choice is something very important and essential in the real world. He expressed his belief in real freedom in the following way: "One of the big differences between the past and the future is that once something has become past, it is, as it were, out of our reach - once a thing has happened, nothing we can do can make it not to have happened. But the future is to some extent, even though it is only to a very small extent, something we can make for ourselves. And this is a distinction which a tenseless logic is unable to express." [4: 48] For this reason Prior argued in favour of a fundamental asymmetry between past and future. The idea of alternative pasts may be conceivable as seen from a epistemological point of view, but he found that from an ontological point of view the idea of alternative pasts should not be accepted.

Prior obviously knew that similar thoughts had earlier been defended by continental philosophers, among whom Henri Bergson (1859-1941) would be one of the clearest examples. In his book from 1889 *Essai sur les données immédiates de la conscience* Bergson had argued that the space-like before-after-calculus (i.e. what was later called the B-approach) was insufficient and misleading as the basis of a proper understanding of time. Bergson denied that time can be adequately represented by space. In this way we can only deal with "time flown" and not with "time flowing", [1: 221]. In fact, he also – like Prior – pointed to the importance of the notion of freedom. He wrote: "Freedom is ... a fact, and among the facts which we observe there is none clearer. All the difficulties of the problem ... arise from the desire to endow duration with the same attributes as extensity, to interpret a succession by a simultaneity, and to express the idea of freedom in a language into which it is obviously untranslatable", [1: 221]. In his discussion of time he even suggested something, which came rather close to what was later called branching time. Bergson suggested to following illustration:

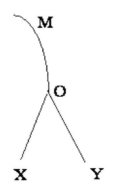

This figure was mainly meant as an illustration of the process of deliberation. The idea is that the deliberating person in question has traversed a series, MO, of conscious states. At the state O he finds the two directions, OX and OY, equally open for him. - However, Bergson argued that this geometrical representation of the process of coming to a decision is deceptive: "This figure does not show me the deed in the doing but the deed already done. Do not ask me then whether the self, having traversed the path MO and decided in favour X, could or could not choose Y: I should answer that the question is meaningless, because there is no line MO, no point O, no path OX, no direction OY. To ask such a question is to admit the possibility of adequately representing time by space and a succession by a simultaneity." [1:180]

According to Bergson the idea of human freedom is in fact indefinable. He argued that "we can analyse a thing but not a process; we can break up extensity, but not duration" [1: 219].

Although Prior knew this philosophical tradition, and also admitted that his own views on time to some extent were similar, he did not find contributions like Bergson's to be particularly useful to him. He had a strong belief in the value of formal logic, and in his opinion explanations like those suggested by Bergson were far too unclear. On the other hand, he also emphasized that logic has to do with real life. He wanted a logic that would take full advantage of formal methods, but which would also be sensitive to the reality of human experience. In an unpublished paper, he described this view: "Perhaps you could call my logic a mixture of Frege and Kolakowski. - I want to join the formal rigorism of the one with the vitalism of the other. Perhaps you regard this as a bastard mixture - a mesalliance. - I think it is a higher synthesis. And I think it important that people who care for rigorism and formalism should not leave the basic flux and flow of things in the hands of existentialists and Bergsonians and others who love darkness rather than light, but we should enter this realm of life and time, not to destroy it, but to master it with our techniques." [17]

Prior's book, *Time and Modality*, from 1957 was the first longer presentation of his tense logical approach to the understanding of reality. Prior demonstrated in the book that the development of tense-logic is very important if we want to establish a deeper understanding of the temporal aspects of reality, i.e. if we want a clear representation of temporal realism. One of the first readers to react on Prior's book was Saul Kripke who was only 17 years old when he wrote to Prior. In his letter Kripke suggested the following: "... in an indetermined system, we perhaps should not regard time as a linear series, as you have done. Given the present moment, there are several possibilities for what the next moment may be like -- and for each possible next moment, there are several possibilities for the next moment after that. Thus the situation takes the form, not of a linear sequence, but of a "tree"..."[21]

In this way Saul Kripke argued that the modal logic S4 corresponds to a branching time system. This presentation of branching time as a logical system is the first ever, and this approach is certainly very different from the ideas included in Bergson's model of the process of deliberation.

The importance of Kripke's approach was clearly recognised by Prior, who in his book *Past, Present and Future* [14] discussed what he called "Kripke's branching time matrix for S4" [14: 27]. However, it should be noted that in such a model, it may in some cases be true that $F(n)p \wedge F(n)\sim p$. In consequence, $\sim(F(n)p \wedge F(n)\sim p)$ will not be a theorem in the system. This would certainly be intuitively acceptable, if $F(n)$ were understood as 'possibly, it will be the case in n time units'. But if we want a logic for $F(n)$ conceived as 'it will be the case in n time units' as opposed to 'possibly, it will be the case in n time units', we have to look for a further elaboration of the tense-logical system and its representation in the branching time model. Much of the recent work on branching time models has been focused on a satisfactory representation of the future operator in terms of branching time (see [2,19, 20]).

Indeterminism is a very important tenet in Prior's philosophical logic. The idea is that there is a fundamental asymmetry between the past and the future. The point is that $P(n)p \vee P(n){\sim}p$ is true in all possible cases (i.e. it is a theorem), whereas the same does not hold for $F(n)p \vee F(n){\sim}p$. Prior's reason for denying that the latter disjunction is a theorem, is that if the proposition p depends on the free choice of some agent, then neither $F(n)p$ nor $F(n){\sim}p$ should regarded as true now. In Prior's opinion, there is no truth about which future decision the agent will make (until the agent has actually made his or her decision). However, regarding the past exactly one of the propositions, $P(n)p$ and $P(n){\sim}p$, is true, since only one of the propositions, p and ${\sim}p$, corresponds with how things were n time units ago. According to Prior, indeterminism is the basis of the asymmetry between past and future expressed here. It should be mentioned that this logical representation of indeterminism depends on the choice of tense-logical system. The above representation is based on the logical system, which Prior himself preferred, i.e. the so-called Peircean system. However, Prior also considered the so-called Ockhamistic system, in which indeterminism would correspond to the rejection of the disjunction $\Box F(n)p \vee \Box F(n){\sim}p$ as a theorem, whereas $F(n)p \vee F(n){\sim}p$ will be accepted as an Ockhamistic theorem. More about the distinctions between the Peircean and the Ockhamistic systems can be found in [14: 113 ff, 6: 211 ff].

It is an important issue within the discussion of temporal logic whether or not it is possible to create a tense-logical system according to which it makes sense to claim that statements about the contingent future can be true now. It has been argued in [19] that this is in fact possible to establish such a logical system.

5   Instants and the Notion of Branching Time

In his later writings Prior significantly contributed to the further development of the notion of branching time. One basic question regarding the branching time diagram has to do with the status of the points in the model. What is an instant? In [14: 187 ff] he suggested a logic of world-states, and he later developed this idea further [15]. His claim was that an instant in a branching time structure is in fact a world-proposition i.e. intuitively, an infinite conjunction of all propositions in a maximal and consistent subset of the set of all well-formed formulae formulated in terms of the logical language we are dealing with. In this way instant propositions are descriptions of possible states of the world, which are as complete as they can be given in the language we have chosen. Following Prior's idea in [15: 128 ff] the set of instant propositions can be characterized by the following three axioms, where a stands for an arbitrary instant proposition, and where p stands for an arbitrary proposition (whether instant proposition or not):

(I1) $\Diamond a$

(I2) $\exists a\colon a$

(I3) $\Box(a \supset p) \lor \Box(a \supset \sim p)$

According to (I1) any instant proposition represents a possible world-state, and (I2) is the claim that there is an instant proposition describing the present state of the world. The last condition, (I3), is the claim that any instant proposition will be total in the sense that for any other proposition, p, the instant proposition either necessarily implies p or it necessarily implies the negation, $\sim p$. It should be noted that any proposition in the logical language can be substituted for p. In consequence, a also implies which instant propositions have been, will be, could have been etc. In terms of the branching time system, this means that the whole structure of the branching time system follows from any single instant proposition. That is, the system has the nice and interesting property that the system as a whole is fully reflected – and in a sense even contained – in any basic part or element of the system i.e. in any instant. This insight might be conceived as a support of Prior's understanding of branching time as a conceptual structure consistent with his presentism. In short, according to Prior's theory the whole structure of time follows logically from the present, i.e., the instant proposition that is true now.

Formally, we may define what it means for a proposition, p, to be true for an instant proposition (or world proposition), a, in this way:

(I4) $T(a,p) \equiv_{def} \Box(a \supset p)$

Prior has demonstrated that given a basic tense-logical system this definition of $T(a,p)$ will have all the properties which a classical B-theorist would like for "truth at an instant". For instance, he demonstrated that given (I1-3) and the definition (I4) along with some basic assumptions concerning the logic of the P-,F-, and $\Diamond$-operators, the equivalences (1-2) become provable theorems. In this way, everything in the B-theory can interpreted as properties of the instant propositions. This also means that the traditional B-theoretical criticism of the A-theory turns out to be empty since the A-theory conceived as a hybrid logic is supposed to include all instant propositions. The A-theoretical criticism of the B-theory for ignoring the importance of the 'Now' and the asymmetry of time, on the other hand, still stands.

In Prior's opinion time is not an object, but rather a construction. He wrote: "What is time? Time is a logical construction. What looks like propositions about time are generalized tensed propositions about other things" [17]. Although time, on this view, is a construction, it is certainly not an arbitrary construction. The point is that our idea of time is an abstract generalization of a number of observations from everyday life concerning what it means to act now on the basis of what is known about the past and the future possibilities.

One very basic assumption in Prior's worldview has to do with the notion of free choice. This should probably be understood as closely related to his ideas of ethics and responsibility. In general, Prior tried to establish a conceptual framework integrating fundamental notions of logic, ethics and time. In terms of branching time notions, it becomes obvious that we may not only ask which future developments are possible and which are necessary, but we may also want to investigate which of the possible futures we should choose and how this choice can be backed up by various kinds of ethical reasoning. (See [15: 65 ff].)

6 Temporal Logic and the Discussion of Time

Given a logical calculus corresponding to Prior's 3rd grade of the tense-logical involvement a variety of temporal ideas and notions can be expressed in a very precise manner. If we assume the tense-logical assumptions corresponding to linear time, including the theorems (3-5), to hold for the fragment of the logic in which the modal operator does not occur, then it will be possible to demonstrate that each instant proposition, a, actually defines a linear set of instant propositions:

$$TRL(a) = \{b|\ T(a, Pb \vee b \vee Fb)\}$$

The linear and maximally ordered sets in the branching time system are normally called chronicles in branching time theory. On the assumptions just mentioned it turns out that there is a chronicle, $TRL(a)$, through a for each instant, a, in the system. The TRL-function corresponds to what has been called "the thin red line" ([2], [19]). In this system we obtain instead of (1):

(6) $T(a,Fq) \equiv \exists b \in TRL(a) : a<b \wedge T(b,q)$

$TRL(a)$ represents not only the past but also the true future relative to a. If such a function can be defined, it will be possible to make distinctions between "necessarily, it is going to be", "possibly, it is going to be", and "it is going to be". Graphically, this may be illustrated in a branching time system in which the TRL-function is indicated using arrows on the selected chronicles as it is shown in this example:

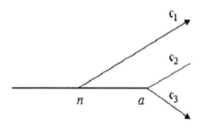

In the above figure it is evident that $TRL(n) = c_1$ and that $TRL(a)=c_3$.

In this framework it will also be possible to discuss whether all chronicles in the branching time system can be presented on the form $TRL(a)$ for some instant proposition, a. An even more abstract question regarding the structure of time would be the question of connectedness: Will any two chronicles have a common past? Or could there be chronicles, which are totally disconnected? It should be mentioned that the question of temporal connectedness cannot even be formulated as an open question if we choose Prior's 4th grade instead of the 3rd grade.

There are many other topics regarding time, which may be discussed on the basis of a framework, based on a hybrid logic corresponding to Prior's 3rd grade. One may, for instance, discuss the representation of durations. Assuming that the instant propositions are conceived as durationless, any duration may be represented as a pair of instant propositions, i.e. (a,b) or alternatively as a proposition like $Pa \land Fb$. Here a is the description of the beginning, and b the end of the duration in question. Alternatively, one may make use of the temporal unit which can be built into the tense operators, i.e., $P(n)$ and $F(n)$.

Having a logical calculus corresponding to Prior's 3rd grade available makes it possible not only to talk about what has happened, what is happening and what is going to happen. The calculus also allows us to reason about what can happen or what could have happened, if things had gone differently in the past.

However, the potential of Prior's temporal logic as a common language for the discussion of time has not been fully explored. One of the aspects of Prior's logic, which needs more investigation, has to do with his idea of a tensed ontology. How can we account for past and future objects given that only the present exists? (See [5]).

One problem, which has been considered very often, has to do with the relation between tense logic and relativistic physics. In fact, this problem was already discussed in the correspondence between Kripke and Prior in 1958. In the correspondence Kripke pointed out that the emphasis on the present (the 'Now') is rather problematic if we assume a scientific discourse taking relativistic physics into serious account. Prior was certainly aware of the challenge from special relativity. However, he also argued that it is in fact possible to maintain the tense-logical position without contradicting the results of relativistic physics. He later elaborated his view (see [14: 197 ff]). Recently, several authors have been interested in the theory of the so-called branching space-time, which has been established under inspiration from various ideas in physics. Here Belnap (2005), Müller ([8], [9]), and Placek [11] have contributed significantly.

Although there are several open questions regarding the use of temporal logic as a conceptual foundation for the construction of a common language for the discussion of time, it is also evident that temporal logic in many cases has been demonstrated to be a very precise and useful tool for the description of the dynamic aspects of reality. On this background, it seems very reasonable to continue and to strengthen the research in the potential of Prior's hybrid tense logic (or a further elaboration of it) as a conceptual basis, a common ground, for the discussion of time whenever there is a need for a precise and formal language in order to clarify the various ideas concerning time.

References

1. Bergson, H.: Time and Free Will, Authorised Translation by P.L. Pogson (First Impression 1910). George Allen & Unwin Ltd., London (1950)
2. Belnap, N.: Branching Histories Approach to Indeterminism and Free Will, Truth and Probability. In: Brown, B., Lepage, F. (edo.) Essays in Honour of Hugues Leblanc, pp. 197–211 (2005)
3. Bräuner, T.: Hybrid Logic and Its Proof-Theory. Applied Logic Series, vol. 37. Springer, Heidelberg (2011)

4. Copeland, J. (ed.): Logic and Reality: Essays on the Legacy of Arthur Prior. Oxford University Press, Oxford (1996)
5. Jakobsen, D., Øhrstrøm, P., Schärfe, H.: A.N. Prior's Ideas on Tensed Ontology. In: Andrews, S., Polovina, S., Hill, R., Akhgar, B. (eds.) ICCS-ConceptStruct 2011. LNCS, vol. 6828, pp. 118–130. Springer, Heidelberg (2011)
6. Jensen, C.S., Snodgrass, R.T. (eds.): Temporal Database Entries for the Springer Encyclopedia of Database Systems: A TIMECENTER Technical Report, Aalborg University & University of Arizona (2008),
   http://timecenter.cs.aau.dk/TimeCenterPublications/TR-90.pdf
7. McTaggart, J.E.: The Unreality of Time. Mind, 457–474 (1908)
8. Müller, T.: Branch dependence in the "consistent histories" approach to quantum mechanics. Foundations of Physics 37, 253–276 (2007)
9. Müller, T., Belnap, N., Kishida, K.: Funny business in branching space-times: infinite modal correlations. Synthese 164, 141–159 (2008)
10. Peirce, C.S.: Collected Papers of Charles Sanders Peirce. In: Hartshorne, C., Weiss, P., Burke, A. (eds). Harward University Press (1931-58)
11. Placek, T.: Stochastic outcomes in branching space-time: analysis of Bell's theorem. The British Journal for the Philosophy of Science 51, 445–475 (2000)
12. Prigogine, I.: From Being to Becoming, Time and Complexity in the Physical Sciences. W. H. Freeman & Co., San Francisco (1980)
13. Prior, A.N.: Time and Modality. Clarendon Press, Oxford (1957)
14. Prior, A.N.: Past, Present and Future. Clarendon Press, Oxford (1967)
15. Prior, A.N.: Papers on Time and Tense. In: P. Hasle, et al. (eds). Oxford University Press, Oxford (2003)
16. Prior, A.N.: The Notion of the Present. In: Fraser, J.T., Haber, F.C., Müller, G.H. (eds.) The Study of Time. Springer, Heidelberg (1972)
17. Prior, A.N.: Unpublished Papers on Time, The Prior Collection, Box 1-11. Bodleian Library, Oxford (1969)
18. Øhrstrøm, P., Hasle, P.: Temporal Logic - From Ancient Ideas to Artificial Intelligence. Kluwer Academic Publishers, Dordrecht (1995)
19. Øhrstrøm, P.: In Defense of the Thin Red Line: A Case for Ockhamism. Humana Mente 8, 17–32 (2009)
20. Øhrstrøm, P.: Time and Logic: A.N. Prior's Formal Analysis of Temporal Concepts. In: Ferré, S., Rudolph, S. (eds.) ICFCA 2009. LNCS, vol. 5548, pp. 66–81. Springer, Heidelberg (2009)
21. Øhrstrøm, P., Schärfe, H., Ploug, T.: Branching Time as a Conceptual Structure. In: Croitoru, M., Ferré, S., Lukose, D. (eds.) ICCS 2010. LNCS(LNAI), vol. 6208, pp. 125–138. Springer, Heidelberg (2010)
22. OWL Time, http://www.w3.org/TR/owl-time (accessed 2011)
23. UNL Web, http://www.unlweb.net/wiki/index.php/Time (accessed 2011)

The Problem with Perceptual Synchrony

Mark A. Elliott[1,2]

[1] School of Psychology
National University of Ireland, Galway, Republic of Ireland
[2] Center for Applied Perceptual Research, Department of Acoustic Design, Kyushu
University 4-9-1,Shiobaru, Minami-ku,Fukuoka 815-0032, Japan
mark.elliott@nuigalway.ie

Abstract. Perceptual synchrony has received attention as result of physiological
studies of neural responses to visual stimuli. The terms synchrony and
synchronization are used to refer to stimulus activity, the psychological-systems
response to that activity and perception although the latter is not necessarily the
same as the systems response. The concern of this paper is the integrity of the
idea of perceptual synchrony. The problem with *perceptual synchrony* is that on
close analysis it is a non sequiter and on this basis it is insufficient to explain
the conditions under which events will be seen as simultaneous. Instead, the
perceptual groupings generally ascribed to perceptual synchrony are better
explained in terms of the intervals of time over which stimulus events integrate.
Considering the agenda of studies that aim to examine the timing of perceptual
grouping, the argument I put forward here recommends interpretation in terms
of *temporal integration* rather than *synchronization*.

Keywords: Temporal Binding, Perceptual Synchrony, Synchronized Stimulus
Activity, Neuro-phenomenological Equivalence, Epiphenomenality, Goodman's
New Problem of Induction, Temporal Integration.

1 Prolegomenon

Our perceptions in space and time consist of organizations of one sort or another: In
vision, we encounter a visual field composed of definable subregions, which we
resolve as objects or items to the extent to which we deploy visual attention to their
locations (that movement to my left is Drosophila, not a mosquito). In audition, we
experience montages of sound that integrate to form coherent auditory scenes, the
chiming of church bells on a background of morning traffic, the slightly asynchronous
ascent of alto and soprano at the beginning of the first movement of Pergolesi's Stabat
Mater. These organizations imply unification, in other words the demarcation of a
group of stimuli, or of a group of stimulus elements that go together to form a
coherent *whole* according to laws established by the Gestalt psychologists. And, as a
general rule, Gestalten arise in spite of variations in featural configuration, the spatial
separation, or even the sensory modality required for coding their separate elements.
It has been claimed that grouping in space, while determined by the spatial
configuration of the grouped elements, is also closely linked to the dynamics of the

A. Vatakis et al. (Eds.): Time and Time Perception 2010, LNAI 6789, pp. 58–66, 2011.
© Springer-Verlag Berlin Heidelberg 2011

systems responsible for coding those elements. It is thus by means of the interaction of processes *in time* that the integration or *binding* of information is achieved [1-3].

This opinion has received support from neurophysiological studies employing grouping stimuli. While now controversial as regards the precise physiological mechanisms concerned [4,5], these studies claim that the presence of simple feature contrasts (defined by luminance, orientation, hue and spatial frequency) within the receptive fields of visual-cortical neurons results in some responding neurons forming an ensemble defined by a common firing rate. This firing rate is usually in excess of 20 Hz with the participating neurons firing in almost perfect synchrony with zero or close to zero phase lag [6-9]. These findings are suggestive of *synchrony* as the neuronal operating characteristic of relevance for feature-feature binding.

In this paper, I will address one major issue in human experimental psychology in its attempts to evaluate the binding by synchrony hypothesis. Experimental psychologists have attempted to resolve two potential problems with the physiological accounts, these being their ability to resolve what I refer to as the *neuro-phenomenological equivalence* and *epiphenomenality* problems. After introducing both problems, I will briefly review the design of experimental paradigms that aim to throw light on these matters and, in particular, I will discuss a common reliance upon perceptual report of whether stimulus events were synchronous or not. Following this, I will outline a logical argument akin in structure to Goodman's New Problem of Induction which shows that the idea of *perceptual synchrony* is a non sequitur: the term is not sufficient to describe the psychological response to event structure in time. Accordingly, I will argue that a number of experimental approaches in psychology have based paradigm design on a misunderstanding of the logic of their independent variable. Having outlined this argument, I conclude by discussing the logical alternative, which is to consider the time over which events integrate, rather than their precise synchronization as of significance in seeking a psychological corroboration of the physiological binding hypothesis.

2   Perceptual Synchrony, Neuro-phenomenological Equivalence and Epiphenomenality

As with the majority of neurophysiological studies, psychological studies of the effects of perceptual synchrony using temporally correlated stimuli and with human subjects are mainly confined to the integration of visual features. These studies have aimed to address two shortcomings inherent to neurophysiological procedures. The first concerns the problem of establishing which, if any, direct equivalences might be made between synchronization at the level of neuronal operation and subjective experiences of what – in terms of one's experience – appears to go together with what (the *neuro-phenomenological equivalence* problem). Although laboratory animals can be trained to perform grouping tasks whilst awake, their responses often remain insufficient to be able to clearly decide what it is that they experience (we assume, perhaps correctly, that they organize their experiential worlds as we organize ours but we don't actually know this for certain). A second shortcoming concerns simulations of grouping. These suggest sustained oscillatory synchronization (i.e., synchronization beyond more than one cycle) to be unnecessary for visual features to be grouped into wholes [10]. In [10], simulations are presented which show low-level binding operations such as *perceptual framing* and boundary completion are achieved as a consequence of fast neuronal synchronization. However unlike physiological observations, these simulations show that it is in principle possible to resynchronize an assembly of desynchronized neurons within a single oscillatory cycle. This raises the possibility that the sustained oscillatory states found to accompany neuronal synchronization are at best *epiphenomenal* and may indeed be *irrelevant* with respects to the organization of sensory space. These simulations raise an *epiphenomenality problem*, a problem, which essentially refers to the correlative and non-causal character of the physiological evidence regarding synchronization (see also perhaps [4] and [6] which attempt to resolve this issue from the neurophysiological perspective). It is worth noting that concerns of this nature have led to a strong call for continued experimental research [11] and perhaps with good reason: in a different domain of interest, studies of other oscillatory phenomena, such as the resonant properties of cochlea, are strongly in favor of the idea of oscillation frequencies as an information rich medium for information transmission, including the feature-related filtering of sensory information [12].

Clearly issues such as these need to be resolved before we can accept the idea that neuronal synchrony brings about grouping. Psychological studies that have proceeded with the explicit (or indeed tacit) aim of showing that grouping comes about as a consequence of perceptual synchrony can be divided into two classes of paradigms: in their simplest form, the first, referred to in terms of the *periodic motion* paradigm [13] involve the alternate presentation of a set of target elements in different phases of the same global presentation frequency [14-15]. Phase is here determined by the inter-stimulus interval (ISI) between presentations of target and background elements and relative to frequency. In these paradigms, an increase in presentation frequency is accompanied by an increase in the phase separation required for target elements to be distinguished from background elements. The second approach, referred to in terms of the *correlated motion* (or *stochastic stimulus*) paradigm, involves the correlation of independent activity across different stimulus elements. Using this technique a coherent whole corresponding to an organization of temporally correlated stimulus elements can emerge from a background of apparently stochastic stimulus activity by virtue of correlated contrast modulation [16] or by virtue of correlated changes in the direction of contrast modulation [17]. Generally, correlations occur with near perfect (i.e., synchronized) temporal precision.

2.1 The Problem with Perceptual Synchrony

A tentative interpretation of the stochastic stimulus paradigm is that it approaches a solution to both neuro-phenomenological and epiphenomenality problems. This is because it is assumed that experiential effects emerge as a consequence of the matching of the temporal responses in neurons coding simple visual features, with the temporal correlation (or synchronous/asynchronous presentation) of the stimuli [16]. However, careful consideration of the notion of perceptual synchrony leads to a series of conclusions so problematic for this interpretation that it begs rejection of the very idea of perceptual synchrony as a possible explanation for the phenomenological effects that either stochastic-stimulus or correlated-motion paradigms appear to bring about. Moreover, rejection of perceptual synchrony highlights some previously expressed suspicions that the effects of stimulus synchrony may not correspond directly with the type of neuronal synchrony observed during grouping [17]. This conclusion significantly reduces the possibility that measures of perceptual synchrony offer the promised solutions to either the neuro-phenomenological or epiphenomenality problems.

So why is perceptual synchrony a problem? The fundamental problem is one of construct validity, in other words the real meaning of the term perceptual synchrony and this stems (but as will be explained, it is not confined to) consideration of perceptual synchrony as synonymous with *perceptual simultaneity* and thus its inclusion in the class of events referred to in terms of *perceptual equivalence*. A *simultaneity (or synchrony) problem* arises when we ask the question "which stimulus events do we actually experience as simultaneous?" At the crux of the problem are events that are not simultaneous but which we see as simultaneous. Some of the experiential effects brought about by periodic motion paradigms might be considered a special case of these: In particular, cases when visual segmentation does not occur even though the ISI between target and background items is greater than zero. In spite of this it might be considered an acceptable claim, irrespective of the actual non simultaneity of two events, that in perception they can be considered simultaneous iff (if and only if) that is how they seem to the observer. The problem is that this obvious definition of perceptual simultaneity is *non-transitive* although simultaneity is, by definition, an equivalence relation. An analogy to this problem is easy to generate and I shall develop an explanation in the following:

Consider any two events A_1 and A_2 that appear to the observer to occur simultaneously, in spite of which they are separated by a small ISI (for arguments sake let's take the lowest known simultaneity threshold of some 4-5 ms [18-19]. Take then some third event that occurs at some time later than either A_1 or A_2 but is experienced as simultaneous with each. Using this method a series of perceptual events $A_1, \ldots, A_n$ may be experienced such that each is experienced as simultaneous both with the immediately subsequent and with more distant events, but A_1 and A_n are experienced as non-simultaneous. The existence proof for non-transitivity as applied to perceptual simultaneity concerns the already very well known demonstrations that apparently continuous experience is subject to subtle discretization [20-23]. The clear non-transitivity of apparent simultaneity in the problem outlined above should also, in principle, preclude the definition of perceived events such as temporally correlated stimuli in terms of their simultaneity because simultaneity, as an equivalence relation, cannot in addition be non-transitive.

Note that the simultaneity problem is similar in structure to the Sorites Paradox attributed to Eubulides of Miletus, an example of which arises when one considers a heap of sand, from which grains are individually removed. Is it still a heap when only one grain remains? If not, when did it change from a heap to a non-heap? However the problem most closely resembles is (in fact it is formally equivalent to) a derivative of the Sorties Paradox referred to as Goodman's New Problem of Induction (or Goodman's Paradox) [24]. This problem concerns the non-transitivity of appearance properties but has the obvious solution to simply circumvent the problem of transitivity by defining two (simultaneous or non-simultaneous) events A_1 and A_2 as perceptually simultaneous iff (1) they appear to be simultaneous and iff (2) there is no third event A_3 such that either A_1 or A_2 appears to be simultaneous with A_3 while the other does not. On this basis, one might argue that the simultaneity problem does not apply to stochastic stimulus paradigms in which target elements A_1 to A_n appear as a single experience (as a function of their correlated motion) relative to background elements, which, while moving at the same time, appear unrelated. This argument would seem to support the potential of stochastic stimulus paradigms for resolution of both the neuro-phenomenological and the epiphenomenality problems, and indeed this counter argument might be valid except for one surprising corollary, which is the entailment that, although two events might *appear to be simultaneous* it is nonetheless impossible for the observer to conclude that they have *experienced them to be simultaneous* in the absence of a third event A_3, which is relative to (i.e., either partially or non-simultaneous with) the relation A_1 - A_2 and thus serves to define A_1 - A_2 as a set, that is as *separate* and (in this case) temporally discrete but unified experience.

2.2 A Solution But Some Implications

Even if this corollary is argued away on the grounds that there are no particular reasons to consider the temporal activity of other stimuli as an important factor for consideration, there are three reasons why the simultaneity problem persists for stochastic stimulus and correlated motion paradigms. The first of these concerns the correlated motion paradigms and is straightforward and procedural: very simply, experimental subjects were asked to make an invalid judgment of stimulus activity. The judgment is invalid because subjects were asked to report a synchrony relation when *no such relation is in principle possible*. As a result it cannot be argued that what they report is not more than a demand characteristic of the experimental procedure. It is difficult to estimate how much of a concern this really presents (it is actually largely an empirical question). But in fact the major problems remain conceptual: various studies have shown that in the absence of a third event, judgments of simultaneity nonetheless appear to be made across an inter-stimulus or stimulus onset interval. For very simple stimuli such as two brief and successive flashes these windows appear to be on the order of 5 ms because paired stimuli separated by longer intervals are seen as separate [18-19]. A simultaneity window of this magnitude is of course of sufficient temporal resolution to be subsumed by the relatively slow frequencies associated with visual-cortical synchronization.

Returning to the potential for stochastic stimulus paradigms to resolve the neuro-phenomenological and epiphenomenality problems, the important question then concerns the magnitude of the window of simultaneity associated with correlated stimulus presentation and whether or not this window would fit within a period of the frequencies associated with visual-cortical synchronization. This leads to the second problem: Even if no particular claim is made concerning a solution to the neuro-phenomenological problem, stochastic stimulus paradigms implicitly claim to have resolved the epiphenomenality problem. In other words they claim groupings *to have emerged*, or to be a consequence of viewing correlated stimulus activity [16-17]. On this basis one might speculate the window of simultaneity to be approximately equivalent (if not entirely synonymous) with the *perceptual moment* which has been established at around 55 milliseconds (or associated with a frequency of 18 Hz [20-21,25-28]. Clearly, the window of simultaneity associated with perceptual simultaneity is greater than a single period of even the lowest frequency associated with neuronal synchronization and this seems to preclude consideration of stochastic stimulus paradigms as direct method for solving the neuro-phenomenological problem.

Unfortunately, the structure of stochastic stimulus paradigms seems relatively uninformative with respects to the precise windows of simultaneity required for their grouping effects to emerge, although this is not true for the periodic motion paradigm. In this case measures exist that are consistent with the idea that for presentations falling within a given window of time all stimuli that appear together will be bound together while stimuli falling outside of these intervals will be seen as separate. The original pattern of effects arising from periodic motion paradigms were clearly defined in terms of the temporal delays that were required between rapidly alternating stimuli for the appearance of one stimulus as distinct relative to the other. Interestingly, for stochastic (random dot) patterns, delays were relatively constant over a range of lower frequencies 1.3 – around 15 - 20 Hz, at which point the required delays were found to decrease in magnitude [14]. Although the reasons for this decrease are not known, it seems plausible to speculate that a general reconfiguration in the timing of processes occurs in the neighborhood of a threshold that divides perceptual moments from other *non-perceptual* intervals. Concerning the relations between binding and perceptual moments our line of argumentation recommends they be treated differently. Indeed evidence from other paradigms aiming to measure the temporal characteristics of binding seems to support this notion (for example, [29]). The finding that spatially superimposed pairings of alternating orientation and color features could be accurately reported below a threshold of some 18.8 Hz suggests dissociation between rapid binding mechanisms operative at frequencies at least greater than 19 Hz and mechanisms responsible for bringing the outcome of the binding process into awareness, operative for combined feature pairs, at frequencies of 18 Hz and lower. Additionally, in [30] the belief is expressed that different attributes of a visual scene are consciously perceived *at different times*, leading to the mis-binding of features such as the colour and the direction of motion or the colour and the orientation of lines. This conclusion is based upon the earlier work of [31] who showed in experiments that colour is perceived before orientation by 63 ms, orientation 52 ms before motion and colour before motion by 118 ms. In the context of our discussion the timing of these asymmetries (equivalent to 16 Hz, 19 Hz and 8.5 Hz) suggests that the *different times* referred to by [30] may in fact be the two sides of a temporal threshold falling at approximately 18 Hz (or 55 ms) and subharmonics (i.e. successive multiples in time) thereof.

So what of the emergence of form from temporally structured displays? A recent appraisal of the effects obtained from periodic motion paradigms argues that perceptual synchrony should be considered a form of the Gestalt principle "Gemeinsames Schicksal" or "common fate", which obtains for stimuli occurring within windows of perceptual simultaneity [32]. However, even if these paradigms should be considered to bring about the temporally defined organization of visual space (a matter currently subject to some disagreement [13,33-34]), they merely serve to specify the set of temporal preconditions and are otherwise silent on the underlying dynamics required for an adequate solution to the neuro-phenomenological problem: This points to a failure to adequately resolve both the neuro-phenomenological problem and (by extension) the epiphenomenality problem. The latter problem is clearly addressed by periodic motion paradigms which emphasize the role of temporal windows for emergence of form from temporally structured displays; however the failure of those paradigms to measure, within the same instant, the temporal dynamics of binding within those windows significantly reduces their potential as measures of any necessity relation that holds between synchrony and the organization of our experience.

3 Conclusions

I have provided a logical argument for considering perceptual synchrony to be a misnomer and to refer to one measure of a temporal window over which two stimulus events will be judged to be in synchrony. Examination of the experimental data tends to corroborate this position while the magnitudes of windows suggested by these data are often equivalent to well-established estimates of the perceptual moment. This conclusion stems from a related conclusion that, contrary to original aims, the perceptual-synchrony paradigms are in principle unable to resolve either the neuro-phenomenological problem or the epiphenomenality problem. This counts against the common claim that neuronal synchrony is a means for the binding of sensory information. However, it is not to say that the information that appears to go together within a given (perceptual) moment is not bound together, it is just to say that it is not bound *only* by virtue of its simultaneous appearance. Instead it becomes bound by virtue of the interval of time over which defines the moment, of which simultaneous appearance is but one instance.

Acknowledgments. The author is indebted to Sean Kelly for his reformulation of Goodman's Paradox, also to three anonymous reviewers for their assistance in improving the flow of argumentation presented in the paper.

References

1. Fraisse, P.: The Psychology of Time. Eyre & Spottiswoode (Publishers) Ltd., London (1963)
2. Milner, P.M.: A model for visual shape recognition. Psych. Rev. 81, 521–535 (1974)
3. von der Malsburg, C.: The Correlation Theory of Brain Function. Internal Report 81-2, Department of Neurobiology, Max-Planck-Institute for Biophysical Chemistry, 3400 Göttingen, Germany (1980)
4. Yuval-Greenberg, S., Tomer, O., Keren, A.S., Nelken, I., Deouell, L.Y.: Transient Induced Gamma-Band Response in EEG as a Manifestation of Miniature Saccades. Neuron 58, 411–429 (2008)
5. Ray, S., Maunsell, J.H.: Differences in gamma frequencies across visual cortex restrict their possible use in computation. Neuron 67, 885–896 (2010)
6. Eckhorn, R., Bauer, R., Jordan, W., Brosch, M., Kruse, W., Munk, M., Reitboeck, H.J.: Coherent oscillations: A mechanism for feature linking in the visual cortex. Biol. Cybern, 60, 121–130 (1988)
7. Gray, C.M., König, P., Engel, A.K., Singer, W.: Oscillatory responses in cat visual cortex exhibit inter-columnar synchronization which reflects global stimulus properties. Nature 338, 334–337 (1989)

8. Livingstone, M.S.: Oscillatory firing and interneuronal correlations in squirrel monkey striate cortex. J. Neurophysiol 75, 2467–2485 (1996)
9. Engel, A.K., König, P., Kreiter, A.K., Singer, W.: Interhemispheric synchronization of oscillatory neuronal responses in cat visual cortex. Science 252, 1177–1179 (1991)
10. Grossberg, S., Somers, D.: Synchronized oscillations during cooperative feature linking in a cortical model of visual perception. Neural Networks 4, 453–456 (1991)
11. Varela, F.J., Thompson, E.: Neural synchrony and the unity of mind: A neurophenomenological perspective. In: Cleeremans, A. (ed.) The Unity of Consciousness: Binding, Integration and Dissociation. Oxford University Press, Oxford (2003)
12. Nobili, R., Mammano, F., Ashmore, J.: How well do we understand the cochlea? Trends Neurosci. 21, 159–167 (1998)
13. Morgan, M., Castet, E.: High temporal synchrony is insufficient for perceptual grouping. Proc. R. Soc. Lond. B 269, 513–516 (2002)
14. Fahle, M.: Figure-ground discrimination from temporal information. Proc. R. Soc. Lond. B 254, 199–203 (1993)
15. Leonards, U., Singer, W., Fahle, M.: The influence of temporal phase differences on texture segmentation. Vis. Res. 36, 2689–2697 (1996)
16. Alais, D., Blake, R., Lee, S.-H.: Visual features that vary together over time group together over space. Nat. Neurosci. 1, 160–164 (1998)
17. Lee, S.-H., Blake, R.: Visual form created solely from temporal structure. Science 284, 1165–1168 (1999)
18. Exner, S.: Experimentelle Untersuchungen der einfachsten psychischen Processe. Pflug. Arch. 11, 403–432 (1875)
19. Westheimer, G., McKee, S.P.: Perception of temporal order in adjacent visual stimuli. Vis. Res. 17, 887–892 (1977)
20. von Baer, K.-E.: Welche Auffassung der lebenden Natur ist die richtige? Und wie ist diese Auffassung auf die Entomologie anzuwenden? In: von Baer, K.-E. (ed.) Reden, gehalten in wissenschaftlichen Versammlungen und kleinere Aufsätze vermischten Inhalt. H. Schmitzdorf, St. Petersburg, pp. 237–284 (1864)
21. Brecher, G.A.: Die Entstehung und biologische Bedeutung der subjectktiven Zeiteinheit – des Momentes. Z. Vergl. Physiol. 18, 204–243 (1932)
22. Pöppel, E.: Mindworks: Time and Conscious Experience. Harcourt, Brace Jovanovich, Orlando Florida (1985)
23. Geissler, H.-G.: New magical numbers in mental activity: On a taxonomic system for critical time periods. In: Geissler, H.-G., Link, S.W., Townsend, J.T. (eds.) Cognition, Information Processing and Psychophysics: Basic Issues. Lawrence Erlbaum Associates, Hillsdale NJ (1992)
24. Goodman, N.: The Structure of Appearances, 3rd edn. Dordrecht Reidel, Boston (1977)
25. Elliott, M.A., Shi, Z., Sürer, F.: The effects of subthreshold synchrony on the perception of simultaneity. Psychol. Res. 71, 687–693 (2007)
26. Elliott, M.A., Shanagher, L.: Temporal event-structure coding in developmental dyslexia: evidence from explicit and implicit temporal processing. Psihologija 43, 359–373 (2010)
27. Giersch, A., Lalanne, L., Corves, C., Seubert, J., Zhuanghua, S., Foucher, J., Elliott, M.A.: Extended visual simultaneity thresholds in patients with schizophrenia. Schizophrenia Bull. 35, 816–825 (2009)
28. Schmidt, H., McFarland, J., Ahmed, M., McDonald, C., Elliott, M.A.: Low-Level Temporal Coding Impairments in Psychosis: Preliminary Findings and Recommendations for Further Studies. J. Abnorm. Psychol. 120, 476–482 (2011)

29. Holcombe, H.O., Cavanagh, P.: Early binding of feature pairs for visual perception. Nat. Neurosci. 4, 127–128 (2001)
30. Bartels, A., Zeki, S.: The theory of multistage integration in the visual brain. Proc. R. Soc. Lond. B 265, 2327–2332 (1998)
31. Moutoussis, K., Zeki, S.: Functional segregation and temporal hierarchy of the visual perceptive systems. Proc. R. Soc. Lond. B 264, 1407–1414 (1997)
32. Kandil, F.I., Fahle, M.: Purely temporal figure-ground segregation. Eur. J. Neurosci. 13, 2004–2008 (2001)
33. Farid, H., Adelson, E.H.: Synchrony does not promote grouping in temporally structured displays. Nat. Neurosci. 4, 875–876 (2001)
34. Dakin, S.C., Bex, P.J.: Role of synchrony in contour binding: some transient doubts sustained. J. Opt. Soc. Am. 19, 678–686 (2002)

New Perspectives on Vierordt's Law: Memory-Mixing in Ordinal Temporal Comparison Tasks

Bon-Mi Gu and Warren H. Meck

Department of Psychology and Neuroscience, Duke University, Durham, NC USA
bg43@duke.edu, meck@psych.duke.edu

Abstract. Distortions in temporal memory can occur as a function of differences in signal modalities and/or by the encoding of multiple signal durations associated with different timing tasks into a single memory distribution – an effect referred to as "memory mixing". Evidence for this type of memory distortion and/or categorization of signal durations as an explanation for changes in temporal context (e.g., duration ranges), as well as for Vierordt's law (e.g., overestimation of "short" durations and underestimation of "long" durations), can be studied by examining proactive interference effects from the previous trial(s). Moreover, we demonstrate that individual differences in the magnitude of this "memory-mixing" phenomenon are correlated with variation in reaction times for ordinal temporal comparisons as well as with sensitivity to feedback effects in the formation of duration-specific memory distributions.

Keywords: Timing and time perception, Interval timing, Memory distributions, Individual differences, Modality differences, Feedback effects, Reaction time.

1 Memory-Mixing and the Encoding of Temporal Information

Subjective time is not necessarily equal to objective time and can be affected by various factors, including memory load and temporal context [1-3]. For example, when subjects are presented with various signal durations and are then instructed to reproduce these durations they tend to bias their reproductions towards the mean of the distribution of signal durations by overestimating short durations and underestimating long durations – an often unrecognized and underappreciated relationship known as Vierordt's law [4-6]. In addition, when auditory and visual signals are intermixed within a session, subjects tend to overestimate auditory signals and underestimate visual signals of equivalent duration [7-12]. The range and modality of experienced signal durations have been shown to contribute to distortions in timing and time perception. Moreover, both of these phenomena have been hypothesized to be related to "memory-mixing" whereby similar clock readings are categorized into a limited number of memory distributions with the decision process involving a comparison of the current clock reading with a sample taken from each of these distributions [2-3,10-11,13]. For example, if auditory signals drive the internal clock faster (on average) than visual signals and memory distributions for a particular target duration are a mixture of these "shorter" visual and "longer" auditory clock readings, then auditory signals will have an increased probability of being judged

A. Vatakis et al. (Eds.): Time and Time Perception 2010, LNAI 6789, pp. 67–78, 2011.
© Springer-Verlag Berlin Heidelberg 2011

"long" relative to visual signals of an equivalent physical duration. Alternatively, "memory-mixing" can occur when different standard durations used within the same temporal context (e.g., test session) are combined into a single memory distribution rather than separate memory distributions being maintained for each standard. As a consequence of the temporal context, "memory-mixing" can produce distortions in scaling of duration that are consistent with Vierordt's law and may be modifiable by training conditions (e.g., blocking of different standards or signal modalities and/or by providing feedback in order to encourage the formation of separate rather than mixed-memory distributions). Furthermore, "memory-mixing" is distinct from the previously described time-order error (TOE) which refers to the influence of the order of presentation on the comparison of successively presented stimuli – see [14-18] for discussion of these different phenomena within the more general field of psychophysics.

1.1   Memory-Mixing and Temporal Context

As described above, the mixing of unimodal stimuli in memory as a function of temporal context is consistent with Vierordt's law [4-6], and the tendency for overestimating shorter durations and underestimating longer durations is one of the most robust temporal phenomena shown under a variety of experimental conditions [3,5]. However, the exact mechanism underlying this effect is currently unknown. A recent study employing functional magnetic resonance imaging examined the neural features whose activation is correlated with the extent of this memory-mixing, and suggested that different brain areas are correlated with clock speed, temporal sensitivity, and the degree of memory-mixing, respectively [19]. In this study, one of two standard signal durations was presented (signal durations were demarcated by 50 msec tones), after which subjects were asked to differentiate whether the following comparison is longer or shorter than the standard. When the percent "longer" response was plotted in relation to the ratios of comparisons to the standard signal durations, the psychometric functions for the short and long standards were horizontally displaced in a manner suggesting the overestimation of the short standard and underestimation of the long standard. Temporal sensitivity in this timing procedure was correlated with the level of activation in the caudate, inferior parietal cortex, and cerebellum – in accordance with current theoretical accounts of interval timing [1,20-24]. Moreover, the degree of "memory-mixing" was correlated with activation of the precuneus and superior temporal gyrus – although the exact contributions of these brain areas in the encoding and/or rehearsal of clock readings remain uncertain.

A recent investigation of temporal context has shown that a Bayesian model can simulate the biased performance of subjects when they were asked to reproduce the presented signal duration [3]. This Bayesian model incorporates the knowledge of the distribution of previous signal durations into the perception of the current signal duration, thus biasing the reproduction of the current interval towards the mean of the distribution. In this model, it is hypothesized that the accuracy of performance trades off with the precision of performance in the presence of temporal uncertainty in such a way that temporal context can optimize performance by sacrificing accuracy but reducing the variability of performance.

In this model, it is hypothesized that a tradeoff exists between accuracy and precision such that the distribution of signal durations (i.e., temporal context) can be used to optimize performance. In other words, precision can be gained at the expense of accuracy (or vice versa). In this case, the implicit knowledge of the underlying distribution from which a sample is drawn would be useful when the current clock reading is uncertain due to the effects of noise and/or inattention. This explains how the intermixing of previous trial's signal durations with the perception of the current trial's signal duration could bias performance. Under certain conditions, however, this statistical analysis can provide an efficient strategy for reducing variability in the presence of uncertainty or noise. Nevertheless, this hypothesis is mainly supported by computer simulation rather than experimental results from behavioral or neurobiological studies.

1.2 Memory-Mixing and Modality Differences

In addition to the "memory-mixing" effects observed in a single sensory modality (e.g., audition), differences between auditory and visual stimuli can also contribute to distortions in timing and time perception [7-12]. The effect of signal modality on time perception has been mostly shown using the duration bisection task where "short" and "long" anchor durations are presented and subjects are required to categorize intermediate durations as being closer to the "short" or the "long" signal duration. The concurrent underestimation of visual signals and overestimation of auditory stimuli has been demonstrated when the auditory and visual signals share the same anchor durations and are presented in the same test session [11].

As a source of this bimodality effect, differences in either *clock speed* or in the probability of closure of an *attentional switch* have been used to account for the findings [11,25-27]. In the case of the *clock speed* account, auditory signals are presumed to drive the pacemaker or oscillatory processes used as the time base for temporal discriminations faster than visual signals, thereby creating proportional differences between the clock readings for physically identical durations. Alternatively, the locus of the modality effect may be at the level of an *attentional switch* that allows pulses to flow from the pacemaker into an accumulator. Auditory signals are purported to be automatically alerting, whereas visual signals require attention to be directed to them in order to initiate and maintain the temporal integration process. According to this hypothesis, the attentional switch flickers/oscillates between an open and closed state with the efficiency of maintaining this closed state varying between auditory and visual signals. In other words, maintaining a closed state is more difficult when timing visual signals than when timing auditory signals due to increased attentional demands. As a consequence, pacemaker pulses are lost at a higher rate for visual signals as a result of this flickering during the signal [9,12].

Under either the *attentional switch* or *clock speed* accounts, auditory and visual signal durations are hypothesized to be stored together in an amodal memory distribution such that visual signals are perceived as "shorter" and auditory signals as "longer" when they are compared to samples taken from this amodal memory distribution – although modality-specific information is acquired and can be used under certain conditions [28]. As the auditory and visual signal durations are intermixed with each other in a single memory distribution, it can be argued that the "memory-mixing" between different modalities contributes to the distortion of perceived duration. Moreover, it has been shown that these amodal memory distributions can be updated in a linear manner as a function of temporal information accumulated for auditory and visual signals on subsequent trials [29,30].

1.3   Memory-Mixing and Sequential Ordinal Comparisons

Ordinality judgments involving standard and comparison durations can be used to investigate "memory-mixing" effects as a function of proactive interference. In this task, two tones of standard and comparison durations were presented with randomly selected inter-stimulus intervals (2.4, 2.7, and 3.0s), and subjects (n=13; 5 males - 8 females; 22-28 year old college students) were asked to determine whether the comparison (2nd) tone was "shorter" or "longer" than the standard (1st) tone. The standard tone duration was either 0.6s or 1.0s, and the comparison duration was randomly selected from 6 durations that were proportionally distributed around each standard duration, as shown in Table 1. In total, 144 trials were presented for 30 min with 12 repetitions for each standard and comparison pairs. The subjects responded by pressing the 'S' or 'L' key corresponding to the "shorter" or "longer" responses in order to classify the comparison duration.

Table 1. Standard and comparison durations for the ordinal comparison task. Comparison durations are proportionally distributed around each standard duration (0.6 and 1.0 s).

Standard (s)	Comparison (s)					
0.60	0.45	0.51	0.56	0.65	0.71	0.80
1.00	0.75	0.85	0.93	1.08	1.18	1.33
Ratios to standard	0.75	0.85	0.93	1.08	1.18	1.33

According to Weber's law and the scalar property of interval timing, the psychometric functions for the 0.6-s and 1.0-s standard durations should superimpose when the percent "longer" response is plotted as a function of the ratio of the comparison duration to the standard duration [31]. In contrast to this prediction, subjects showed the standard "memory-mixing" effect as revealed by overestimation of the "short" standard duration/underestimation of the "short" comparison durations and underestimation of the "long" standard duration/overestimation of the "long" comparison durations (Fig. 1a). This "memory-mixing" effect is consistent with previous reports using a temporal comparison task [19] and a temporal reproduction task [3]. The basic idea here is that subjects don't actually use the standard duration presented on the current trial, but rather a conglomeration of the standards presented on a sequence of previous trials, i.e., a memory distribution composed of "short" and "long" standards. In this sense, standard signals are underestimated for the "long" set of comparison signals and overestimated for the "short" set of comparison signals. In addition, the plot of reaction (RT) time as a function of the ratio of the comparison duration to the standard duration shows similar leftward shifts for the 1.0-s standard and rightward shifts for the 0.6-s standard (Fig. 1b). In psychophysical tasks of this sort, RT is generally thought to reflect the level of difficulty in the decision process as a function of the similarity in the current clock reading and the sample taken from memory [32]. Moreover, the observation that the shortest RTs are obtained for long comparison signals judged "longer" and for short comparison signals judged "shorter" appears to an example of the "semantic congruity effect" described by Petrusic and colleagues for situations in which the time to select the smaller of two relatively small quantities is faster than the time to select the larger. Moreover, the magnitude of the semantic congruity effect has been shown to be larger for incorrect than for correct RTs due to linguistic factors involved in the encoding of the stimuli [33,34].

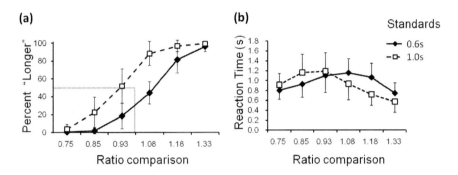

Fig. 1. (a) Mean ± SD percent "longer" response for the 0.6-s and 1.0-s standard conditions indicating the standard "memory-mixing" effect. (b) Mean ± SD reaction time (s) in each standard condition.

1.4   Effects of the Previous Trial on Memory-Mixing

The effects of proactive interference from the standard duration presented on the previous trial (n-1) were analyzed in order to determine the potential impact of "memory-mixing" of standards on the current trial (n) as illustrated in Fig. 2. The 1.08 ratio comparison for the 0.6-s standard and the 0.93 ratio comparison for the 1.0-s standard were selected for analysis due to their intermediate levels of "short" vs. "long" response classification. Comparison signal durations on trial (n) were recategorized according to the standard duration used on the previous trial (n-1). The results of this reanalysis showed that if the current trial's standard was different from the previous trial's standard, the error rate was significantly increased. In other words, the presentation of 1.0-s standard on trial (n-1) leads to the overestimation of a 0.6-s standard on trial (n), whereas the presentation of a 0.6-s standard on trial (n-1) leads to the underestimation of a 1.0-s standard on trial (n). Two-way ANOVAs were conducted to test the effect of the standard on the current trial (n), the standard on the previous trial (n-1), and the interaction of the previous and current trial's standard durations on error rates. As expected, the interaction between the previous and current trial's standard durations was shown to be significant ($F[1,48] = 7.57$, $p < 0.01$). However, when the interaction between the previous and current trial's standard durations was evaluated for the conditions in which the memory of the previous trial's standard did not interfere with the classification of the current comparison (e.g., standard:comparison ratio of 1.08 for the 1.0-s standard, and standard:comparison ratio of 0.93 for the 0.6-s standard), there was no reliable effect on error rate ($F[1,48] < 1.0$).

This pattern of results that the increased error rate was not induced by sequential changes in the standard signal duration (e.g., "task-switching" effect) or the response classification used on the previous trial, but occurred as a result of the formation of a memory distribution representing the accumulation of a series of standard signal durations (e.g., "memory-mixing" effect). These data provide support for the proposal that subjects contrast the comparison duration of a specific trial with a sample selected from a distribution of previously experienced standard durations rather than the standard duration presented on that specific trial.

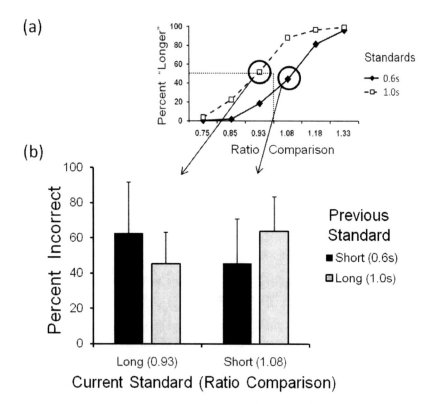

Fig. 2. (a) Mean percent "longer" response for the 0.6-s and 1.0s standard conditions indicating the basic "memory-mixing" effect. (b) Mean ± SD percent incorrect (error rate) for the classification of comparison durations on the current trial (n) as a function of the standard duration on the previous trial (n-1) for the 0.93 ration from the "long" set of comparison durations and the 1.08 ratio from the "short" set of comparison durations. A significant interaction was observed between the current and previous trial's standard duration on timing performance as a function of the range of comparison signals, p < 0.05/ Please see text for additional statistical details.

2   Individual Differences in Memory-Mixing

Although the "memory-mixing" effect that we have been describing is quite reliable, large individual differences can be observed as illustrated in Fig. 3. Interestingly, the subject with a relatively large displacement of the "short" and "long" timing functions (high degree of "memory-mixing") displayed relatively low variation in the reaction times for their response classifications, whereas the opposite was true for the subject with little separation of the timing functions (low degree of "memory-mixing"). Indeed, the "memory-mixing" index was negatively correlated with the observed variability in reaction time across individuals (r = -0.66, p < 0.05) as shown in Fig. 4. For this correlation analysis, the degree of "memory-mixing" was calculated by averaging over the percent "longer" response differences between each comparison for the two standard functions.

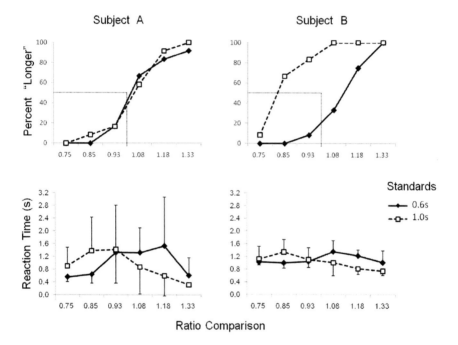

Fig. 3. Individual differences in percent "longer" and reaction time measures. A representative subject exhibiting little or no displacement of the 0.6-s and 1.0-s functions is shown in the upper left panel (Subject A) and a representative subject exhibiting a large displacement of the two functions is shown in the upper right panel (Subject B). The lower panels illustrate the correlation between the "memory-mixing" represented by this displacement and reaction time for these individual subjects, i.e., low levels of "memory-mixing" are associated with a high degree of variability in reaction times (lower left panel), whereas high levels of "memory-mixing" are associated with a low degree of variability in reaction times (lower right panel).

It is uncertain why variability in reaction time should be related to the level of "memory-mixing". One possible explanation for this negative correlation, however, would be the difference in attention during the processing of the standard duration. Those subjects who pay less attention to the current standard would utilize the arguably more automatic and less variable process of sampling from a previously established memory distribution rather than engaging the more variable process of controlled attention to time the duration of the current standard on a trial-by-trial basis [30,35]. Moreover, it has not been determined whether the degree of "memory-mixing" for unimodal signal durations would correlate with the magnitude of any observed modality difference across individuals. Although they appear to be similar, the type of "memory-mixing" resulting from differences in the timing of auditory and visual signals may differ from the type of "memory-mixing" observed for different signal durations within a single modality. It has been hypothesized that the size of the modality effect is related to the relative difference in clock speed between auditory and visual signals and/or the efficiency in maintaining closed state of an attention switch [9,11,36]. On the other hand, higher levels of "memory-mixing" for unimodal signals are likely caused by paying less attention to the duration of current signals and/or stronger residual components of previously timed signals. Further investigation of the individual differences associated with these two "memory-mixing" phenomena should provide the means for identifying these sources of variance [10,37].

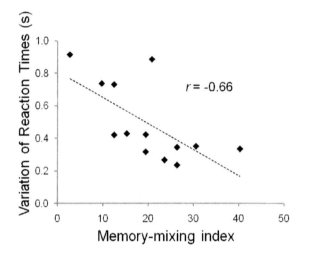

Fig. 4. Relation between "memory-mixing" and variation of reaction time for individual subjects (n=13). A significant negative correlation was observed between the "memory-mixing" index and the standard deviation of the mean reaction times, r = 0.66, $p < 0.05$.

3   Feedback Effects on Memory-Mixing

The observation of reliable individual differences in "memory-mixing" begs the question as to whether it is possible to increase or decrease the degree of "memory-mixing" by experimental manipulation? One can assume that if differences in attention to the standard duration during the encoding phase of the trial contribute to variation in the degree of "memory-mixing", then it might be possible that manipulation of this encoding phase would alter the degree of "memory-mixing". Feedback is well known to increase timing efficiency [38,39]. Reward cues, for example, have been shown to increase the encoding of information through mesolimbic dopamine activation [40,41] and also, the proportion of feedback has been shown to affect the accuracy and precision of timing functions – especially as a function of dopaminergic manipulations [22,38-42]. Presumably this feedback aids in the formation of modality-specific or standard-duration specific memory representations within the context of the procedures described above.

In order to determine whether feedback can affect the degree of "memory-mixing", the word "WRONG" was presented on the computer screen along with an aversive buzzer sound when subjects made an incorrect response and the word "CORRECT" was presented along with a pleasant bell sound when they made a correct response. Following the implementation of this feedback procedure, some subjects showed a dramatically reduced "memory-mixing" effect as illustrated in Fig. 5. Further studies will have to be conducted in order to determine the most reliable and effective form of feedback for different subjects, including the loss or gain of money, in order to extend and verify the exact nature of these feedback effects on "memory-mixing" [43-45].

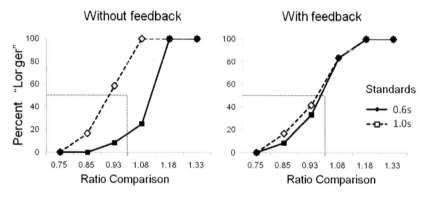

Fig. 5. Feedback effects on "memory-mixing." Mean percent "longer" response is plotted as a function of the ratio comparison between the standard and comparison durations for the 0.6-s and 1.0-s standards. The amount of separation between the different psychometric functions is hypothesized to reflect the degree of "memory-mixing" without feedback (left panel) and with feedback (right panel). Feedback significantly reduced the degree of "memory-mixing" in a subset of subjects sensitive to this specific kind of auditory/visual feedback; $t(5) = 4.1$ $p < 0.05$.

4   Summary

The classic hallmarks of Vierordt's law, i.e., the overestimation of "short" durations and the underestimation of "long" durations within a specific range of signal durations (i.e., temporal context) has been shown to be a common property of temporal memory distortions. A general mechanism of "memory-mixing" is proposed to account for these effects whether they are the result of modality differences and/or proactive interference. Subjects can be "released" from the interference effects of "memory-mixing" by providing appropriate feedback and/or by blocking trials in such a way as to discourage the formation of such distortions in temporal memory. Moreover, individual differences in "memory-mixing" provide a unique opportunity to study the effects of instructional ambiguity, positive and negative feedback, as well as unimodal and bimodal distractors [46,47]. Such encoding processes may also provide a target for pharmacological investigation in select patient populations in which dopaminergic function can be manipulated, e.g., attention deficit hyperactivity disorder, obsessive-compulsive disorder, Parkinson's disease, and schizophrenia [48-51].

References

1. Buhusi, C.V., Meck, W.H.: What Makes us tick? Functional and Neural Mechanisms of Interval Timing. Nat. Rev. Neurosci. 6, 755–765 (2005)
2. Grondin, S.: Overloading Temporal Memory. J. Exp. Psychol. Hum. Percept. Perform. 31, 869–879 (2005)
3. Jazayeri, M., Shadlen, M.N.: Temporal Context Calibrates Interval Timing. Nat. Neurosci. 13, 1020–1026 (2010)
4. Mamassian, P., Landy, M.S.: It's That Time Again. Nat. Neurosci. 13, 914–916 (2010)
5. Lejeune, H., Wearden, J.H.: Vierordt's The Experimental Study of the Time Sense and its Legacy. Eur. J. Cogn. Psychol. 21(1868), 941–960 (2009)
6. Woodrow, H.: Time Perception. In: Stevens, S.S. (ed.) Handbook of Experimental Psychology, pp. 1224–1236. Wiley, New York (1951)
7. Cheng, R.K., Dyke, A.G., McConnell, M.W., Meck, W.H.: Categorical Scaling of Duration as a Function of Temporal Context in Aged Rats. Brain Res. 1381, 175–186 (2011)
8. Cheng, R.K., Scott, A.C., Penney, T.B., Williams, C.L., Meck, W.H.: Prenatal Choline Availability Differentially Modulates Timing of Auditory and Visual Stimuli in Aged Rats. Brain Res. 1237, 167–175 (2008)
9. Penney, T.B.: Modality Differences in Interval Timing: Attention, Clock Speed, and Memory. In: Meck, W.H. (ed.) Functional and Neural Mechanisms of Interval Timing, pp. 209–234. CRC Press, Boca Raton (2003)
10. Penney, T.B., Allan, L.G., Meck, W.H., Gibbon, J.: Memory Mixing in Duration Bisection. In: Rosenbaum, D.A., Collyer, C.E. (eds.) Timing of Behavior: Neural, Psychological and Computational Perspectives, pp. 165–193. MIT Press, Cambridge (1998)
11. Penney, T.B., Gibbon, J., Meck, W.H.: Differential Effects of Auditory and Visual Signals on Clock Speed and Temporal Memory. J. Exp. Psychol. Hum. Percept. Perform. 26, 1770–1787 (2000)
12. Penney, T.B., Tourret, S.: Modality Effects in Short Interval Timing. Psychologie Française 50, 131–143 (2005)
13. Allan, L.: The Influence of Scalar Timing Model on Human Timing Research. Behav. Processes 44, 101–117 (1998)
14. Allan, L.G., Gibbon, J.: A New Temporal Illusion or the TOE Once Again? Percept. Psychophys 55, 227–229 (1994)
15. Brown, G.D.A., McCormack, T., Smith, M., Stewart, N.: Identification and Bisection of Temporal Durations and Tone Frequencies: Common Models for Temporal and Nontemporal Stimuli. J. Exp. Psychol. Hum. Percept. Perform. 31, 919–938 (2005)
16. Eisler, H., Eisler, A., Hellström, A.: Psychophysical Issues in the Study of Time Perception. In: Grondin, S. (ed.) Psychology of Time, pp. 75–109. Emerald Group Publishing, Bingley (2008)
17. Grondin, S.: Timing and Time Perception: A Review of Recent Behavioral and Neuroscience Findings and Theoretical Directions. Atten. Percept. Psychophys 72, 561–582 (2010)
18. Hairston, I.S., Nagarajan, S.S.: Neural Mechanisms of the Time-Order Error: An MEG Study. J. Cogn. Neurosci. 19, 1163–1174 (2007)

19. Harrington, D.L., Boyd, L.A., Mayer, A.R., Sheltraw, D.M., Lee, R.R., Huang, M., Rao, S.M.: Neural Representation of Interval Encoding and Decision Making. Cogn. Brain Res. 21, 193–205 (2004)
20. Gooch, C.M., Wiener, M., Wencil, E.B., Coslett, H.B.: Interval Timing Disruptions in Subjects with Cerebellar Lesions. Neuropsychologia 48, 1022–1031 (2010)
21. Lustig, C., Matell, M.S., Meck, W.H.: Not "Just" a Coincidence: Frontal-Striatal Synchronization in Working Memory and Interval Timing. Memory 13, 441–448 (2005)
22. Meck, W.H.: Neuropsychology of Timing and Time Perception. Brain Cogn. 58, 1–8 (2005)
23. Meck, W.H.: Neuroantomical Localization of an Internal Clock: A Functional Link Between Mesolimbic, Nigrostriatal, and Mesocortical Dopaminergic Systems. Brain Res. 1109, 93–107 (2006)
24. Meck, W.H., Penney, T.B., Pouthas, V.: Cortico-Striatal Representation of Time in Animals and Humans. Cur. Opin. Neurobiol. 18, 145–152 (2008)
25. Lustig, C., Meck, W.H.: Paying Attention to Time as One Gets Older. Psychol. Sci. 12, 478–484 (2001)
26. Wearden, J.H., Edwards, H., Fakhri, M., Percival, A.: Why "Sounds are Judged Longer than Lights": Application of a Model of the Internal Clock in Humans. Q. J. Exp. Psychol. B. 51, 97–120 (1998)
27. Wearden, J.H., Todd, N.P., Jones, L.A.: When Do Auditory/Visual Differences in Duration Judgments Occur? Q. J. Exp. Psychol. 59, 1709–1724 (2006)
28. Meck, W.H., Church, R.M.: Abstraction of Temporal Attributes. J. Exp. Psychol. Anim. Behav. Process. 8, 226–243 (1982)
29. Gamache, P.L., Grondin, S.: The Lifespan of Time Intervals in Reference Memory. Perception 39, 1431–1451 (2010)
30. Gibbon, J., Church, R.M.: Representation of Time. Cogn. 37, 23–54 (1990)
31. Gibbon, J., Church, R.M., Meck, W.H.: Scalar Timing in Memory. Ann. NY Acad. Sci. 423, 52–77 (1984)
32. Meck, W.H.: Selective Adjustment of the Speed of Internal Clock and Memory Processes. J. Exp. Psychol. Anim. Behav. Process. 9, 171–201 (1983)
33. Petrusic, W.M.: Semantic Congruity Effects and Theories of the Comparison Process. J. Exp. Psychol. Hum. Percept. Perform. 18, 962–986 (1992)
34. Petrusic, W.M., Baranski, J.V.: Semantic Congruity Effects in Perceptual Comparisons. Percept. Psychophys. 45, 439–452 (1989)
35. Chen, Y., Huang, X., Luo, Y., Peng, C., Liu, C.: Differences in the Neural Basis of Automatic Auditory and Visual Time Perception: ERP Evidence From an Across-Modal Delayed Response Oddball Task. Brain Res. 1325, 100–111 (2010)
36. Penney, T.B., Meck, W.H., Roberts, S.A., Gibbon, J., Erlenmeyer-Kimling, L.: Interval-Timing Deficits in Individuals at High Risk for Schizophrenia. Brain Cogn. 58, 109–118 (2005)
37. Gibbon, J., Church, R.M.: Sources of Variance in an Information Processing Theory of Timing. In: Roitblat, H.L., Bever, T.G., Terrace, H.S. (eds.) Animal Cognition, pp. 465–488. Erlbaum, Hillsdale (1984)
38. Lustig, C., Meck, W.H.: Chronic Treatment with Haloperidol Induces Deficits in Working Memory and Feedback Effects of Interval Timing. Brain Cogn. 58, 9–16 (2005)
39. Rakitin, B.C., Malapani, C.: Effects of Feedback on Time Production Errors in Aging Participants. Brain Res. Bul. 75, 22–33 (2008)
40. Adcock, R.A., Thangavel, A., Whitfield-Gabrieli, S., Knutson, B., Gabrieli, J.D.: Reward-Motivated Learning: Mesolimbic Activation Precedes Memory Formation. Neuron. 50, 507–517 (2006)

41. Koepp, M.J., Gunn, R.N., Lawrence, A.D., Cunningham, V.J., Dagher, A., Jones, T., Brooks, D.J., Bench, C.J., Grasby, P.M.: Evidence For Striatal Dopamine Release During a Video Game. Nature 393, 26–268 (1998)
42. Malapani, C., Rakitin, B., Levy, R., Meck, W.H., Deweer, B., Dubois, B., Gibbon, J.: Coupled Temporal Memories in Parkinson's Disease: A Dopamine-Related Dysfunction. J. Cogn. Neurosci. 10, 316–331 (1998)
43. Droit-Volet, S., Meck, W.H., Penney, T.B.: Sensory Modality and Time Perception in Children and Adults. Behav. Processes. 74, 244–250 (2007)
44. Droit-Volet, S., Meck, W.H.: How Emotions Colour Our Perception of Time. Trend Cogn. Sci. 11, 504–513 (2007)
45. Meck, W.H.: Distortions in the Content of Temporal Memory: Neurobiological Correlates. In: Fountain, S.B., Bunsey, M.D., Danks, J.H., McBeath, M.K. (eds.) Animal Cognition and Sequential Behavior: Behavioral, Biological, and Computational Perspectives, pp. 175–200. Kluwer Academic Press, Boston (2002)
46. Klapproth, F.: Single-Modality Memory Mixing in Temporal Generalization: An Effect Due to Instructional Ambiguity. NeuroQuantology 7, 8–94 (2009)
47. Vatakis, A., Spence, C.: Temporal Order Judgments for Audiovisual Targets Embedded in Unimodal and Bimodal Distractor Streams. Neurosci. Lett., 5–9 (2006)
48. Allman, M.J., Meck, W.H.: Pathophysiological Distortions in Time Perception and Timed Performance. Brain (in press 2011)
49. Coull, J.T., Cheng, R.K., Meck, W.H.: Neuroanatomical and Neurochemical Substrates of Timing. Neuropsychopharmacology 36, 3–25 (2011)
50. Gu, B.-M., Park, J.-Y., Kang, D.-H., Lee, S.J., Yoo, S.Y., Jo, H.J., Choi, C.-H., Lee, J.-M., Kwon, J.S.: Neural Correlates of Cognitive Inflexibility During Task-Switching in Obsessive-Compulsive Disorder. Brain 131, 155–164 (2008)
51. Gu, B.-M., Yin, B., Cheng, R.K., Meck, W.H.: Quinpirole-Induced Sensitization to Noisy/Sparse Periodic Input: Temporal Synchronization as a Component of Obsessive-Compulsive Disorder. Neurosci. 179, 143–150 (2011)

Reproduction of Duration: How Should I Count the Ways?*

Joseph Glicksohn and Rotem Leshem

Department of Criminology and The Leslie and Susan Gonda (Goldschmied)
Multidisciplinary Research Center, Bar-Ilan University, Israel
jglick@bgu.ac.il

Abstract. We take a close look at the task of *prospective time reproduction*, wherein an individual is aware of the fact that she will subsequently be asked to reproduce a demarked duration. Our participants were either explicitly instructed not to count, or were allowed to count. When participants are allowed to count, their reproductions (R) tend to be a linear function of target duration (D). When instructed not to count, they exhibited a shorter $\log(R)$ mean value than those who were allowed to count. Participants not counting are thus less veridical in time estimation. Given that for them $\beta<1$, this suggests that subjective time for them is not a linear function of physical time. We further contrast four major indices relating reproduced time to target duration: R/D, D/R, $|R-D|$, and $|R-D|/D$. While the D/R ratio score detected the difference between groups; this was not the case for the other measures.

Keywords: Time estimation, Time reproduction, Psychophysics, Ratio score, Absolute discrepancy, Absolute error.

1 Introduction

Subjective time has always been a favourite subject of investigation for scholars, poets, and other students of perception [1], each of whom has addressed the vagaries of definition which plague the field [2]. The task that we have chosen to analyze is that of *prospective time reproduction*, wherein an individual is aware of the fact that he or she will subsequently be asked to reproduce a demarked duration.[1] Of all the various tasks

---

* Our title incorporates a play on words alluding, on the one hand, to the first line of Elizabeth Barrett Browning's famous love sonnet 43 ("How do I love thee? Let me count the ways."), while also referring to one of the factors under investigation here—namely, whether there is a difference in psychophysical function and in the various indices presented here, for participants who are allowed to count and for those explicitly instructed not to count, while performing the task of time reproduction.

[1] Our participants were aware of the fact that they were engaged in a task of time reproduction—hence the paradigm is *prospective*. A *retrospective* paradigm, wherein the participant is not aware of the fact that she will subsequently be required to reproduce a target duration, would be effective for the first time duration reproduced, but following this the participant would, of course, be fully aware of the task requirement—hence implementing a prospective time reproduction. See [1] for references to studies conducted under either paradigm.

A. Vatakis et al. (Eds.): Time and Time Perception 2010, LNAI 6789, pp. 79–91, 2011.

of time estimation—and especially in contrast with that of time production (i.e., the request to produce a target duration)—time reproduction seems to be the most problematic, for three reasons: methodology, modeling, and measurement.

First, the methodology is problematic, given that there is no consensus in the literature regarding the reliability and validity of the task. Time reproduction has been viewed as being inherently "untrustworthy because it necessarily confounds factors affecting the subjective durations of the initial, presentation event and the subsequent, reproduction event; differences in attentional and set characteristics of these two events cannot be controlled and may introduce time-order errors" [3, p.168]. It has been claimed to be "typically the most difficult" [4, p.22], yet the most accurate task [5], producing the least variable results [6]. In short, we have no consistent view here regarding the very nature of the task.

Secondly, the task is problematic because it is unclear whether time reproduction is a separate variant of time estimation, requiring its own type of modeling, or whether it and time production can be modeled along the same lines [7]. Presumably, the same type of model for both tasks could be adopted if the data generated by both were consistently related (sometimes found [8], and sometimes not [9]). Some authors claim that time production and time reproduction indices should be negatively correlated [10], others that they should be positively correlated in the sense that *reproduction* is *re-production* [11,12], at least for those cases in which "introducing a delay between the two parts of a reproduction trial makes this task more nearly like a combination of the separate estimation and production tasks" [13, p.178]. Some authors have concluded that time production and time reproduction involve inherently *different* processes [9]. There is, however, a growing consensus in the literature that time production and time reproduction employ *different* components of the *same* internal clock: Time production being more attuned with internal clock speed [14,15] and attention [16,17], whereas time reproduction, while also being dependent on attention [18,19], relies heavily on working memory [20,21]. Others have argued against the notion of an internal clock [22,23], but would, presumably, still suggest that time reproduction and working memory are inherently related.

Thirdly, there is the problem of measurement (or, data evaluation). Reproduced time (R) is to be related to target duration (D). Of course, this is part and parcel of the more general problem of relating subjective time to physical time [5]. How is this done? We find a total of three different approaches in the literature, none of which is derived from any particular model, nor are they necessarily specific to the task of time reproduction: (1) computing the R/D ratio [24,25]—one can also consider the D/R variant [26]; (2) computing an absolute discrepancy ($|R-D|$) score [27]; (3) computing an absolute error ($|R-D|/D$) score [28,29]. What are the benefits of one measure over the others? In computing the R/D ratio, "the time estimates are expressed as proportions of physical durations, [hence] they are directly comparable across the different durations" [10, p.108]. More importantly, such a measure is completely compatible with the notion of a ratio comparison of "a currently evolving interval" [30, p.171] to a retrieved duration ('standard') at the memory stage in interval timing. Computing the $|R-D|$ score "reflects the magnitude of the participant's errors in timing regardless of directionality" [27, pp.354-355], and is compatible with "an absolute discrepancy rule" for response output in interval timing [31, p.145]. The $|R-D|/D$ score is "more sensitive at detecting differences between treatment conditions than are measures of directional error" [32, p.622] and, further, "measures based on absolute error or variability may be especially sensitive indicators of timing performance ... Absolute error represents a mix of both overestimations and underestimations and as such reflects a more generalized disruption of timing" [29, p.612].

Time reproduction is also somewhat an insular task, in that two specific models have been proposed for its depiction, with little or no reference to other tasks: the "parallel-clock" model for time reproduction [33], and the "dual klepsydra" model (DKM) [34]. In the "parallel-clock" model, "two sensory registers ('clocks') are in use: one accumulates subjective time units from the start of the first to the end of the second duration. The other accumulates subjective time units during ... reproduction" [33, p. 22]. The task of time reproduction involves a comparison of both registers, such that when the difference between the two is equivalent to the state of the second, then both durations are viewed as being equal. The "parallel-clock" model "disposes of any memory" [35, p.71], that is "no time is required for transferring data from the sensory register to memory" [36, p.271] because "the total subjective duration and the 2nd duration are each accumulated in a separate sensory register" [37]. Neither of these changing values are subsequently affected because the two sensory registers (or, clocks) do not suffer from such capacity constrictions as would be the case with a working-memory register, in which "the outcome from the accumulator corresponding to the current time is transiently stored" [15, p.368]. There is an online "comparison between two magnitudes that change continuously in parallel (hence the *Parallel*-Clock Model')" [36, p.271].

The recently proposed that the DKM for time reproduction [38,39] relies heavily on memory (i.e., leaky accumulators, or klepsydrae), while disposing of any 'pacemaker-counter' scheme. According to this model, two inflow/outflow systems ('klepsydrae') are in use: one is filled with constant flow from the start to the end of the first duration; after a waiting time, the second is then filled with constant flow. The task of time reproduction involves a comparison of both klepsydrae, such that when their two states are equal, then both durations are viewed as being equal.

Given our interest in contrasting various indices of time perception [40], we compute the parameters of the psychophysical function for time reproduction, using the "parallel-clock" model, and investigate to what degree simple experimental manipulations are captured by the function. These manipulations involve a factor of chronometric counting (whether the participants were explicitly instructed not to count, or whether they were allowed to count), and a waiting interval (whether they were required to wait 2 seconds or 4 seconds before reproducing the target interval). Chronometric counting by participants is explicitly prohibited by the proponents of the "parallel-clock" model [33,35], who argue that counting will impact on the psychophysical exponent. Waiting time has been investigated by proponents of the DKM [38,39], who argue that waiting will impact on the reproduction function.[2] Our present interest is in seeing to what degree these two factors will have an influence on the four major indices relating reproduced time to target duration. Our design (see below) allows for a comparison amongst conditions, and we investigate whether the different indices are sensitive enough to such an experimental manipulation.

---

[2] Unfortunately, we could not also investigate the DKM indices, and will have to wait until the software for computing these indices becomes available (Jiri Wackermann, personal communication).

2 Method

2.1 Participants and Design

Our 24 participants (22 female and 2 male) were drawn from an undergraduate pool.[3] Their age ranged between 20 and 26. They were randomly allocated to four groups of a 2×2 design, having the following factors: Whether the participants were explicitly instructed not to count, or whether they were allowed to count[4]—we shall subsequently refer to this factor as Count—and whether they were required to wait 2 seconds or 4 seconds before making each of their reproductions—we shall subsequently refer to this factor as Wait.

2.2 Apparatus, Stimuli, and Procedure

Five target intervals—2, 4, 8, 16 and 32 seconds—were demarked by a coloured disk appearing on a grey background, presented focally for the required interval. Disk diameter was 8 cm, viewed from a comfortable viewing distance (50 cm). For reproduction, the same disk was redisplayed, and the duration of its appearance was terminated by the participant on pressing the spacebar, after an estimated duration subjectively equivalent to that of the original presentation. To aid the participant here, interval and the colour of the disk were matched as follows: red (2 sec), yellow (4 sec), green (8 sec), purple (16 sec) and blue (32 sec). Allocation of colour to duration had been done randomly, but was then set for all participants serving in the study. All materials were prepared as visual stimuli using Canvas 2.0 software, and presented on a colour monitor. The experiment was controlled by a SuperLab routine, run on an Apple Power Macintosh, and presented on a colour monitor having a refresh rate of 67 Hz.

The second author, who served as experimenter, explicitly instructed the participants that they had to wait either 2 seconds or 4 seconds, and she measured these waiting times using a stopwatch. The five target durations were each replicated 5 times, and all 25 durations were presented in a random order within participants, with a different random order for each participant. For one group ($n = 12$), time reproduction was done after waiting 2 seconds following each target interval; for the other group ($n = 12$), this was done after a waiting period of 4 seconds. Within each group, half the participants ($n = 6$) were explicitly instructed not to count; the others were allowed to count.

2.3 Data Screening

Clear aberrant values were deleted (for an example, see Fig. 1), and these were not replaced by some other value. We view such an aberrant value as indicating what has been referred to as a *stimulus-independent lapse* [41]. Of the 600 (24×25) reproductions, a total of 22 (3.7%) were discarded. A total of 4 participants exhibiting

---

[3] Given the existence of sex differences in time estimation [40], it is plausible that our male and female participants might well differ in their performance in the present study. Unfortunately, we are not able to investigate this here, given the small number of male participants.

[4] The participants were given no specific instruction. From our previous work in this domain (e.g., [40]), we know that they usually report counting.

aberrant performance (i.e., more than one aberrant reproduction in their data set) were dropped from the sample. The final sample thus comprised a total of 20 participants, and it is their data that are presented below. These were evenly split ($n = 10$) into the two groups of Wait.

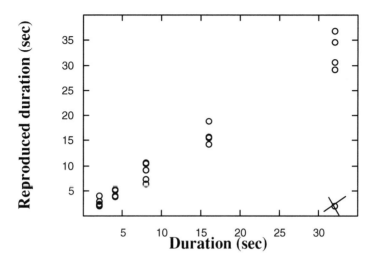

Fig. 1. Data Screening: An example of an aberrant value for one individual

Individual psychophysical functions were computed using 5 durations × 5 replications = 25 data points. Mean time reproduction values (using both untransformed data and log-transformed data) were computed for each target duration based on these 5 replications—except for those participants, for whom one aberrant reproduction was deleted, leaving for these 4 replications. The intra-individual standard deviation (SD) for each target duration was computed using these replications, relative to the participant's mean time reproduction.

3 Results and Discussion

3.1 Individual Time Reproduction Functions

We computed individual psychophysical functions, using the "parallel clock" model, wherein the exponent (β) and subjective zero (ϕ) are derived from the *slope* and *intercept* respectively of the *linear* plot of R regressed on ($D+R$), as follows [42, 43]: $\beta = \log(0.5)/\log(slope)$; $\phi = intercept/(1 - slope)$. The exponent ranged between 0.78 and 1.12 (median=0.939), and has a symmetric distribution. Does the exponent change as a function of both Count and Wait? To answer this, we ran a two-way analysis of variance (ANOVA) on both the exponent and the subjective zero (in separate analyses). For the exponent, we uncovered a main effect for Count [$F(1, 16)$ = 4.63, $MSE = 0.007$, $p < .05$, Cohen's d=0.93], and no other effects (for Wait, $F < 1$), indicating that when participants were instructed not to count, they exhibited a lower exponent (β=0.91) than those who were allowed to count (β=0.99). No effects were uncovered for the subjective zero (F values for both Count and Wait < 1). Eisler and Eisler [43, p.202] have suggested that when β<1, this indicates both that the number of units accumulated has decreased, and that the participant's attention has "slipped." More importantly for present purposes, it would seem that when participants are allowed to count, their reproductions tend to be a linear function of target duration. Given this pattern of results, we discarded our factor of Wait, and restricted our subsequent analyses to the factor of Count.

3.2 Mean Reproduction, Coefficient of Variation (CV), and Mean Log(reproduction)

Given our profile of time reproductions for each participant, namely reproductions for each of 2, 4, 8, 16, and 32 second target durations, we subsequently analyzed the data by means of a two-way ANOVA, with repeated measures on target duration (subsequently referred to as Duration), and with a grouping factor of Count. We uncovered a main effect for Duration [$F(4, 72) = 936.94$, $MSE = 2.635$, $p < .0001$], together with a main effect for Count [$F(1, 18) = 7.49$, $MSE = 11.77$, $p < .05$, $d = 1.23$], and a Duration × Count interaction [$F(4, 72) = 7.36$, $MSE = 2.645$, $p < .0001$].

As can be seen in Fig. 2a, while reproduced duration increases with Duration, so does the standard deviation (SD). In fact, it is because of this very dependence of the SD on the mean, that we shall subsequently present an analysis based on a logarithmic transformation of the reproduction data. Turning to the CV (i.e., SD divided by mean R) as dependent variable, and using the same ANOVA, we uncovered a main effect for Duration [$F(4, 72) = 3.87$, $MSE = 0.007$, $p < .01$], together with a main effect for Count [$F(1, 18) = 26.72$, $MSE = 0.010$, $p < .0001$, $d = 2.323$], and no significant interaction.

To what extent do these results conform to the expectations of scalar expectancy theory (SET) [44]? Firstly, the expected *linear* relationship between reproduced (R) and target (D) durations [45] is found when participants are allowed to count, but is exchanged for a monotonically increasing one when they are requested not to count (see Fig. 2a). Secondly, the expected increase in SD with target duration [46] is confirmed. Thirdly, the expectation of a constant coefficient of variation (CV) [47, p.62] is not found. We do note, however, that with only 5 data points based on which we computed the mean, SD and CV for each reproduced duration, we cannot really make a strong statement here with respect to this issue.

We then looked at log(R), which we would argue is preferable over R. Given our choice of target durations, all of which are powers of 2, we employed a logarithmic transformation to base 2, of both reproduced and target durations, the target durations rendering thereby a linear scale ranging between 1 and 5, with a midpoint value of 3. Now the data exhibited linearity, between reproduced and target durations, when both are log-transformed (see Fig. 2b). We find a main effect for Duration [$F(4, 72) = 794.36$, $MSE = 0.04$, $p < .0001$], together with a main effect for Count [$F(1, 18) = 4.67$, $MSE = 0.33$, $p < .05$, $d = 0.97$], and no interaction. When participants were

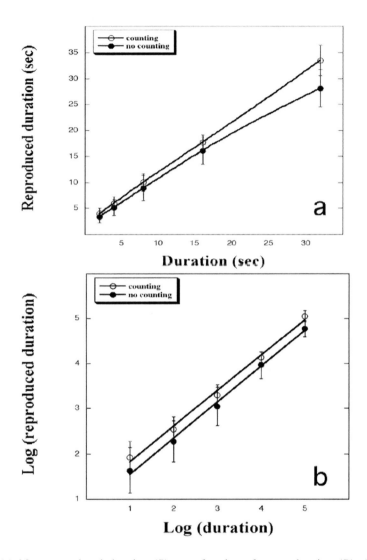

Fig. 2. (a) Mean reproduced duration (*R*) as a function of target duration (*D*); (b) mean log(reproduction) as a function of log(duration), both using log to base 2. Error bars are standard deviations (*SD*), for group (between participants) mean reproductions.

instructed not to count, they exhibited a shorter log(*R*) mean value (*M*=3.14) than those who were allowed to count (*M*=3.39). In the present context, this indicates that participants not counting are less veridical in time estimation. When coupled with the fact that for them $\beta < 1$, this suggests that for these participants, subjective time is not a linear function of physical time.

3.3 Comparing Different Dependent Variables: (1) *R/D* and *D/R* Ratios, (2) Absolute Discrepancy (|*R-D*|), and (3) Absolute Error (|*R-D*|/*D*)

3.3.1 *R/D* and *D/R* Ratios

Analyzing the data by means of a two-way ANOVA, with repeated measures on Duration, and with a grouping factor of Count, we uncover a main effect for Duration using the *R/D* ratio [$F(4, 72) = 45.79$, $MSE = 0.054$, $p < .0001$], but no such effect for Count [$F(1, 18) = 2.39$, *ns*, $d = 0.69$], nor one for their interaction.

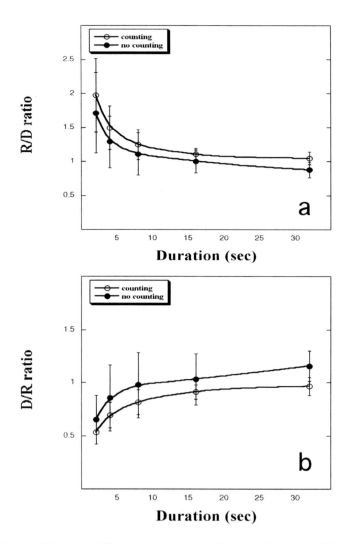

Fig. 3. (a) Mean *R/D* ratio ($\pm$ *SD*) as a function of *D*; (b) mean *D/R* ratio ($\pm$ *SD*) as a function of *D*

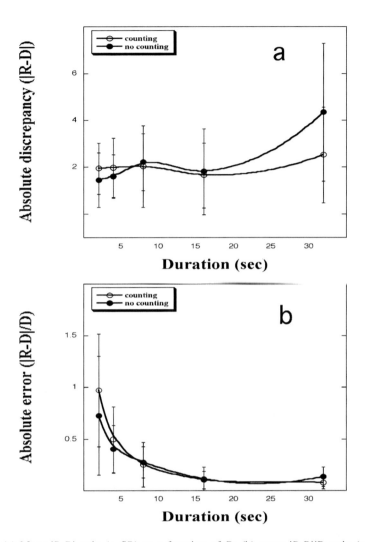

Fig. 4. (a) Mean |R-D| ratio (± SD) as a function of D; (b) mean |R-D|/D ratio (± SD) as a function of D

We then looked at the reversed, D/R ratio [26][5]. For the mean D/R ratio, we uncover, as before, a main effect for Duration [F(4, 72) = 48.97, MSE = 0.013, p < .0001], but this time also one for Count [F(1, 18) = 4.75, MSE = 0.117, p < .05, d = 0.98], but no interaction. For participants who were instructed not to count, D/R = 0.933, while for

---

[5] As one reviewer acknowledged, it might be surprising to see that both R/D and D/R are analyzed. In fact, we have benefited here from Richard Block's insightful comment to us regarding another study [40], suggesting looking at both such measures. To paraphrase his logic here: If the target duration is 8 seconds, and the reproduced duration is 6 seconds, the R/D ratio is 0.75, and the D/R ratio is 1.33—and these are not equally distant from the value of 1.00.

those who were allowed to count, $D/R = 0.783$. Furthermore, note that for the R/D ratio, SD progressively decreases with Duration (see Fig. 3a), while for the D/R ratio, SD fluctuates (see Fig. 3b).

3.3.2 Absolute Discrepancy ($|R\text{-}D|$) and Absolute Error ($|R\text{-}D|/D$)

Turning now to our two other measures, we uncover a main effect for Duration for the absolute discrepancy ($|R\text{-}D|$) [$F(4, 72) = 4.83$, $MSE = 1.96$, $p < .05$], and for the absolute error ($|R\text{-}D|/D$) [$F(4, 72) = 34.01$, $MSE = 0.058$, $p < .0001$], but no such effect for Count, nor one for their interaction. For participants who were instructed not to count, $|R\text{-}D| = 2.28$, and $|R\text{-}D|/D = 0.33$, while for those who were allowed to count, $|R\text{-}D| = 2.02$, and $|R\text{-}D|/D = 0.38$, these respective values not being significantly different (see Fig. 4). Hence, when employing these indices, no effect is uncovered for Count. Furthermore, note that for $|R\text{-}D|$, SD fluctuates (see Fig. 4a), and for $|R\text{-}D|/D$, SD progressively decreases with Duration (see Fig. 4b).

4 Conclusions

Counting entails either more accurate (i.e., veridical) [33,35,48-51], or at least as accurate [46] time reproductions. Our use of a $\log(R)$ score [52] is fully compatible with the use of a geometric mean (GM) for time reproduction data [53], in that the arithmetic average of the log-transformed reproductions R_1 and R_2, namely [$\log(R_1) + \log(R_2)]/2 = \log(R_1R_2)^{1/2}$, is the same as $\log(GM[R_1R_2])$. Furthermore, the logarithmic transformation is consistent with two notions current in the literature: (1) that a power function holds for the data [42, 54, 55], linearized using a logarithmic transformation; (2) that numbers have a logarithmic rather than linear representation [56]. The latter case pertains to the spatial mapping of number (i.e., the demarcation of a series of numbers on an analog scale)—the smallest number being to the left, the largest being to the right, and the intervening numbers in between—and especially to the spatial representation of their numerical magnitude (i.e., the translation of each number to a magnitude on the analog scale)—the distance between numbers reflecting their difference in magnitude. A number of authors have referred to this analog representation as comprising a "compressed logarithmic mapping" [57, p.1217], the distance between the smaller numbers/magnitudes (e.g., 4, 7, 12) being made much larger than that between the larger numbers/magnitudes (e.g., 80, 90, 100), or as being indicative of the implementation of an intuitive "logarithmic-ruler counter" [58], which might subsequently be replaced by a linear mapping. Hence, given the fact that participants might well be counting off intervals during the task [49], and/or the notion that "pulses, possibly generated by a neural oscillator, are counted during a time interval, and that the sum of counts constitutes the experienced duration" [43, p.195], the resultant value should be on a logarithmic scale. The fact that the $|R\text{-}D|$ and the $|R\text{-}D|/D$ scores did not detect a main effect for Count provides further evidence supporting the argument that the use of these measures should be reconsidered [40]. That it was specifically the D/R ratio, and not the R/D ratio, which uncovers the effect for Count is somewhat surprising, and is worthy of further investigation.

   In conclusion, we have shown in this paper that a number of commonly used indices for relating subjective time to physical time, or as specifically here, for relating reproduced (R) to target (D) duration, seem to be suspect. When participants are allowed to count, their reproductions tend to be a linear function of target duration. This distinction (Count) is detected in the psychophysical exponent of the "parallel clock" model for time reproduction, is seen in the CV of R, and is seen in the $\log(R)$ measure. It is detected by the D/R ratio, and not the R/D ratio, and is not at all detected by the $|R-D|$ and the $|R-D|/D$ scores.

Acknowledgments. We thank our three reviewers for their constructive and insightful comments on a previous draft of this chapter.

References

1. Roeckelein, J.E.: The Concept of Time in Psychology: A Resource Book and Annotated Bibliography. Greenwood Press, Westport (2000)
2. Bindra, D., Waksberg, H.: Methods and Terminology in Studies of Time Estimation. Psychol. Bull. 53, 155–159 (1956)
3. Blankenship, D.A., Anderson, N.H.: Subjective Duration: A Functional Measurement Analysis. Percept. Psychophys. 20, 168–172 (1976)
4. Kerns, K.A., McInerney, R.J., Wilde, N.J.: Time Reproduction, Working Memory, and Behavioral Inhibition in Children with ADHD. Child Neuropsychol. 7, 21–31 (2001)
5. Zakay, D.: The Evasive Art of Subjective Time Measurement: Some Methodological Dilemmas. In: Block, R.A. (ed.) Cognitive Models of Psychological Time, pp. 59–84. Lawrence Erlbaum Associates, Inc., Hillsdale (1990)
6. Rammsayer, T.H.: On the Relationship Between Personality and Time Estimation. Pers. Individ. Differ. 23, 739–744 (1997)
7. Thomas, E.A.C., Brown Jr, I.: Time Perception and the Filled-Duration Illusion. Percept. Psychophys. 16, 449–458 (1974)
8. Glicksohn, J., Ron-Avni, R.: The Relationship Between Preference for Temporal Conceptions and Time Estimation. Eur. J. of Cogn. Psychol. 9, 1–15 (1997)
9. Wackermann, J., Späti, J., Ehm, W.: Individual Response Characteristics in Time Reproduction and Time Production Tasks. In: Monahan, J.S., Sheffert, S.M., Townsend, J.T. (eds.) Fechner Day 2005. Proceedings of the 21st Annual Meeting of the International Society for Psychophysics, pp. 359–364. International Society for Psychophysics, Traverse City (2005)
10. Brown, S.W.: Time, Change, and Motion: The Effects of Stimulus Movement on Temporal Perception. Percept. Psychophys. 57, 105–116 (1995)
11. Killeen, P.R.: Counting the Minutes. In: Macar, F., Pouthas, V., Friedman, W.J. (eds.) Time, Action and Cognition: Towards Bridging the Gap, pp. 203–214. Kluwer Academic Publishers, Dordrecht (1992)
12. Poynter, D.: Judging the Duration of Time Intervals: A Process of Remembering Segments of Experience. In: Levin, I., Zakay, D. (eds.) Time and Human Cognition: A Life-Span Perspective, pp. 305–331. Elsevier Science Publishers, Amsterdam (1989)
13. Carlson, V.R., Feinberg, I.: Time Judgment as a Function of Method, Practice, and Sex. J. Exp. Psychol. 85, 171–180 (1970)
14. Baudouin, A., Vanneste, S., Isingrini, M., Pouthas, V.: Differential Involvement of Internal Clock and Working Memory in the Production and Reproduction of Duration: A Study on Older Adults. Acta Psychol. 121, 285–296 (2006)
15. Pouthas, V., Perbal, S.: Time Perception Depends on Accurate Clock Mechanisms as Well as Unimpaired Attention and Memory Processes. Acta Neurobiol. Exp. 64, 367–385 (2004)

16. Burle, B., Casini, L.: Dissociation Between Activation and Attention Effects in Time Estimation: Implications for Internal Clock Models. J. Exp. Psychol.-Hum. Percept. Perform 27, 195–205 (2001)
17. Casini, L., Macar, F.: Multiple Approaches to Investigate the Existence of an Internal Clock using Attentional Resources. Behav. Processes 45, 73–85 (1999)
18. Macar, F., Grondin, S., Casini, L.: Controlled Attention Sharing Influences Time Estimation. Mem. Cogn. 22, 673–686 (1994)
19. Seri, Y., Kofman, O., Shay, L.: Time Estimation Could be Impaired in Male, but not Female Adults with Attention Deficits. Brain Cogn. 48, 553–558 (2002)
20. Fortin, C., Breton, R.: Temporal Interval Production and Processing in Working Memory. Percept. Psychophys. 57, 203–215 (1995)
21. Rubia, K., Smith, A.: The Neural Correlates of Cognitive Time Management: A Review. Acta Neurobiol. Exp. 64, 329–340 (2004)
22. Lewis, P.A., Miall, R.C.: Remembering the Time: A Continuous Clock. Trends Cogn. Sci. 10, 401–406 (2006)
23. Lustig, C., Matell, M.S., Meck, W.H.: Not "Just" a Coincidence: Frontal-Striatal Interactions in Working Memory and Interval Timing. Memory 13, 441–448 (2005)
24. Brown, S.W.: Time Perception and Attention: The Effects of Prospective versus Retrospective Paradigms and Task Demands on Perceived Duration. Percept. Psychophys. 38, 115–124 (1985)
25. Brown, S.W.: Attentional Resources in Timing: Interference Effects in Concurrent Temporal and Nontemporal Working Memory Tasks. Percept. Psychophys. 59, 1118–1140 (1997)
26. Rammsayer, T.H., Rammstedt, B.: Sex-Related Differences in Time Estimation: The Role of Personality. Pers. Individ. Differ. 29, 301–312 (2000)
27. Barkley, R.A., Murphy, K.R., Bush, T.: Time Perception and Reproduction in Young Adults with Attention Deficit Hyperactivity Disorder. Neuropsychology 15, 351–360 (2001)
28. Angrilli, A., Cherubini, P., Pavese, A., Manfredini, S.: The Influence of Affective Factors on Time Perception. Percept. Psychophys. 59, 972–982 (1997)
29. Brown, S.W., Boltz, M.G.: Attentional Processes in Time Perception: Effects of Mental Workload and Event Structure. J. Exp. Psychol.-Hum. Percept. Perform. 28, 600–615 (2002)
30. Gibbon, J., Malapani, C., Dale, C.L., Gallistel, C.R.: Toward a Neurobiology of Temporal Cognition: Advances and Challenges. Curr. Opin. Neurobiol. 7, 170–184 (1997)
31. Matell, M.S., Meck, W.H.: Cortico-Striatal Circuits and Interval Timing: Coincidence Detection of Oscillatory Processes. Cognit. Brain Res. 21, 139–170 (2004)
32. Brown, S.W.: Influence of Individual Differences in Temporal Sensitivity on Timing Performance. Perception 27, 609–625 (1998)
33. Eisler, H.: The Parallel-Clock Model: A Tool for Quantification of Experienced Duration. In: Buccheri, R., Saniga, M., Stuckey, W.M. (eds.) The Nature of Time: Geometry, Physics and Perception, pp. 19–26. Kluwer Academic, Amsterdam (2003)
34. Wackermann, J.: From Neural Mechanics to the Measure of Subjective Time: The Klepsydra model. In: Oliveira, A.M., Teixara, M., Borges, G.F., Ferro, M.J. (eds.) Fechner Day 2004: Proceedings of the Twentieth Annual Meeting of the International Society for Psychophysics, pp. 164–169. International Society for Psychophysics, Coimbra (2004)
35. Eisler, H.: Time Perception from a Psychophysicist's Perspective. In: Helfrich, H. (ed.) Time and Mind, pp. 65–86. Hogrefe & Huber, Seattle (1996)
36. Eisler, A.D., Eisler, H., Montgomery, H.: A Quantitative Model for Retrospective Subjective Duration. NeuroQuantology 4, 263–291 (2004)
37. Eisler, H.: Applicability of the Parallel-Clock Model to Duration Discrimination. Percept. Psychophys. 29, 225–233 (1981)

38. Wackermann, J., Ehm, W.: The Dual Klepsydra Model of Internal Time Representation and Time Reproduction. J. Theor. Biol. 239, 482–493 (2006)
39. Wackermann, J., Ehm, W., Späti, J.: The 'Klepsydra Model' of Internal Time Representation. In: Berglund, B., Borg, E. (eds.) Fechner Day 2003: Proceedings of the Nineteenth Annual Meeting of the International Society for Psychophysics, pp. 331–336. International Society for Psychophysics, Larnaca Bay (2003)
40. Glicksohn, J., Hadad, Y.: Sex Differences in Time Production Revisited. J. Individ. Differ. (in press)
41. Wichmann, F.A., Hill, N.J.: The Psychometric Function: I. Fitting, Sampling, and Goodness of Fit. Percept. Psychophys. 63, 1293–1313 (2001)
42. Eisler, H.: Experiments on Subjective Duration 1868-1975: A Collection of Power Function Exponents. Psychol. Bull. 83, 1154–1171 (1976)
43. Eisler, A.D., Eisler, H.: Subjective Time in a Patient with Neurological Impairment. Psychologica 28, 193–206 (2001)
44. Wearden, J.H.: "Beyond the Fields we Know..." Exploring and Developing Scalar Timing Theory. Behav. Processes 45, 3–21 (1999)
45. Wearden, J.H.: Applying the Scalar Timing Model to Human Time Psychology: Progress and Challenges. In: Helfrich, H. (ed.) Time and Mind II: Information-Processing Perspectives, pp. 21–39. Kluwer, Dordrecht (2003)
46. Hinton, S.C., Rao, S.M.: "One-Thousand One... One-Thousand Two... " Chronometric Counting Violates the Scalar Property in Interval Timing. Psychon. Bull. Rev. 11, 24–30 (2004)
47. Wearden, J.H.: Do Humans Possess an Internal Clock with Scalar Timing Properties? Learn. Motiv. 22, 59–83 (1991)
48. Boltz, M.: Time Estimation and Attentional Perspective. Percept. Psychophys. 49, 422–433 (1991)
49. Fetterman, J.G., Killeen, P.R.: A Componential Analysis of Pacemaker-Counter Timing Systems. J. Exp. Psychol.-Hum. Percept. Perform. 16, 766–780 (1990)
50. Grondin, S., Meilleur-Wells, G., Lachance, R.: When to Start Explicit Counting in a Time-Intervals Discrimination Task: A Critical Point in the Timing Process of Humans. J. Exp. Psychol.-Hum. Percept. Perform. 25, 993–1004 (1999)
51. Hinton, S.C., Harrington, D.L., Binder, J.R., Durgerian, S., Rao, S.M.: Neural Systems Supporting Timing and Chronometric Counting: An fMRI Study. Cognit. Brain Res. 21, 183–192 (2004)
52. Eisler, A.D., Eisler, H., Derwinger, A.: Time Perception in Extravert and Introvert Personalities. In: Guirao, M. (ed.) Procesos Sensoriales y Cognitivos, pp. 371–387. Ediciones Dunken, Argentina (1997)
53. Richards, W.: Time Estimates Measured by Reproduction. Percept. Mot. Skills 18, 929–943 (1964)
54. Anderson, R.B.: The Power Law as an Emergent Property. Mem. Cogn. 29, 1061–1068 (2001)
55. Grondin, S.: From Physical Time to the First and Second Moments of Psychological Time. Psychol. Bull. 127, 22–44 (2001)
56. Dehaene, S.: The Neural Basis of the Weber-Fechner Law: A Logarithmic Mental Number. Trends Cogn. Sci. 7, 145–147 (2003)
57. Dehaene, S., Izard, V., Spelke, E., Pica, P.: Log or Linear? Distinct Intuitions of the Number Scale in Western and Amazonian Indigene Cultures. Science 320, 1217–1220 (2008)
58. Siegler, R.S., Opfer, J.E.: The Development of Numerical Estimation: Evidence for Multiple Representations of Numerical Quantity. Psychol. Sci. 14, 237–243 (2003)

Duration Discrimination Performance: No Cross-Modal Transfer from Audition to Vision Even after Massive Perceptual Learning

Simon Grondin[1] and Rolf Ulrich[2]

[1] Université Laval, École de psychologie,
2325 rue des Bibliothèques, G1V 0A6, Québec, Québec, Canada
simon.grondin@psy.ulaval.ca
http://darwin.psy.ulaval.ca/~perception/
[2] University of Tübingen, Department of Psychology
Friedrichstrasse 21, 72072 Tübingen, Germany
ulrich@uni-tuebingen.de

Abstract. In the present study, we tried to improve the discrimination of short temporal intervals marked by two brief visual signals with an extensive and massive training involving the discrimination of intervals marked by brief auditory signals. Two groups completed two sessions of visual interval discrimination (pre- and post-test). Between the two sessions, participants were either discriminating intervals marked by auditory signals (experimental group) or waiting for a period equivalent to the auditory training (control group). Once a method (called jackknife) is applied to reduce the statistical noise inherent in individual psychometric functions, the results show that visual duration discrimination is improved in the post-test portion of the experiment, but this effect applies to both groups. Therefore, it is not possible to argue that the gain is due to the auditory training. The discrimination threshold in the visual condition remained much higher than the threshold observed in the auditory mode.

1 Introduction

The discrimination of brief temporal intervals is much better when these intervals are marked by auditory signals rather than by visual or tactile signals ([1-4]; for a review see [5]). Given this basic fact, one cannot expect to improve auditory duration discrimination on the basis of visual or tactile duration discrimination. However, the question of cross-modal transfer of temporal learning is relevant in the opposite direction: could temporal discrimination training in audition improve the subsequent duration discrimination performance in another modality?

It is known that practice exerts moderate influence on auditory duration discrimination [6-7]. Nevertheless, there are within-modality transfers, for interval discrimination at specific durations, in the auditory [8-9] and in the visual modes [10]. Moreover, the timing literature also shows some cases of transfer of temporal learning across skin locations for tactile duration discrimination [11]. Even more striking is the fact that there is evidence that the learning obtained in auditory

A. Vatakis et al. (Eds.): Time and Time Perception 2010, LNAI 6789, pp. 92–100, 2011.
© Springer-Verlag Berlin Heidelberg 2011

duration discrimination can be transferred to an interval production task, would the intervals, in the discrimination and production tasks, be in the same range [12].

However, there are some signs in the literature that not much temporal learning can be transferred between sensory modalities. In one experiment by Grondin et al. [13], it was first shown that, after five 300-trial sessions of visual duration discrimination, performance did not much improve from Session 1 to 5. After these sessions, Grondin et al. conducted multiple sessions where simultaneous presentations of auditory and visual signals were used for marking empty intervals to be discriminated. Discrimination was better with marking signals delivered in both modalities instead of only in the visual one. This indicates that as soon as auditory signals are available for marking time, duration discrimination is improved. Once the auditory signals were withdrawn, there remained only a slight improvement of visual duration discrimination. In other words, even this type of training (learning by association between auditory and visual markers) resulted in small progress. In a final step of Grondin et al.'s experiment, additional auditory training seemed to provide some gain, but a fragile one given that the levels of performance in visual conditions tended to diminish rapidly. Indeed, in this experiment, the capacity to maintain benefits after auditory exposure depended on task difficulty level (which was set in this experiment according to the initial capabilities of observers).

In another attempt for improving visual duration discrimination with audition, Grondin et al. [14] reported data for sessions involving only auditory duration discrimination, only visual duration discrimination, or some visual trials within a context where mainly auditory intervals were presented. The performance levels remained constant in the different experimental conditions in the auditory condition: the Weber fraction around 6% with or without the insertion of visual interval. However, with visual trials, the Weber fraction was slightly above 10% in sessions involving only visual stimuli, but close to 15% when auditory signals were also presented. Instead of helping discrimination, the auditory context interfered with the ability to process visually marked intervals, in spite of the fact that the participants knew that they should keep paying attention to the visual signals.

In a further study [6], participants were trained to discriminate between two empty temporal intervals marked by brief auditory signals. The main goal of this study was to examine whether temporal learning generalizes to empty intervals with the same duration, but marked by brief visual signals. In addition, the authors wanted to assess to what extent temporal learning generalizes to other conditions within the same sensory modality; therefore, their experiment also included conditions involving longer intervals marked with auditory intervals and filled auditory intervals of the same duration as the one used for training. In contrast to previous findings showing a transfer from the haptic to the auditory modality [11], the results of Lapid et al. [6] did not show a transfer from the auditory to the visual modality, though they showed a transfer within the auditory modality.

In brief, it is still difficult to draw a definite conclusion regarding the potential benefits that the training in auditory duration discrimination would have on visual duration discrimination. The potential effect, if any [6], seems to be thin and not permanent [13], if not damageable [14]. The lack of success in past experiments on this question may be due to an inefficient distribution of training sessions. Indeed, one aspect of the potential cross-modal transfer in timing performances that remains unexplored, as far as we know, is the effect that can be exerted by massive, instead of distributed, training sessions. The effect of extensive and massive auditory training on visual duration discrimination is the question addressed in the present study.

Discriminating auditory intervals versus discriminating visual intervals leads to the unequal levels of performance. For the auditory training portion of the experiment, we have chosen to adopt a simple task, which is the discrimination between one short (240 ms) or one long (260 ms) interval. In the auditory mode, such parameters should lead to a level close to 75% of correct responses. In the visual mode, the discrimination of such intervals is much more difficult. Therefore, we have adopted the same intervals for the first blocks of trials in the visual condition, and added much easier blocks of trials, with intervals lasting 220 ms vs. 280 ms. Finally, we applied a novel statistical method, the jackknife method [15-18], in an attempt to overcome the statistical noise that is often inherent in individual psychometric functions. This noise hampers the estimation of the difference threshold for determining discrimination performance at an individual level. The jackknife method operates on aggregated psychometric functions rather than on the level of individual functions like traditional approaches in psychophysics. Since aggregated data are less prone to statistical noise than individual data, the jackknife method is likely to provide more reliable estimates of the difference threshold compared to previous approaches. This in turn may enhance the statistical power of the subsequent data analysis.

2 Method

2.1 Participants

Twenty volunteer students or employees at Université Laval, aged between 20 and 35 years old, took part in this experiment. They received $40 for their participation. The experiment lasted about 3.5 hours.

2.2 Apparatus and Stimuli

Participants sat in a dimly lit room. A red LED, controlled by a stimulus generator connected to a microcomputer, was placed at approximately 70 cm in front of the participants and used to mark the visually-marked intervals. The 1-kHz auditory signals were presented through Sennheisen HD 477 headphones (70 dB SPL). The computer's keyboard was used as a response device with the participants indicating, by pressing the appropriate button, whether the interval presented was short or long. The parameters of the task were under control of an E-Prime program.

2.3 Procedure

At the beginning of each main part, a 250-ms standard interval was presented ten times. Each interval was marked by two successive 20-ms stimuli, visual in Parts 1 and 7, and auditory in Parts 2-6. Within each part, there were 6 blocks of 60 trials, with a 20-sec inter-block pause. Each trial began with a 500-ms preparation period, after which the interval to be categorized as short or long was presented. The observer then provided a response and a 1-sec feedback was presented.

Ten participants were assigned to each of two conditions. In one condition, the experiment consisted of seven parts, the first and the last ones involving visually-marked intervals. In the five remaining parts, the participants received duration discrimination training with auditory intervals. There was a potential 5-min pause between the parts during which participants could come out of the room, if they wished to. Each part lasted about 25 minutes, making the whole experiment approximately 3.5 hours long.

Ten participants were assigned to the control group where Parts 1 and 7 were the same; however, in-between, there was no auditory training but only a long rest period in the testing room, with the possibility to leave briefly.

In the two visual parts (control condition), intervals for the first three blocks lasted either 240 or 260 ms and the next three lasted 220 or 280 ms. There were 30 trials per block for each temporal interval. For the auditory parts, there were 30 short (240 ms) and 30 long (260 ms) presented randomly within each block. For each of the five auditory parts, there were 360 trials; therefore, participants of the experimental group received 1800 trials of auditory duration discrimination within about 2.5 hours.

2.4 Data Analyses

For each participant and for each of the two visual conditions (pre and post), a 4-point psychometric function was traced, plotting the four empty intervals on the *x-axis* and the probability of responding "long" on the y-*axis*.

The *cumulative normal distribution* (CND) was fitted to the resulting curves. Two indices of performance were estimated from each psychometric function, one for sensitivity and one for the perceived duration. As an indicator of temporal sensitivity, estimates of one standard deviation (SD) on the psychometric function were determined. Using one SD (or variance) is a common procedure to express temporal sensitivity [19]. The other dependent variable was the bisection point (BP). The BP can be defined as the *x* value corresponding to the 0.50 probability of "long" responses on the y-axis. Longer perceived durations are reflected by smaller BP values.

The data presented below are (1) the mean results of individual psychometric functions as described in the preceding paragraph and (2) the result of the jackknife method. The jackknife method consists in the following steps. In a first step, the individual psychometric functions for each experimental condition are averaged and an estimate SD(all) from this aggregated function is computed. Secondly, the individual score for each condition is computed in the following way. For Participant 1, the estimate of SD is based on the data of all subjects except that of Participant 1, say, SD(-1). For Participant 2, the estimate of SD is based on all subjects except Participant 2, i.e., SD(-2). The procedure is repeated for each of the 10 participants, i.e., up to SD(-10). For Participant 1, the score, SD(1), kept for final analysis is: 10*SD(all) – 9*SD(-1); and for Participant 2, SD(2) = 10*SD(all) - 9*SD(-2); ... and for Participant 10, SD(10) = 10*SD(all) - 9*SD(-10). The jackknife method was applied for estimating both SD and BP.

3   Results

3.1   Mean Individual Results

The mean SD in each experimental block indicate that the experimental (M=59.80) and control (35.74) groups have unequal performances in the first part of the experiment (baseline in visual duration discrimination). In the last part of the experiment (second visual duration discrimination estimate), the SD is slightly increased in the experimental group (61.84) and decreased in the control group (29.75). However, a 2x2 ANOVA with repeated measures on the part factor (pre vs. post) revealed that there are no significant effects, main or interaction.

The BP results seem to indicate that there is an increase of the mean value in the auditory training group but in the control group, the results go in the opposite direction (see Table 1). Once again though, the 2x2 ANOVA revealed no significant effect.

3.2   With the Jackknife Method

In spite of the large mean differences between groups, especially with the SD variable, no effect reported above was significant. This situation may be partly caused by the large variability of the individual scores (a variability that occurred even if the scores were based on 90 trials per data point on each individual psychometric function). In order to attenuate this variability effect, we have adopted the jackknife procedure.

Table 1. Mean Standard Deviation (SD) and Bisection Point (BP) in the experimental and control groups before and after using the jackknife procedure

| | Without jackknife | | With jackknife | |
	Auditory training	Control	Auditory training	Control
SD - Pre	59.80	35.74	40.58	32.22
SD - Post	61.84	29.75	31.13	28.03
BP – Pre	252.52	256.28	250.94	254.38
BP – Post	256.01	253.65	252.02	252.94

As indicated in Table 1, the effect of individual differences (very high SD estimates in some cases in the experimental group especially) is largely reduced with the method. Indeed, there is now a reduction in the experimental group from the first to the second estimate of the visual duration discrimination. The 2x2 ANOVA with repeated measures on the part factor (pre vs. post) revealed that this effect is significant, $F(1,18) = 4.68$, $p<.05$, $\eta^2=.21$. The group effect ($p=.42$) and the interaction ($p=.41$) are not significant (see Fig. 1).

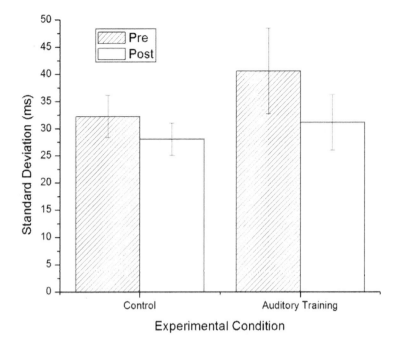

Fig. 1. Mean Standard Deviation, based on the jackknife analysis, in the pre- and post-tests for the experimental and control groups. Bars are SE.

Table 1 also reveals that, for the BP, the differences between conditions are now reduced following the application of the jackknife method. The 2x2 ANOVA reveals that no effect is significant.

3.3   Performance in Auditory Duration Discrimination (Experimental Group)

The mean percentages of correct responses in each of the five parts of auditory duration discrimination are the following: .683 (SE=.035), .704 (.038), .715 (.038), .716 (.038) and .709 (.043). A one-way ANOVA with repeated measures reveals that the differences between the means are only marginally significant, $F(4, 36) = 2.495$, $p=.081$, $\eta^2=.22$.

4   Discussion

The main finding revealed by this study is that performance for visual duration discrimination can be improved. When two performance estimates are completed within a 4-hour period, the second estimate shows better performance (smaller SD). However, and most importantly, this improvement cannot be attributed to the auditory training occurring between the two estimates with visual signals. Although the improvement was in average larger in the experimental group, there was no significant interaction.

The present finding joins previous ones where minimal or temporary gain, when any, was observed on visual duration discrimination after temporal training in the auditory mode [6,13,14]. What the present study shows is that the previous unsuccessful attempts cannot be attributed to the spacing of the training sessions in auditory. The auditory training here was massive and extensive, but it was still insufficient to exert a significant improvement in discrimination performance relative to the control condition. Indeed, the performance levels were increased in the visual condition, but remained far from what is obtained in the auditory mode. A specific look at the performance levels in the blocks of trials involving for the 240- and the 260-ms intervals, visual discrimination went from 58.5% (mean of both groups) of correct responses in the first session to 62.3% in the last session, which remains far from 70.6% obtained in the auditory training sessions. In other words, the visual vs. auditory difference for the discrimination of brief temporal intervals remains present, which is consistent with the modality differences typically reported in the literature (for reviews, see [20-21]).

From a theoretical standpoint, our data show the difficulty to gain any benefit in the visual modality, in term of temporal discrimination, from the training in the auditory mode. Strictly speaking, this means that there is no possible transfer of temporal information processing, just as if the reading of the output of a central clock could not be trained. This may be interpreted as if there is no such central clock. Consequently, the data could rather be interpreted as an indirect support to the idea that temporal processing is modality-specific, each modality having its own limitations [21].

There are some limitations in the design of the present study. For instance, it cannot be excluded that multiple trials of training caused some fatigue, although the performance levels in the auditory condition remained quite stable over the different parts of the experiment. Therefore, the potential gain that would accompany massive training may be masked partly by some fatigue. Maybe that employing another training schedule would have led to different conclusions. As well, it cannot be excluded that using different parameters (instead of 240 vs. 260 ms) for either the auditory or visual portions of the experiment would have lead to different results; and the present study remains restricted to the 250-ms range anyway.

The analysis of the BP, before and after the jackknife analyses, revealed no significant effect. In other words, whether or not there was massive auditory training, there was no subsequent change in the perceived duration of the intervals marked by visual signals. This result is consistent with some previous findings with empty intervals [14,22], but inconsistent with other findings when auditory and visual intervals are compared [6].

The present study also indicates that the jackknife method is a promising tool for improving the signal-to-noise ratio of psychometric functions. This in turn may enable especially reliable estimates of SD and BP from such functions. Of course, a methodological study is required to assess thoroughly the potential of this tool before it can be recommended as standard procedure. We are currently conducting extensive simulations to evaluate the potential virtue of this method for analyzing psychometric functions.

Acknowledgments. This research was made possible by a research grant awarded to SG by the Natural Sciences and Engineering Council of Canada and the Deutsche Forschungsgemeinschaft UL116/12-1. We would like to thank Félix Désautels for his help with data collection and analyses. We also extend special thanks to Joseph Glicksohn and one anonymous reviewer for their comments on an earlier version of this paper. This work was conducted under the European project COST ISCH Action TD0904 "Time In MEntaL activitY: theoretical, behavioral, bioimaging and clinical perspectives (TIMELY; www.timely-cost.eu)". Address correspondance to Simon Grondin, École de psychologie, Université Laval, 2325 rue des Bibliothèques, Québec, Qc, Canada G1V 0A6 (simon.grondin@psy.ulaval.ca).

References

1. Grondin, S.: Duration discrimination of empty and filled intervals marked by auditory and visual signals. Perception & Psychophysics 54, 383–394 (1993)
2. Grondin, S., McAuley, J.D.: Duration discrimination in crossmodal sequences. Perception 38, 1542–1559 (2009)
3. Grondin, S., Rousseau, R.: Judging the relative duration of multimodal short empty time intervals. Perception & Psychophysics 49, 245–256 (1991)
4. Ulrich, R., Nitschke, J., Rammsayer, T.: Crossmodal temporal discrimination: Assessing the predictions of a general pacemaker-counter model. Perception & Psychophysics 68, 1140–1152 (2006)
5. Grondin, S.: Sensory modalities and temporal processing. In: Helfrich, H. (ed.) Time and Mind 2002, pp. 75–92. Hogrefe & Huber, Goettingen, Ge (2003)
6. Lapid, E., Ulrich, R., Rammsayer, T.: Perceptual learning in auditory temporal discrimination: No evidence for a cross-modal transfer to the visual modality. Psychonomic Bulletin & Review 16, 382–389 (2009)
7. Rammsayer, T.: Effects of practice and signal energy on duration discrimination of brief auditory intervals. Perception & Psychophysics 55, 454–464 (1994)
8. Karmarkar, U.R., Buonomano, D.V.: Temporal specificity of perceptual learning in an auditory discrimination task. Learning and Memory 10, 141–147 (2003)
9. Wright, B.A., Buonomano, D.V., Manhcke, H.W., Merzenich, M.M.: Learning and generalization of auditory temporal-interval discrimination in humans. The Journal of Neuroscience 17, 3956–3963 (1997)
10. Westheimer, G.: Discrimination of short time intervals by human observers. Experimental Brain Research 129, 121–126 (1999)
11. Nagarajan, S.S., Blake, D.T., Wright, B.A., Byl, N., Merzenich, M.M.: Practice-related improvements in somatosensory interval discrimination are temporally specific but generalize across skin location, hemisphere, and modality. Journal of Neuroscience 18, 1559–1570 (1998)
12. Meegan, D.V., Aslin, R.N., Jacobs, R.A.: Motor timing learned without motor training. Nature Neuroscience 3, 860–862 (2000)
13. Grondin, S., Bisson, N., Gagnon, C., Gamache, P.-L., Matteau, A.-A.: Little to be expected from auditory training for improving visual temporal discrimination. NeuroQuantology 7, 95–102 (2009)
14. Grondin, S., Gamache, P.-L., Tobin, S., Bisson, N., Hawke, L.: Categorization of brief temporal intervals: An auditory processing context impair visual performances. Acoustical Science & Technology 29, 338–340 (2008)

15. Miller, J., Patterson, T., Ulrich, R.: Jackknife-based method for measuring LRP onset latency differences. Psychophysiology 35, 99–115 (1998)
16. Miller, J., Ulrich, R., Schwarz, W.: Why jackknifing yields good latency estimates. Psychophysiology 46(2), 300–312 (2009)
17. Smulders, F.T.Y.: Simplifying jackknifing of ERPs and getting more out of it: Retrieving estimates of participants' latencies. Psychophysiology 47, 387–392 (2010)
18. Ulrich, R., Miller, J.: Using the jackknife-based scoring method for measuring LRP onset effects in factorial designs. Psychophysiology 38, 816–827 (2001)
19. Grondin, S.: Methods for studying psychological time. In: Grondin, S. (ed.) Psychology of time, pp. 51–74. Emerald Group Publishing, Bingley (2008)
20. Grondin, S.: From physical time to the first and second moments of psychological time. Psychological Bulletin 127, 22–44 (2001)
21. Grondin, S.: Timing and time perception: A review of recent behavioral and neuroscience findings and theoretical directions. Attention, Perception, & Psychophysics 72, 561–582 (2010)
22. Grondin, S.: Overloading temporal memory. Journal of Experimental Psychology: Human Perception and Performance 31, 869–879 (2005)

An Investigation on Temporal Aspects in the Audio-Haptic Simulation of Footsteps

Luca Turchet and Stefania Serafin

Department of Architecture, Design and Media Technology,
Aalborg University Copenhagen
{tur,sts}@create.aau.dk

Abstract. In this paper, we present an experiment whose goal is to assess the role of temporal aspects in sonically and haptically simulating the act of walking on a bump or a hole. In particular, we investigated whether the timing between heel and toe and the timing between footsteps affected perception of walking on unflat surfaces. Results show that it is possible to sonically and haptically simulate a bump or a hole only by varying temporal information.

Keywords: Footstep sounds, physical models, auditory feedback, haptic feedback.

1 Introduction

Previous research on simulating walking sounds using physics based engines has focused on the act of walking on flat surfaces [2,4,3,14,11]. In the virtual reality community, few locomotion interfaces are able to render uneven grounds, and they have the disadvantage of being costly and cumbersome [5,6,8]. Recently, research has shown that it is possible to simulate the act of walking on unflat surfaces by only using visual cues [10]. Three parameters of camera motion were considered in the simulation: orientation, velocity and height, and their combination. The experiments were run both actively, having users wear an head mounted display, as well as passively, having users look at a video of the simulations. Results show that such visualization techniques successfully simulate bumps and holes located in the ground. These results are a development of previous research on pseudo-haptic simulation [9]. This research was extended by implementing a multimodal (audio-visual) simulation of walking on a bump or a hole [16]. Results in this case showed that the auditory cues reinforce the visual cues when coherent cues are provided in both modalities. When subjects were exposed to conflicting cues, for example by simulating visually the act of walking on a bump and auditorily the act of walking on a hole, usually the visual cues are dominant, apart from when the velocity effect is the visual parameter varied. This might be due to the higher temporal resolution of the auditory system versus the visual system [21].

In this paper, we are interested in exploring the possibility of implementing such pseudo-haptic feedback from the sonic and haptic point of view. Recently,

A. Vatakis et al. (Eds.): Time and Time Perception 2010, LNAI 6789, pp. 101–115, 2011.

we developed a system which can provide combined auditory and haptic sensations that arise while walking on aggregate and solid surfaces. The system is composed of an audio-haptic synthesis engine, and a pair of shoes enhanced with sensors and actuators. Such engine is based on physical models, that drive both the haptic and audio synthesis. A complete description of such system and of all its components is given elsewhere in detail [12], [17].

In a previous study [15], we used the synthesis engine in order to run an experiment whose goal was to assess the role of temporal aspects in sonically simulating the act of walking on a bump or a hole. In particular, we investigated whether the timing between heel and toe and the timing between footsteps affected perception of walking on unflat surfaces. In the experiment the footstep sounds where prerecorded. Results showed that it is possible to simulate a bump or a hole only by using temporal information [15].

Starting from those results, in this paper we are interested in understanding whether at haptic level it is possible to simulate the act of walking on a bump or a hole. Such haptic information is generated by means of the same techniques applied in [15] for the auditory simulation of bumps and holes, i.e., varying the temporal distances between the vibrations corresponding to the heel and to the toe as well as those between footsteps.

2   Simulation Hardware and Software

In this section we briefly describe the system used in the experiments presented in this paper. As mentioned in section 1, the complete description of such system can be found in our previous research [20], [17].

We developed a system which simulates both offline and in real-time the auditory and haptic sensation of walking on different surfaces. Specifically, the sensation of walking on solid surfaces is simulated by using and impact model [7], while to simulate walking on aggregate grounds, we used a physically informed sonic models (PhiSM) algorithm [1].

In order to provide both audio and haptic feedback, haptic shoes enhanced with pressure sensors have been developed. In detail, such shoes are pair of lightweight sandals (Model Arpenaz-50, Decathlon, Villeneuve d'Ascq, France). This particular model has light, stiff foam soles that are easy to gouge and fashion. Four cavities were made in the tickness of the sole to accommodate four vibrotactile actuators (Haptuator, Tactile Labs Inc., Deux-Montagnes, Qc, Canada). These electromagnetic recoil-type actuators have an operational, linear bandwidth of 50–500 Hz and can provide up to 3 G of acceleration when connected to light loads. As indicated in Fig. 1, two actuators were placed under the heel of the wearer and the other two under the ball of the foot. They were bonded in place to ensure good transmission of the vibrations inside the soles. When activated, vibrations propagated far in the light, stiff foam. The sole has force sensors intended to pick the foot-floor interaction force in order the drive the audio and haptic synthesis. They were not used in the present study.

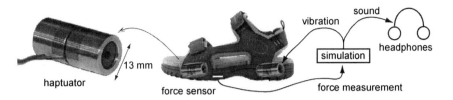

Fig. 1. System (one shoe shown). Left: recoil-type actuation from Tactile Labs Inc. The moving parts are protected by an aluminum enclosure able to bear the weight of a person. Middle: approximate location of the actuators in the sandal. Right: system diagram showing the interconnections. Here the force signal was not used.

The involved hardware provides a control in real-time of an audio-haptic synthesis engine. Such engine is based on physical models which are driven by a signal, in the audio domain, expressing the ground reaction force (GRF), i.e., the reaction force supplied by the ground at every step. In our simulations the GRF corresponds to the amplitude envelope extracted from an audio signal containing a footstep sound.

As previously mentioned, the engine can work both offline and in realtime. The two approaches differ for the way the input GRF is generated. Concerning the realtime implementation, various systems for the generation of such input have been developed and tested [20], [17], [12], [13], [18], [19]. In the offline implementation, the input signal consists of an audio file from which the GRF is extracted. Such file consists of a recording of a person walking on a real surface. Better results in terms of the GRF detection can be found on audio recordings of walking on solid surfaces and with a small amount of background noise. The different envelope profiles of each step in the file are extracted and fed to the engine which produces the synthesized footstep sounds according to the choice of the surface to be simulated.

In the experiment presented in this paper, we adopted the offline use of the engine. To control the engine, we created different audio files placing at various temporal patterns the recording of an unique real footstep sound on concrete. Such sound was chosen among those available in the Hollywood Edge sound effects library.[1] Three types of surface profiles have been created starting from the footstep sound generator: bumps, holes, and flat surfaces (see Figure 2). The details about the simulation of such surface profiles are shown in section 3.4. For the purpose of the experiment, two types of surfaces, one solid (wood) and one aggregate (gravel), were chosen. The reason for choosing two materials was to assess whether the surface type affected the quality of the results.

3   Experiment Design

We conducted one experiment whose goal was to ascertain the participants' ability to recognize if the sounds and the haptic sensations they were exposed to

---

[1] Hollywood Edge sound effects library: `www.hollywoodedge.com`

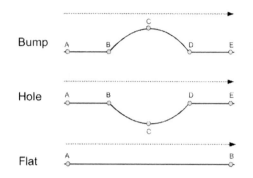

Fig. 2. The three types of surfaces modeled

corresponded to walking on a bump, a hole or a flat surface. Specifically, subjects were exposed to one of the three following conditions:

1. Condition 1: auditory simulation of bumps and holes
2. Condition 2: haptic simulation of bumps and holes
3. Condition 3: audio-haptic simulation of bumps and holes

The results of the experiment related to the first condition have been already published in our previous research [15] and they are illustrated in section 4.1. In this paper we are interested in extending to the haptic level those results achieved with the auditory cues. Indeed the technique used for the simulation of the three types of surface profiles at haptic level is exactly the same proposed for the auditory level. In detail, the audio files used as input to the audio-haptic synthesis engine were created placing at different temporal intervals the footstep sound generator (see section 3.4). The basic idea is that in a real environment, a person generally walks slower on ascending slopes, and faster on descending slopes. We transposed this information in our experiment by modifying the time intervals both between footsteps and between the heel and toe information in each footstep.

The goal of condition 2 was to assess whether at haptic level it is possible to simulate the act of walking on a bump or a hole by means of this technique, when subjects are not walking but are sitting on a chair and passively receive the haptic stimuli. In this haptic condition, a noise signal masked the auditory input generated by the haptic shoes as result of the activation of the actuators. In particular, participants were presented with a continuous 70 dB spl pink noise over the headphones described in section 3.2. In condition 3, we were interested in understanding whether the addition of haptic feedback to the auditory one enhanced the recognition of the proposed surface profiles as well as the realism of the simulation.

3.1 Participants

Forty-five participants were divided in three groups (n=15) to perform the experiment. The three groups were composed respectively of 11 men and 4 women, aged between 20 and 29 (mean=23.6, standard deviation=2.84), 11 men and 4 women, aged between 21 and 32 (mean=24.86, standard deviation=3.48) and 11 men and 4 women, aged between 20 and 28 (mean=23.06, standard deviation=2.40). All participants reported normal hearing conditions. All participants were naive with respect to the experimental setup and to the purpose of the experiment. The participants took on average about 15, 17 and 21 minutes for experiments 1, 2 and 3 respectively.

3.2   Setup

The experiment was carried out in an acoustically isolated laboratory where the setups for the experiments were installed. They consisted of a simple graphical user interface with which participants were asked to interact, and a spreadsheet to collect their answers. The interface was created using the Max/MSP program[2] and was composed only by buttons to be pressed. Each button was numbered, and by pressing it an audio or audio-haptic stimulus was triggered and conveyed to the user by means of headphones[3] and the haptic shoes respectively. The choice of delivering auditory feedback using headphones was motivated by the fact that we wanted the subjects to be isolated from external noise. Users were asked to press each button according to their numerical order, and to write the corresponding answers on the spreadsheet.

3.3   Task

During the experiment subjects were sitting on a chair, listening to the sounds through headphones and feeling the haptic vibrations through the haptic shoes, and interacting with the interface mentioned in section 3.2.

They were given the list of three different surfaces (bump, hole, flat), presented as forced alternate choice. The task consisted of recognizing to which surface the walk corresponded after the presentation of the stimulus. In addition to the classification of the surfaces subjects were also asked to evaluate the degree of certainty of their choice on a scale from 1 to 7 (1=very low certainty, 7=very high certainty). Furthermore, in conditions 2 and 3 they were asked to evaluate, again on a seven point Likert scale, the degree of realism and the degree of quality of the perceived stimulus. Participants were allowed to listen to the sounds as much as they wanted before giving an answer. When moving to the next stimulus they could not change the answer to the previous stimuli.

3.4   Haptic and Auditory Simulation

As described in section 3, the technique used for the simulation of bumps, holes and flat surface consisted of temporal intervals variations. The temporal patterns used were designed to simulate 14 different surface profiles. Specifically 2 flat, 6

---

[2] Max/MSP: www.cycling74.com
[3] Sennheiser HD 600, http://www.sennheiser.com

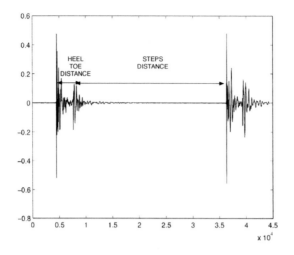

Fig. 3. Temporal distances between (named "steps distance" in the Figure), and within (named "heel-toe distance" in the Figure) footsteps. x-axis: Time (s). y-axis: Amplitude.

bumps and 6 holes were designed. Such patterns involved three types of temporal distances. The first was the temporal distance between footsteps (i.e., the time interval between the end of the sound generated by the toe and the beginning of the sound generated by the heel of the next step), the second was the temporal distance between heel and toe (i.e., the time interval between the end of the sound generated by the heel and the beginning of the sound generated by the toe in the same step), the third consisted of the combination of the previous two (see Figure 3).

The characteristics of the 14 files used to drive the sound engine are illustrated in table 1. In such table the suffixes _step, _h_t and _comb indicate the type of temporal distance used for each file (footsteps distance, heel-toe distance and their combinations respectively). The equations in the "Number of steps" column indicate how the steps where placed in reference to Figure 2. As an example, the stimulus bump_2_step was composed by 19 steps, 4 steps to go from point A to point B, 6 steps to go from point B to point C, 5 steps to go from point C to point D, and 4 steps to go from point D to point E). In order to model two different types of bumps and holes, for each category of surface modeling (by means of the three temporal distance types), two slopes where chosen. In all the three conditions participants were exposed to 28 trials, where 14 surface profiles were presented twice in randomized order. In condition 1 and 2 (see sections 4.1 and 4.2) the simulated surface profiles are all those presented in table 1, while in condition 3 only 7 of them was used and presented both in audio and audio-haptic conditions (see section 4.3).

The audio-haptic synthesis engine was set in order to synthesize footstep sounds and vibrations on two different kinds of materials: wood and gravel. Each surface profile was presented with both wood and gravel.

Table 1. Features of the 14 files used as input to the audio-haptic engine. For a detailed description, see the text.

	Duration (sec.)	Number of steps	Footsteps temporal distance increment (ms.)	Footsteps temporal distance range (ms.)	Heel-toe increment (ms.)	Heel-toe range (ms.)
flat_1	12	19	-	550 (fixed)	-	69 (fixed)
flat_2	16	19	-	750 (fixed)	-	69 (fixed)
bump_1_step	27	$31 = 4+12+11+4$	50	$550 \longrightarrow 1150$	-	69 (fixed)
bump_2_step	16	$19 = 4+6+5+4$	100	$550 \longrightarrow 1150$	-	69 (fixed)
hole_1_step	18	$31 = 4+12+11+4$	-50	$750 \longrightarrow 150$	-	69 (fixed)
hole_2_step	11	$19 = 4+6+5+4$	-100	$750 \longrightarrow 150$	-	69 (fixed)
bump_1_h_t	24	$31 = 4+12+11+4$	-	550 (fixed)	30	$0 \longrightarrow 360 \ (+ 69)$
bump_2_h_t	14	$19 = 4+6+5+4$	-	550 (fixed)	60	$0 \longrightarrow 360 \ (+ 69)$
hole_1_h_t	24	$31 = 4+12+11+4$	-	550 (fixed)	-20	$240 \longrightarrow 0 \ (+ 69)$
hole_2_h_t	13	$19 = 4+6+5+4$	-	550 (fixed)	-40	$240 \longrightarrow 0 \ (+ 69)$
bump_1_comb	32	$31 = 4+12+11+4$	50	$550 \longrightarrow 1150$	30	$0 \longrightarrow 360 \ (+ 69)$
bump_2_comb	19	$19 = 4+6+5+4$	100	$550 \longrightarrow 1150$	60	$0 \longrightarrow 360 \ (+ 69)$
hole_1_comb	22	$31 = 4+12+11+4$	-50	$750 \longrightarrow 150$	-20	$240 \longrightarrow 0 \ (+ 69)$
hole_2_comb	15	$19 = 4+6+5+4$	-100	$750 \longrightarrow 150$	-40	$240 \longrightarrow 0 \ (+ 69)$

The haptic signal was separated in order to activate coherently the actuators placed under the heel and the toe. In our simulation the actuators placed under the heel of the right foot were activated simultaneously with those of the left foot, using the same signal. Analogously, the haptic signal for the toes was conveyed simultaneously to the actuators placed under the toes of both the feet.

4   Results

In this section we show the results for condition 1 (audio condition), condition 2 (haptic condition) and condition 3 (comparison between audio and audio-haptic conditions). In section 4.1 we report the results found in a previous work [15], where the 14 surface profiles described in section 3.4 were used to simulate a bump or a hole only by using auditory cues.

4.1   Results of Condition 1 (Audio Condition)

The results of the condition 1 for wood and gravel are shown in tables 2 and 3 respectively. In both tables, the first column shows the different conditions as described in table 1. The second, third and fourth columns illustrate the choices of the subjects (bump, hole or flat) for the different conditions they were exposed to. The fifth, sixth and seventh column report the average certainty expressed by the subjects after performing their choice; the fifth column reports the total certaintly in both correct and wrong answers, while the sixth and seventh column report the certainty in correct and uncorrect answers respectively. Finally, the last column reports the percentage of correct answers.

As the tables show, subjects could successfully recognize bumps and holes using only the auditory cues described in the previous section. In fact, as can be seen in the last column of tables 2 and 3, the percentage of correct answers is

Table 2. Results of condition 1 (audio condition) for the wood surface

	Bump	Hole	Flat	Mean certainty Total	Mean certainty Correct answers	Mean certainty Wrong answers	% Correct answers
flat_1	1		14	6	6.1429	4	93.33
flat_2		1	14	5.6667	6	1	93.33
bump_1_step	13	2		5.4286	5.5385	4.5	93.33
bump_2_step	14	1		5.4667	5.5714	4	93.33
hole_1_step	1	14		4.8	4.7857	5	93.33
hole_2_step	2	13		4.9333	5	4.5	86.66
bump_1_h_t	13	1	1	5.6	5.8469	4	86.66
bump_2_h_t	12	2	1	5.1333	5.4167	4	80
hole_1_h_t		15		4.2667	4.2667		100
hole_2_h_t	3	12		4.4	4.8182	3.25	80
bump_1_comb	14	1		5.4	5.5	4	93.33
bump_2_comb	14	1		5.1333	5.3571	2	93.33
hole_1_comb	1	14		5.1333	5.2143	4	93.33
hole_2_comb	1	14		4.9333	5	4	93.33

Table 3. Results of condition 1 (audio condition) for the gravel surface

	Bump	Hole	Flat	Mean certainty Total	Mean certainty Correct answers	Mean certainty Wrong answers	% Correct answers
flat_1		3	12	5.2667	5.6667	3.6667	80
flat_2	1	1	13	5.4667	6	2	86.66
bump_1_step	12	2	1	5.8469	5.75	4.6667	80
bump_2_step	13	1		5.4667	5.9231	2.5	86.66
hole_1_step		14	1	5.4667	5.7857	1	93.33
hole_2_step		15		6	6		100
bump_1_h_t	14	1		5.5333	5.7857	2	93.33
bump_2_h_t	11	2	2	4.5333	4.8182	3.75	73.33
hole_1_h_t	1	12	2	4.5333	4.5833	4.3333	80
hole_2_h_t		15		4.4	4.4		100
bump_1_comb	13	2		5.3333	5.6667	4	86.66
bump_2_comb	13	1	1	5.2667	5.7692	2	86.66
hole_1_comb	2	12	1	5.2667	5.3333	5	80
hole_2_comb	2	13		5.2667	5.8469	1.5	86.66

high for all conditions, reaching also 100 % of correct answers in three conditions, and with a lowest score of 73 % which was reached only in one condition.

Observing columns 6 and 7, morever, it is possible to notice how subjects are quite certain when they express a correct answer. In both surfaces, indeed, the mean certainty for correct answers is always above average. On the other hand, in situations where the answer was incorrect the degree of certainty is also extremely low. This is the case, for example, in the second flat stimulus for the wood surface and the first hole stimulus in the gravel surface.

A t-test was performed to examine whether significant differences were present in the recognition rate among the two surfaces and among the different conditions in the same surface. Overall, no significant differences were measured in the recognition rate among the two surfaces. Moreover, no significant differences were measured in the recognition rate for the different conditions in the same material. For example, no difference was measured in the recognition rate of the first simulated bump footstep versus the second simulated bump footstep. No significant difference was furthermore measured between the recognition rate obtained when changing the temporal information between footsteps versus the one obtained when changing the temporal information within footsteps. Also, the combination of the two temporal information did not significantly enhance the recognition of a bump or a hole. This, however, is also due to the fact that the temporal information taken individually already provided a high recognition rate.

4.2   Results of Condition 2 (Haptic Condition)

Tables 4 and 5 illustrate the results of condition 2 for wood and gravel respectively. The structure of these tables is the same of tables 2 and 3, with the addition of the two columns expressing the average scores of the degree of realism and of the degree of quality.

The first noticeable element emerging from both tables is that it is possible to simulate bumps, holes and flat surfaces by means of haptic stimuli using only the variation of the temporal information. Indeed, on average, subjects could successfully recognize the simulated surfaces using only the haptic cues described in section 3.4, both with wood and gravel. As a matter of fact, the percentage of correct answers is quite high in most of the conditions, reaching also 100 % of correct answers in two conditions, while only in three conditions the score is under 50 %.

From a comparison between all the conditions it is possible to notice that on average the stimuli involving only the variations in the heel-toe distance (i.e., those with suffix _h_t) are recognized with the lowest scores in comparison with the other conditions. Such tendency is also confirmed by values in column 5 which expresses the total degree of certainty for each stimulus (both of correct and wrong answers) and therefore it is an indication of the difficulty of the choice. Indeed in both the tables such values are on average lower for the stimuli with suffix _h_t than all the other conditions.

A chi-square test and a t-test were performed to examine whether significant differences were present in the recognition rate among the two surfaces and among the different conditions in the same surface. Overall, no significant differences were measured in the recognition rate among the two surfaces, nor in the recognition rate for the different conditions in the same material. Moreover no significant difference was measured between the recognition rate obtained when changing the temporal information between footsteps versus the one obtained when changing the temporal information within footsteps. In addition, the combination of the two temporal information did not significantly enhance the recognition of a bump or a hole. Finally, a t-test performed on the realism and on the quality evaluations, did not reveal any significant difference between the two materials nor among the conditions.

Table 4. Results of condition 2 (haptic condition) for the wood surface

	Bump	Hole	Flat	Mean certainty Total	Mean certainty Correct answers	Mean certainty Wrong answers	% Correct answers	Mean Realism	Mean Quality
flat_1	2		13	5.2	5.3077	4.5	86.66	3.9231	4
flat_2	2		13	5.1333	5.3077	4	86.66	3.6154	4.1333
bump_1_step	13		2	4.8	4.7692	5	86.66	4.0769	4.0667
bump_2_step	15			5.2	5.2		100	3.9333	3.8
hole_1_step	2	11	2	4.6667	4.4	5.2	73.33	3.0909	3.6
hole_2_step	2	13		4.6667	4.6923	4.5	86.66	3.7692	3.9333
bump_1_h_t	7	5	3	3.6667	4.1429	3.25	46.66	3	3.4
bump_2_h_t	9	6		4.4667	4.7778	4	60	3.4444	3.4667
hole_1_h_t	1	8	6	3.8	4.375	3.1429	53.33	3.25	3.2
hole_2_h_t		12	3	3.8667	4.25	2.3333	80	3.75	3.2
bump_1_comb	11	4		4.2667	4.2727	4.25	73.33	3.1818	3.2
bump_2_comb	11	3	1	4.7333	5.1818	3.5	73.33	4.0909	3.7333
hole_1_comb	2	13		4.4	4.3846	4.5	86.66	3.5385	3.8
hole_2_comb	1	12	2	4.6667	5.3333	2	80	3.25	3.2

Table 5. Results of condition 2 (haptic condition) for the gravel surface

	Bump	Hole	Flat	Mean certainty Total	Mean certainty Correct answers	Mean certainty Wrong answers	% Correct answers	Mean Realism	Mean Quality
flat_1			15	4.4667	4.4667		100	3.6	3.8667
flat_2	1	1	13	5.2667	5.6923	2.5	86.66	4.7692	4.3333
bump_1_step	12		3	4.9333	5	4.6667	80	3.9231	3.7333
bump_2_step	11	2	2	4.4667	4.7273	3.75	73.33	3.3636	3.33
hole_1_step		12	3	4.8	4.9167	4.3333	80	3.6667	3.7333
hole_2_step		12	3	5.5333	5.75	4.6667	80	4.25	4.2
bump_1_h_t	8	6	1	4.4	5	3.7143	53.33	2.875	3.5333
bump_2_h_t	11	1	3	3.8667	4.1818	3	73.33	3.7273	3.8667
hole_1_h_t	1	7	7	4.3333	4.2857	4.375	46.66	3.8571	4
hole_2_h_t	3	6	6	3.7333	3.6667	3.7778	40	3.5	3.4667
bump_1_comb	13	1	1	5.2	5.2308	5	86.66	3.7692	4
bump_2_comb	10	4	1	4.4	5.1	3	66.66	3.5	3.5333
hole_1_comb	1	13	1	4.8	4.8462	4.5	86.66	3.3077	3.4667
hole_2_comb		14	1	4.8	4.9286	3	93.33	4.2143	4

4.3   Results of Condition 3 (Audio and Audio-Haptic Condition)

In this experiment we used only a subset of the 14 files used in the previous conditions. This was due in order to avoid that the experiment became too long for the participants, and therefore started answering randomly. In particular, we selected 7 stimuli to be presented both with the modality audio and audio-haptic (suffixes _A and _AH respectively in tables 6 and 7), and both with wood and gravel. Precisely we used those with suffix _2 in table 1, with the exception of the flat stimulus for which we used the one with suffix _1.

The first noticeable element emerging from both tables is that subjects could successfully recognize the simulated surfaces with high precision both at audio and audio-haptic level. An exception is the stimulus hole_h_t_A with wood material for which the score is 40 %, differing from the percentage obtained by the same stimulus in condition 1. Anyways a chi-square test revealed that such difference is not statistically significant so we can state that all the results concerning the audio modality are consistent with those found in condition 1.

Table 6. Results of condition 3 (audio and audio-haptic condition) for the wood surface

	Bump	Hole	Flat	Mean certainty Total	Mean certainty Correct answers	Mean certainty Wrong answers	% Correct answers	Mean Realism	Mean Quality
flat_A			15	6	6	-	100	3.7333	3.6
flat_AH		1	14	6.0667	6.4286	1	93.33	4.9286	4.4667
bump_step_A	11	2	2	4.7333	5.1818	3.5	73.33	3.2727	3.6667
bump_step_AH	12	2	1	5.2667	5.5833	4	80	3.9167	4.6
hole_step_A	1	14		5.6667	5.7143	5	93.33	3.6429	4
hole_step_AH	2	12	1	5.1333	5.6667	3	80	4.75	4.4667
bump_h_t_A	13	2		4.9333	5.3846	2	86.66	3.6154	3.33
bump_h_t_AH	13	2		4.6667	5.2308	1	86.66	4.3846	4.0667
hole_h_t_A	2	6	7	3.7333	4.5	3.2222	40	2.8571	3
hole_h_t_AH	2	11	2	4.0667	4.1818	3.75	73.33	3.6364	4.4
bump_comb_A	12	3		4.2	4.8333	1.6667	80	3.25	4.6667
bump_comb_AH	14	1		5.0667	5.2857	2	93.33	4.2143	4.3333
hole_comb_A	1	12	2	4.9333	5.25	3.6667	80	3.5	3.8
hole_comb_AH	2	13		5.3333	5.5385	4	86.66	4.3846	4.6

Table 7. Results of condition 3 (audio and audio-haptic condition) for the gravel surface

	Bump	Hole	Flat	Mean certainty Total	Mean certainty Correct answers	Mean certainty Wrong answers	% Correct answers	Mean Realism	Mean Quality
flat_A			15	5.3333	5.3333	-	100	3.8	4.2
flat_AH	1	1	13	5.6667	5.8462	4.5	86.66	5.1538	5.2667
bump_step_A	12	2	1	4.5333	4.6667	4	80	3.75	4
bump_step_AH	12	2	1	5.3333	5.5833	4.3333	80	4.3333	4.8667
hole_step_A	1	14		5.1333	5.2857	3	93.33	4.2857	4.7333
hole_step_AH	1	13	1	5.0667	5	5.5	86.66	4.4615	4.9333
bump_h_t_A	12	1	2	4.1333	4.25	3.6667	80	2.9167	3.6667
bump_h_t_AH	12	1	2	5.4	5.25	6	80	4.5833	4.8667
hole_h_t_A		10	5	4.2667	4.4	4	66.66	2.8	3.7333
hole_h_t_AH	3	12		4.6667	4.75	4.3333	80	4.3333	5.3333
bump_comb_A	14	1		5.1333	5.2143	4	93.33	3.9286	4
bump_comb_AH	12	3		5.1333	5.3333	4.3333	80	4.0833	4.6
hole_comb_A	1	13	1	4.9333	5.1538	3.5	86.66	4	4.5333
hole_comb_AH	2	13		5.7333	6.2308	2.5	86.66	4.7692	5.2667

As regards the degree of certainty of the correct answers, most of the times conditions with audio-haptic modality present higher values than the audio modality, Despite an in-depth analysis with t-test did not show any statistically significant difference between the corresponding pairs, the ANOVA analysis revealed that at global level the AH condition gives rise to higher evaluation in the case of gravel material (p-value = 0.0449).

As concerns the degree of realism and the degree of quality, results are always higher for the bimodal stimuli rather than the unimodal ones (see figure 4). The ANOVA analysis shows that such differences are statistically significative, (p-value < 0.0001 and p-value < 0.0001 for realism in the conditions wood and gravel respectively, and p-value = 0.002862 and p-value = 0.003386 for quality in the conditions wood and gravel respectively). In addition an in depth analysis performed with t-test, revealed also significant differences for the pairs of stimuli (audio, audio-haptic) in table 8.

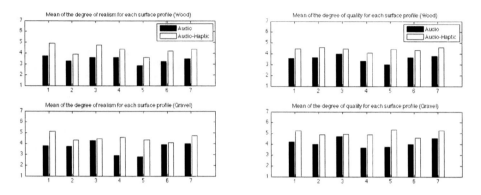

Fig. 4. Average scores of the degree of realism (left) and quality (right), for audio and audio-haptic conditions in condition 3. Surface profile from left to right: 1-flat, 2-bump_step, 3-hole_step, 4-bump_h_t, 5-hole_h_t, 6-bump_comb, 7-hole_comb.

Table 8. Statistically significative differences for average scores of the degree of realism and quality, between audio and audio-haptic conditions in condition 3

Stimulus	Material	P-value realism	P-value quality
flat	wood	0.03381	-
flat	gravel	0.01425	-
hole_h_t	wood	-	0.01834
bump_h_t	gravel	0.001482	0.04558
hole_h_t	gravel	0.02296	0.00732

Considering the total degree of certainty (column 5), it is possible to notice that on average the stimuli involving only the variations in the heel-toe distance present lower values in comparison with the other conditions. This is an indication of a greater difficulty in the participants' choices for these stimuli rather than the others.

Finally, an ANOVA analysis performed on the evaluations of the degree of certainty of correct answers, of realism and of quality, did not reveal any significant difference between the two materials.

5 General Discussion

From a comparison between results of the three condtions it is possible to notice that the use of the proposed techniques allows to simulate the act of walking on a bump, a hole, or a flat surface by passively presenting audio, haptic and audio-haptic stimuli. The most important result is that the haptic modality plays an important role in this kind of tasks. In particular, results of condition 3 show that haptic cues significantly reinforces the auditory cues. Indeed, participants gave rise to higher evaluations in presence of audio-haptic stimuli rather than the audio-stimuli, for what concerns the realism and the quality of the presented stimuli, as well as they were more certain in giving their correct answers. When the haptic is presented alone it is still possible to simulate quite well the act of walking over a bump, a hole or a flat surface, as results of condition 2 show. From a comparison with the results of condition 1 what emerges is that the auditory modality seems to be dominant on the haptic one in this kind of tasks. A common trend noticed in all the conditions is that the material does not have any particular influence on the participants evaluations, i.e., there is no statistically significant difference in the responses between the presented solid and aggregate surfaces. Another trend more or less common to the three conditions is that on average the stimuli involving only the variations in the heel-toe distance present lower values in comparison with the other conditions for what concerns the total degree of certainty, and this is an indication of a greater difficulty in the participants' choices for these stimuli rather than the others. This also means that participants found more natural the variations in the temporal distance between steps rather than the ones in the temporal distances between heel and toe. In addition, in all the conditions the combination of the two temporal information did not significantly enhance the recognition of a bump or a hole. Subjects were allowed to listen to the simulations as many times as they wished, but in general they listened only once, and this was enough to provide an answer. At the end of the test some informal interviews were performed, where subjects declared that the stimuli were clear. Subjects were also surprised by the ability of the feet to distinguish the simulations.

6   Conclusion and Future Work

In this paper, we described a between subject audio-haptic experiment whose goal was to assess the role of temporal aspects in recognizing whether a person is walking on a flat surface, a bump or a hole.

Results show that varying temporal aspects between footsteps allow to successfully simulating the act of walking on a bump, hole, or flat surface, especially in the auditory modality. Moreover, in the recognition task, haptic cues show to significantly reinforce auditory cues, as the results of condition 3 show. All three conditions were run by using the synthesis engine offline. The reason why we asked subjects to seat was to create an environment similar to a home situation, e.g., when subjects are watching a movie. Indeed, we plan to use the same engine with visual feedback, in order to assess the role of haptic feedback in enhancing the experience of watching an audio-visual scene.

In the future, we are interested in running the same experiments interactively, to understand whether our technique can be used to simulate bumps and holes in a virtual reality setup.

Acknowledgment. The research leading to these results has received funding from the European Community' s Seventh Framework Programme under FET-Open grant agreement 222107 NIW - Natural Interactive Walking.[4]. The authors

---

[4] Natural Interactive Walking Project: `www.niwproject.eu`

would like to thank Professor Vincent Hayward and Amir Berrezag for providing the haptic shoes used in this experiment.

References

1. Cook, P.: Physically Informed Sonic Modeling (PhISM): Synthesis of Percussive Sounds. Computer Music Journal 21(3), 38–49 (1997)
2. Cook, P.: Modeling Bill's Gait: Analysis and Parametric Synthesis of Walking Sounds. In: Proceedings of the AES 22nd International Conference on Virtual, Synthetic, and Entertainment Audio, pp. 73–78 (2002)
3. Farnell, A.: Marching onwards: procedural synthetic footsteps for video games and animation. In: Proceedings of the Pure Data Convention (2007)
4. Fontana, F., Bresin, R.: Physics-based sound synthesis and control: crushing, walking and running by crumpling sounds. In: Proc. Colloquium on Musical Informatics, pp. 109–114 (2003)
5. Hollerbach, J., Checcacci, D., Noma, H., Yanagida, Y., Tetsutani, N.: Simulating side slopes on locomotion interfaces using torso forces. In: Haptic Symposium, Citeseer, pp. 91–98 (2003)
6. Hollerbach, J., Mills, R., Tristano, D., Christensen, R., Thompson, W., Xu, Y.: Torso force feedback realistically simulates slope on treadmill-style locomotion interfaces. The International Journal of Robotics Research 20(12), 939 (2001)
7. Hunt, K.H., Crossley, F.R.E.: Coefficient of restitution interpreted as damping in vibroimpact. ASME Journal of Applied Mechanics 42(2), 440–445 (1975)
8. Iwata, H., Yano, H., Nakaizumi, F.: Gait master: A versatile locomotion interface for uneven virtual terrain. vr, page 131(2001)
9. Lécuyer, A., Burkhardt, J., Etienne, L.: Feeling bumps and holes without a haptic interface: the perception of pseudo-haptic textures. In: Proceedings of the SIGCHI Conference on Human Factors in Computing Systems, page 246. ACM, New York (2004)
10. Marchal, M., Lecuyer, A., Cirio, G., Bonnet, L., Emily, M.: Walking Up and Down in Immersive Virtual Worlds: Novel Interactive Techniques Based on Visual Feedback. In: Proceedings of IEEE Symposium on 3D User Interface (2010)
11. Miner, N., Caudell, T.: Using wavelets to synthesize stochastic-based sounds for immersive virtual environments. ACM Transactions on Applied Perception 2(4), 521–528 (2005)
12. Nordahl, R., Serafin, S., Turchet, L.: Sound synthesis and evaluation of interactive footsteps for virtual reality applications. In: Proc. IEEE VR (2010)
13. Serafin, S., Turchet, L., Nordahl, R., Dimitrov, S., Berrezag, A., Hayward, V.: Identification of virtual grounds using virtual reality haptic shoes and sound synthesis. In: Proc. Eurohaptics Symposium on Haptics and Audio-visual Environments (2010)
14. Serafin, S., Turchet, L., Nordahl, R.: Extraction of ground reaction forces for real-time synthesis of walking sounds. In: Proc. Audiomostly (2009)
15. Serafin, S., Turchet, L., Nordahl, R.: Do You Hear A Bump Or A Hole? An Experiment on Temporal Aspects in the Recognition of Footsteps Sounds (2010)
16. Turchet, L., Marchal, M., Lécuyer, A., Nordahl, R., Serafin, S.: Influence of auditory and visual feedback for perceiving walking over bumps and holes in desktop VR. In: Proceedings of the 17th ACM Symposium on Virtual Reality Software and Technology, pp. 139–142. ACM, New York (2010)

17. Turchet, L., Nordahl, R., Berrezag, A., Dimitrov, S., Hayward, V., Serafin, S.: Audio-haptic physically based simulation of walking sounds. In: Proc. of IEEE International Workshop on Multimedia Signal Processing (2010)
18. Turchet, L., Nordahl, R., Serafin, S.: Examining the role of context in the recognition of walking sound. In: Proc. of Sound and Music Computing Conference (2010)
19. Turchet, L., Serafin, S., Dimitrov, S., Nordahl, R.: Conflictual audio-haptic feedback in physically based simulation of walking sounds. In: Proc. of Haptic Audio Interaction Design Conference (2010)
20. Turchet, L., Serafin, S., Dimitrov, S., Nordahl, R.: Physically based sound synthesis and control of footsteps sounds. In: Proceedings of Digital Audio Effects Conference (2010)
21. Welch, R., Warren, D.: Immediate perceptual response to intersensory discrepancy. Psychological Bulletin 88(3), 638 (1980)

Enhanced Audiovisual Temporal Sensitivity When Viewing Videos That Appropriately Depict the Effect of Gravity on Object Movement

Argiro Vatakis[1,2] and Charles Spence[1]

[1] Crossmodal Research Laboratory, Department of Experimental Psychology,
University of Oxford, U.K.
[2] Cognitive Systems Research Institute (CSRI), Athens, Greece
argiro.vatakis@gmail.com, charles.Spence@psy.ox.ac.uk

Abstract. We report a study designed to examine how knowledge of the effects of gravity may change the temporal processing of audiovisual events. Specifically, normally-oriented and inverted audiovisual video-clips of different objects being dropped were presented at a range of different stimulus onset asynchronies. Participants made temporal order judgments regarding whether the auditory/visual stream appeared to have been presented first. The results revealed that inverting the visual-display of the falling object led to a significant difference in participant's ability to judge the temporal order of the auditory/ visual components of the desynchronized video-clips. That is, participants were more sensitive to audiovisual asynchrony when viewing normally-oriented video-clips of the falling object as compared to viewing the same clips inverted. These results demonstrate that people's understanding of the effects of gravity on object movement can affect their temporal sensitivity when violations of the fundamental physical parameters determining the movement of real objects are introduced.

Keywords: Gravity, Inversion, Temporal perception, Multisensory, Audition, Vision.

1 Introduction

Early in life, people demonstrate an excellent ability to walk in a well-balanced manner or to catch objects that have accidentally fallen from their hands. Not only we are highly skilled with such acts but we are also very accustomed to the stereotypical behavior of objects falling under the influence of gravity. That is, we expect that when an object is released from a height, it will move downward and accelerate. Any other kind of behavior would seem both unnatural and surprising [1-3].

Our high-level skills in interception and balance and the familiarity that we demonstrate with the behavior of objects could be attributed, at least in part, to the knowledge and experience we possess regarding the laws governing gravity on Earth (other accounts support the use of sensory information or intrinsic representational gravity, and not necessarily knowledge, in order to successfully interact with falling objects). Specifically, we are aware of the fact that, under the influence of gravity, all

A. Vatakis et al. (Eds.): Time and Time Perception 2010, LNAI 6789, pp. 116–124, 2011.

objects accelerate at the same rate when moving through the air (e.g., [4]). This notion of gravitational acceleration in visual motion has been observed from very early on in life, as demonstrated in studies where 5-7 month old infants begin implicitly to expect downward-moving objects to accelerate and upwardly-moving objects to decelerate [4-7]. Adults are also able to predict very accurately the time-to-contact (TTC) of a falling object with a surface [6, 8-9]. Finally, people utilize visual cues concerning the effects of gravity to perceive causality and the naturalness of motion [7, 10], to determine the absolute distance and size of falling objects [11-12], and to interpret biological motion [13].

The knowledge and experience that people have with the action of gravitational forces in nature has rendered this phenomenon as something natural and expected of object behavior. For instance, cues associated with gravity are widely utilized in the cinema in order to elicit illusions of size, where small objects appear full-sized when the frame speed is slowed down (e.g., [12, 14]). Consequently, sensory and motor mechanisms have evolved in order to account for the effects of gravity on objects, particularly those that are in motion (e.g., [7, 15-16]). It is therefore expected that our perception would be sensitive to the effects of gravity [17]. To date, however, researchers have typically looked at the effects of gravity on people's perception of unimodal visual events. It has been hypothesized that the notion of gravity has been transformed and stored as an abstract representation that is accessible by the visual system and, thus, by any related neuronal mechanism (see [6, 18]). Support for this abstract representation of the influence of gravity comes from the observation that, in the absence of gravity-determined sensory cues, astronauts exposed to a falling object in the Spacelab initially expected the effects of Earth's gravity to come into play and it took them several days in flight to adapt to this new environment [19].

Given the limited amount of multisensory research on the topic, and the importance of identifying the specific effects that gravitational forces exert on perceptual processing, we conducted the present study. In particular, we were interested in investigating the effects of gravity on the temporal processing of complex audiovisual events by looking at the sensitivity of humans to violations of the fundamental physical parameters determining the movement of real-objects. We presented normally-oriented and inverted audiovisual video clips of different objects (a ball, a piece of metal, and a book) being dropped vertically onto either a hard surface or water. We utilized these types of events due to the fact that in the case of a bouncing ball, for example, the relation between temporal and spatial parameters is defined only by gravity since there are no other forces affecting the movement. Additionally, we utilized normally-oriented and inverted presentations without altering any elements (e.g., the speed) in order to examine how gravity alone affects temporal perception. The video clips were presented either in synchrony or else desynchronized (see below for details) and the participants performed a temporal order judgment (TOJ) task in which they had to report which modality stream, either auditory or visual, they perceived to be leading.

1.1 Methods

Participants 19 participants (10 female) aged 20 to 34 years (mean age of 25 years) took part in this experiment. All of the participants were naïve as to the purpose of the study and all reported having normal hearing and normal or corrected-to-normal visual acuity. The experiment was performed in accordance with the ethical standards laid down in the 1990 Declaration of Helsinki, as well as the ethical guidelines laid down by the Department of Experimental Psychology, University of Oxford. The experiment lasted for approximately 40 minutes.

Apparatus and materials. The experiment was conducted in a completely dark sound-attenuated testing booth with the participants seated facing straight-ahead. The visual stimuli were presented on a 17-inch (43.18 cm) TFT colour LCD monitor (SXGA 1240x1024-pixel resolution; 60-Hz refresh rate), placed at eye level, approximately 68 cm from the participant. The auditory stimuli were presented by means of two Packard Bell Flat Panel 050 PC loudspeakers; one placed 25.4 cm to either side of the centre of the monitor. The audiovisual stimuli consisted of black and white video clips presented against a black background using Presentation (Version 11.0; Neurobehavioral Systems Inc., CA). The stimuli and background were well contrasted. The video clips (300x280-pixel, Cinepak Codec video compression, 16-bit Audio Sample Size, 24-bit Video Sample Size, 30 frames/sec) were processed using Adobe Premiere 6.0. The stimuli consisted of normally-oriented or inverted video clips of: a small rubber ball falling into a glass of water, a metal object falling into the same glass of water, and a thick hardcover book falling onto a table. All of the clips were 466 ms long, with the duration of the event being equal to that of the entire clip, with both the auditory and visual signals being dynamic over the same period of time (e.g., starting from the beginning with book and ending with the point of contact with the table, respectively; the actual time that the ball, metal, or book was in motion between the hand and the glass or hard surface, respectively was 190 ms; Note here that the hand shown in the video only performed a release-motion, that is, there was no upward or downward movement of the hand). In order to achieve accurate synchronization of the dubbed video clips, each original clip was re-encoded using XviD codec (single pass, quality mode of 100%).

At the beginning and end of each video clip, a still image and background acoustic noise was presented for a variable duration. The duration of the image and noise was unequal with the difference in their duration being equivalent to the particular SOA tested (values reported below) in each condition. This aspect of the experimental design ensured that the auditory and visual streams always started at the same time, thus avoiding the possibility that the participants might have been cued as to the nature of the audiovisual asynchrony with which they were being presented. In order to achieve a smooth transition at the start and end of each video clip, cross-fading was added between the still image and the video clip. The participants responded using a standard computer mouse, which they held with both hands, using their right thumb to make 'vision-first' responses and their left thumb to make 'audition-first' responses (or vice versa, the response buttons were counterbalanced across participants).

Design. Seven possible SOAs between the auditory and visual streams were used: ±200, ±133, ±66, and 0 ms. These SOAs were chosen on the basis of previous studies conducted on the temporal perception of object actions; cf. [20]). Negative values indicate that the auditory stream was presented first, whereas positive values indicate that the visual stream was presented first. The participants completed one block of 18 practice trials before the main experimental session in order to familiarize themselves with the task and the video clips. The practice block was followed by 5 blocks of 126 experimental trials, consisting of three presentations of each of the 6 video clips at each of the 7 SOAs per block of trials. The various SOAs were presented randomly within each block of trials using the method of constant stimuli (see [21]).

Procedure. The participants were informed that they would be presented with a series of normally-oriented and inverted video clips. The participants were also informed that on each trial they would have to decide whether the auditory or visual component appeared to have been presented first and that they would sometimes find this task difficult, in which case they should make an informed guess as to the order of stimulus presentation. The participants were encouraged to avoid guessing and to try to respond as accurately as possible. The participants did not have to wait until the video clip had finished before making their response, but a response had to be made before the experiment would advance to the next trial.

1.2 Results

The proportions of 'vision-first' responses were converted to their equivalent z-scores under the assumption of a cumulative normal distribution (cf. [22]). The data from the 7 SOAs were used to calculate best-fitting straight lines for each participant for each condition, which, in turn, were used to derive values for the slope and intercept (Normally-oriented presentation: Ball and Metal, r2 = .99, p < .01, for both; Book: r2 = .98, p < .01; Inverted: Ball and Metal, r2 = .99, p < .01, for both; Book: r2 = .98, p < .01; the r2 values reflect the correlation between the SOAs and the proportion of 'vision-first' responses, and hence provide an estimate of the goodness of the data fits; see Fig. 1A). The slope and intercept values were used to calculate the just noticeable difference (JND = 0.675/slope; since ± 0.675 represents the 75% and 25% points on the cumulative normal distribution) and the point of subjective simultaneity (PSS = - intercept/slope) values (see [23] for more details).

The JND provides a measure of perceptual sensitivity: More specifically, it provides a measure of the temporal asynchrony between two sensory signals (in this case, one auditory and the other visual) required in order for participants to judge the temporal order of the auditory and visual streams correctly 75% of the time. The PSS provides an estimate of the amount of time by which the event in one sensory modality had to lead the event in the other modality in order for synchrony to be perceived (or rather, for participants to choose the 'vision-first' and 'sound-first' responses equally often). For all of the analyses reported here, Bonferroni-corrected t-tests (where p < .05 prior to correction) were used for all post-hoc comparisons. The JND and PSS data for each of the normally-presented and inverted audiovisual events were analysed using repeated measures analysis of variance (ANOVA) with the factors of Event Type (ball falling into water, metal falling into water, and a book falling onto a table) and Orientation of the video (normal vs. inverted).

Analysis of the JND data revealed a significant main effect of the Orientation of the video [F(1,18) = 4.56, p<.05], with participants being significantly more sensitive at discriminating the temporal order of the auditory and visual streams when viewing the normally-oriented object action video clips (M = 69 ms) than when viewing the inverted video clips (M = 73 ms; see Fig. 1B). There was no main effect of Event

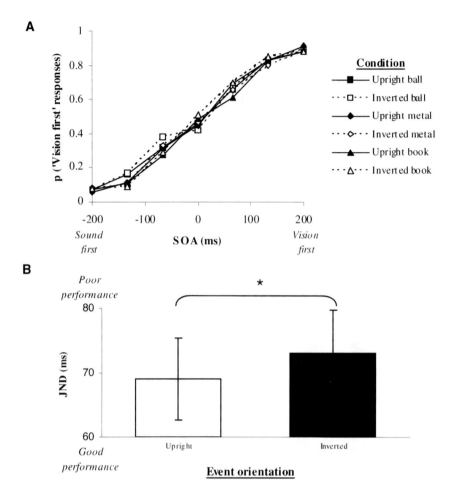

Fig. 1. A. Mean percentage of 'vision-first' responses plotted as a function of the SOA. B. Average JNDs for the normally-presented and inverted audiovisual stimuli. The error bars represent the standard errors of the means. Significant differences (P < .05) are highlighted by an asterisk.

Type [F(2,36) = 2.22, p=.13] (ball, M = 76 ms; metal, M = 70 ms; book, M= 68 ms), nor any interaction between Event Type and Orientation [F(2,36) = 1.45, p=.25]. A similar analysis of the PSS data revealed no main effects or interactions (for Orientation [F(1,18) = 2.06, p=.20]; for Event Type [F(2,36) = 1.21, p=.31]; and for the interaction term [F(2,36) = 1.20, p=.31]).

2 Discussion

The results of the experiment reported here demonstrate that people's ability to judge the temporal order of the auditory and visual components of desynchronized naturalistic video clips of objects falling under the influence of gravity is modulated by the orientation of the video (i.e., normal vs. inverted): People are more sensitive to audiovisual asynchrony when viewing normally oriented videos than when viewing the same video clips when presented in an inverted orientation. Although the magnitude of this effect was small (mean change in the JND of 4 ms), it was nevertheless significant. This result is consistent with the view that the experience and knowledge that people possess concerning the typical effects of gravity on an object's movement can affect people's temporal sensitivity when violations of the fundamental physical parameters determining real-object movements are introduced. (Note that mental rotation cannot account for these findings given that participants did not have to make any judgments in terms of the identity of the stimuli but rather just to determine the temporal order in which the auditory and visual signals were presented. Thus, there was no particular reason for the participants to have attempted to rotate the inverted display back into their normal orientations, and hence mental rotation does not seem to provide a particularly likely explanation for the findings reported here.) The violations in this study were related to the fact that our participants presumably expected the inverted video clips to show an object decelerating as it ascended and anticipated a downward moving object as opposed to an object that was moving upward with a constant acceleration (as was the case here). It should, however, be noted that this result, impaired temporal sensitivity for the inverted videos, cannot be accounted for simply by suggesting an effect of familiarity on temporal perception (i.e., that people are less sensitive at judging the temporal order of unfamiliar, as opposed to more familiar, events), since no such inversion effect on temporal sensitivity was observed in any of our previous inversion experiments in which we compared people's ability to judge the temporal order of normal-orientation versus inverted-orientation speech and music video clips [20].

While a number of researchers have previously suggested that the inversion of objects that are falling under the influence of gravity exerts some influence on people's temporal perception of those events, it is important to note that very few studies have actually examined such putative effects empirically. One such attempt was made recently using the 'kappa effect', which occurs when participants have to judge the duration of intervals marked by a series of stimuli occurring successively along a straight line. In the case of constant temporal separation and variable spatial distance between stimuli, the perceived temporal separation tends to increase as the actual spatial distance increases (see [24-26]). In order to examine how people's understanding of gravity influences the 'kappa effect' in event perception, Noguchi et al. sequentially presented three circular stimuli on an inclined slope. The first two stimuli were displayed successively at fixed positions (depicting an object moving down the slope), and the third stimulus was presented in one of a number of different positions further down, or further up, the slope. Thus, the researchers were able to manipulate the temporal interval, the spatial distance, and the direction of movement (i.e., 'sliding' vs. 'ascending' of the three stimuli). The participants in this study had to try and estimate the perceived duration of the temporal gap that elapsed between the presentation of the second and third stimulus. The results showed that the perceived velocity of climbing tended to be slower than that of slipping, thus suggesting that people's temporal perception can be affected by their experience and knowledge of the effects of gravitational forces on objects [25-26].

More recently, Vatakis and Spence [20, 27] used videos of dynamic audiovisual stimuli in order to investigate the effects of stimulus inversion on the temporal perception of complex audiovisual stimuli. The participants in their study were presented with videos of speakers uttering speech and non-speech tokens, musical notes being played on the piano, and monkey vocalizations. The results of these studies showed that the inversion of the dynamic visual-stream had absolutely no effect on the sensitivity (i.e., JND) of participants' judgments concerning the temporal order in which the dynamic auditory and visual stimuli were presented. By contrast, the inversion of the visual-stream resulted in it having to lead the auditory-stream by a greater interval in order for the PSS to be reached when people viewed audiovisual speech stimuli but not when they viewed musical notes being played on a piano, monkey vocalizations, or even humans imitating monkey vocalizations. Vatakis and Spence argued that their results were consistent with the view that the visual inversion of a face results in the loss of configural information due to and the recruitment of additional neural processing when viewing face stimuli as compared to other types of stimuli (see [28]). The present findings show a small but significant difference in the JND for normal versus inverted event presentation, but most importantly, inversion of the video had absolutely no effect on the PSS. Thus, our previously-observed finding that inversion only affects people's accuracy in judging the temporal order of the auditory and visual streams of speech stimuli still stands. In addition, Vatakis and Spence's [20] previous findings with non-speech stimuli further supports the effects of knowledge and experience of gravitational forces in the present findings. That is, in both the present and these previous studies, the PSS remained non-significantly different for normal versus inverted stimulus presentations for non-speech stimuli.

It must be noted here that the limited number of studies conducted on the perceptual effects of the influence of gravity on object motion have all utilized unimodal visual stimuli (e.g., [29]). That is, no previous study has investigated the effect of people's knowledge about gravity on multisensory information processing. In terms of the results of the present study, it seems likely that the JND effect on crossmodal TOJs reported in the present study was driven by the reduced sensitivity to the visual timing information when the videos were inverted. Given that in the present study we tested only two types of events (i.e., an object being dropped on a solid and a liquid surface) with relatively discrete and brief auditory signals, we are currently running follow-up experiments utilizing other relevant events of different durations with more extended continuous sounds (e.g., a marble rolling down a metal surface). Additionally, given that in the present study we did not require participants to fixate at a particular location on the screen, we cannot determine the effect of lower versus upper visual field perceptual processing in our results. That is, research has shown evidence that the control of visually guided motor actions is better processed in the lower visual field [30]. Thus, in follow-up experiments we plan to address this possible visual field confound by having participants fixate at certain screen locations during both our normally-oriented and inverted stimulus presentations.

Acknowledgments. We would like to thank Annika Linke and Sophia Zeeden for their valuable help with the stimulus recordings. A.V. was supported by a Newton Abraham Studentship from the Medical Sciences Division, University of Oxford. Correspondence regarding this article should be addressed to A.V. at the Cognitive Systems Research Institute (CSRI), Athens, Greece, E-MAIL: argiro.vatakis@gmail.com.

References

1. Baures, R., Benguigui, N., Amorim, M.A., Siegler, I.A.: Intercepting free falling objects: Better use Occam's razor than internalize Newton's law. Vis. Res. 47, 2982–2991 (2007)
2. Kim, I.K., Spelke, E.S.: Infants' sensitivity to effects of gravity on visible object motion. J Exp. Psychol. JEP 18, 385–393 (1992)
3. Shanon, B.: Aristotelianism, Newtonianism and the physics of the layman. Percept. 5, 241–243 (1976)
4. Zago, M., Lacquaniti, F.: Visual perception and interception of falling objects: A review of evidence for an internal model of gravity. J. Neural Eng. 2, 198–208 (2005)
5. Friedman, W.J.: Arrows of time in infancy: The representation of temporal-causal invariances. Cognit. Psychol. 44, 252–296 (2002)
6. Indovina, I., Maffei, V., Bosco, G., Zago, M., Macaluso, E., Lacquanita, F.: Representation of visual gravitational motion in the human vestibular cortex. Sci. 308, 416–419 (2005)
7. Kim, I.K., Spelke, E.S.: Perception and understanding of effects of gravity and inertia on object motion. Dev. Sci. 2, 339–362 (1999)
8. Lacquaniti, F., Carrozzo, M., Borghese, N.A.: Time-varying mechanical behavior of multi-jointed arm in man. J. Neurophysiol. 69, 1443–1464 (1993)
9. McBeath, M.K., Shaffer, D.M., Kaiser, M.K.: How baseball outfielders determine where to run to catch fly balls. Sci. 268, 569–573 (1995)
10. Twardy, C.R., Bingham, G.P.: Causation, causal perception, and conservation laws. Percept. & Psychophys. 64, 956–968 (2002)
11. Muchisky, M.M., Bingham, G.P.: Perceiving size in events via kinematic form. In: Kruschke, J.K. (ed.) Proceedings of the 14th Annual Conference of the Cognitive Science Society, pp. 1002–1007. Erlbaum, Hillsdale (1992)
12. Watson, J.S., Banks, M.S., von Hofsten, C., Royden, C.S.: Gravity as a monocular cue for perception of absolute distance and/or absolute size. Percept. 21, 69–76 (1992)
13. Jokisch, D., Troje, N.F.: Biological motion as a cue for the perception of size. J. Vis. 3, 252–264 (2003)
14. Spottiswoode, R.: The focal encyclopedia of film and television techniques. Hastings House, New York (1969)
15. Howard, I.P.: Human visual orientation. Wiley, New York (1982)
16. Schone, H.: Spatial orientation (C. Strausfeld, trans.).Princeton University Press, Princeton (1984)
17. Shepard, R.N.: Perceptual-cognitive universals as reflections of the world. Psychonomic Bull. Rev. 1, 2–28 (1994)
18. Smetacek, V.: Balance: Mind-grasping gravity. Nat. 415, 481 (2002)
19. McIntyre, J., Zago, M., Berthoz, A., Lacquaniti, F.: Does the brain model Newton's laws? Nat. Neurosci. 4, 693–694 (2001)
20. Vatakis, A., Spence, C.: Investigating the effects of inversion on configural processing with an audiovisual temporal-order judgment task. Percept. 37, 143–160 (2008)
21. Spence, C., Shore, D.I., Klein, R.M.: Multisensory prior entry. J Exp. Psychol. Gen. 130, 799–832 (2001)
22. Finney, D.J.: Probit analysis: Statistical treatment of the sigmoid response curve. Cambridge University Press, London (1964)
23. Coren, S., Ward, L.M., Enns, J.T.: Sensation & perception, 6th edn. Harcourt Brace, Fort Worth (2004)

24. Cohen, J., Hansel, C.E.M., Sylvester, J.D.: A new phenomenon in time judgment. Nat. 172, 901 (1953)
25. Masuda, T., Wada, Y., Noguchi, K.: The role of represented direction of gravity force in time perception: Which is more important, physical or phenomenal direction? Percept. 34(ECVP Abstract Supplement) (2005)
26. Wada, Y., Masuda, T., Noguchi, K.: Temporal illusion called 'kappa effect' in event perception. Percept. 34(ECVP Abstract Supplement) (2005)
27. Vatakis, A., Spence, C.: How 'special' is the human face? Evidence from an audiovisual temporal order judgment task. Neuroreport 18, 1807–1811 (2007)
28. Bentin, S., Allison, T., Puce, A., Perez, E., McCarthy, G.: Electrophysiological studies of face perception in humans. J Cognit. Neurosci. 8, 551–565 (1996)
29. Fonseca, J.V., Soares, T.M.B., Nascimento, S.M.C.: Visual sensitivity to changes in acceleration of gravity tested with free-falling objects. Percept. 34(ECVP Abstract Supplement) (2005)
30. Danckert, J., Goodale, M.A.: Superior performance for visually guided movements in the inferior visual field. Exp. Brain Res. 137, 303–308 (2001)

About Musical Time – Effect of Age, Enjoyment, and Practical Musical Experience on Retrospective Estimate of Elapsed Duration during Music Listening

Michelle Phillips and Ian Cross

Centre for Music and Science, Faculty of Music, University of Cambridge,
11 West Road, Cambridge, CB3 9DP, UK
Mep41@cam.ac.uk

Abstract. 237 participants listened to a 37 second extract of original music for solo piano, and were asked to retrospectively verbally estimate elapsed duration. Differences were found for age (mean estimate for ages 5-8: 76.11 seconds, ages 9-10: 66.38, 11-13: 54.88 seconds, ages 14 to adult: 65.17 seconds) and a correlation found between adult age and estimate. Estimates were found to be significantly longer for those who enjoyed the music, compared to those who disliked it. Elapsed duration was also judged significantly more accurately by experienced musicians and also marginally significantly more accurately by school teachers. Results are discussed in terms of memory, attention, and emotion.

Keywords: Music perception, music and time, retrospective estimation, age, enjoyment, memory, attention, emotion.

The phenomenological experience of elapsed duration is dependent on multiple and complex factors. These include, but are not limited to, working memory capacity, division of attention, and emotional state. Moreover, estimates of duration differ according to experimental paradigm employed (prospective or retrospective), length estimated (i.e., the sub- or supra-second level), and means of testing (verbal estimation, production, reproduction, or comparison).

Whether musical time conforms to current models of psychological time (for a review see [20]) - such as internal clock or contextual change models (see [4]), or more recently proposed models of timing based on neural networks [9-10,14] – or whether 'temporal production and estimation have special meanings in musical contexts' [23, p. 214], remains as yet unclear. However, studies demonstrate that musical features do appear to influence the experience of elapsed duration, and that the extent and nature of this influence varies depending on multiple musical parameters.

This study explores the effect of individual characteristics and preferences on estimates of elapsed duration during music listening, specifically, the effects of age, enjoyment, and level of musical training. Results are discussed with reference to memory, attention and encoding of musical information, and emotion.

A. Vatakis et al. (Eds.): Time and Time Perception 2010, LNAI 6789, pp. 125–136, 2011.
© Springer-Verlag Berlin Heidelberg 2011

1   Background

How we plan, conceive of, structure, and reflect on our daily lives and experiences depends on the notion of time. Our lives exist in time, or rather, the events of our lives occupy and shape the time available to us over our biological existence. Most investigations of psychological time employ one of four methods of measurement - verbal estimation, reproduction, production, and comparison (for a summary see [19]) – and relies on one of two timing paradigms; the prospective paradigm (or 'experienced duration'), in which a person is aware an estimation of elapsed duration will be required; and the retrospective paradigm (or 'remembered duration'), in which the person is unaware such judgment will be required. The former has largely been explored and theorised in terms of levels and foci of attention (for instance, the more attention paid to the passing of time, rather than the salient event, the longer the estimate) [4], and the latter chiefly in terms of memory resources (as the sequence of events experienced must be recalled, and time elapsed gauged) [4].

Prospective estimation of time is usually discussed in relation to internal-clock models [4], or, more recently, neural models [9] of time perception, while retrospective experience is most often represented by a form of 'contextual-change' model [4], which proposes that estimations of duration rely on recall of the number of 'changes' perceived in environmental context during the salient interval (the more changes registered, the longer the estimate of duration). Models also vary depending on the length of interval concerned, with different processes considered to be relevant for various lengths of duration whether at the sub- or supra-second level [26]. Neurological studies, which have implicated areas involved in time estimation including the cerebellum, cortex areas (SMA), and basal ganglia (for a summary see [20]), also suggest regions involved depend on length of duration in question [26,29].

Studies of experienced elapsed duration have most frequently employed the prospective paradigm, as this allows for collection of multiple data points per participant, whereas retrospective estimations require participants' ignorance of the purpose of the study (i.e., perception of time) until after the salient event. However, the latter paradigm perhaps better reflects the everyday experience of temporal duration, as daily events are rarely consciously timed but their duration may be reflected on in retrospect. Moreover, much existing empirical literature concerning time estimation employs intervals in the range of 100ms to 2-3 seconds, often examining implicit, or motor, responses. The retrospective paradigm is more directly applicable to the explicit estimation of longer durations (from a few seconds to an interval of minutes or more), but studies of this nature are currently few in comparison with their prospective equivalents.

It should however be borne in mind that the fine-grained distinctions and binary delineations in time perception models and paradigms sketched out above are often problematic, in that any one category in isolation may fail to sufficiently explain empirically obtained results, and hence risk limiting the scope of such findings. Importantly, studies exist which propose prospective and retrospective duration estimation may rely on similar mechanisms [7], and models have been developed which assign equal importance to processes of attention and memory [8], rather than aligning the former chiefly with prospective estimates, and the latter with retrospective. The theory of 'break points' in the different brain areas involved depending on the length of time in question has also been empirically challenged [29].

Data for the current study were collected during a nine-week residency at the Science Museum, London (each Tuesday-Thursday from 17th January to 17th March 2011, as part of the 'Live Science' programme in the 'Who Am I?' gallery). The study took place in a dedicated research room, in which temperature, ambient noise, lighting, visual information and stimulus volume were carefully controlled throughout the study (by use of a thermometer and a decibel monitor in the case of the first two measures). The chosen environment allowed for wide demographic penetration, and data from a breadth of age ranges from age 5 to adult.

The study employed a retrospective paradigm and verbal estimation method. Verbal estimation is one of the most common methods of assessing experienced duration during music listening (e.g., [3,25,36]). This is partly due to its suitability for assessing intervals in excess of 30 seconds, which is considered to be the upper limit of intervals suitable for the reproduction paradigm [19], and also due its relevance for the music listening experience, which rarely involves the tracking of passing seconds and minutes.

Study of the effect of music listening on retrospective estimation of time is a relatively new, yet growing, field of interest. Empirical investigation has suggested that atmospheric music influences perception of time [1-2,31], and that estimates may be influenced by music's mode [36], familiarity [2], and harmonic variation [15]. This study aimed to assess whether two common findings concerning the perception of time – that there is an effect of age on time perception, and that enjoyment influences our perception of the passing of time – hold when the event concerned involves music listening. In addition, the study aimed to examine whether there is any evidence to support the notion that musical training may enhance awareness of elapsed duration during music listening, i.e., whether experienced musicians give significantly more accurate retrospective estimations compared to non-musicians.

Age has been shown to effect estimation of elapsed duration, with older adults and children giving less accurate estimations than other age groups [30], and older adults giving longer verbal estimations than younger [5]. It is thus predicted that the current study will find that estimates of the duration of the experience of listening to a piece of music become longer with age in teenagers and adults (hypothesis 1, H1). Time perception studies have also examined differences in time perception of young children, often in the age range of 5-8 years of age [12]. However, studies examining the development from age 5 (when a concept of time is thought to be under-developed, or at least not yet verbally expressible, see [17] for a review), to post age-8 (when a concept of duration is considered to emerge [17,32]), and into puberty, have been rare. As children develop a sense of units of time as expressed in seconds and minutes around the age of 8, it is predicted that the current study will demonstrate more variable, and hence on average higher, estimates from the age group 5-8 compared to that following development of durational expression at age 11-13 (hypothesis 2, H2).

Models and theories of time perception are increasingly recognising the significant role played by emotion in experience of elapsed duration; early internal-clock models such as those based on scalar timing [18] now incorporate an arousal component (see e.g., the 'attentional-gate' model, [4]), consumer studies acknowledge to an ever-greater extent the influence of affective state on experience of subjective time [1,20-21], and neurological studies have even begun to explore the notion that time may indeed *only* be represented as a series of emotional moments [10]. Both arousal and valance (or enjoyment/liking/pleasantness of the stimulus) have been shown to influence estimates of duration, although studies vary with regard to whether negative or positive valence leads to higher arousal, and hence longer estimates [11].

The purpose of engagement in music listening is considered to be linked to music's power to induce emotion [23]. Hence it is no surprise that experience of duration during music listening appears to be no exception in the link between psychological time and emotion. Studies have suggested that retrospective estimates vary depending on music's valence, with positively valenced music leading to higher estimates [3], and on subjective ratings of enjoyment [1,36], where ratings of higher pleasantness have been shown to correlate with higher estimations [36]. It is hence predicted that the current study will demonstrate higher estimates from those who rate enjoyment of the music higher than others (hypothesis 3, H3).

Musicians have been shown to demonstrate more accurate motor timing than non-musicians [16,34] but little is known of musicians' estimation of durations exceeding the millisecond to 1-2 second range. On the basis of these previous studies, and given that awareness of elapsed duration during music engagement is a key skill in musicianship, it is predicted that the current study will demonstrate more accurate estimates from experienced musicians (age 18-40, see below for criteria used for categorisation) compared to non-musicians (hypothesis 4, H4).

As familiarity with a musical stimulus has been shown to significantly effect estimation of elapsed duration during music listening and ratings of preference of musical stimuli [2,33], a bespoke composition for piano solo, *Time To Go*, by Matthew Woolhouse, was used in this study. The piece was selected from a number of possible compositions after receiving feedback from prospective participants (who did not go on to participate in the current study, as it was required that they be unfamiliar with the chosen stimulus). The listeners rated the composition highly in terms of ease of listening and entertainment value, and hence it was considered an ecologically valid selection. Other criteria that influenced the choice of piece include the tempo (100bpm, which is considered to be the preferred tapping rate for young adults [20], who represent the average age of Science Museum visitors eligible to participate in the study[1]) and timbre (piano solo, and hence effectively modified using software employed, *Logic Pro* and *Audacity*).

2 Method

2.1 Participants

Participants were museum visitors who volunteered to take part in the experiment. The age range of the 237 participants (118 female) was 5 to 79 years (mean: 27.18 years), after exclusion of 25 participants due to various data corruptions.[2]

---

[1] Although school children represent a large portion of museum visitors, they were unable to participate due to lack of parental consent.

[2] These include the following: other museum visitors walking into the room during the listening stage of the experiment, interruption of the listening stage by the museum voiceover announcement, visitors' failing to follow experimental instructions, and non-normal hearing.

After they had taken part in the experiment, all participants were asked to confirm they had not been aware that the experiment would ask for an estimation of time before they took part, and data for any who were of aware of the purpose of the study were excluded.

2.2 Stimulus

All participants heard a 37 second extract (one-second fade out to end) taken from the beginning of an original tonal composition by Matthew Woolhouse, *Time To Go*, for solo piano (major key, consistent tempo of 100bpm). The stimulus was created using *Logic Pro* and *Audacity* from a midi recording made by the composer.

2.3 Procedure

Participants were informed that the experiment concerned 'music and the mind', and that they would be asked to listen to a piece of music and answer a series of questions, following which they would be offered the opportunity to discuss the project and results collected to date. They were told that the entire experience would last approximately 10 minutes and asked to sign a consent form.

Participants first listened to the 37-second stimulus through Sennheiser HD201 closed-back headphones, and were then asked to press 'next' on the computer at which they were sitting, and respond to a series of questions (designed for the current study). The first of these asked 'Without looking at your watch or a clock, how long do you think you were listening to the music?' (and gave a 'minutes' and 'seconds' box, one above the other).[3] In terms of practical musical experience, participants were asked 'Have you ever had any formal music training at any time in your life (i.e. instrumental or singing lessons)?' and 'Do you currently play a musical instrument and/or sing?' If participants responded 'yes' to either question, they were also asked to state how long this engagement had lasted (in years). To obtain ratings of enjoyment, participants were asked 'How much did you enjoy listening to the music?' (1 = I didn't like it at all, 7 = I liked it a lot). The question, and the use of a seven-point scale, was based on previous studies employing the retrospective paradigm to investigate experience of elapsed duration during music listening [25,36]. However, the term 'pleasant' (used for [25,36], in which participants were all university students) was rejected in favour of the simpler terms 'enjoy' and 'like', in order for the question to be as clear as possible for all ages (from 5 years old).

The study was granted ethical approval by the Psychology Research Ethics Committee of the University of Cambridge.

3 Results

Analysis was conducted using one-tailed t tests (as all hypotheses predict direction) and Pearson product-moment correlation coefficients, except where stated otherwise. Participants were separated into four age categories: 5-8 ($N = 9$), 9-10 ($N = 13$), 11-13 ($N = 17$) and 14 to adult ($N = 126$).

---

[3] The question formulation, and the use of two response boxes, was based on previous studies of retrospective estimation using music and a verbal estimation method [see e.g., 1,3,25,36].

Responses ranged from 6 to 300 seconds.[4] 49 of the 237 responses were underestimates of the actual duration of 37 seconds (20.7% of total response, the remainder being overestimates) and the average duration reported across all participants was 72.25 seconds.

While public access to the experiment allowed sampling across a wide range of ages and levels of musical expertise, it also meant that the make-up of the population of participants was, from time to time, subject to considerable change. 71 of the total 237 participants took part in the experiment during a school holiday week which occurred within the period of the experiment. Analysis confirmed a significant effect [t(233) = -3.684, p < 0.001] of the altered environment during this school holiday (age range: 5 to 67, mean age: 20.34, mean estimate: 89.8 seconds) on duration estimation, compared to the 166 non-school holiday participants (age range: 5 to 79, mean age: 30.49, mean estimate: 64.83 seconds). This difference is largely owing to the differences in the under-18 population. Comparison of under-18 year olds only between the school-holiday (N = 47, mean age: 10, mean estimate: 96.49 seconds) and non-school-holiday (N = 48, mean age: 11, mean estimate: 61.27 seconds) groups also revealed a significant difference in estimation [t(93) = -3.214, p. <0.01]. Owing to these differences, data collected during the school holiday period has been excluded from all analyses detailed below.[5]

3.1 Age – Children (Three Groups: 5-8, 9-10, 11-13)

Mean estimates were: ages 5-8: 76.11 seconds, ages 9-10: 66.38 seconds, and ages 11-13: 54.88 seconds (see Fig. 1).

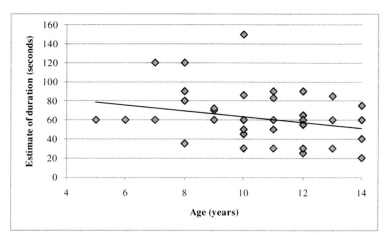

Fig. 1. Duration estimates for 37-second extract by participants 5-14 years of age

---

[4] Two outliers (defined as more than 2SD from the mean) were removed from the total data set for all analyses discussed in this study; one outlier of 1,200 seconds from the school holiday under 18 group and one of 600 seconds from the non-school holiday 5-8 group.

[5] For examples of studies exploring the notion that 'our feeling for time is fundamentally inseparable from our subjective [emotional] experience of the environment' [see 11, p.512]. However, influence of *overall* atmosphere or holiday environment on experience of elapsed duration is currently little understood.

A significant difference was detected between the 5-8 and 11-13 [t(24) = -2.048; p < 0.03] categories, with older children giving shorter responses (no significant difference was detected between the 5-8 and 9-10, or 9-10 and 11-13 groups). The data also revealed that estimates in children became more accurate between the ages of 5 and 14 (Pearson's r = -0.2712, t = -1.826, DF = 42, p < 0.04).

3.2 Age – 14 to Adult

In participants aged 14 and above (N = 126, mean age: 36.63, mean estimate: 65.17 seconds) a correlation was also found between age and duration estimate [r = 0.288, t = 3.348, DF = 124, p < 0.01], with estimates increasing in line with age (see Fig. 2).

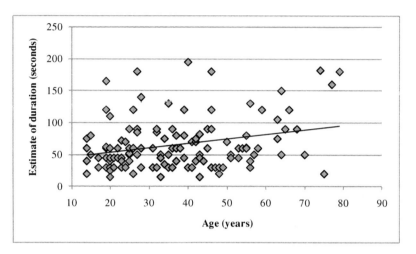

Fig. 2. Duration estimates for 37 second extract by participants aged 14 years of age and over

3.3 Enjoyment

Analysis of duration estimates of participants age 14 and above (N = 73, mean age: 39, mean rating: 4.89), and excluding experienced musicians and teachers (for reasons discussed below), revealed a significant effect of enjoyment, with those who reported enjoying the music giving higher estimations of elapsed duration (Pearson's r = 0.1941, t = 1.667, DF = 71, p < 0.05). There was no evidence of correlation for younger participants.

3.4 Musical Experience

A subset of the data was used to explore the effects of musical experience. Time estimations of non-musicians (defined as those who do not currently play a musical instrument and who responded with a maximum of 1 year to the question 'Have you ever had any formal music training at any time in your life (i.e., instrumental or singing lessons)?') were compared with experienced musicians (defined as having over 5 years' musical training and/or those who have engaged in regular playing of a musical instrument for the last 10+ years). 18 years of age was selected as the lower limit, as UK schools offer instrumental tuition from year four (age 8-10) [27], and hence 18 would be the lower limit of participants possessing 10+ years of training. 13 of a total of 17 (76.47%) experienced musicians were evenly distributed within the range 18-40 (with the remaining third including disparate ages), and hence 40 was selected as the upper limit for inclusion of data from both non-musician and experienced musician categories. This delineation also ensured average age was relatively consistent across the two experimental groups (mean age = 28.41 and 27.15 respectively), as was enjoyment rating (average rating = 5.16 and 4.46 respectively).

Average estimates for the groups were 68.97 seconds for non-musicians (N = 32, mean age: 28.41) and 47.08 seconds for experienced musicians (N = 13, mean age: 27.15) respectively. Analysis revealed a significant effect of musical training [$t(43)$ = -1.767; $p < 0.05$], with experienced musicians giving shorter, more accurate estimates.

3.5 Profession - Teaching

Qualitative data gathered during the study suggested that teachers considered themselves to have an accurate sense of elapsed duration. Due to the high volume of school trips visiting the Science Museum, a comparison was possible between estimates of teachers and non-teachers. Current teachers with over ten years' teaching experience (N = 6, mean age: 46, age range: 39-50) were compared to non-teachers within the same age range (N = 13, mean age: 43, age range: 39-48)[6].

Average estimates for the teacher and non-teacher conditions were 46.67 seconds and 82.46 seconds respectively. Analysis revealed a marginally significant effect of being employed in the teaching profession [$t(17)$ = -1.467, $p < 0.09$].

4   Discussion

The current study used a retrospective paradigm to examine verbal estimations of elapsed duration of a 37 second extract of bespoke tonal music. Age was found to be a determining factor in duration estimates, with 5-8 year olds giving significantly higher responses than children aged 11-13 (thus supporting H1). For participants aged 14 to adult, estimates were found to correlate significantly with age; increased age resulted in longer estimates (H2). Estimates of elapsed duration also became longer with increased rating of enjoyment (H3). Finally, estimates given by experienced musicians were found to be significantly shorter than non-musicians (H4). There was also some evidence that teachers' estimates of elapsed duration were also marginally significantly shorter than non-teachers.

Retrospective estimation of elapsed duration of a salient event requires recall of the information processed in memory. A contextual-change model would suggest that the more changes perceived in the interval, the higher the estimate. However, a purely memory-based interpretation does not suffice to explain the above findings, and a more attention-based explanation appears more relevant here.

---

[6] Results collected during the school holidays were excluded, due to factors discussed above. There was no overlap between teachers and experienced musicians.

Firstly, the finding that estimates of elapsed duration become longer with enjoyment appears to challenge the notion that 'time flies when you're having fun'; however, this is consistent with previous studies and models demonstrating a difference between prospective estimates (when elapsed duration is estimated as being shorter if enjoyment is high) and retrospective (when the reverse is the case). The result is also in line with previous studies demonstrating a correlation between perceived time during music listening and valence [3]. The retrospective paradigm (in which attention is not consciously divided between the tracking of time and the salient event, when an attentional-gate model may be useful) invites the application of an information processing theory here; higher enjoyment of the event results in higher levels of engagement, more attention paid to the salient event, and hence a richer encoding of the information presented. When retrieved from memory, the information encoded is more extensive and detailed compared to those whose engagement was at a lower level, and a longer assessment of elapsed duration results.

Experienced musicians were found to give significantly shorter estimates than non-musicians, which could also be considered in relation to the above theory - musicians may have encoded the musical information more efficiently than non-musicians. A musician's memory of the music as chunks of information (e.g., chords rather than separate notes) could lead to a shorter estimate compared to a non-musician. This would also be consistent with the contextual change model of time, which suggests that experience of time becomes longer as stimulus complexity increases [4], as a greater amount of information is processed and stored over the time interval. Experienced musicians may have found the stimulus less complex than non-musicians, and thus recalled shorter elapsed duration. Moreover, musical processing requires attention to hierarchical structures in time, with expectations of metrical pattern being formed based on rhythmic patterns [22]. With extensive expertise in processing metrical information, musicians may have been able to allocate attention to the music (at a constant 100bpm) more efficiently, and thus encode the information in a less detailed, more schematic way. Furthermore, owing to more accurate timing processing, musicians may have formed more accurate expectations of metrical events, compared to non-musicians. Non-musicians would therefore have experienced a greater level of violation of expectation (compared to musicians), resulting in an increase of affect (summarised in [28]), and thus longer responses.

The notion of attention remains central to the finding in relation to teachers. The teachers all visited the museum with their respective school groups, and attention is likely to have been diverted from the salient event (music listening), in favour of thinking through the distribution of the children in the gallery, and the logistics of the school visit. This diversion of attention would have resulted in lower levels of encoding of the musical information, and hence shorter estimates. However, participant numbers in the teacher and non-teacher conditions ($N = 6$ and $N = 13$, standard deviations = 24.22 and 56.73 seconds, respectively) were relatively small, and further research with larger sample sizes is required to further investigate this trend.

Results for the age group 5-8 compared to 11-13 year olds confirm that verbal expression of experienced time is not yet developed at this age, and hence the method may not have adequately reflected time perception [13]. However, results relating to participants age 14 to adult may be interpreted, as those discussed above, in terms of attention allocation and resource. Studies have shown that the greater attention paid to a task, the shorter the estimate of elapsed duration (summarised in [6]). Teenagers may not have devoted as much attention to listening to the music as adults, which would lead less musical information encoded in memory, and subsequently to shorter estimates. Age differences could be present in the data because of differences in time perception that are apparent in temporal behaviour (spontaneous tapping rates) between children (350ms), young adults (600ms), and adults (700ms), as summarised by [20]. The 100bpm tempo would feel faster to older adults than to younger adults, and this could lead to an increase in pacemaker rate and higher arousal, and thus to longer estimates of elapsed duration.

Attention processes have often been neglected in retrospective estimation literature, in favour of theories of memory. However, the findings of the current study challenge this tendency, and call for attention to feature more adequately in retrospective models, particularly where emotional stimuli are employed. Moreover, the results herein could offer new directions for research concerning the effect of emotion on time perception, as it is recognised that: i) the field requires a standardisation of emotional stimuli in order to further elapsed duration models [11], ii) time discrimination has been shown to be better when the intervals contain *auditory* rather than *visual* information [35], and iii) music is considered an effective inducer of emotion [24]. There is therefore scope for affective musical stimuli to become the standard emotional stimuli required by the field of time perception and emotion.

Finally, the results of this study suggest that current theories of experience of elapsed duration are relevant to music listening, providing the process of attention is sufficiently accounted for in retrospective models. However, the findings also call for redefinition of these models in musical situations - musical structure exists, and is perceived, as a series of hierarchically organised events in time, and it is according to the perception of such a hierarchy (dependent on various factors, including musical experience and engagement) that experience of elapsed duration during music listening must be modelled.

Acknowledgements. Many thanks to the Science Museum, London, for providing the opportunity and space for data collection, and to SEMPRE for the generous funding of this research residency. Thanks also to Matthew Woolhouse (Centre for Music and Science, University of Cambridge) for allowing his composition, *Time To Go*, to be used as the stimulus for this study, and to Jessica Grahn (University of Western Ontario) and colleagues in the Centre for Music and Science.

References

1. Areni, C., Grantham, N.: (Waiting) Time Flies When the Tune Flows: Music Influences Affective Responses to Waiting by Changing the Subjective Experience of Passing Time. Adv. Consum. Res. 36, 449–455 (2009)
2. Bailey, N., Areni, C.S.: When a Few Minutes Sound like a Lifetime: Does Atmospheric Music Expand or Contract Perceived Time? J. Retailing 82(3), 189–202 (2006)
3. Bisson, N., Tobin, S., Grondin, S.: Remembering the Duration of Joyful and Sad Musical Excerpts: Assessment with Three Estimation Methods. NeuroQuantology 7(1) (2009)

4. Block, R.A., Zakay, D.: Prospective and Retrospective Duration Judgments: A Meta-analytic Review. Psychon. B. Rev. 4(2), 184–197 (1997)
5. Block, R.A., Zakay, D., Hancock, P.A.: Human Aging and Duration Judgments: A Meta-analytic Review. Psychol. Aging 13(4), 584–596 (1998)
6. Brown, S.W.: Time and Attention: Review of the Literature. In: Grondin, S. (ed.) Psychology of Time, pp. 111–138. Emerald Group Publishing Ltd., Bingley (2008)
7. Brown, S.W.: Time Perception and Attention: the Effects of Prospective versus Retrospective Paradigms and Task Demands on Perceived Duration. Percept. Psychophys. 38, 115–124 (1985)
8. Buhusi, C.V., Meck, W.H.: Relative Time Sharing: New Findings and an Extension of the Resource Allocation Model of Temporal Processing. Philos. T. R. Soc. B 364(1525), 1875–1885 (2009)
9. Buonomano, D.V., Bramen, J., Khodadadifar, M.: Influence of the Interstimulus Interval on Temporal Processing and Learning: Testing the State-Dependent Network Model. Philos. T. R. Soc. B 364(1525), 1865–1873 (2009)
10. Craig, A.D.: Emotional Moments across Time: a Possible Neural Basis for Time Perception in the Anterior Insula. Philos. T. R. Soc. B 364(1525), 1933–1942 (2009)
11 Droit-Volet, S., Meck, W.H.: How Emotions Colour Our Perception of Time. Trends Cogn. Sci. 11(12), 504–513 (2007)
12. Droit-Volet, S., Tourret, S., Wearden, J.: Perception of the Duration of Auditory and Visual Stimuli in Children and Adults. Q. J. Exp. Psychol. 57A(5), 797–818 (2004)
13. Droit-Volet, S.: Stop Using Time Reproduction Tasks in a Comparative Perspective without Further Analyses of the Role of the Motor Response on the Temporal Performance: the Case of Children. Eur. J. Cogn. Psychol. 22(1), 130–148 (2010)
14. Eagleman, D.M., Pariyadath, V.: Is Subjective Duration a Signature of Coding Efficiency? Philos. T. R. Soc. B 364(1525), 1841–1851 (2009)
15. Firmino, É.A., Bueno, J.L.O., Bigand, E.: Travelling through Pitch Space Speeds up Musical Time. Music Percept. 26(3), 205–209 (2009)
16. Franek, M., Mates, J., Radil, T., Beck, K., Pöppel, E.: Finger Tapping in Musicians and Nonmusicians. Int. J. Psychophysiol. 11(3), 277–279 (1991)
17. Friedman, W.J.: Developmental Perspectives on the Psychology of Time. In: Grondin, S. (ed.) Psychology of Time, pp. 345–366. Emerald Group Publishing Ltd., Bingley (2008)
18. Gibbon, J., Church, R.M., Meck, W.H.: Scalar Timing in Memory. Ann. N. Y. Acad. Sci. 423, 52–77 (1984)
19. Grondin, S.: Methods for Studying Psychological Time. In: Grondin, S. (ed.) Psychology of Time, pp. 51–74. Emerald Group Publishing Ltd., Bingley (2008)
20. Grondin, S.: Timing and Time Perception: a Review of Recent Behavioral and Neuroscience Findings and Theoretical Directions. Atten. Percept. Psycho. 72(3), 561–582 (2010)
21. Hornik, J.: Time Estimation and Orientation Mediated by Transient Mood. J. Socio-Econ. 21(3), 209–229 (1992)
22. Jones, M.R., Boltz, M.: Dynamic Attending and Responses to Time. Psychol. Rev. 96(3), 459–491 (1989)
23. Jones, M.R.: Musical Events and Models of Musical Time. In: Block, R.A. (ed.) Cognitive Models of Psychological Time, pp. 207–238. Lawrence Erlbaum Associates Inc., Hillsdale (1990)
24. Juslin, P.N., Laukka, P.: Expression, Perception, and Induction of Musical Emotions: a Review and a Questionnaire Study of Everyday Listening. J. New Music Res. 33, 217–238 (2004)

25. Kellaris, J.J., Kent, R.J.: The Influence of Music on Consumers' Temporal Perceptions: Does Time Fly when You're Having Fun? J. Consum. Psychol. 1(4), 365–376 (1992)
26. Koch, G., Oliveri, M., Caltagirone, C.: Neural Networks Engaged in Milliseconds and Seconds Time Processing: Evidence from Transcranial Magnetic Stimulation and Patients with Cortical or Subcortical Dysfunction. Philos. T. R. Soc. B 364(1525), 1907–1918 (2009)
27. Lamont, A., Hargreaves, D.J., Marshall, N.A., Tarrant, M.: Young People's Music in and out of School. Br. J. Music Educ. 20(3), 229–241 (2003)
28. Large, E.W.: Resonating to Musical Rhythm: Theory and Experiment. In: Grondin, S. (ed.) Psychology of Time, pp. 189–232. Emerald Group Publishing Ltd., Bingley (2008)
29. Lewis, P.A., Miall, R.C.: The Precision of Temporal Judgement: Milliseconds, Many Minutes, and beyond. Philos. T. R. Soc. B 364(1525), 1897–1905 (2009)
30. McCormack, T., Brown, G.D.A., Maylor, E.A.: Developmental Changes in Time Estimation: Comparing Childhood and Old Age. Dev. Psychol. 35(4), 1143–1155 (1999)
31. Noseworthy, T.J., Finlay, K.: A Comparison of Ambient Casino Sound and Music: Effects on Dissociation and on Perceptions of Elapsed Time while Playing Slot Machines. J. Gambl. Stud. 25, 331–342 (2009)
32. Piaget, J.: The Child's Conception of Time; translated (from the French) by A. J. Pomerans. Routledge & K. Paul, London (1969)
33. Peretz, I., Gaudreau, D., Bonnel, A.-M.: Exposure Effects on Music Preference and Recognition. Mem. Cognition 26(5), 884–902 (1998)
34. Rammsayer, T., Altermuller, E.: Temporal Information Processing in Musicians and Nonmusicians. Music Percept. 24(1), 37–48 (2006)
35. Ulrich, R., Nitschke, J., Rammsayer, T.: Crossmodal Temporal Discrimination: Assessing the Predictions of a General Pacemaker-Counter Model. Atten. Percept. Psycho. 68(7), 1140–1152 (2006)
36. Ziv, N., Omer, E.: Music and Time: the Effect of Experimental Paradigm, Musical Structure and Subjective Evaluations on Time Estimation. Psychol. Music 39(2), 182–195 (2010)

The Impact of Attention on the Internal Clock in Prospective Timing: Is It Direct or Indirect?

Pierre-Luc Gamache[1], Simon Grondin[1,*], and Dan Zakay[2,*]

[1] École de psychologie. Université Laval, Québec, QC, Canada GIV0A6
[2] The Inter-Disciplinary Center, School of Psychology, Herzeliya, Israel
```
Pierre-Luc.Gamache.1@ulaval.ca
Simon.Grondin@psy.ulaval.ca
dzakay@post.tau.ac.il
```

Abstract. A debate about the nature of the influence of attention on prospective timing exists. According to one approach, attention directly influences the internal clock and determines how many pulses emitted by a pacemaker will be accumulated in a given time unit ("direct-impact" hypothesis). According to a different view ("indirect-impact" hypothesis), attention does not influence the internal clock directly but rather indirectly. In order to test the "direct-impact" hypothesis, an experiment was conducted, in which the amount of attentional resources available for timing was determined before the onset of a target interval. It was found that prospective timing of a target interval was affected by the manipulation, which took place before it even started. Although the results do not allow discarding the "indirect-impact" hypothesis, they are certainly consistent with the "direct-impact" hypothesis. Further research is needed in order to determine which approach can provide the best explanation for the findings.

Keywords: Attention, Attentional Gate Model, Internal Clock, Prospective Duration Estimation.

1 Introduction

Time perception researchers draw a distinction between prospective and retrospective timing [1-4]. Prospective timing refers to a situation where, for a given period of time, a person is aware that a duration judgment will have to be made following this period. In retrospective timing, the person is only aware that a judgment about time has to be made after the targeted interval ends [5-6]. The present article focuses on the role of attention in prospective timing and more specifically on how attention can affect the internal clock.

Important support for a central role of attention in prospective timing comes from resource allocation manipulations, more specifically from using a dual-task paradigm. In the context of time estimation, a typical finding obtained with this paradigm is that the manipulation of a non-temporal task has a direct influence on temporal performance; in particular, increasing the difficulty of a non-temporal task results in impaired temporal performances [5, 7]. Moreover, when two temporal tasks are processed

---

* Corresponding author.

A. Vatakis et al. (Eds.): Time and Time Perception 2010, LNAI 6789, pp. 137–150, 2011.
© Springer-Verlag Berlin Heidelberg 2011

simultaneously, there is an impairment of temporal performance in both tasks [8]. It has also been shown that, when performing simultaneously a non-temporal and a temporal duration discrimination task, the efficiency varies as a function of the amount of attention dedicated to the tasks. As more attention is devoted to time, duration is perceived as longer and fewer discrimination errors occur [9-10].

A robust characteristic of prospective timing is that when target intervals of equal durations are encoded under high or low mental load conditions (i.e., with a difficult or an easy concurrent non-temporal task, respectively), they are under- or over-reproduced, respectively. A mirror picture is obtained for production: equal target durations are over- or under-produced under high or low mental load conditions, respectively. The Attentional-Gate Model (AGM) [11] provides a good explanation for this mirror effect [12]. According to the AGM, a pacemaker emits pulses at a given rate, determined by the level of arousal, and these pulses are filtered through an attentional gate that leads to an accumulator. The more attention allocated to time, the wider the opening of the gate and thus the more pulses amassed in the accumulator. Under high mental load conditions the gate is not widely opened and the number of pulses accumulated in the accumulator is lower than when the concurrent non-temporal task is an easy one (and the gate is widely opened). Reproduced intervals reflect the number of pulses in the accumulator and thus equal clock-time intervals will be reproduced as longer intervals when the target interval is encoded under low than under high mental load conditions.

In production tasks, a representation of a target interval is retrieved from memory and is stored in reference memory. The internal clock is then starting to operate in a process similar to that of reproduction. The process is stopped when a match between the number of pulses accumulated in the accumulator and the representation in reference memory is achieved. This will take a longer period when the production is made under high mental load than when production is made under low mental load. The reason for that is that under low mental load more attentional resources are allocated for timing, the attentional-gate is widely opened and the flow of pulses to the accumulator is faster than under high mental load conditions which narrow the attentional-gate. Since according to the AGM, the attentional gate is a central part of an internal clock, a basic assumption of the model is that attention has a direct impact on the internal clock ("direct-impact" hypothesis).

In contradiction to the AGM, the Basic Internal Clock Module (BICM) [13] argues that the internal clock is only comprised of a pacemaker and an accumulator and that attention does not have any direct impact on it ("indirect-impact" hypothesis). According to this view, the BICM is not affected directly by mental load conditions. However, when attention is distracted from timing, the accumulator resets back to zero and then starts counting pulses anew. A reset event may occur, according to this model, with a probability that is higher the more intensive the distraction level is. Thus, when encoding of a target interval is done under high mental load conditions, the probability of a reset event is higher than when encoding is done under low mental load conditions. As a result respective reproduction will be longer when timing is done under low than under high mental load conditions. The mirror effect of production is explained in a similar way. In more general terms, BICM assumes that time estimation has to compete with other tasks for attentional resources, and even though this does not affect the accumulation of pulses it might cause the model to sometimes "forget" to pay attention to time.

Thus, both the AGM and BICM models provide explanations for the mirror effect, but each explanation rests on different grounds. Whereas the AGM posits that an attentional-gate is a central part of an internal clock and attention has a direct impact on it, the BICM model posits that an attentional-gate is not needed and attention does not have a direct effect on the internal clock.

The aim of the present study is to test the "direct-impact" hypothesis. The rationale for the test is based on the following assumption: If attention allocation for timing can be manipulated such that the attention allocation policy is determined before the onset of a target interval, and if during the target interval itself no attentional distraction exists, then no impact of the attentional manipulation on perceived targets' interval durations should be recorded, if the indirect-impact hypothesis is valid. However, if this attentional manipulation has an impact on perceived duration of target intervals without the existence of concurrent attentional distractions, this will indicate that attention have a direct impact on the internal clock.

1.1 Manipulating Foreperiods

One method by which attention allocation for timing during encoding of a time interval can be determined before the start of a target interval is by manipulating the characteristics of the foreperiod. Grondin and Rammsayer [14] manipulated the duration of the foreperiod – that is, the period of time preceding an interval to be timed – in a duration discrimination task. Typically, foreperiods are used to study participants' preparation for responding to a signal in a reaction time experiment [15-16]. Grondin and Rammsayer obtained two main results. Firstly, the target intervals following foreperiods are perceived as longer when the foreperiods are actually longer. Secondly, foreperiods' length only has an impact when they are varied randomly from trial to trial. When the same foreperiods are held constant within a session, there is no effect on perceived target intervals' durations. Grondin and Rammsayer suggested a potential explanation for the foreperiod effect, based on the AGM [11]. Using this theoretical framework, Grondin and Rammsayer hypothesized that the probability of occurrence of the first signal marking time increases with the passage of time, with the result that more attention is allocated to temporal information. Consequently, the gate opens more widely when longer foreperiods are used, leading to greater temporal accumulation during brief target intervals, which immediately followed foreperiods, i.e., longer perceived durations of the target intervals.

The foreperiod effects observed by Grondin and Rammsayer [14] could also be accounted for by the notion of temporal uncertainty (TU) [17]. TU refers to the degree of certainty by which the duration of a forthcoming interval can be predicted. The higher the TU, the more attentional resources are allocated for timing the foreperiod. Attention allocation policies adapt to the TU of a given context. Since the probability of occurrence of the signal increases as a function of foreperiod length, the TU associated with the foreperiod diminishes conversely. Therefore, the attentional resources disengaged from the foreperiod's time dimension and become available for anticipating the forthcoming target interval. Consequently, lengthening foreperiod duration decreases TU, while increasing its variability generates more TU. Such manipulations directly impact the level of temporal uncertainty and thus lead to variable levels of attentional resources being allocated to timing. The study of Grondin and Rammsayer demonstrates how manipulations, which might change the amount of attentional resources allocated for timing, can affect prospective timing, even though they took place before the start of the target interval.

1.2 The Present Study

The general purpose of the present study is to test the attentional preparation account of the foreperiod and TU effects on perceived duration by replicating Grondin and Rammsayer's [14] findings and by adding a new manipulation of a different type by which attention allocation policy can be influenced. For this purpose, two manipulations affecting attentional processing during the foreperiod are proposed. The first manipulation concerns the duration range of the foreperiods to be used. More specifically, if the influence of foreperiod length is due to attention, it should be cancelled out, or at least reduced, when very long foreperiods are used, given that, at some point, no additional attentional resources should be available for attending to the signal to be timed.

The second manipulation concerns the notion of TU and its impact on attention allocation policies. We wanted to find out if instructions delivered to generate expectations that foreperiod could vary have an influence on perceived duration and sensitivity. Inducing TU about the length of the foreperiod via instructions should lead to shorter perceived duration and to weaker temporal sensitivity because, as more attention is allocated to the temporal dimension of the foreperiod, less attention should be available for timing the target interval. These experimental manipulations enabled the testing of the "direct-impact" and "indirect-impact" hypotheses.

As explained earlier, if the PFs durations and levels of TU associated with its variability are found to affect perceived durations of brief target intervals which follow foreperiods, and no attentional distraction exists during the target interval itself, then attention must have a direct impact on the internal clock.

2   Method

2.1   Participants

The participants were 19 female and 13 male adult volunteers ranging in age from 19 to 25 years. All participants were undergraduate or graduate students at Laval University and were paid $32 (Canadian) for taking part in this experiment. All participants had normal hearing.

2.2   Apparatus and Stimuli

The presentation of the auditory intervals and the recording of the participant's responses were computer-controlled using E-prime 3.0 software. The auditory stimuli were 1000-Hz square wave tones. The intervals to be discriminated were silent durations (empty intervals). The empty intervals were marked by onset and offset tones 10-ms in duration, presented binaurally through headphones (Sony MDR-V600) with an intensity of approximately 70 dB SPL.

2.3 Procedure

Each trial consisted of the presentation of a single empty interval. An experimental session was initiated by 10 presentations of a 100-ms standard interval followed by five blocks of 80 trials each. On each trial, an empty interval shorter or longer than the 100-ms standard interval was presented. There were four durations shorter (79, 85, 91, and 97 ms) and four durations longer (103, 109, 115, and 121 ms). Within each block, each of these eight intervals was presented 10 times in random order. Also, what is called the foreperiod is the period of time from completion of the participant's response to the preceding trial to the onset of the following stimulus presentation.

Participants were divided in four groups –8 participants in each group– according to two between-subject independent variables, with two levels each. The first between-subject variable is called "foreperiods mixing mode". Participants were randomly assigned to one of two equal groups, corresponding to the two levels of the variable. In the variable foreperiods group (VF), foreperiods were completely randomized across interval durations. In the constant foreperiods (CF) group, foreperiods were held constant within a session, but varied from session to session. Within each mixing mode group, participants were divided in two halves, regarding the instructions they were told before the experimental sessions.

Half the subjects were informed that the foreperiod might vary from trial to-trial (group "cued as variable"), while the other half received no information regarding the foreperiod (group "uncued"). Table 1 summarizes the different experimental conditions.

For all participants, there were seven foreperiod durations (300, 400, 500, 600, 1200, 1800, and 2400 ms). In the VF group, these were grouped in two different types of sessions, which introduced a two-level within-subject independent variable called "duration range": Short (300, 400, 500 and 600 ms, randomly mixed) and Long (600, 1200, 1800 and 2400 ms, randomly mixed). There were four sessions of each type, one session consisting in 5 blocks of 80 trials. In the CF group, there were seven sessions, one with each foreperiod. That is, in the CF group, foreperiod constitutes a seven-level within-subject independent variable.

Participants were seated at a table in a dimly lit, sound attenuated room. Participants' task was to decide whether the presented empty interval was shorter or longer than the 100-ms standard interval by pressing "1" (short) or "3" (long) on the computer's keyboard. The instructions for the participants emphasized accuracy: there was no requirement to respond quickly. After each response, a variable foreperiod preceded the next empty interval to be presented. Each participant was run individually. Each experimental session lasted approximately 25 min.

2.4 Data Analysis

All trials were kept for analysis. For each participant and for each foreperiod, an 8-point psychometric function was traced, plotting the eight comparator intervals on the x-axis and the probability of responding "long" on the y-axis.

The cumulative normal distribution was fitted to the resulting curves. Two indices of performance were estimated for each psychometric function, one for sensitivity and one for the perceived duration. As an indicator of temporal sensitivity, estimates of the standard deviation (SD) on the psychometric function were determined. For this purpose, the difference between the x values corresponding to .84 and .16 probabilities of "long" responses, on the y-axis, was divided by 2. Using one SD (or variance) is a common procedure to express temporal sensitivity [18-19].

The other dependent variable was temporal bisection point (BP). The bisection point can be defined as the x value corresponding to the .50 probability of "long" responses on the x-axis. The observed shift of the bisection point for different foreperiod conditions can be interpreted as an indication of differences in perceived duration. Thus, longer perceived durations are reflected by smaller bisection point values. This implies the assumption that with the uncertainty conditions of the present experiment, participants employed the same response criterion for all foreperiod conditions and that the differences in the distributions of "long" and "short" responses depend on the perceived duration in each foreperiod condition [20].

Table 1. Summary of the different experimental conditions

Instructions	Variable		Constant
Informed ("The foreperiod may vary")	*SHORT range*	*LONG range*	
	Four durations:	Four durations:	Seven durations:
	300, 400, 500 and 600 ms	600, 1200, 1800 and 2400 ms	300, 400, 500, 600, 1200, 1800, 2400 ms
Not informed (No information about the foreperiod)	*SHORT range*	*LONG range*	
	Four durations:	Four durations:	Seven durations:
	300, 400, 500 and 600 ms	600, 1200, 1800 and 2400 ms	300, 400, 500, 600, 1200, 1800, 2400 ms

* Double lines are used to separate conditions performed by different subjects.

3 Results

The results are presented first for the variable experimental group followed by the results in the constant group.

3.1 Variable Group

Perceived duration and sensitivity patterns observed in the variable group are illustrated in Figure 1. To validate the presence of statistically significant effects, a split-plot ANOVA 2 x 2 x 4 (Instructions x Duration range x Relative foreperiod length) was performed on each dependent variable. Regarding the BP (Figure 1, Upper Panel), the main effect of the relative foreperiod length was significant, $F(3, 42) = 44.99$, $p < .001$, $\eta^2_p = .76$. The Relative foreperiod duration x Duration range interaction was also significant, $F(3, 42) = 5.40$, $p = .003$, $\eta^2_p = .28$. Post-hoc multiple comparisons were conducted using Tukey HSD (with $\alpha = 0.05$ and $q_{HSD} = 4.52$). There was no significant difference between any of the means in the long range, while in the short range, the shortest foreperiod (300 ms) generated significantly higher BPs than the two longest foreperiods of both ranges (500, 600short, 1800 and 2400 ms). There was no main effect of Instructions (cued as variable vs. uncued), $F(1,14) = 1.33$, $p = .268$, $\eta^2_p = .087$.

For SD (Figure 1, lower Panel) the Relative foreperiod length was significant, $F(3, 42) = 7.59$, $p < .001$, $\eta^2_p = .35$. Moreover, the Relative foreperiod length x Duration range interaction was also significant, $F(3,42) = 6.51$, $p = .001$, $\eta^2_p = .32$. Post-hoc Tukey tests ($\alpha = 0.05$ and $q_{HSD} = 4.52$) reveal that the 2400 ms foreperiod generated significantly lower variability than the 300, 400, and 500 ms foreperiods in the short range condition, and than the 600 ms in the long range condition. There was no Instructions effect, $F(1,14) = 0.92$, $p = .353$, $\eta^2_p = .062$.

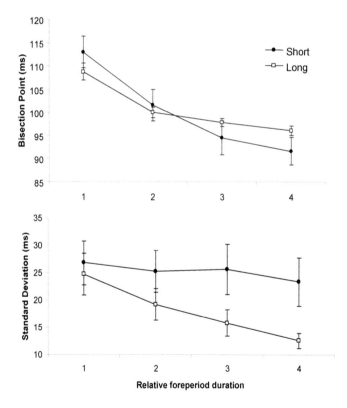

Fig. 1. Mean bisection point (upper panel) and mean standard deviation (lower panel) (± standard error of the mean) as a function of the relative foreperiod length (1, 2, 3, 4) and the duration range (short vs. long), in the mixed foreperiod group (for short foreperiods: 1 = 300 ms, 2 = 400 ms, 3 = 500 ms, 4 = 600 ms ; for long foreperiods : 1 = 600 ms, 2 = 1200 ms, 3 = 1800 ms, 4 = 2400 ms)

These results showed that longer foreperiods result in longer perceived duration, but this applies most importantly with foreperiods belonging to the *short* range. As regards SD, longer foreperiods resulted in better temporal sensitivity but interestingly, this beneficial effect was observable only in the *long* duration range.

3.2 Constant Group

Perceived duration and sensitivity patterns observed in the constant group are depicted in Figure 2. A 2 x 7 (Instructions X foreperiod) ANOVA according to a split-plot design was performed on each dependent variable (BP and SD). For BP, there was no foreperiod effect, $F(6, 84) = 1.82$, $p = .106$, $\eta^2_p = .12$. However, the instructions effect (cued as variable vs. uncued) was significant, $F(1,14) = 4.81$, $p = .046$, $\eta^2_p = .26$ (Figure 2, upper Panel). Regarding the SD, there is a foreperiod effect, $F(6, 84) = 4.15$, $p = .001$, $\eta^2_p = .23$, and a significant linear decrease as a function of the foreperiod length, $F(1, 14) = 16.25$, $p = .001$. A pair wise comparison test adjusted with the Bonferroni procedure revealed that only the 300 vs. 1800 ms comparison led to a significant difference ($p = .024$). The Instructions effect was not significant.

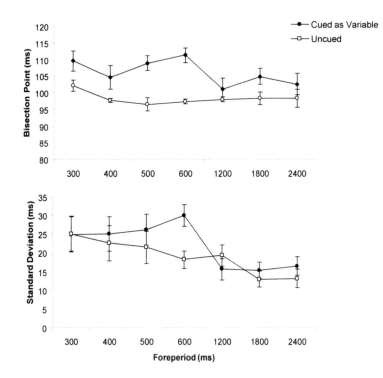

Fig. 2. Mean bisection point (upper panel) and mean standard deviation (lower panel) (± standard error of the mean) (+ standard error of the mean) as a function of the foreperiod length, in the constant foreperiod group

3.3 Comparison of Variable and Constant Groups

A 2 x 2 ANOVA on the between-subjects factors (Foreperiod Mixing Mode and Instructions) was conducted on the mean BP and mean SD. In both cases, no main effect was significant.

The Instructions X Mixing mode interaction was significant for the BP, $F(1,32) = 4.84$, $p = .036$, $\eta^2_p = .15$ (Figure 3), but not for SD.

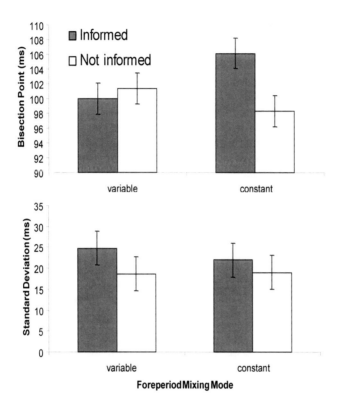

Fig. 3. Mean bisection point (upper panel) and mean standard deviation (lower panel) (± standard error of the mean) (± standard error of the mean) as a function of the instructions and the foreperiod mixing mode

4 Discussion

The purpose of the experiment conducted in this study was to test the "direct- impact hypothesis." This was done by trying to influence perceived durations of brief target intervals by manipulating foreperiods' characteristics and level of TU during foreperiods, before the onset of target intervals. Thus, we should first check whether these manipulations produced the expected outcomes.

The variable foreperiod effect on temporal discrimination reported by Grondin and Rammsayer [14] and Bendixen, Grimm, and Schröger [21] has been replicated here.

In the variable foreperiod paradigm, longer foreperiods resulted in longer perceived duration, but there was no such effect when foreperiods were held constant within a session.

Our results support the main predictions regarding temporal uncertainty and attentional limits. Firstly, reducing temporal uncertainty regarding the foreperiod by increasing its length led to longer perceived duration of brief target intervals, which followed foreperiods, and, as expected, this was true in the variable condition only. Moreover, in the constant group, generating temporal uncertainty via instructions influenced the perceived duration of target intervals. False expectations about the foreperiod's variability in this condition resulted in shorter perceived duration.

As regards SD, the results did not reveal a pattern comparable to the one observed for perceived duration. Temporal sensitivity increased with longer foreperiods in the long range condition only. Although perceived duration was affected by the foreperiod in the short range condition, there was no difference for temporal sensitivity between the 300, 400, 500, and 600 ms foreperiods. As in Grondin and Rammsayer [14], the effects observed across the different experimental conditions were more consistent for perceived duration than for temporal sensitivity. It should be noted, however, that the pattern of results obtained here regarding discrimination performance and foreperiod's duration might be domain specific and therefore should be further tested in different domains (see [12]). It should be noted that the notion of a foreperiod, as used in the present study, is related to the inter-trial interval and thus may involve a confounding with time pressure. A short foreperiod means not only high temporal uncertainty in variable foreperiod conditions, but also less time to recover from one trial and prepare for the forthcoming one. This confounding should be eliminated in future research using the current paradigm.

4.1 The Attentional-Gate Model and Temporal Uncertainty

Temporal uncertainty refers to the level of unpredictability of a temporal signal [2], and this uncertainty has a direct impact on timing performance [23-24]. Indeed, with high temporal uncertainty, more attention is required to process temporal information efficiently. In the present experiment, two manipulations were intended to affect temporal uncertainty: foreperiod length (and variability) and instructions given to the participants.

The effect of the first manipulation can be accounted for by the temporal uncertainty notion within the frame of the AGM [24]. TU has a direct impact on attention allocation policies, with greater TU resulting in a greater amount of attentional resources being allocated to time. Introducing variability in the foreperiod creates uncertainty about its duration. With high levels of TU about the foreperiod, more attentional resources are allocated to process it, and fewer resources are thus available to process brief target intervals, which immediately follow foreperiods. As foreperiod length increases, the probability of occurrence of the interval's onset increases, thereby reducing uncertainty about the time remaining in the foreperiod. In other words, with long foreperiods, more attention is available for timing the target interval. According to the attentional-gate model, time signals from an emitting pacemaker are filtered through a gate, and the gate's degree of opening is a function of attention. More attention leads to a wider gate opening and, consequently, to a greater accumulation of temporal information. In brief, reducing TU during the foreperiod allows more attention to be allocated to the target interval, produces a wider opening of the attentional gate, and leads to more accumulation of temporal information. The final result of this cascade is greater perceived duration and greater temporal sensitivity. The current interpretation is further supported by findings, which demonstrated the lengthening effect of allocating more attention on perceived durations of brief intervals (e.g., [25-26]). Similarly, Enns, Brehaut and Shore [27] reported that brief flashes in attended locations were perceived to last longer than the same flashes in unattended locations.

Regarding the instructions given to participants, it was anticipated that they would induce a form of uncertainty based on expectations rather than on the experience gained from previous trials. The results with the variable group suggest that temporal variability was easily detected with experience and, consequently, that instructions had no additional impact. Therefore, when foreperiods were variable, there was no difference between groups based on the instructions they received. However, a significant instruction-dependent difference was observed when foreperiods were held constant within a session. In this case, expecting foreperiod variability, when there was no such variability, led to shorter perceived duration.

We propose the following explanation to account for the effects of instructions and foreperiod length on perceived duration. The basic assumption is that one always attends to the time dimension of any stimulus [28]. When one is instructed that foreperiods are going to be constant or variable, one will test the foreperiods first in order to verify whether the instructions are correct or not. When it is not only the instructions that are "variable" but the foreperiods as well, it takes only a few trials to confirm this consistency; temporal uncertainty then increases and attentional resources are allocated to timing, up to a limit imposed by the length of the foreperiod. When the foreperiod is constant, one has to keep testing the hypothesis suggested by the instructions. This means allocating attentional resources to the foreperiod on a constant basis, which makes it impossible to allocate all attentional resources to timing later on. Therefore, timing is performed using fewer resources and this leads to shorter perceived durations due to a reduced opening of the attentional-gate. When instructions are "constant" and foreperiods variable, one trial might be enough to conclude that the foreperiods are actually variable. In this case, no more testing is needed and temporal uncertainty is created, as in the previous scenario. Finally, when foreperiods are constant and consistent with the instructions, the hypothesis is confirmed after a while and no more testing is needed; in other words, no more attentional resources are allocated for testing the foreperiods' duration and no temporal uncertainty is created.

The previous explanation predicts that shortening will occur only when participants are not informed about the variability of the foreperiod, and foreperiods are variable because the variable-variable condition does not require that resources be allocated for further testing. In the constant-variable condition, variability wins out because there is no need for further testing; there is also no need for further testing in the case of constant-constant sessions. However, in the variable-constant condition, it is impossible to confirm the hypothesis since foreperiod variability might be induced at any point in the session; as a result, participants have to test the hypothesis throughout the session, which places a constant demand on resources.

This study provides additional evidence of the critical role of attention in prospective timing. It highlights the impact of temporal uncertainty on attentional resources allocation by showing that it can be induced by random foreperiod duration, but only up to a given duration, due to the limits of attention resources. It also illustrates the role of temporal expectations, which are apparently tested against the actual perceptual input, a testing that is demanding in terms of resources and, thus, has an impact on the amount of resources left for the timing process itself, which comes after the foreperiod interval. Therefore, temporal expectations should be taken into account while designing and interpreting timing experiments. Following this study, a question that remains open for further exploration is why temporal sensitivity is not affected by TU.

5 Summary and Conclusions

The main purpose of the present study was to test the "direct-impact" hypothesis regarding the nature of the impact attention has on the internal clock in prospective timing. As discussed earlier, the findings obtained in the study clearly demonstrated that perceived durations of brief target intervals were affected by manipulating the characteristics of foreperiods before the onset of target intervals. Since no attentional distractions of any sort existed during target intervals it is plausible to assume that what affected perceived durations was the amount of attentional resources available for timing at the onset of a target interval. Target intervals were brief, and therefore available attentional resources were those available for timing at the end of the preceding foreperiod. The available resources affected timing via the attentional-gate, which is a central part of the internal clock. This argument is supported by the compatibility between the length of obtained perceived durations and predictions based on the AGM, in the different experimental conditions. Overall, these findings indicate that attention has a direct impact on the internal clock in prospective timing. While the findings are well explained by the AGM model it seems that the BICM model can also provide an explanation for them, by using a more general attentional theory within the framework of a cognitive architecture (see [29]). Another possibility that should be considered is that temporal uncertainty might increase the probability of a reset event due to distractions during a timing task. Further research is needed in order to enable an accurate definition of the internal clock and its components as well as the nature of its interaction with attention in prospective timing tasks.

Acknowledgments. This research was made possible by a Scholarship awarded to PLG by the Natural Sciences and Engineering Council of Canada (NSERC) and a research grant awarded to SG by NSERC.

References

1. Tobin, S., Bisson, N., Grondin, S.: An ecological approach to prospective and retrospective timing of long durations: A study involving gamers. PLoS One 5(2), e9271 (2010)
2. Zakay, D.: Gating or switching? Gating is a better model of prospective timing. Behavioural Processes 50, 1–7 (2000)
3. Zakay, D.: Attention et jugement temporel/Attention and Duration Judgment. Psychologie Française 50, 65–79 (2005)

4. Zakay, D., Block, R.A.: The distinction between prospective and retrospective duration judgments: An executive-control functions' perspective. Acta Neurobiologiae Experimentalis 64, 319–332 (2004)
5. Block, R.A.: Models of psychological time. In: Block, R.A. (ed.) Cognitive Models of Psychological Time, pp. 1–35. Erlbaum, Hillsdale (1990)
6. Grondin, S.: Timing and time perception: A review of recent behavioural and neuroscience findings and theoretical directions. Attention, Perception, & Psychophysics 72, 561–582 (2010)
7. Brown, S.W.: Attentional resources in Timing: Interference effects in concurrent temporal and nontemporal working memory tasks. Perception & Psychophysics 59, 1118–1140 (1997)
8. Brown, S.W., Stubbs, D.A., West, A.N.: Attention, multiple timing, and psychophysical scaling of temporal judgements. In: Macar, F., Pouthas, V., Friedman, W. (eds.) Time, Action, Cognition: Towards Bridging the Gap, pp. 129–140. Kluwer, Dordrecht (1992)
9. Grondin, S., Macar, F.: Dividing attention between temporal and nontemporal tasks: A performance operating characteristic—POC—analysis. In: Macar, F., Pouthas, V., Friedman, W. (eds.) Time, Action, Cognition: Towards Bridging the Gap, pp. 119–128. Kluwer, Dordrecht (1992)
10. Macar, F., Grondin, S., Casini, L.: Controlled attention sharing influences time estimation. Memory & Cognition 22, 673–686 (1994)
11. Zakay, D., Block, R.A.: Temporal cognition. Current Directions in Psychological Science 6, 12–16 (1994)
12. Zakay, D.: Time estimation methods: Do they influence prospective duration estimates. Perception 22, 91–101 (1993)
13. Taatgen, N.A., Van Rijin, H., Anderson, J.: An integrated theory of prospective time interval estimation: The role of cognition, attention and learning. Psychological Review 114, 577–598 (2007)
14. Grondin, S., Rammsayer, T.H.: Attention preparation and duration discrimination. The Quarterly Journal of Experimental Psychology 56A, 731–765 (2003)
15. Los, S.A., Van Den Heuvel, C.E.: Intentional and unintentional contributions to nonspecific preparation during reaction time foreperiods. Journal of Experimental Psychology: Human Perception and Performance 27, 370–386 (2001)
16. Niemi, P., Näätänen, R.: Foreperiod and simple reaction time. Psychological Bulletin 89, 133–162 (1981)
17. Zakay, D.: On prospective time estimation, temporal relevance and temporal uncertainty. In: Macar, F., Pouthas, V., Friedman, W. (eds.) Time, Action and Cognition, pp. 109–118. Kluwer, Dordrecht (1992)
18. Grondin, S., Meilleur-Wells, G., Lachance, R.: When to start explicit counting in time-intervals discrimination task: A critical point in the timing process of humans. Journal of Experimental Psychology: Human Perception and Performance 25, 993–1004 (1999)
19. Killeen, P.R., Weiss, N.A.: Optimal timing and the Weber function. Psychological Review 94, 455–468 (1987)
20. Grondin, S.: Judgments of the duration of visually marked empty time intervals; Linking perceived duration and sensitivity. Perception & Psychophysics 60, 319–330 (1998)
21. Bendixen, A., Grimm, S., Schröger, E.: Human auditory event-related potentials predict duration judgments. Neuroscience Letters 383, 284–288 (2005)
22. Bausenhart, K.M., Rolke, B., Ulrich, R.: Temporal preparation improves temporal resolution: Evidence from constant foreperiods. Attention, Perception and Psychophysics 79, 1504–1514 (2008)

23. Block, R.A., Hancock, P.A., Zakay, D.: How cognitive load affects duration judgments: A meta analytic review. Acta Psychologica 134, 330–343 (2010)
24. Zakay, D., Block, R.A.: The role of attention in time estimation processes. In: Pastore, M.A., Artieda, J. (eds.) Time, Internal Clocks and Movement, pp. 143–164. Elsevier, Amsterdam (1996)
25. Barnes, R., Jones, M.R.: Expectancy, attention and time. Cognitive Psychology 41, 254–311 (2000)
26. Correa, A., Sanabria, D., Spence, C., Tudela, P., Lupianez, J.: Selective temporal attention enhances the temporal resolution of visual perception: Evidence from a temporal order judgment task. Brain Research 1070, 202–205 (2006)
27. Enns, J.T., Buehaut, J.C., Shore, D.I.: The duration of a brief event in the mind's eye. The Journal of General Psychology 126, 355–372 (1999)
28. Nobre, A.C., Correa, A., Coull, J.T.: The hazards of time. Current Opinion in Neurobiology 17, 465–470 (2007)
29. Taatgen, N.A., Van Rijin, H., Anderson, J.: Time perception: beyond single interval estimation. In: Proceedings of the Sixth International Conference on Cognitive Modeling, pp. 296–301. Erlbaum, Mahwah (2004)

Child and Time

Sylvie Droit-Volet

Université Blaise Pascal, Laboratoire de Psychologie Sociale & Cognitive, CNRS
(UMR 6024), 34 Avenue Carnot, 63000 Clermont-Ferrand, France
Sylvie.droit-volet@univ-bpclermont.fr

Abstract. During the decades following Piaget's work, it has been believed that correct judgments of durations require sophisticated reasoning abilities that emerge at about 8 years of age. However, a number of researchers have demonstrated that young children's poor judgments in classical Piagetian tasks are not due to their inability to judge time correctly, but rather to their limited attentional capacities. Recent research has therefore concentrated on further investigating the development of abilities to discriminate durations in young children on the basis of the temporal tasks initially used with animals within the framework of the internal clock theories. This manuscript reviews and discusses the results of these studies.

Keywords: Child, Time Perception, Timing, Attention.

1 Introduction

> *"What is real time unless it is time which has been or could be experienced."*
> ***Bergson (1968)***

What is time really? Time is what my watch shows me, most men and women would reply. And what does this watch show you? The movements of a hand about an axis. So time is movement! And do humans confuse time with movement, then? But time cannot be reduced to the way we measure it. The distance traveled that we read from our watches is only one representation of time among others invented by human beings in order to be able to measure its passing with precision. So what, truly, is time? What, after all, does it matter what time is, what does it matter whether it exists or not? If we experience it then, psychologically, it exists. As Bergson [1] says, "time is purely and simply an item of data relating to our experience… and we want to hold onto that experience".

By adopting this postulate, psychologists have left the debate about the true nature of time to philosophers and physicists so that they, for their part, are free to try to study its psychological reality through the feelings and behaviors of human beings in the face of time. As a result, they have been led to ask a number of questions. If time exists at the psychological level, why should children, who have no sophisticated representation of time, not also be capable of precise temporal estimates? Is there a "primitive sense" of time? What neurological mechanism is responsible for this sense of time? If such an internal mechanism for measuring time exists, then why and under

A. Vatakis et al. (Eds.): Time and Time Perception 2010, LNAI 6789, pp. 151–172, 2011.

what conditions do young children find it difficult to estimate time correctly? How can we explain the illusions to which they are frequently subjected in which time stretches and contracts as the context changes? Are they due to a specific problem in measuring time or to a more general cognitive problem? Over the last twenty years, this series of questions has reawakened considerable interest in the study of time. Nevertheless, due to methodological reasons, which are fairly easy to understand, studies of time estimation behaviors in children are still quite rare. We shall, nevertheless, attempt to summarize the most recent works conducted in this field by focusing on the behaviors involved in the estimation of durations in tasks similar to those employed in animals. As the young philosopher, Jean-Marie Guyau [2], said in his essay on the genesis of the idea of time, it is in the expectation and frustration of the child who cries as he stretches out his arms to his nurse that the idea of the future, the idea of time, is born.

2   The Pioneering Studies of Time Estimation Capabilities in Children

The work conducted by Jean Piaget has greatly influenced studies of child psychology in a number of different fields. In his constructivist theory of children's intellectual development, Piaget described how young children explore their environment by means of their senses and actions. The primitive understanding of the physical world, therefore, appears to be grounded in sensorimotor knowledge. It is only at the transitional period of 7-8 years, when children accede to the concrete operational stage, that they think logically and manipulate the symbolic representations, which enable them to solve complex problems. As far as duration is concerned, Piaget's theory consequently considers that young children are unable to evaluate time accurately since their time judgments are derived from their feelings concerning their internal states or from their sensorimotor experience. For example, children estimate durations as a function of the quantity of work accomplished or effort produced. Children, who were asked to transfer lead disks or wooden disks to a wooden box for a given period, thought that the task of transferring the lead weights took longer than that of transferring the wood because it required greater effort [3]. Numerous studies which have varied the nature of the non-temporal information (e.g., number of changes, speed, light intensity) presented during the period to be estimated have confirmed that young children initially estimate durations as a function of their content [4-8]. However, children's ability to estimate time accurately emerges earlier than these pioneering psychologists thought. In most cases, the estimation of time does not require logical reasoning about time. As we will see below, infants with only limited conceptual capacities are able to estimate time. Finally, the fact that children distort time in certain conditions does not mean that they do not possess a basic time discrimination capability. The question is to determine the contexts in which children's time judgments are or are not accurate and why?

When only a small number of cues are used or the duration of events is familiar, children's temporal estimations improve [9-12]. This finding led Fraisse [13] to suggest that children's time estimates may be based only on a single cue. In other words, if children are to process time correctly, their attention must not be distracted by non-temporal information. Their attention must be to focus on time. They must be aware of the relevance of time. Pouthas, Droit, Jacquet, and Wearden [14] showed that children younger than 10 years of age, although with some exceptions at 7 years, did not spontaneously think about the temporal features of a task. That is why the temporal instructions given by adults play such an important role in the establishment of temporal behavior in young children. In a temporal operant conditioning situation, in which the responses were reinforced after a fixed interval of 30 s (FI), Droit, Pouthas, and Jacquet [15] showed that 60% of children aged from 4 to 6 years exhibited erratic response patterns when given minimal instructions, but succeeded in regulating their time-related behavior as soon as they were given temporal instructions.

When temporal behaviors are governed by verbal rules or when participants have to be aware of time in order to process it accurately, we talk about the explicit processing of time. A fundamental distinction must be drawn between the implicit and the explicit processing of time [16]. The former is involved in the processing of short durations, in motor timing as in the case of finger tapping, in time conditioning and in implicit temporal learning involving multiple trials and a long series of sessions such as those used in studies in animals. The latter is mainly involved in the processing of longer durations, in the judgment of new and unpredictable events, and in temporal tasks involving smaller numbers of trials. Precisely, most of the experiments conducted in human adults have used instructions and a small number of trials. The presented events are often new and the participants are not exposed to any repeated experience of their durations. In addition, as noted by Zakay [17], in real life, time is rarely relevant for an optimal adaptation to the environment. Finally, humans frequently make explicit judgments, with the result that accurate time judgments may well be the exception rather than the rule. Moreover, human adults use counting strategies because they are well aware of the inaccurate nature of their temporal estimates in most situations. To summarize, because the majority of the employed experimental conditions have used an explicit judgment of time, human subjects, and children in particular, have often been found not to judge time accurately. Their time estimations are distorted and they judge durations to be shorter or longer than they actually are. Consequently, time judgments in humans cannot be reduced to the reading of a sort of internal clock. As suggested by grounded time theory [18,19], time judgments are also derived from affective states and sensorimotor experiences. This is why, in our description of the development of time-related knowledge, we talk in terms of "multiple time" in the case of younger children and "unique time" when referring to children older than 7 years [20-22]. This "multiple time" takes the form of items of temporal knowledge specific to each event duration experienced in a particular context. In contrast, "unique time" reflects an awareness of a homogeneous time, which is independent of context, i.e., the concept of time referred to by Fraisse [13]. However this may be, after the work of the early psychologists had shown that children's temporal judgments are context-dependent, the main aim of the next generation of psychologists was to find empirical data demonstrating children's ability to estimate time accurately.

3   Temporal Conditioning

In order to find empirical demonstrations of children's ability to estimate time accurately, psychologists have employed the same temporal tasks that have been successfully used to investigate timing in animals. First of all, they adapted temporal conditioning paradigms with arbitrary temporal intervals, which do not correspond to any biological rhythm, for use in children. The most frequently cited study in this domain is the study of the classical conditioning of an autonomic reflex (pupillary dilation and constriction) conducted by Brackill and Fizgerald [23] in 1 month old infants. In this study, a 4 s change in lighting conditions (light offset or light onset) occurred at a constant temporal interval (20 s; unconditioned stimulus, UCS) and was systematically found to produce a pupillary reflex (UCR). During the test trials when the UCS was not applied, the infants' pupils continued to contract or dilate. This clearly demonstrates that the infants had perceived the passage of time during the interval. The evidence relating to the temporal conditioning of heart rate responses and their deceleration in anticipation of the UCS is somewhat weaker [24]. However, Colombo and Richman [25] recorded the heart rates of 4-month-old infants during the repetitive presentation of a 2 s stimulus at an interval of 3 or 5 s, and observed a deceleration in the infants' heart rates each time the stimulus was omitted. These different findings are consistent with the observations of Brannon and co-workers [26,27] who found that the brain activity of 10-month-old infants exhibited a change in negative polarity (mismatch negativity) amplitude when a temporal deviation occurred in a stream of tones produced at a regular 1500 ms interstimulus interval. For a regular or rhythm temporal structure of stimuli, if infants are able to predict the occurrence of a stimulus at a precise temporal interval, then we can conclude that they have perceived the temporal regularity of events.

Faced with these findings showing that children are able to anticipate the temporal occurrence of events, researchers have used operant conditioning procedures to attempt to examine whether young children are also able to regulate their temporal behavior. Viviane Pouthas [28-29] used a Differential Reinforcement of Low response rate (DRL) schedule, replacing the lever in the Skinner box by a large red button and the food by slides displayed on a screen. In this experimental condition, when children aged of 2 to 5 years had to delay their responses by a given period in order to see a slide, some of them succeeded in spacing their responses at a given temporal interval (DRL 10 or 15 s). However, most of them failed to withhold their responses. The fixed-interval schedule of reinforcement (FI) has been tested in an attempt to overcome this problem of behavioral inhibition in young children. In contrast to the DRL, the responses produced during the fixed temporal interval have no consequence in FI. In this condition, some of the children aged from 4 to 7 years exhibited a low or a high rate of responding, i.e., they either waited for the required temporal interval before responding or they pressed the button constantly [15,30-32]. However, as in the DRL, most of the children produced erratic patterns when they did not receive any explicit temporal instructions, even after 10 training sessions [15,32-33]. It is very regrettable that the poor performances achieved by children are not always reported in the literature given that they illustrate a behavioral reality at a given age. Indeed, within the framework of operant temporal conditioning, young children's poor performances can be explained in terms of the difficulty they experience in preventing themselves from responding rather than on the basis of a specific timing deficit. It is well known that young children have limited motor inhibition capacities [34]. Moreover, temporal regulation in children has been found to improve when they are kept busy and engaged in motor activities (collateral activities) during the waiting period [29, 35]. Droit [36] compared two schedules of temporal reinforcement, one in which

3-year-old children had to produce a given temporal interval between two button presses (DRL 5 s) and the other in which they had to keep the button pressed down for a critical duration (differential reinforcement of response duration, DRRD). In both conditions, an external clock indicated the target duration over a total of four training sessions. During the four test sessions that followed, only the children in the DRRD condition succeeded in producing accurate timing responses. In the DRRD condition, some 3-year-olds even reported that they had pressed hard on the button while they were timing their responses. The inhibition of motor responses is thus a critical factor in the emergence of temporal behaviors in children.

Finally, it is in infants that temporal performance in FI seems to be the best. Lowe, Beasty, and Bentall [37] reported examples of infants who were able to wait in an FI condition. More precisely, the response pattern they produced was similar to that observed in animals, i.e., a pause followed by a progressive increase in responses through to the end of the fixed interval. More surprising still, Darcheville, Rivière, and Wearden [38-39] observed low-rate patterns of responding in infants aged from 3 to 23 months for different FI values ranging from 10 to 80 s. The infants made long pauses that were appropriate given the duration of the fixed interval. They then touched the touch-sensitive screen to obtain reinforcement [40]. Taken overall, these results obtained in children by means of temporal conditioning procedures reveal that very young children can implicitly learn temporal intervals or event durations and adjust their temporal behavior accordingly. However, as children become older, their behavior seems to become resistant to simple control by reinforcement over time. Consequently, one of the major challenges involved in the development of time discrimination abilities is to find an experimental task that can be used both in verbal and non-verbal children, i.e., at all the levels of the ontogenetic scale.

4   Early Ability to Discriminate Time in Bisection: Weber's Law Holds!

After many attempts to use temporal conditioning procedures, simpler temporal discrimination tasks similar to those used in animals have been tested in children, namely the temporal generalization task [41-43], and the temporal bisection task [43-44]. Of these tasks, the one that has been most frequently used is probably the temporal bisection task [45]. This task was originally used in rats by Church and Deluty in 1977 [46], and was then adapted for use in human adults by Allan and Gibbon [47] and Wearden [48]. In this task, the participants are presented with two signal durations: a short (S) and a long (L). In the test phase, they are then presented with comparison durations, which are either equal to S and L or have an intermediate value between S and L. The participants must either categorize the comparison durations as short or long [47] or judge whether these durations are more similar to the short or to the long standard duration [48]. In addition, some studies have also provided feedback for the two anchor durations during the test phase [47,49,50] while others have not [51-53]. Despite these experimental variants, the psychometric functions obtained in bisection in human adults are close to those observed in animals. The proportion of comparison durations judged as more similar to L (p(long)) systematically increases with the stimulus duration value. According to Church and Deluty [46], the results obtained in bisection in rats suggest "that they have some sort of internal clock that they can read" (p. 223). Consequently, Wearden [48] concluded that humans possess an internal clock that is in many ways similar to that found in animals.

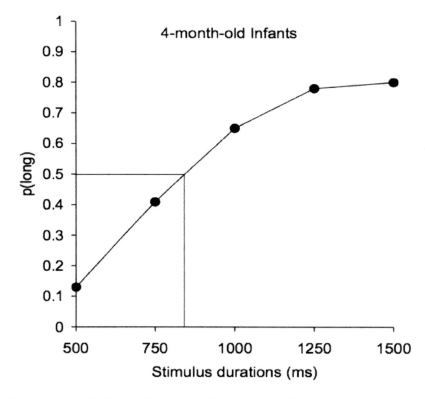

Fig. 1. Psychometric function in a temporal bisection task in 4-month-old infants. Proportion of long responses (p(long)) plotted against stimulus durations.

We recently succeeded in adapting this temporal bisection procedure for use in infants as young as 4 months old [54]. During a training phase, the infants were presented with two sounds, namely a short (0.5 s) and a long sound (1.5 s). They were then trained to look to the left after S and to the right after L (counterbalanced order), with a correct response resulting in the appearance of a picture on the side toward which the infant had looked (left or right; reinforcement). During the test phase, the infants were presented with S and L and sound durations of intermediate values (750, 1000, 1250 ms). In this phase, S and L were followed by reinforcements either immediately or after a 3 s interval. The first look to the right, to the left or elsewhere, and the time spent by the infants looking in these directions for a period of 3 s following the sound were recorded. As shown in Figure 1, in this bisection procedure, the infants exhibited orderly psychometric functions with p(long) increasing with the stimulus duration (i.e., they looked to the right for longer after L). This indicates that they were sensitive to changes in sound durations. In addition, in bisection, three indexes of temporal performance are calculated: the Bisection Point (BP), the Difference Limen (DL), and the Weber Ratio (WR). The BP is the point of subjective equality, i.e. the stimulus duration (t) that gives rise to p(long) = .50. The DL is the just noticeable difference ($t(p$(long) = .75) - $t(p$(long) = .25) /2), i.e., the smallest change in stimulus durations that is detected and produces a change in behavior.

The WR is the DL divided by the BP. Participants with a low WR exhibit a fairly high sensitivity to change in duration and produce very steep psychometric functions in bisection tasks. In contrast, participants with a high WR exhibit variable temporal discrimination capabilities. In others words, their sensitivity to time is poor, and their psychometric functions particularly flat. In our study, the infants obtained a BP of 860, a value which was closer to the geometric mean ($\sqrt{S} \times L$) (GM) than to the arithmetic mean ($S + L$ /2) (AM) of the two anchor durations (500/1500). In addition, their WR was .32, thus indicating that they could discriminate differences in durations of 275 ms. This finding is consistent with the results obtained by means of a habituation paradigm in 6-month-old infants by VanMarle and Wynn [55] and by Brannon, Suanda, and Libertus [56]. These authors showed that the infants looked longer at the same event (Sylvester the cat moving his head from right to left during a sound, in one study, and a cow puppet opening and closing its mouth in the other) when its presentation duration varied by a ratio of 1:2 regardless of the absolute value of the durations tested (i.e., 0.5 vs. 1 s, 2 vs. 4 s and 1.5 vs. 3 s).

In addition, to account for the infant data obtained in bisection tasks, we modeled their data using the mathematical models proposed by the Scalar Timing Theory [57,58], namely the Sample Known Exactly (SKE) model developed by Gibbon [59] for animals and the Difference Modified (DM) model developed by Wearden [48] for human adults. These two models use the same parameters. They differ only in the type of decision rule employed. In the DM model, this decision rule is based on differences, whereas in the SKE model it is based on ratios. The DM model responds long if $|S^*-t| > |L^*-t|$ and short if $|S^*-t| < |L^*-t|$. In contrast, the SKE model responds long if $(L^*/t) < (t/S^*)$, and vice versa. It appears that the modified SKE model fits the data observed in infants better than the DM model, while the reverse appears to be true for older children [44]. This finding is explained by a smooth age-related rightward shift in the localization of the BP from a value close to the geometric mean to a value closer to the arithmetic mean of the two anchor durations, although a BP at the GM has also been observed in older children in certain experimental conditions [60]. The BP has systematically been found to be close to the GM rather than the AM of S and L in animals [46,61-62], while, with only a few exceptions [47], it has regularly been found to be closer to the AM than the GM in human adults. The development of decision processes is thus a major factor that may explain age-related changes in the establishment of the BP [63-64]. In addition, Wearden, and Ferrara [65-66] have demonstrated that the localization of the BP is mainly determined by the ratio between the two standard durations. A small ratio (< 1:2) - when it is not easy to distinguish between S and L - shifts the BP from the AM to the GM of S and L. We can thus assume that infants find it more difficult than older children or adults to bisect durations that differ by a ratio of 1:3. Using a habitation paradigm, Brannon et al. [56] showed that 6-month-old infants were able to discriminate two durations that differed by a ratio of 1:2 ratio (1.5 vs. 3 s) but not of 2:3 (1 vs. 1.5, 2 vs. 3 s) while older infants aged 10 months succeeded in both conditions. Furthermore, in our temporal bisection model, which enables us to account for infants' bisection performances, we found it necessary to add a parameter, which corresponds to the probability of producing a random response on each trial, irrespective of the stimulus duration. In particular, this parameter explains the high proportion of long responses for the shortest comparison durations. We can therefore conclude that the clock system that is thought to be responsible for the perception of time in animals and human adults is probably functional at an early age. However, infants' ability to discriminate time is often masked by the high proportion of random responses that are produced. This is probably due to the inattentiveness of the subjects or to the experimental procedures used which, despite all the experimental ingenuity shown by researchers, rapidly become boring for young children.

Studies conducted in older children which have used a wide variety of durations, both shorter (0.2/0.8; 0.15/1.05; 0.5/1; 0.4/1.6 s) [43, 63,67-68] and longer than 1 s (1.25/2.5; 1/4; 2/8; 4/8; 4/10; 8/20, 15/30 s) [44,60,69-71], and which have primarily involved a ratio of 1:2 or 1:4, have obtained orderly psychometric functions from children in all age groups, from 3 to 10 years. At all ages, these children detect the differences in stimulus durations and the probability that they will respond long varies in consequence. This observation, however, applies to duration ratios ≥ 2:3 (Zélanti & Droit-Volet, in preparation). In the case of smaller ratios (3:3.6), 30 % and 45 % of 5-year-old children, respectively, succeeded in producing quite orderly psychometric functions with a short (0.5/0.6 s) and a long duration (4/4.8-s), while 80 % and 95 %, respectively, of children aged 8 years succeeded in these two duration conditions. In addition, according to the scalar properties of timing, which have received widespread confirmation both in animals and human adults, time estimates are accurate on average, while temporal sensitivity also remains constant as durations vary [72]. This is exactly what we have found in children of different ages [41,44,67]. Children's temporal behaviors conform perfectly to the scalar property of variance. Two methods are currently used to test this property. The first consists in calculating the WR, which is itself a sort of coefficient of variation (SD/M), and verifying whether it remains constant with different durations. The second consists in testing the superposition of the psychometric functions when plotted on the same relative scale. We found that children's WR remained constant with different durations and that their psychometric functions superimposed well both for durations longer and shorter than 1 s as shown in Figure 2. We nevertheless found a violation of the scalar property for very long durations (15/30 s) [68]. Therefore, Weber's law holds in children at different levels of the ontogenetic scale. Overall, these results confirm that there is a primitive temporal discrimination mechanism that works well in young children.

5   Age Similarities and Changes in Time Discrimination Capacities

A debate is currently underway concerning the type of mechanism involved in the processing of time. According to the internal clock models [57-58,73], the raw material for the representation of time comes from a pacemaker-like system that emits pulses. At the onset of the stimulus to be timed, an attentional switch connecting the pacemaker to the accumulator closes, thus allowing the pulses emitted by the pacemaker to flow into the accumulator. At the offset of the stimulus, the switch reopens and stops the flow of pulses. The time estimate thus depends on the number of pulses accumulated during the elapsed period: The more pulses that are accumulated, the longer the duration is judged to be. Numerous neuroscience researchers have tried to identify the neural substrates of this type of internal clock system. However, they have so far been unable to identify a simple neural mechanism dedicated to the processing of time. Brain activations during temporal tasks are always dependent on the type and complexity of the task used [74]. This has led Eagleman [75] to conclude that "the neural basis of time perception remains shrouded in mystery". However, current hypotheses consider that two main brain structures play a critical role in time perception: (1) the prefrontal cortex and (2) the striatum, or more precisely the caudate and putamen of the dorsal striatum via dopaminergic modulations [76]. In the striatal beat frequency model, Matell and Meck [77-78] suggested that the neural inputs that constitute the time code arise from the oscillatory activity of large areas of the cortex. At the onset and the offset of the stimulus to be timed, the oscillatory activity of a subset of these cortical neurons is synchronized. The striatal spiny neurons that receive inputs from the cortex detect patterns of oscillatory firing (or beats) that match other patterns stored in memory. They then fire to indicate that the interval has

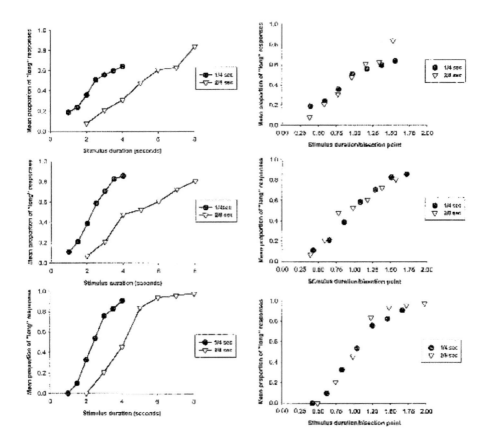

Fig. 2. Superimposition of psychometric functions for different duration ranges (1/4 and 2/8s) in 3-, 5-, and 8 year-old children

elapsed. In other words, the striatum of the basal ganglia plays a central role in timing by reading the temporal code provided by oscillating neurons in the cortex. Other recent models have nevertheless completely abandoned the idea that there is a specialized brain system for representing time. They argue that the neural circuits are inherently capable of processing temporal information as a result of state-dependent changes in network dynamics [79,80]. Time is therefore an emergent property of changes in neural firing patterns. However, these models only account for the automatic processing of short durations of tens or hundreds of milliseconds (< 500 ms). Whatever the case, the time courses of maturation of the prefrontal cortex and the striatum are totally different. Subcortical structures that are phylogenetically older mature earlier. The structures that constitute the basal ganglia (e.g., caudate, putamen, substantia nigra) are effectively the first of the telencephalic structures to begin to myelinate. In contrast, the prefrontal cortex matures slowly [81]. More precisely, the frontal cortex matures relatively quickly from birth through to 2 years of age before reaching a stable volume at the age of 5 years old. However, it then continues to develop gradually until the end of adolescence, a period characterized by neural elimination and reorganization and an increase in white matter [82,83]. Finally, the type of temporal judgment required and the underlying processes may partly explain similarities and differences in temporal performance as a function of children's age.

The basal ganglia influence time perception via the dopaminergic (DA) system. Many pharmacological studies have shown that the administration of a drug that increases the level of DA in the brain (metamphetamine, cocaine) speeds up subjective time, thus producing a lengthening of the stimulus duration to be encoded [61-62,84-86]. In response to negative emotions such as fear, when the organism detects a danger, there is also a release of DA in the brain. According to Kienast et al. [87], the feeling of stress is directly dependent on the DA storage capacity in the brain. Numerous studies on the perception of time have shown that time is overestimated in response to a threatening stimulus (e.g., angry faces, threatening events) compared to a neutral stimulus [88-92]. More interestingly here, the lengthening effect produced by highly arousing emotional stimuli (angry faces) has been observed in children of different ages (from 3 to 8 years) in the absence of any developmental effect [93]. These results have since been replicated in children aged 5 and 8 years as well as in adults, although the magnitude of the emotional effect has been found to be larger in the youngest children (Fig. 3) [94-95]. One of the stimuli that are renowned for speeding up the internal clock is the presentation of periodic events (repetitive clicks, flickers) [96]. As recently concluded by Wearden et al. [97], the click train effect on the perception of time due to a speeding up of the internal clock is one of the more robust effects to be observed in time psychology. In this condition, in exactly the same way as in adults, children's psychometric functions in bisection shift toward the left in flicker compared to no-flicker conditions [98]. In other words, in the same way as in adults, children overestimate time in the presence of flickers. Between 3 and 8 years, there is no age-related difference in the flicker effect on time perception. Furthermore, the magnitude of this leftward shift in bisection functions does not appear to be constant but instead proportional to the duration values. This observation is more compatible with a multiplicative effect due to a speeding up of the internal clock than with an additive effect related to an earlier closure of the attentional switch. Although the mechanisms underlying the production of temporal overestimation in the presence of click trains or flickers are far from clear [99-100], when considered in combination with those found in response to highly arousing emotions, these findings illustrate that the mechanisms underlying the perception of time conform to the scalar property of time at all ages. Weber's law holds under all circumstances.

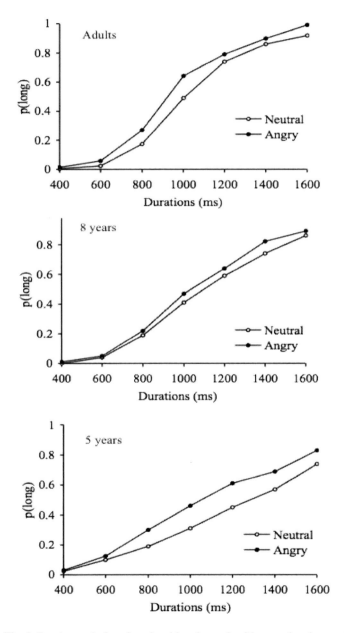

Fig. 3. Psychometric functions in a bisection task with neutral and angry faces

Beyond phylogenetic and ontogenetic similarities in the perception of time, there are also developmental changes in the ability to discriminate time. All the bisection studies cited above have revealed that children's sensitivity to time improves with age. As Figure 4 illustrates, when the durations are easy to discriminate (ratio of 1:4 or 1:2), and whatever the absolute value of the durations shorter than 1 s, between 1 and 4 s, or longer than 4 seconds, the slope of the psychometric functions in bisection always increases with age. Children aged 3 and 5 years systematically produce flatter psychometric functions than older children. At the age of 8 years, the slope of the bisection curve becomes close to that produced by adults, although some age differences subsist and especially for very long durations (> 8 s) [68]. A calculation of the mean WR values obtained in our bisection studies reveals that the mean WR values obtained were .17 for adults, .21 for 8-year-olds and .32 for 5-year-olds, with the greatest inter-study variations in these values being observed for the youngest children and the longest durations (> 4 s) (see Table 1). The question, which we now have to answer, is why young children have a lower sensitivity to time. To try to find the sources of this developmental change in time sensitivity, we have modeled children's bisection data on the basis of parameters taken from bisection models used in animals and human adults. We have also experimentally manipulated variables, which specifically affect memory, attention and decisional processes, and, more recently, we have evaluated the differences in cognitive abilities by means of neuropsychological tests. Taken together, our findings demonstrate that the development of attention-related cognitive capacities as well as that of the executive functions, which depend upon the slow maturation of the frontal cortex, explain in great part developmental changes in the ability to discriminate time.

Table 1. Bisection Point (BP), Difference Limen (DL) and Weber Ratio (WR) for the children aged 5 years old and 8 years old, as well as in the adults for durations that differ by a ½ ratio in different duration ranges [68]

	PB		DL		WR	
	M	SD	M	SD	M	SD
5 years						
0.5/1-s	0.88	0.32	0.34	0.23	0.39	0.20
1.25/2.5-s	1.76	0.30	0.52	0.14	0.32	0.17
4/8-s	5.16	1.40	1.86	0.52	0.42	0.32
15/30-s	21.74	5.88	8.34	3.47	0.44	0.19
9 years						
0.5/1-s	0.81	0.08	0.17	0.05	0.21	0.06
1.25/2.5-s	1.80	0.19	0.37	0.09	0.21	0.07
4/8-s	5.63	0.89	1.40	0.33	0.26	0.10
15/30-s	19.92	5.39	6.97	2.83	0.40	0.27
Adults						
0.5/1-s	0.77	0.06	0.13	0.02	0.17	0.02
1.25/2.5 s	1.82	0.14	0.32	0.05	0.18	0.03
4/8-s	5.73	0.44	0.97	0.18	0.17	0.03
15/30-s	21.5	2.74	5.02	1.40	0.23	0.06

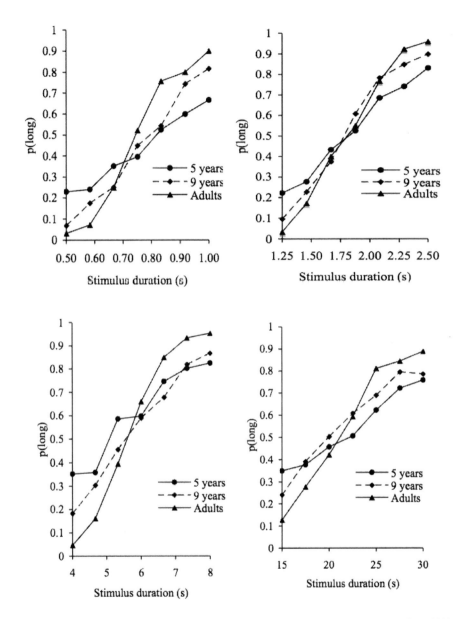

Fig. 4. Psychometric functions in different duration ranges in children and adults (from [68])

6 The Cognitive Sources of Children's Lesser Ability to Discriminate Time

As suggested above, several models have been proposed to account for bisection performance in animals and humans based on the scalar timing theory [48,50,57]. These models have generally provided good fits for the bisection data on the basis of two parameters. The first parameter, c, is the coefficient of variability of the representation of standard durations (S and L) in memory. This parameter is a kind of sensitivity parameter that controls the slope of the psychometric function in bisection. When the memory representation of S and L is fuzzier, the psychometric function becomes flatter. The second parameter, β, is related to the localization of the BP. This is a sort of decisional bias toward responding long when faced with ambiguous cases, i.e. when the participants cannot tell whether the comparison value is closer to S or L. In these models, the main source of temporal variance lies in the memory processes rather than in the perception of time, which is thought to be accurate. The models that have used these two parameters also fit well with children's data in bisection tasks, even though it has often been necessary to include an additional parameter relating to random responses [44,67]. This therefore suggests that children's lower sensitivity to time might be due to their fuzzier memory representations of the standard durations. However, in their model, McCormack et al. [43] added another parameter, q, which represents noise in the perceived duration. In accordance with Weber's Law, the proportion of noise in the perceived duration should be proportional to the length of the duration. Children would therefore have a "noisier" perception of time.

Finally, the question that has to be answered is what is it that leads to greater variability in young children's memory representations of standard durations. One initial hypothesis consists in the idea that there may be a specific problem relating to the memory retention of standard durations. Rattat and Droit-Volet [71,101-102] showed that the bisection task is a temporal task involving explicit memory, and that young children remember durations better in an implicit than in an explicit memory task. In bisection, when a long retention delay (15 min, 24 h) or an interference task has been introduced between the phase in which the standard durations are presented and the test phase, psychometric functions have been seen to become flattened in 5-year-olds and their time sensitivity poorer. Under the same conditions, 8-year-olds and the adults change their strategies. They no longer refer to the representation of standard durations in memory but instead partition the comparison durations into short and long. However, using a temporal bisection task, Droit-Volet and Rattat [70] showed that developmental differences in time sensitivity subsist even in a partition task when no standard durations are stored in reference memory. A second hypothesis would therefore consist in supposing that the representation of standard durations in reference memory results from what has previously been encoded, i.e., during the perception of time before inclusion in reference memory. Delgado and Droit-Volet [103] tested the reference memory of standard durations in bisection by introducing variance in the samples of standard durations and showed that the value of the memory parameter, c, used in the bisection model depends directly on the initial noise introduced during the encoding of temporal samples.

Instead of pointing to a major problem of retention in the memory for durations, developmental studies suggest that the difficulties young children experience in focusing and sustaining their attention on the continuous flow of time accounts for the variability of their time judgments. This explains why time estimation is often impaired in children with Attention Deficit Hyperactivity Disorder (ADHD) [104-106]. Recently, Zélanti and Droit-Volet [68] used a series of neuropsychological tests to assess cognitive abilities in children. The results enabled them to point out significant correlations between temporal sensitivity (WR) and the attention/concentration index of the Children's Memory Scale (CMS) [107]. The higher the attention/concentration score, the lower the WR value, and the better sensitivity to time. The attention/concentration index of the CMS also involves working memory. According to the leading models in this domain [108-109], working memory consists of a central executive system, which manages attentional resources by directing attention toward relevant information, suppressing irrelevant information and keeping the information present in memory active. Precisely, the working memory capacity assessed in our study by means of the backward memory span test, (and, in particular, the visuospatial component) also predicted the age differences in time sensitivity for the long durations (> 1 s, and more particularly > 4 s). For short durations of less than 1 s, the short-term memory span (forward memory span) was the only reliable factor allowing us to predict age changes in bisection performance. Our findings on working memory and time in children are entirely consistent with those of recent studies that have studied temporal reproduction in adults and shown that temporal precision improves with increased working memory capacity [110- 112].

As reported above, according to scalar timing theory, the clock system consists of a pacemaker, a switch and an accumulator. When the behavioral data obtained in bisection tasks suggest the presence of an effect related to clock rate (multiplicative effect), this may be due to variations in the speed of the pacemaker or to the flickering of the switch-accumulator system [113]. In behavioral studies, it is difficult to distinguish between these two types of mechanism (pacemaker vs. accumulator/switch) because they have the same effects on temporal performance (multiplicative effect). Nevertheless, studies conducted among children suggest that the development of time sensitivity is better explained in terms of an impairment to the switch/accumulator system than the idea that the pacemaker runs more slowly in children than in adults, although both explanations are possible. More precisely, the accumulator/switch system would be less efficient in young children due to their limited attentional capacities. The accumulator/switch system is indeed thought to depend on both mental load in working memory and attentional demands [114]. While the passage of time is being tracked, it would be more difficult for the switch to stay closed in children than in adults. In other words, the "child switch" would be more variable and would flicker more often than the "adult switch".

It does indeed appear that the accurate processing of time involves all the dimensions of attention: oriented attention, divided attention, selective attention and sustained attention. At the risk of losing some of the temporal information, attention must be prepared so that the subject can capture the beginning of the forthcoming stimulus. Droit-Volet [115] showed that a signal warning participants of the onset of a visual stimulus which they had to time produced a temporal overestimation of this stimulus because the attentional switch have closed earlier. More importantly, however, this warning signal also reduced the variability in time discrimination in the younger children. The warning signal thus reduced the children's variability in the attentional capture of the onset of a visual stimulus to be timed. Furthermore, if individuals are to be able to process time correctly, they must have sufficient attentional resources available to them. As a number of studies have demonstrated, when attention is divided between a temporal and a non-temporal task, time is judged shorter [116,117,118]. Using a dual-task paradigm, it has been demonstrated that 5-year-olds, who possess a limited pool of attentional resources, produce greater temporal underestimations than older children [119-122]. The development of selective attention capacities also allows children to resist attentional distractors and focus their attention on the processing of time. The introduction of attentional distractors in a temporal bisection task has thus been found to impair children's time discrimination to a greater extent at the age of 5 years than at the age of 8 [121]. In sum, children's distractibility and their deficit in inhibitory control prevent them from correctly apprehending the continuous flow of time.

The attentional control deficit exhibited by young children explains why they are more subject than adults to temporal illusions. Two temporal illusions have been widely investigated in time psychology: (1) the visual-auditory illusion, and (2) the empty-filled illusion. The visual-auditory illusion consists in the fact that the duration of an auditory signal is judged longer than that of a visual signal presented for the same period. The empty-filled illusion is reflected in the fact that an empty duration (temporal interval between two short signals) is judged to be shorter than a filled duration (duration of a signal). Developmental studies of these visual-auditory temporal illusions have shown that theses illusions are greater in 5-year-olds than in 8-year-olds or adults [67,123-124]. Similarly, the scale of the empty-filled illusion has been shown to decrease as children develop [125]. A greater level of attention is indeed involved in the control of the switch-accumulator system during the processing of visual rather than auditory signals as well as that of empty compared to filled durations. In the case of visual signals, young children have to keep their attention focused on the computer screen, whereas in the case of empty durations, they must not become distracted during the temporal interval, i.e., they must wait without doing anything.

In addition to attentional processes, as previously suggested, the development of decision processes may also modify time judgments in children [63-64]. However few studies have focused on the decisional strategies and the "metacognition of time". We do not know the precise role of the development of knowledge and beliefs concerning time in our own time judgments. This is a new avenue of research that we have decided to investigate. In our studies, we have nevertheless already shown that children have a lesser feeling of knowing (whether the duration is long or short) and that this affects the localization of their PB in bisection. According to the mathematic models of bisection, children's feeling of knowing should be related to the variability of their representation of time in memory [41]. What, ultimately, is the cause of this lesser feeling of knowing concerning time discrimination: children's awareness of their poor temporal abilities or a general problem of metacognition? Finally, developmental studies reveal that the explicit judgments of time are highly dependent upon contexts, because the flow of time must always remain in the attentional focus or awareness. It therefore seems to be very important to investigate in greater detail the differences between implicit and explicit time judgments in children.

Acknowledgments. This work was supported by a grant from the ANR (Agence Nationale de la Recherche) N° ANR-07-NEURO-048-02, France. It was also supported by the European COST Action TD0904 (TIMELY).

References

1. Bergson, H.: Durée et simultanéité. Presses Universitaires de France (1968)
2. Guyau, J.-M.: La genèse de l'idée de temps. Paris, F. Alcan (1890)
3. Piaget, P.: Le développement de la notion de temps chez l'enfant. Paris, P.U.F. (1946)
4. Zuili, N., Fraisse, P.: L'estimation du temps en fonction de la quantité de movements effective dans une tâche. Etude génétique. L'Année Psychologique 66, 383–396 (1966)
5. Fraisse, P., Vautrey, P.: La perception de l'espace, de la vitesse et du temps chez l'enfant de 5 ans. Enfance 5, 102–119 (1952)
6. Levin, I.: The development of time concepts in young children: Reasoning about duration. Child Development 48, 435–444 (1977)
7. Levin, I.: Interference of time-related and unrelated cues with duration comparison of young children: Analysis of Piaget's formulation of the relation of time and speed. Child Development 50, 469–477 (1979)
8. Arlin, M.: The effect of physical work, mental work, and quantity on children's time perception. Perception & Psychophysics 45(3), 209–214 (1989)
9. Berndt, T.J., Wood, D.J.: The development of time concepts through conflict based on a primitive capacity. Child Development 45, 825–828 (1974)
10. Richie, D.M., Bickard, M.H.: The ability to perceive duration: Its relations to the development of the logical concept of time. Developmental Psychology 24, 318–323 (1988)
11. Levin, I.: Principles underlying time measurement: The development of children's constraints on counting time. In: Levin, I., Zakay, D. (eds.) Time and Human Cognition: A Life-span Perspective?, pp. 145–181. Elsevier, Amsterdam (1989)
12. Friedman, W.: Children's representations to the daily activities. Child Development 61, 1399–1412 (1990)
13. Fraisse, P.: Psychologie du temps. Presses Universitaires de France, Paris (1967)
14. Pouthas, V., Droit, S., Jacquet, A.Y., Wearden, J.: Differentiation of response duration in children of different ages: Developmental changes in relation between verbal and non verbal behavior? J. Exp. Analysis of Behavior 53, 21–31 (1990)
15. Droit, S., Pouthas, V., Jacquet, A.Y.: Temporal learning in 4 1/2- and 6-year-old children: Role of instructions and prior knowledge. J. Exp. Child Psychology 50, 305–321 (1990)
16. Lewis, P., Miall, C.: Remembering the time: A continuous clock. Trends in Cognitive Sciences 10(9), 401–406 (2006)
17. Zakay, D.: On prospective time estimation, temporal relevance and temporal uncertainty. In: Macar, F., Pouthas, V., Friedman, W. (eds.) Time, Action and Cognition Toward Bridging the Gap, pp. 141–153. Kluwer Academic Publishers, Dordrecht (1992)
18. Droit-Volet, S.: What emotions tell us about Time. In: Llyod, D., Arstila, V. (eds.) Subjective Time: The Philosophy, Psychology, and Neuroscience of Temporality. MIT Press, Cambridge (in press)
19. Droit-Volet, S., Gil, S.: The time-emotion paradox. Journal of Philosophical Transactions of the Royal Society, B-Biological Sciences 364, 1943–1953 (2009)
20. Droit-Volet, S.: Adaptation to time in young children: An initial force rule governing temporal behavior. J. Exp. Child Psychology 68, 236–249 (1998)
21. Droit-Volet, S., Rattat, A.C.: Are time and action dissociated in young children's time estimation? Cognitive Development 14, 573–595 (1999)
22. Rattat, A.C., Droit-Volet, S.: Le transfert d'apprentissage de durée d'action chez le jeune enfant: l'effet facilitateur de la variété des actions? Enfance 54, 141–153 (2002)

23. Brackbill, Y., Fitzgerald, H.E.: Stereotype temporal conditioning in infants. Psychophysiology 9, 569–577 (1972)
24. Stamps, L.S.: Temporal conditioning of heart rate responses in newborn infants. Developmental Psychology 13(6), 624–629 (1977)
25. Colombo, J., Richman, W.A.: Infant timekeeping: Attention and temporal estimation in 4-month-olds. Psychological Science 13, 475–479 (2002)
26. Brannon, E.M., Libertus, M., Meck, W., Woldorff, M.: Electrophysiological measures of time processing in infant and adult Brains: Weber's law holds. J. Cognitive Neuroscience 20, 193–203 (2008)
27. Brannon, E.M., Roussel, L.W., Meck, W., Woldorff, M.: Timing in the baby brain. Cognitive Brain Research 21, 227–233 (2004)
28. Pouthas, V.: Adaptation à la durée chez l'enfant de 2 à 5 ans. Année Psy. 81, 33–50 (1981)
29. Pouthas, V.: Timing behavior in young children: A developmental approach to conditioned spaced responding. In: Michon, J., Jackson, J. (eds.) Time, Mind and Behavior, pp. 100–109. Springer, Berlin (1985)
30. Bental, R.P., Lowe, C.F.: The role of verbal behavior in human learning: III instructional effects in children. J. Experimental Analysis of Behavior 47, 177–190 (1987)
31. Bentall, R.P., Lowe, C.F., Beasty, A.: The role of verbal behavior in human learning: II Developmental differences. J. Experimental Analysis of Behavior 43, 165–181 (1985)
32. Zeiler, M.D., Kelley, C.A.: Fixed-ratio and fixed interval schedules of cartoon presentation. J. Exp. Child Psychology 8, 306–313 (1969)
33. Long, E.R., Hammack, J.T., May, F., Campbell, B.J.: Intermittent reinforcement of operant behavior in children. J. Exp. Analysis of Behavior 1, 315–339 (1958)
34. Dempster, F.N., Brainerd, C.J.: Interference and inhibition in cognition. Academic Press, New York (1995)
35. Pouthas, V., Jacquet, A.Y.: A developmental study of timing behavior in 4 1/2- and 7-year-old children. J. Exp. Child Psychology 43, 282–299 (1987)
36. Droit, S.: Temporal regulation of behavior with an external clock in 3-year-old children: differences between waiting and response duration tasks. J. Exp. Child Psy. 58, 332–345 (1994)
37. Lowe, C.F., Beasty, A., Bentall, R.P.: The role of verbal behavior in human learning: Infant performance on Fixed-Interval Schedules. J. Exp. Analysis of Behavior 39, 157–164 (1983)
38. Darcheville, J.C., Rivière, V., Wearden, J.H.: Fixed-interval performance and self-control in children. J. Experimental Analysis of Behavior 57, 187–199 (1992)
39. Darcheville, J.C., Rivière, V., Wearden, J.H.: Fixed-interval performance and self-control in infants. J. Experimental Analysis of Behavior 60, 239–254 (1993)
40. Clément, C., Lattal, K.A., Rivière, V., Darcheville, J.-C.: Understanding the ontogenesis of temporal regulation in infants and children: An evaluation of the procedures. European Journal of Behavior Analysis 8, 41–48 (2007)
41. Droit-Volet, S.: Scalar timing in temporal generalization in children with short and long stimulus durations. The Quarterly J. Exp Psy. 55A, 1193–1209 (2002)
42. Droit-Volet, S., Clément, A., Wearden, J.: Temporal Generalization in children. J. Exp. Child Psy. 80, 271–288 (2001)
43. McCormack, T., Brown, G.D.A., Maylor, E.A., Darby, A., Green, D.: Developmental changes in time estimation: Comparing childhood and old age. Develop. Psy. 35, 1143–1155 (1999)

44. Droit-Volet, S., Wearden, J.H.: Temporal bisection in children. J. Exp. Child Psy. 80, 142–159 (2001)

45. Kopec, C.D., Brody, S.D.: Human performance on the temporal bisection task. Brain and Cognition 74, 262–272 (2010)

46. Church, R.M., Deluty, M.Z.: Bisection of temporal intervals. J. Exp. Psy. 3, 216–228 (1977)

47. Allan, L.G., Gibbon, J.: Human bisection at the geometric mean. Learning and Motivation 22, 39–58 (1991)

48. Wearden, J.H.: Human performance on an analogue of an interval bisection task. The Quarterly J. Exp. Psychology 43, 59–81 (1991)

49. Melgire, M., Ragot, R., Samson, S., Penney, T.B., Meck, W., Pouthas, V.: Auditory/visual duration bisection in patients with left or right medial-temporal lobe resection. Brain and Cognition 58, 119–124 (2005)

50. Penney, T., Gibbon, J., Meck, W.: Differential effects of auditory and visual signals on clock speed and temporal memory. J. Exp. Psy.: H.P.P. 26, 1770–1787 (2000)

51. Allan, L.G.: Are the referents remembered in temporal bisection? Learning and Motivation 33, 10–31 (2002)

52. Smith, J.G., Harper, D.N., Gittings, D., Abernethy, D.: The effect of Parkinson's disease on time estimation as a function of stimulus duration range and modality. Brain and Cognition 64, 130–143 (2007)

53. Wearden, J.H., Todd, N.P.M., Jones, L.A.: When do auditory/visual differences in duration judgment occur? The Quarterly J. Exp. Psychology 59, 1709–1724 (2006)

54. Provasi, J., Rattat, A.C., Droit-Volet, S.: Temporal bisection in 4-month-old infants. J. Exp. Psy.: Animal Behavior Processes 37(1), 108–113 (2010)

55. VanMarle, K., Wynn, K.: Six-month-olds infants use analog magnitudes to represent durations. Developmental Science 9, 41–49 (2006)

56. Brannon, E.M., Suanda, S., Libertus, K.: Temporal discrimination increases in precision over development and parallels the development of numerosity discrimination. Developmental Science 10(6), 770–777 (2007)

57. Gibbon, J.: Scalar expectancy theory and Weber's law in animal timing. Psychological Review 84, 279–325 (1977)

58. Gibbon, J., Church, R.M., Meck, W.H.: Scalar timing in memory. In: Gibbon, J., Allan, L. (eds.) Annals of the New York Academy of Sciences, 423: Timing and Time Perception, pp. 52–77. New York Academy of Sciences, New York (1984)

59. Gibbon, J.: On the form and location of the bisection function for time. Journal of Mathematical Psychology 24, 58–87 (1981)

60. Droit-Volet, S., Clément, A., Fayol, M.: Time, number and length: Similarities and differences in bisection behavior in children and adults. The Q. J. Exp. Psy. 61(12), 1827–1846 (2008)

61. Meck, W.H.: Affinity for the dopamine D2 receptor predicts neuroleptic potency in decreasing the speed of an internal clock. Pharmacol. Biochem. Behav. 25, 1185–1189 (1986)

62. Meck, W.H.: Selective adjustment of speed of internal clock and memory processes. J. Exp. Psy.: Animal Behavior Processes 9, 171–201 (1983)

63. Droit-Volet, S., Izaute, M.: The effect of feedback on timing in children and adults: the temporal generalization task. The Quarterly J. Exp. Psy. 58(3), 507–520 (2005)

64. Droit-Volet, S., Izaute, M.: Improving time discrimination in children and adults in a temporal bisection task: The effects of feedback and no-forced choice on decision and memory processes. The Quarterly J. Exp. Psy. 62(6), 1173–1188 (2009)

65. Wearden, J.H., Ferrara, A.: Stimulus spacing effects in temporal bisection by humans. The Quarterly J. Exp. Psycholgy 48B(4), 289–310 (1995)
66. Wearden, J.H., Ferrara, A.: Stimulus range effects in temporal bisection by humans. The Quarterly J. Exp. Psychology 49B(1), 24–44 (1996)
67. Droit-Volet, S., Tourret, S., Wearden, J.H.: Perception of the duration of auditory and visual stimuli in children and adults. Quarterly J. Exp. Psychology 57, 797–818 (2004)
68. Zélanti, P., Droit-Volet, S.: Cognitive abilities explaining age-related changes in time perception of short and long durations. J. Exp. Child Psychology 109(2), 143–157 (2011)
69. Droit-Volet, S., Clément, A.: Time perception in children and adults: Effects of continuous and discontinuous signal. Current Psychology of Cognition 23(3), 229–248 (2005)
70. Droit-Volet, S., Rattat, A.C.: A further analysis of temporal bisection behavior in children with and without reference memory: The similiarity and the partition task. Acta Psychologica 125, 240–256 (2007)
71. Rattat, A.C., Droit-Volet, S.: Variability in 5- and 8-year-olds' memory for duration: An interfering task in temporal bisection. Behavioural Processes 55, 81–91 (2001)
72. Wearden, J.H., Lejeune, H.: Scalar properties in human timing: Conformity and violations. The Quarterly Journal of Experimental Psychology 61, 569–587 (2007)
73. Treisman, M.: Temporal discrimination and the indifference interval: Implications for a model of the "internal clock". Psychological Monographs 77, 1–13 (1963)
74. Livesey, A.C., Wall, M.B., Smith, A.T.: Time perception: Manipulation of task difficulty dissociates clock functions for other demands. Neuropsychologia 45, 321–331 (2007)
75. Eagleman, D.M.: News & Views: Distortions of time during rapid eye movements. Nature Neuroscience 87, 850–851 (2005)
76. Coull, J.T., Cheng, R.K., Meck, W.H.: Neuroanatomical and neurochemical substrates of timing. Neuropsychopharmacology 36(1), 3–25 (2011)
77. Matell, M.S., Meck, W.H.: Neuropsychological mechanisms of interval timing behavior. Bioessays 22, 94–103 (2000)
78. Matell, M.S., Meck, W.H.: Cortico-striatal circuits and interval timing: Coincidence-detection of oscillatory processes. Cognitive Brain Research 21, 139–170 (2004)
79. Karmarkar, U.R., Buonomano, D.V.: Timing in the absence of clocks: Encoding time in neural network states. Neuron 53, 427–438 (2007)
80. Mauk, M., Buonomano, D.: The neural basis of temporal processing. Annual Review of Neurosciences 27, 207–340 (2004)
81. Tsujimoto, S.: The Prefrontal Cortex: Functional Neural Development During Early Childhood. The Neuroscientist 14(4), 345–358 (2008)
82. Casey, B.J., Tottenham, N., Liston, C., Durston, S.: Imaging the developing brain: What have we learned about cognitive development. Trends in Cognitive Sciences 9, 104–110 (2005)
83. Sowell, E.R., Thompson, P.M., Holmes, C.J., Batth, R., Jernigan, T.L., Toga, A.W.: Localizing Age-Related Changes in Brain Structure between Childhood and Adolescence Using Statistical Parametric Mapping. NeuroImage 9, 587–597 (1999)
84. Maricq, A.V., Roberts, S., Church, R.M.: Metamphetamine and time estimation. J. Exp. Psy.: Animal Behavior Processes 7, 18–30 (1981)
85. Rammsayer, T.: Is there a common dopaminergic basis of time perception and reaction time? Neuropsychobiology 21, 37–42 (1989)
86. Rammsayer, T.: Effects of pharmacologically induced dopamine-receptor stimulation on human temporal information processing. NeuroQuantology 7, 103–113 (2009)
87. Kienast, T., et al.: Dopamine in amygdala gates limbic processing of aversive stimuli in humans. Nature Neuroscience 11, 1381–1382 (2008)

88. Bar-Haim, Y., Kerem, A., Lamy, D., Zakay, D.: When time slow down: The influence of threat on time perception in anxiety. Cognition & Emotion, 1–9 (2009)
89. Droit-Volet, S., Brunot, S., Niedenthal, P.M.: Perception of the duration of emotional events. Cognition and Emotion 18, 849–858 (2004)
90. Droit-Volet, S., Mermillod, M., Cocenas-Silva, R., Gil, S.: The effect of expectancy of a threatening event on time perception in human adults. Emotion 10(6), 908–914 (2010)
91. Langer, J., Wapner, S., Werner, H.: The effect of danger upon the experience of time. American Journal of Psychology 74, 94–97 (1966)
92. Watts, F.N., Sharrock, R.: Fear and time estimation. P. & Motor Skills 59, 597–598 (1984)
93. Gil, S., Niedenthal, P., Droit-Volet, S.: Anger and temporal perception in children. Emotion 7, 219–225 (2007)
94. Droit-Volet, S., Meck, W.H.: How emotions colour our time perception. Trends in Cognitive Sciences 1(12), 504–513 (2007)
95. Gil, S., Droit-Volet, S.: How do emotional facial expressions influence our perception of time? In: Masmoudi, S., Yan Dai, D., Naceur, A. (eds.) Attention, Representation, and Human Performance: Integration of Cognition, Emotion and Motivation. Psychology Press, Taylor & Francis, London (2011)
96. Treisman, M., Faulkner, A., Naish, P.L.N., Brogan, D.: The internal clock: Evidence for a temporal oscillator underlying time perception with some estimates of its characteristic frequency. Perception 19, 705–743 (1990)
97. Wearden, J.H., Smith-Spark, J.H., Cousins, R., Edelstyn, N.M.J., Cody, F.W.J., O'Boyle, D.J.: Effect of click trains on duration estimated by people with Parkinson's disease. The Quarterly J. Exp. Psychology 62, 33–40 (2009)
98. Droit-Volet, S., Wearden, J.H.: Speeding up an internal clock in children? Effects of visual flicker on subjective duration. Quarterly J. Exp. Psychology 55, 193–211 (2002)
99. Droit-Volet, S.: Speeding up a master clock common to time, number and length? Behavioural Processes 85, 126–134 (2010)
100. Jones, L.A., Allely, C.A., Wearden, J.H.: Click trains and the rate of information processing: Does "speeding up" subjective time make other psychological processes run faster? The Quarterly J. Exp. Psy. 64, 363–380 (2010)
101. Rattat, A., Droit-Volet, S.: Development of long-term memory for duration in a temporal bisection task. The Quarterly J. Exp. Psy. 58B(2), 163–176 (2005)
102. Rattat, A.C., Droit-Volet, S.: Implicit long-term memory for duration in young children. The European Journal of Cognitive Psychology 19, 271–285 (2007)
103. Delgado, M.L., Droit-Volet, S.: Testing the representation of time in reference memory in the bisection and the generalization task: The utility of a developmental approach. The Quarterly Journal of Experimental Psychology 60(6), 820–836 (2007)
104. Meaux, J.B., Chelonis, J.J.: Time perception differences in children with and without ADHD. J. Pediatr. Health Care 17(2), 64–71 (2003)
105. Smith, A., Taylor, E., Warner Rogers, J., Newman, S., Rubia, K.: Evidence for a pure time perception deficit in children with ADHD. J. Child Psy. and Psychiatry 43(4), 529–542 (2002)
106. Toplak, M.E., Dockstader, C., Tannock, R.: Traitement de l'information temporelle dans le TDAH: les résultats à ce jour et de nouvelles méthodes. Journal of Neurosciences Methods 151, 15–29 (2006)
107. Cohen, M.J.: Examiner's manual: Children's memory scale (1997)
108. Baddeley, A.D., Hitch, G.: Working memory. In: Bower, G. (ed.) The Psychology of Learning and Motivation, pp. 47–90. Academic Press, New York (1974)

109. Baddeley, A.D., Logie, R.H.: The multiple-component model. In: Miyake, A., Shah, P. (eds.) Models of Working Memory: Mechanisms of Active Maintenance and Executive Control, pp. 28–61. Cambridge University Press, New York (1999)
110. Baudouin, A., Vanneste, S., Pouthas, V., Isingrini, M.: Age-related changes in duration reproduction: Involvement of working memory processes. Brain and Cognition 62, 17–23 (2006)
111. Fink, A., Neubauer, A.C.: Individual differences in time estimation related to cognitive ability, speed of information processing and working memory. Intelligence 33, 5–26 (2005)
112. Ulbrich, P., Churan, J., Fink, M., Wittman, M.: Temporal reproduction: Further evidence for 2 processes. Acta Psychologica 125, 51–65 (2007)
113. Lejeune, H.: Switching or gating? The attentional challenge in cognitive models of psychological time. Behavioural Processes 44, 127–145 (1998)
114. Ivry, R.B., Schlerf, J.E.: Dedicated and intrinsic models of time perception. Trends in Cognitive Sciences 12, 273–280 (2008)
115. Droit-Volet, S.: Alerting attention and time perception in children. J. Exp. Child Psychology 85(4), 372–394 (2003)
116. Brown, S.: Attentional resources in timing: Interference effects in concurrent temporal and non-temporal working memory tasks. Perception & Psychophysics 59, 1118–1140 (1997)
117. Fortin, C., Rousseau, R.: Interference from short-term memory processing on encoding and reproducting brief durations. Psychological Research 61, 269–276 (1998)
118. Macar, F., Grondin, S., Casini, L.: Controlled attention sharing influences time estimation. Memory and Cognition 22, 673–686 (1994)
119. Arlin, M.: The effects of quantity and depth of processing on children's time perception. J. of Experimental Child Psychology 42, 84–98 (1986)
120. Gautier, T., Droit-Volet, S.: Attention and time estimation in 5- and 8-year-old children: A dual-task procedure. Behavioural Processes 58, 56–66 (2002)
121. Gautier, T., Droit-Volet, S.: The impact of attentional distraction on temporal bisection in children. International Journal of Psychology 37, 27–34 (2002)
122. Zakay, D.: The role of attention in children's time perception. J. Exp. Child Psy. 54, 355–371 (1992)
123. Droit-Volet, S., Meck, W., Penney, T.: Sensory modality effect and time perception in children and adults. Behavioural Processes 74, 244–250 (2007)
124. Szelag, E., Kowalska, J., Rymarczyk, K., Pöppel, E.: Duration processing in children as determined by time reproduction: implications for a few seconds temporal window. Acta Psychologica 110, 1–19 (2002)
125. Droit-Volet, S.: A further investigation of the filled duration illusion with the comparison between children and adults. J. Exp. Psy.: Animal Behavior Processes 34, 400–414 (2008)

Electrophysiological Evidence for an Accumulation Process in the Timing of Emotional Stimuli

Nathalie Mella[1,2] and Viviane Pouthas[2]

[1] University of Geneva, bl du Pont d'Arve 40,
1211 Geneva, Switzerland
[2] Unit of Cognitive Neurosciences and Cerebral Imaging, CNRS, Paris, France
nathalie.mella-barraco@unige.ch, viviane.pouthas@upmc.fr

Abstract. Emotion and time perception are in constant interaction in everyday life activities. While growing literature explored the mechanisms underlying emotional timing, the neural correlates remain unknown. The present experiment explored evoked-related potentials associated to the estimation of emotional sounds duration and to its modulation by attention. Electroencephalographic activity and skin conductance response were recorded during a time estimation task, in which participants were instructed to attend either to time or to emotion. Attending to emotion increased autonomic arousal and lengthened subjective duration of stimuli. Conversely, focusing attention away from emotion decreased physiological arousal and shortened time estimates. ERP results showed that subjective time dilation was associated to enhanced amplitude of the Contingent Negative Variation - a slow negative wave involved in time processing. This result supports models of time perception assuming that subjective time is based on an accumulation process in the brain.

Keywords: Time perception, Emotion, ERP, CNV, Arousal.

1 Introduction

Timing events is critical for adaptive behaviors. This ability is especially important in presence of events that have an adaptive value and thus generate an emotional response. This last decade, there had been growing behavioral studies that have explored the links between emotion and time perception [1]. To date however, little is known about the neural correlates of emotional timing. Behavioral experiments using standardized material suggest that emotional events seemed to last longer than non emotional [2-7]. This effect has been observed in early childhood [8] as well as in adults and was demonstrated in both the visual [9] and the auditory modalities [6]. The most prominent hypothesis proposed to account for the temporal dilation is that autonomic arousal generated by emotional situations speeds up the rate of a neural timing system [1,5,6,10]. Such a hypothesis comes from a dominant theory of time perception postulating that the representation of time is given by an internal clock, composed of a pacemaker that generates pulses at a given rate and a counter in which pulses are accumulated [11-13]. The subjective duration of an event will depend on

A. Vatakis et al. (Eds.): Time and Time Perception 2010, LNAI 6789, pp. 173–185, 2011.
© Springer-Verlag Berlin Heidelberg 2011

the number of accumulated pulses: the more pulses accumulated the longer the subjective duration. Several studies have shown that the clock speed was affected by manipulations generating modification in arousal level, for example drugs [14-15] or visual/auditory clicks trains [16-17]. In line with these observations, experienced emotion is thought to accelerate the pacemaker rate by inducing a higher level of arousal. More temporal information would be accumulated and duration would then appear longer. This assumption was confirmed by a recent study demonstrating that the emotional effect on time perception was associated to a higher level of autonomic arousal, attested by skin conductance response (SCR) [5]. The present experiment aimed at deepened knowledge of the mechanisms by which emotion affects time processing by the use of the electroencephalographic (EEG) method.

EEG studies have described sensitivity to temporal information processing of the contingent negative variation (CNV), a slow negative wave developing over frontal and central areas between a warning signal and a subsequent imperative stimulus. A CNV develops when subjects reproduce or judge the duration of a given interval relative to a standard [18-23]. Previous studies have demonstrated that CNV was a sensitive index to subjective duration [18-20,24]. Latency of the CNV is more specifically related to decision processes involved in timing [25] while its amplitude has been associated to the length of experienced duration [18-19]. Using both a production and a comparison task, Macar and collaborators [19] reported greater CNV amplitudes on fronto-central area associated to longer than those associated to shorter estimates in the production task. Similarly, in the comparison task CNV amplitude measured on fronto-central site was found to reflect the judged interval duration (short, equal, or long), despite the fact that its objective duration was strictly the same. Using a temporal discrimination paradigm, Bendixen et al. [18] found larger CNV amplitudes to physically identical stimuli when they were judged as longer than the memorized standard duration as compared to being classified as shorter. Relation between CNV amplitude modulation and subjective duration is consistent with the postulate of an accumulator-type neural activity for the representation of duration [26-27]. Considering these previous findings, one may expect that emotion-related differences in subjective duration be reflected by modulation of the CNV.

To test this hypothesis, we used a paradigm adapted from Mella and collaborators [5], in which participants were instructed to attend either to time or to emotion while estimating the duration of neutral and negative sounds of varying emotional intensity. In addition to EEG measures, SCR was recorded to control for the level of autonomic arousal. Considering previous findings, we expected that for highly arousing negative sounds the duration will be judged as longer than that of less arousing sounds when attention is oriented toward emotion. Such an effect should be less important when attention is oriented toward time. As arousal is assumed to be responsible for the subjective duration modulation by emotion, SCR should be higher when time estimates are longer. Furthermore, considering that CNV may be an index of experienced duration, we expected that emotional modulation on time judgements would be reflected in CNV amplitude modulations.

2 Method

2.1 Participants

Twelve right-handed volunteers (six females) took part in the experiment (mean age: 24 ± 1.94). Informed consent was obtained for each of them. Prior to experiment, we ensured that none of them had a history of neurological or psychiatric disorders, and that they were not taking any medication. The experiment was conducted in accordance with the Declaration of Helsinki and has been approved by the local ethical committee.

2.2 Stimuli

The training phase was conducted using a pure beep-like tone of 500Hz lasting either 2000, 1800, or 2200ms. For the test phase, 32 sounds rated for valence and emotional intensity were selected in the IADS (International Affective Digitalized Sounds System [28]. 16 neutral sounds (mean arousal 4.39), 8 low negative sounds (mean arousal 5.71), and 8 high negative sounds (mean arousal 7.58). As the original sounds lasted 6s, fragments of 2s were selected for each of them. A prior experiment demonstrated that such a manipulation did not affect judgments of valence and emotional intensity of the selected sounds [6]. Fragments of 1s and 4s, which were used as fillers, were also selected from 8 sounds (4 neutral, 2 low arousing negative, and 2 high arousing negative). Intensity of all sounds had been averaged to 75dB using Adobe Audition.

2.3 Experimental Procedure

Once the electrode cap and electrodes for peripheral measures had been fitted, participants were comfortably seated in a small dimly lit room, in front of the stimulus presentation monitor. Auditory stimuli were presented binaurally via headphones. Participants' judgments were given with a three-button control device held in their dominant hand.

The experiment consisted in two phases - a training phase and a test phase. During the training phase, participants had to memorize the standard duration of a pure tone (2s). This standard was first presented ten times, followed by 30 trials in which the duration could either be slightly shorter (1800ms), equal (2000ms), or slightly longer (2200ms). Trials were equiprobable and occurred randomly. Participants had to decide whether the presented sound was shorter, equal, or longer than the standard, using their index finger, middle finger or ring finger respectively to indicate their responses on the three-button panel. Three seconds after the end of the sound, feedback was provided on the screen. The standard duration was considered to be correctly memorized when at least 80% of correct responses were reached. The training phase was repeated once if necessary.

In the test phase, each trial began with a fixation cross lasting 1s. Then, an attentional cue was presented on the screen for 1s, informing participants to attend either to Time (a "T" was given on the screen) or to Emotional intensity (an "I" was given on the screen). In the "T" condition, participants were asked to focus on the sounds duration in order to inhibit emotion. In the "T" condition, participants were asked to focus on the emotional intensity of the sounds, keeping in mind that a duration judgment will also be asked. After a 780-820ms varying delay, sounds of IADS were presented. 80% of these sounds were of the same duration as the standard (2s), 10% were shorter (1s) and 10% longer (4s). In both conditions of attentional cue, participants had to decide (1) whether the presented sound was of shorter, equal or longer duration than the standard duration and (2) whether its emotional intensity was low, middle or high. Judgments were given with the same three buttons panel (index finger: shorter/low intensity; middle finger: equal/middle intensity; ring finger: longer/high intensity). To reinforce the attentional cue, order of responses was fixed: a judgment about time was first asked in the "T" condition, and then a judgment concerning the emotional intensity and vice-versa in the "I" condition.

The test phase was composed of 4 sequences of 32 trials with sounds lasting 2s, balancing the emotional intensity and the attention conditions. 8 trials with shorter and longer durations, considered as fillers, were added to each sequence. Intertrial intervals varied between 2 and 3s. Prior to the test phase, participants were given some practice trials. In order to limit eye movements, they received the instruction to avoid blinking from the onset of the attentional cue to the sound offset and to fix the fixation cross presented on the screen during the whole sound duration.

2.4 Skin Conductance Response Data Collection and Reduction

SCR was recorded using an MP-150 psychophysiological monitoring system (Biopac Systems, Santa Barbara, CA). It was measured using two Ag–AgCl electrodes filled with isotonic NaCl unibase electrolyte that were attached to the palmar surface of the middle phalanges of the third and fourth fingers of the non-dominant hand. Before the electrodes were attached, the skin was cleaned with abrasive gel and alcohol. Raw SCR signals were recorded at a sampling rate of 2 KHz, amplified and band-pass filtered online at 0.05-10 Hz. Signals were sampled off-line at 2Hz and a log $(SCR(\mu S) + 1)$ transformation was performed in order to normalize the data and to include zero responses [29]. The amplitude of SCR was determined by the maximum level recorded within the 1-6s time window following the sound onset from which was subtracted a baseline computed within 1s before the sound onset. Maximum SCRs were then averaged for each condition and subjected to statistical analyses.

2.5 EEG Data Collection and Reduction

Continuous EEG activity was recorded with a MICROMED EEG system from 72 electrodes evenly distributed over the scalp, according to the 10/10 extended system, using an ElectroCap. Continuous EEG was recorded at a sampling rate of 1024 Hz. Electrode impedances were kept under 5 kΩ. The signal was amplified and band-pass filtered online at 0.16–160 Hz. Four facial bipolar electrodes placed on the outer canthi of the eyes and in the inferior and superior areas of the director eye orbit monitored, respectively, horizontal and vertical EOG. Trials containing artifacts were manually rejected. Blinks and vertical eye movements were automatically corrected with dedicated software developed in our laboratory [30]. Due to intensive blinking, data from one participant (male) had been removed from analyses. All scalp electrodes were off-line referenced to both earlobes. ERPs were computed for each participant at all recording sites with epochs extending from 200ms before the sound onset to 2000ms after (including a 200ms prestimulus baseline). Signal was then low-pass filtered below 12 Hz in order to increase the signal-to-noise ratio by eliminating those frequencies that were irrelevant to the measurements of interest and ERPs were averaged across participants.

2.6 Data Analyses

Subjective reports and SCR data
Mean index for time judgments (M_T) was computer by subtracting the number of "shorter" responses ($N_{shorter}$) to the number of "longer" responses (N_{longer}), divided by the total number of responses (N_{total}). Similarly, the mean index for the evaluation of emotional intensity (M_I) was computed by subtracting the number of "low emotional" responses (N_{low}) to the number of "high emotional" responses (N_{high}), divided by the total number of responses (N_{total}):

$$M_T = (N_{longer} - N_{shorter}) / N_{total}$$

and

$$M_I = (N_{high} - N_{low}) / N_{total}$$

These indexes as well as maximum amplitudes of SCR were submitted to repeated measures analyses of variance (ANOVA) with two factors: "Attention" (attend to time (T), attend to emotional intensity (I)) × "Emotional intensity" (neutral, low arousing negative, high arousing negative). When needed, posthoc analyses were used (Newman Keuls).

ERP data
Inspection of the ERP cartography showed in each condition a negative component between 50 ms and 150 ms (N1) peaking over frontocentral electrodes followed by a positive component between 150 and 250ms (P2), peaking over central-parietal sites. This was followed by a broadly distributed negative component over medial and bilateral frontal and central sites (CNV-like) between 350 and 800ms.

Thus, for each participant and each condition, maximum amplitudes for the N1 and the P2 components were measured over FCZ and CPZ, respectively. Furthermore, mean CNV amplitudes were computed between 350 and 800ms over right, medial and left frontal and central sites (F5, FZ, F6, C5, CZ, and C6). Repeated measures analyses of variance (ANOVA) were carried out including different factors according to the ANOVA: emotional intensity (low, middle, high), attention (T, I), scalp region (e.g., frontal, central) and lateralization (e.g., left, right).

Additionally, correlations analyses between brain potentials and temporal judgments were carried out. Firstly, we investigated whether temporal judgment (M_T) covariated with electrical activity of interest, i.e., amplitude of the CNV. Secondly, we investigated whether the effect of attention observed on temporal judgments covariated with those observed over the CNV amplitude.

3 Results

3.1 Subjective Reports

Evaluation of emotional intensity
The ANOVA conducted on the index of subjective emotional intensity (M_I) revealed a main effect of "Emotional Intensity" [F (2; 20) = 92.21, p < .0001; η^2_p = .90], indicating that neutral sounds were judged of lowest intensity (mean = -0.57) than low arousing negative sounds (mean = 0.02), themselves judged of lowest intensity than high arousing negative sounds (mean = 0.55). Main effect of "Attention" was also significant [F (1; 10) = 21.54, p < .001; η^2_p = .69]: when participants attended to time, sounds were judged less intense than when they attended to emotional intensity.

Temporal judgment
Fig. 1 shows mean temporal judgment of 2s sounds as a function of "Emotional intensity" and "Attention". The ANOVA showed a main effect of "Emotional Intensity" [F (2; 20) = 6.41, p < .05; η^2_p = .39], indicating that high arousing negative sounds were judged as longer than low arousing negative and neutral sounds. Posthoc comparisons showed significant differences between conditions. When participants attended to emotional intensity, high arousing negative sounds were judged significantly longer than in all other conditions (all ps < .001) (see Fig. 2). No differences due to "Attention" were observed with neutral or low arousing negative sounds (all ps > .05).

The main effect of "Attention" as well as the "Emotional intensity" x "Attention" interaction were not significant [F (1; 10) = 0.46, p > .05; F (2; 20) = 1.35, p > .05, respectively].

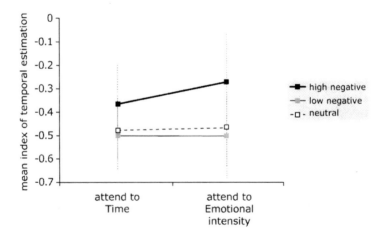

Fig. 1. Mean subjective duration for 2s sounds indicated by the following ratio: (number of "longer" responses   number of "shorter" responses) / total number of responses, as a function of attention (**T**: attend to time, **I**: attend to emotional intensity) and of the emotional intensity level (low intensity for neutral sounds, medium intensity for low negative sounds, and high intensity for high negative sounds)

3.2 SCR Analyses

The ANOVA carried out on maximum SCR amplitudes showed a significant main effect of "Emotional intensity" [F (2; 20) = 5.17, p < .05; η^2_p = .32], indicating that negative sounds of high emotional intensity were associated to a greater SCR than neutral and negative sounds of low intensity (all ps < .05). The main effect of "Attention" was also significant [F (1; 10) = 6.18, p < .05; η^2_p = .36], indicating that a greater SCR when participants attended to emotional intensity than when they attended to time. The "Emotional intensity" × "Attention" interaction was not significant [F (2; 20) = 1.65, p > .05] but post-hoc comparisons showed that SCR was significantly greater for high arousing emotional stimuli when participants attended to emotional intensity than in all other conditions (all ps < .05). While mean SCRs did not differ (all ps > .05) with the attention instruction for neutral and low arousing negative sounds, a significantly greater level of SCR was observed for high arousing negative stimuli when participants attended to emotional intensity than when they attended to time (p < .05) (see Fig. 2).

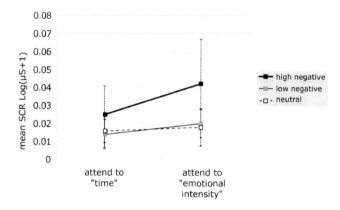

Fig. 2. Mean SCR amplitude (in log (μS+1)) as a function of attention and the emotional intensity level (low intensity for neutral sounds, medium intensity for low negative sounds and high intensity for high negative sounds). Bars represent SEMs.

3.3 ERPs Analyses

The ANOVA carried out on mean CNV amplitudes showed a significant interaction between "Emotional intensity" and "Scalp region" [F (2; 20) = 7.62, p < .05; η^2_p = .29], indicating that while no differences were observed over central sites, CNV amplitude was greater with highly arousing negative sounds than with neutral or less arousing negative sounds over frontal sites (all ps < .001). Results also revealed a significant interaction between "Emotional intensity" and "Lateralization" [F (4; 40) = 2.66, p < .05; η^2_p = .21], indicating that CNV amplitudes were greater over the right sites than over the left sites, whatever the sounds arousal level (all ps > .05).

Interestingly, a significant interaction between "Emotional intensity", "Attention", "Scalp region", and "Lateralization" was observed [F (4; 40) = 2.44, p < .05; η^2_p = .26]. Posthoc comparisons showed that while there were neither effects of "Attention" over left, medial and right central sites nor over left and medial frontal sites (all *ps* > .05), whatever the sounds arousal level, the right frontal site displayed a significantly greater CNV amplitude associated to highly arousing sounds when participants attended to emotional intensity than when they attended to time ($p < .05$) (see Fig. 4). By contrast, CNV amplitudes associated to neutral and less arousing negative sounds showed no differences between "attention" conditions (all *ps* > .05) (see Fig. 3).

Main effects of "Scalp region" and "Lateralization" were also significant [F (1; 10) = 28.42, $p < .05$; $\eta^2_p = .34$] and [F (2; 20) = 40.46, $p < .01$; $\eta^2_p = .47$], respectively.

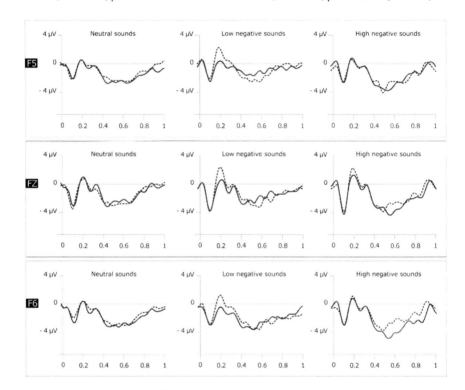

Fig. 3. Temporal course of the CNV. Grand-average ERPs of eleven subjects elicited by neutral sounds, negative sounds of low intensity and negative sounds of high emotional intensity, when participants attended to time (dotted line) or to emotional intensity (plain line), over the left, medial and right frontal electrodes *(F5, FZ, F6)*. The red line constitutes the time window of analysis, in the condition where an effect of Attention was observed. The horizontal axis represents the time (ms), the 0 being the onset of the stimulus.

3.4   Correlations between Brain Potentials and Subjective Time

Correlation analyses were conducted using the CNV amplitude over the right frontal site (where amplitudes were maximal and were attention and emotional intensity interaction was observed).

Correlations between temporal judgments and right frontal CNV amplitude were not significant (all *ps* > .05). Correlations analyses concerning the effect of attention showed a significant positive correlation for negative sounds of high intensity ($r = .77$, $p < .01$), indicating that individuals who had the greatest effect of attention on time judgments were also those who had the greatest effect of attention on mean CNV amplitude. For neutral sounds and negative sounds of low intensity, correlations were also positive but not significant ($r = .36$ and $r = .14$, respectively, all $ps > .05$).

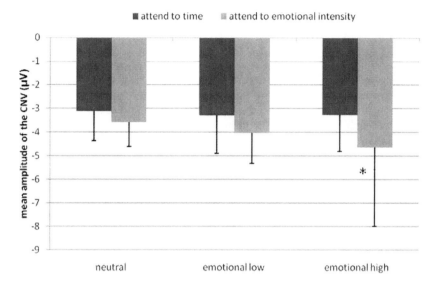

Fig. 4. Mean amplitude and SEMs of the CNV (in µV) over the right frontal site (F6) elicited by neutral sounds, negative sounds of low intensity, and negative sounds of high emotional intensity, when participants attended to time or to emotional intensity. The effect of Attention was significant only with negative sounds of high emotional intensity.

4 Discussion

4.1 Behavioral and SCR Results

Consistently with previous studies [4-6], time judgments were affected by the emotional intensity of sounds: the duration of highly arousing negative sounds were judged longer than that of neutral or less arousing negative sounds. This subjective temporal dilation was associated to a higher SCR level, which is considered as a reliable index of autonomic arousal. Replicating previous results [5], our result gives further support to an arousal effect of emotion on time perception and more generally to the postulate of an arousal-sensitive internal clock implicated in the timing of few seconds [5,13]. Furthermore, attention affected temporal judgments and autonomic arousal only when participants were exposed to highly arousing sounds. When participants attended to time, highly arousing sounds were judged shorter than when they attended to emotional intensity. Similarly, the level of SCR decreased. Consistently with a dampening of autonomic arousal, emotional intensity ratings were lower. Then, regulating emotion by attentional control alters its related effect on time judgment [5]. Alternatively, one may consider that attending to emotional intensity enhanced the emotion-induced arousal effect on time judgments. In this case, the absence of attentional effect on the timing of neutral and less arousing sounds may be explained by the fact that there was little emotional intensity to focus on. Both alternative views argue in favor of an effect of attention on arousal, as shown by the modulation of autonomic arousal, emotional intensity judgments and the emotional effect on time judgments.

4.2 ERPs Results

As expected, amplitude of the CNV was modulated by the emotional intensity of the sounds. Over frontal sites, amplitudes were greater with high arousing stimuli than with those of lower intensity, i.e., neutral and negative sounds of low intensity. This effect was modulated by attention over the right frontal site but not over medial and left sensors: CNV amplitude, associated to highly arousing sounds, was larger when participants attended to emotional intensity than when they attended to time. Then, for a same objective duration, sounds, which were perceived to be longer, were associated to greater CNV amplitude. Implication of right frontal areas in temporal estimation has been widely documented [31-35]. In an fMRI study, Coull and collaborators [32] manipulated the amount of attention allocated either to the duration or to the colour of a stimulus. They showed that attending to time recruited the right prefrontal cortex, in addition to AMS, insula, putamen, intraparietal sulcus and right premotor and temporal cortices. Coupling EEG and TEP methods Pouthas and collaborators [35] showed that the temporal course of the CNV paralleled a right frontal activity. Consistently, our results demonstrate a relation between right frontal ERP and temporal judgements. They give further support to previous observation of an existing relation between amplitude of the CNV and online experience of duration [18,36]. The nature of such a relation remains to be clarified. It has been proposed that the CNV amplitude reflects the accumulation process underlying temporal judgement [37], which would imply that a greater amount of temporal information is accumulated in highly arousing context, leading to a longer subjective duration. Such an accumulation process has been observed in neurophysiological animal studies that showed specific climbing neuronal activity - interpretable as representing a temporal integrator-like function - involved in the encoding of short durations [26,27]. In humans, fMRI studies reported correlations between the duration being measured and signal in different parts of the brain [38,39]. Wittmann and collaborators [39] reported an accumulatory-type activity within the insula and suggested that this may encode of duration of multiple seconds. In the same line, covariation of regional brain activity with CNV amplitude was found in the thalamus, cingulated cortex, and insula [40]. It is noteworthy that these regions, in particular the anterior cingulate cortex (ACC) and insula, are thought to be involved in subjective feeling states and interoceptive awareness [41,42], which has been proposed constitute the basis for time processing [43]. According to Craig, the insula integrates the salience of the environment via representation of the body condition, and then motivational, hedonic and social conditions represented in other interconnected parts of the brain. This hierarchical integration of the salience leads to a unified representation of a "global emotional moment" at the immediate moment of time—'now'. Accordingly, the succession of "global emotional moments" would be used for subjective time estimation. On this account, one may speculate that modulation of the CNV amplitudes by highly arousing stimuli reflect climbing neuronal activity in the insula, which would index the accumulation of physiological changes in body states or the representation of "global emotional moments".

Interestingly, our correlation results showed that, while temporal judgments and CNV amplitudes did not correlate, the effect of attention on temporal judgement and on CNV amplitude did (r = .77), which enlightens the role of attention in the arousal-induced modulation of both the CNV amplitude and temporal judgements. Some studies have demonstrated that CNV amplitude may be modulated by peripheral arousal state, for example, increased heart rate [44]. In a non temporal task inducing a CNV, Nagai and collaborators [40] reported that, while ACC and insula regions were influenced by peripheral autonomic arousal state of the subjects, enhanced activity in parietal and medial prefrontal cortical regions was common to both CNV amplitude and increasing SCR. These regions are known to show activity enhancement during sustained attention tasks, suggesting that arousal level enhances attention to different features of emotional stimuli, including its duration.

5 Conclusion

The present study brings contribution to a better understanding of how emotion modulates our sense of time. In line with previous behavioural findings, it suggests that physiological arousal plays a key role in the experience of emotional duration, showing that its modulation correspondingly modulates emotional effect on time judgements. Such modulations could be indexed by electrocortical activity, supporting the hypothesis that the representation of duration in the multiple-seconds range is underlined by the accumulation of brain activity [45].

References

1. Droit-Volet, S., Gil, S.: The time-emotion paradox. Philos. Trans. R. Soc. Lond. B Biol. Sci. 364, 1943–1953 (2009)
2. Dalby, P.-R.: Facial EMG and the subjective experience of emotion in idiopathic Parkinson's disease in response to affectively laden visual stimuli. Dissertation Abstracts International: Section B: The Sciences and Engineering 55 (1994)
3. Droit-Volet, S., Bigand, E., Ramos, D., Bueno, J.L.: Time flies with music whatever its emotional valence. Acta Psychol (Amst) 135, 226–232 (2010)
4. Droit-Volet, S., Brunot, S., Niedenthal, P.: Perception of the duration of emotional events. Cognition and Emotion 18, 849–856 (2004)
5. Mella, N., Conty, L., Pouthas, V.: The role of physiological arousal in time perception: psychophysiological evidence from an emotion regulation paradigm. Brain Cogn. 75, 182–187 (2011)
6. Noulhiane, M., Mella, N., Samson, S., Ragot, R., Pouthas, V.: How emotional auditory stimuli modulate time perception. Emotion 7, 697–704 (2007)
7. Tipples, J.: Negative emotionality influences the effects of emotion on time perception. Emotion 8, 127–131 (2008)

8. Gil, S., Niedenthal, P.M., Droit-Volet, S.: Anger and time perception in children. Emotion 7, 219–225 (2007)
9. Droit-Volet, S., Tourret, S., Wearden, J.: Perception of the duration of auditory and visual stimuli in children and adults. Q. J. Exp. Psychol. A 57, 797–818 (2004)
10. Droit-Volet, S., Meck, W.H.: How emotions colour our perception of time. Trends Cogn. Sci. 11, 504–513 (2007)
11. Church, R.M., Broadbent, H.A.: A connectionist model of timing, in Neural network of conditioning and action. In: Commons, M., Grossberg, S., Staddon, J. (eds.), pp. 225–240. Erlbaum, New York (1991)
12. Gibbon, J., Church, R.M., Meck, W.H.: Scalar timing in memory. Ann. N Y Acad. Sci. 423, 52–77 (1984)
13. Treisman, M.: Temporal discrimination and the indifference interval. Implications for a model of the "internal clock". Psychol. Monogr. 77, 1–31 (1963)
14. Matell, M.S., Berridge, K.C., Wayne Aldridge, J.: Dopamine D1 activation shortens the duration of phases in stereotyped grooming sequences. Behav. Processes 71, 241–249 (2006)
15. Meck, W.H.: Neuropharmacology of timing and time perception. Brain Res. Cogn. Brain Res. 3, 227–242 (1996)
16. Burle, B., Casini, L.: Dissociation between activation and attention effects in time estimation: Implications for clocks models. Journal of Experimental Psychology: Human Perception and Performance 27, 195–205 (2001)
17. Penton-Voak, I.S., Edwards, H., Percival, A., Wearden, J.H.: Speeding up an internal clock in humans? Effects of click trains on subjective duration. J. Exp. Psychol. Anim. Behav. Process 22, 307–320 (1996)
18. Bendixen, A., Grimm, S., Schroger, E.: Human auditory event-related potentials predict duration judgments. Neurosci. Lett. 383, 284–288 (2005)
19. Macar, F., Vidal, F., Casini, L.: The supplementary motor area in motor and sensory timing: Evidence from slow brain potential changes. Exp. Brain Res. 125, 271–280 (1999)
20. Pfeuty, M., Ragot, R., Pouthas, V.: When time is up: CNV time course differentiates the roles of the hemispheres in the discrimination of short tone durations. Exp. Brain Res. 151, 372–379 (2003)
21. Praamstra, P., Kourtis, D., Kwok, H.F., Oostenveld, R.: Neurophysiology of implicit timing in serial choice reaction-time performance. J. Neurosci. 26, 5448–5455 (2006)
22. Ruchkin, D.S., McCalley, M.G., Glaser, E.M.: Event related potentials and time estimation. Psychophysiology 14, 451–455 (1977)
23. Walter, W.G., Cooper, R., Aldridge, V.J., McCallum, W.C., Winter, A.L.: Contingent Negative Variation: An Electric Sign of Sensorimotor Association and Expectancy in the Human Brain. Nature 203, 380–384 (1964)
24. Pfeuty, M., Ragot, R., Pouthas, V.: Relationship between CNV and timing of an upcoming event. Neurosci. Lett. 382, 106–111 (2005)
25. Macar, F., Vidal, F.: The CNV peak: an index of decision making and temporal memory. Psychophysiology 40, 950–954 (2003)
26. Durstewitz, D.: Neural representation of interval time. Neuroreport 15, 745–749 (2004)
27. Reutimann, J., Yakovlev, V., Fusi, S., Senn, W.: Climbing neuronal activity as an event-based cortical representation of time. J. Neurosci. 24, 3295–3303 (2004)
28. Bradley, M.M., Lang, P.J.: International affective digitized sounds (IADS): Stimuli, instruction manual and affective ratings, in Technical Report C-1, Psychophysiology, T.C.f.R.I., Editor: University of Florida (1999)
29. Cacioppo, J.T., Tassinary, L.G., Berntson, G.G.: Hanbook of psychophysiology. In: Cacioppo, J.T., Tassinary, L.G., Berntson, G.G. (eds.). Cambridge University Press, Cambridge (2007)

30. Gratton, G., Coles, M.G., Donchin, E.: A new method for off-line removal of ocular artifact. Electroencephalogr Clin. Neurophysiol. 55, 468–484 (1983)

31. Belin, P., McAdams, S., Thivard, L., Smith, B., Savel, S., Zilbovicius, M., Samson, S., Samson, Y.: The neuroanatomical substrate of sound duration discrimination. Neuropsychologia 40, 1956–1964 (2002)

32. Coull, J.T.: fMRI studies of temporal attention: allocating attention within, or towards, time. Brain Res. Cogn. Brain Res. 21, 216–226 (2004)

33. Kagerer, F.A., Wittmann, M., Szelag, E., Steinbuchel, N.: Cortical involvement in temporal reproduction: evidence for differential roles of the hemispheres. Neuropsychologia 40, 357–366 (2002)

34. Monfort, V., Pouthas, V., Ragot, R.: Role of frontal cortex in memory for duration: an event-related potential study in humans. Neurosci. Lett. 286, 91–94 (2000)

35. Pouthas, V., Garnero, L., Ferrandez, A.M., Renault, B.: ERPs and PET analysis of time perception: spatial and temporal brain mapping during visual discrimination tasks. Hum. Brain Mapp. 10, 49–60 (2000)

36. Macar, F., Vidal, F., Casini, L.: The supplementary motor area in motor and sensory timing: evidence from slow brain potential changes. Exp. Brain Res. 125, 271–280 (1999)

37. Meck, W.H., Penney, T.B., Pouthas, V.: Cortico-striatal representation of time in animals and humans. Curr. Opin. Neurobiol. 18, 145–152 (2008)

38. Jech, R., Dusek, P., Wackermann, J., Vymazal, J.: Cumulative blood oxygenation-level-dependent signal changes support the 'time accumulator' hypothesis. Neuroreport 16, 1467–1471 (2005)

39. Wittmann, M., Simmons, A., Aron, J., Paulus, M.P.: Accumulation of neural activity in the posterior insula encodes the passage of time. Natu. Precedings See (2008)

40. Nagai, Y., Critchley, H.D., Featherstone, E., Fenwick, P.B., Trimble, M.R., Dolan, R.J.: Brain activity relating to the contingent negative variation: an fMRI investigation. NeuroImage 21, 1232–1241 (2004)

41. Craig, A.D.: How do you feel? Interoception: the sense of the physiological condition of the body. Nat. Rev. Neurosci. 3, 655–666 (2002)

42. Critchley, H.D., Wiens, S., Rotshtein, P., Ohman, A., Dolan, R.J.: Neural systems supporting interoceptive awareness. Nat. Neurosci. 7, 189–195 (2004)

43. Craig, A.D.: Emotional moments across time: a possible neural basis for time perception in the anterior insula. Philos. Trans. R. Soc. Lond. B. Biol. Sci. 364, 1933–1942 (2009)

44. Tecce, J.J.: Contingent negative variation (CNV) and psychological processes in man. Psychol. Bull. 77, 73–108 (1972)

45. Wittmann, M.: The inner experience of time. Philos. Trans. R. Soc. Lond. B. Biol. Sci. 364, 1955–1967 (2009)

Temporal Information Processing and Mental Ability: A New Perspective

Stefan J. Troche and Thomas H. Rammsayer

Institute for Psychology, University of Bern, Muesmattstr. 45, 3012 Bern, Switzerland
stefan.troche@psy.unibe.ch

Abstract. According to the temporal resolution power (TRP) hypothesis, individual differences in mental ability (MA) can be explained by differences in the neural oscillations of the central nervous system which find expression in the acuity of temporal information processing: Faster neural oscillations do not only lead to better temporal information processing but also to faster speed of information processing and to better coordinated mental operations which, in turn, lead to higher MA. Empirical evidence for this hypothesis is reviewed in this chapter. Also, critical findings challenging the TRP hypothesis are compiled. For example, it is not yet clear whether the relations of MA to temporal and non-temporal discrimination ability can be dissociated from each other. In addition, the role of attention as a possible underlying mechanism of the relation between TRP and MA needs further exploration.

Keywords: Time perception, Mental ability, Intelligence, Temporal resolution power, Sensory discrimination, Working memory, Mismatch negativity.

1 Introduction

For a long time, it has been known that better performance on sensory discrimination tasks is highly associated with higher mental ability (MA) [1-3]. The mechanisms underlying this relationship, however, are not at present understood. Most of these studies used pitch, brightness, loudness, or colour discrimination tasks and high correlations can only be obtained if performances on several tasks are combined by means of factor analysis. Rammsayer and Brandler [4,5] probed whether such a relation between sensory discrimination and MA would also hold for performance on duration discrimination and other psychophysical tasks assessing various aspects of temporal information processing such as temporal generalization, rhythm perception, and temporal-order judgment.

Rammsayer and Brandler [4,5] used three *duration discrimination tasks* in which participants were required to decide which of two successively presented intervals was of longer duration. Two out of the three discrimination tasks used filled intervals (white-noise bursts) with standard durations in the range of milliseconds (50 ms) and seconds (1,000 ms), respectively. In the third duration discrimination task, stimuli were empty intervals with the onset and the offset of the intervals marked by clicks and a standard duration of 50 ms.

A. Vatakis et al. (Eds.): Time and Time Perception 2010, LNAI 6789, pp. 186–195, 2011.
© Springer-Verlag Berlin Heidelberg 2011

In two *temporal generalization tasks*, participants were initially required to memorize a standard duration of 75 or 1,000 ms, respectively. In the subsequent test phase, standard and nonstandard stimuli were presented and participants had to decide whether or not the presented stimulus was of the same duration as the initially learned standard interval.

In a *rhythm perception task*, participants had to detect a deviation from a regular sequence of click-to-click intervals. The participants' task was to indicate whether they had perceived a regular or an irregular rhythmic pattern.

Finally, in a *temporal-order judgment task,* a tone and a red light were presented with a very short delay between the onsets of the two stimuli. It was determined how long the delay had to be, so that the participants were able to correctly indicate, with a probability of .75, whether the tone or the light was presented first.

Human timing and time perception as reflected by these psychophysical timing tasks is often explained by the general assumption of a hypothetical internal clock based on neural counting [6-8]. Main features of such an internal-clock device are a pacemaker and an accumulator. The pacemaker emits pulses and the number of pulses relating to a physical time interval is recorded by the accumulator. Thus, the number of pulses counted during a given time interval is the internal representation of the interval. The higher the clock rate, the finer is the temporal resolution of the internal clock which is equivalent to higher temporal sensitivity as indicated by better performance on all sorts of timing tasks (for a concise review see [5]).

Based on these considerations, Rammsayer and Brandler [4] proposed neural oscillations to be functionally equivalent to the pulses emitted by the pacemaker. It seems reasonable to assume that a higher frequency of pulses corresponds with higher temporal resolution power (TRP) of the central nervous system and, hence, with better timing accuracy.

The basic notion of neural oscillations controlling a hypothetical master clock can be traced back to Surwillo [9]. He proceeded on the assumption that an internal master clock in the brain is responsible for the coordination of different mental operations. More specifically, he proposed that speed and efficiency of information processing are positively related to clock rate. Later, Burle and Bonnet [10,11] provided converging evidence for the existence of some kind of master clock in the human information processing system. Thus, there had been early ideas that eventually became manifest in the TRP approach to MA.

The basic idea of the TRP approach to MA acts on the assumption that a higher neural oscillation rate corresponds with higher TRP of the central nervous system and, hence, with better timing accuracy [4]. In a series of experiments, Rammsayer and Brandler [4,5,12] carried out principal component analyses on performance measures of the above-mentioned psychophysical timing tasks. Their results supported the view that performance on various timing tasks can be assigned to one common latent dimension of temporal information processing. This dimension was referred to as TRP and found to be related to MA, which was derived from a battery of psychometric intelligence tests. The observed correlations ranged from $r = .47$ to .56 indicating that better timing performance is accompanied by higher MA [5, 13-15]. Proceeding from these findings, Rammsayer and Brandler [5] put forward the TRP hypothesis to explain individual differences in MA. According to this theoretical account, TRP of the brain represents a basic property of the central nervous system, which may be crucial for both temporal information processing, as well as, different aspects of cognitive abilities.

2 Temporal Resolution Power, Speed of Information Processing, and Mental Ability

An idea akin to the TRP approach was put forward by Jensen [16,17] to explain the highly consistent association between MA and speed of information processing as measured, for example, with simple and choice reaction times in the Hick task (e.g., [18]) or the inspection time paradigm [19]. Within his so-called *Oscillation Theory*, Jensen [17] proposed that individual differences in speed of information processing are due to individual differences in the oscillation rate of excitatory and refractory states of a neuron (or group of neurons). If, for example, a stimulus is presented during the refractory state, the mental representation of the stimulus can be transmitted faster when the refractory state is short, i.e., when the oscillation rate is high. A faster oscillation rate leads to less decay of information before entering short-term memory and to a lower strain of working memory (WM) capacity because fewer elements of the stimuli (or a complex task) have to be stored in WM. Slower oscillation rates, however, may lead to an overstrain of WM capacity and, consequently, to a breakdown and response errors. As a result, the neuronal oscillation rate does not only contribute to speed but also to efficiency of information processing.

In contrast to Jensen's [17] model of neuronal oscillation rate, the TRP hypothesis provides a more direct link between neural oscillations and manifest behavior, i.e., performance on psychophysical timing tasks assessing temporal sensitivity and timing accuracy. Proceeding from the assumption that TRP is functionally equivalent to the neuronal oscillations, which control speed of information processing, individual differences in TRP should be able to account for the relation between speed of information processing and MA. This assumption was investigated by Helmbold, Troche, and Rammsayer [13]. They used a reaction time (RT) task based on the Hick paradigm [20] to obtain a measure of speed of information processing. This RT task is one of the most frequently used elementary cognitive tasks to investigate the relation between speed of information processing and MA [21]. Typically, the Hick task consists of three or four conditions with different amounts of information to be processed. Participants are required to simply react to a (visual) stimulus or to make simple decisions at which of two, four, or eight positions a stimulus was presented. Individuals with higher MA show consistently faster RT and less intraindividual variability of RT compared to individuals with lower MA. Furthermore, the increase of RT with complexity of the condition is less pronounced in individuals with higher MA (e.g., [22]).

Helmbold et al. [13] used confirmatory factor analyses and structural equation modelling to investigate the interplay among TRP, MA, and speed of information processing. A latent variable *Speed of Information Processing* was derived from central tendencies and intraindividual variabilities of RTs obtained with different conditions of the Hick task. The latent variable *TRP* was measured with seven psychophysical timing tasks, while *MA* was assessed with a battery of ten different intelligence scales. MA was reliably related to both *Speed of Information Processing* ($r = -.49$) and *TRP* ($r = .59$) indicating faster and less variable RTs as well as better timing performance in individuals with higher compared to lower MA. In additional analyses of the common and unique contributions of *TRP* and *Speed of Information Processing* to *MA*, the effect of *Speed of Information Processing* on *MA* was nearly completely mediated by *TRP* (see Fig. 1). This finding is in line with the assumption of the TRP hypothesis that TRP is the basic brain mechanism underlying the relation between speed of information processing and MA.

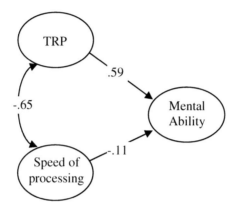

Fig. 1. The interplay of speed of information processing, temporal resolution power (TRP), and mental ability (adapted from [13])

3   Temporal Resolution Power, Working Memory Capacity, and Mental Ability

The TRP hypothesis also states that higher TRP should lead to better coordination of mental operations providing a direct link from TRP to efficiency of information processing. Individual differences in the coordination of information processing should be particularly salient when information processing is subjected to capacity limits. WM is one of the best-investigated stages of information processing with limited capacity, which is closely associated with MA [23]. Although there are several different views and definitions of WM [24], maintenance of information and its concurrent processing can be considered the least common denominator of all these divergent views [25-27].

To test the assumption that higher TRP represents a major prerequisite for better coordination of information processing, and as a consequence, for higher MA, Troche and Rammsayer [14] investigated the interplay of TRP, WM capacity, and MA. For this purpose, a sample of 200 participants performed three psychophysical timing tasks (duration discrimination with empty intervals, temporal-order judgment, and temporal generalization) and three WM tasks (a numerical memory-updating task, a figural dot-span task, and a verbal monitoring task). According to the above given definition, in all three WM tasks the amount of information to be maintained and the number of required mental operations was continually increased until the individual upper limit of the WM capacity was reached. It is this situation in which higher TRP should lead to higher WM capacity due to better coordinated mental operations. Beside the psychophysical timing and WM tasks, measures of speed- and reasoning-related facets of MA were obtained from intelligence subtests of the Berlin Intelligence Structure test [28]. Using structural equation modelling, the data could be best described in accordance with the idea that TRP leads to better coordination of mental operations (i.e., higher WM capacity) and, in turn, to higher reasoning- and speed-related MA (see Fig. 2).

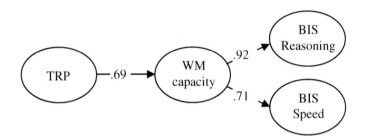

Fig. 2. TRP predicts WM capacity, which, in turn, is related to reasoning- as well as speed-related aspects of MA as measured with the Berlin Intelligence Structure (BIS) test (adapted from [14])

4 The Relations of Mental Ability to Duration and Frequency Discrimination

As already mentioned, MA seems to be related to performance on any kind of sensory discrimination. Such relations were shown for frequency [29], color [30], or texture and shape in the tactile modality [31]. Therefore, it could be argued that general, unspecific discrimination performance rather than specific processing of temporal information may account for the observed association between TRP and MA. In a first study on this topic, Helmbold, Troche, and Rammsayer [32] tried to dissociate the relations of MA to duration and frequency discrimination. Using a frequency- and a duration-generalization task to predict MA by (non-temporal) frequency and (temporal) duration discrimination performance, 24% of MA variance could be explained by both tasks. Only 9%, however, was commonly accounted for by duration- and frequency-discrimination performance, while 9% and 6% of variability in MA were explained uniquely by duration and frequency discrimination, respectively. Helmbold et al. [32] concluded that the relation between TRP and MA is twofold with one part of this relation due to rather unspecific, general discrimination ability and another part specifically due to the processing of temporal information.

Also, a subsequent study by Troche, Houlihan, Stelmack, and Rammsayer [33] suggested that the relations of MA to duration and frequency discrimination are, at least partly, dissociable from each other. In this study, event-related potentials (ERPs) were recorded while subjects performed experimental tasks. In one task, a long sequence of standard tones of 200 ms duration and 1000 Hz frequency was interrupted by infrequently occurring deviant tones of 275 ms duration and 1000 Hz. In the other task, the deviants were of the same duration as the standard tone but of higher frequency (1045 Hz). Participants' task was to press a key as soon as they detected a deviant tone. The ERP was determined separately for the standard and deviant tones. To isolate the neural activity related to the detection of change, the ERP waveform to the standards was subtracted from the waveforms to the deviants. The resulting difference waveform is called mismatch negativity (MMN), which is most prominent at frontal electrode sites and peaks at about 200 ms after stimulus onset. Because MMN can be observed even when participants do not pay attention to the stimuli, it was concluded that MMN reflects a sensory pre-attentive process [34,35]. With increasing difference between standard and deviant tones, MMN amplitude increases and latency decreases. Therefore, MMN seems to be an important mechanism involved in the discrimination process. This view is supported by studies reporting a functional relationship between behavioral discrimination performance and MMN amplitude [36,37].

In the study by Troche et al. [33], larger MMN amplitudes were related to better discrimination performances. This was true for duration and frequency discrimination. Larger duration and frequency MMN was also associated with higher MA. A more detailed analysis of these associations revealed that duration and frequency MMN shared some common variance with MA. Most importantly, however, duration but not frequency MMN explained also unique portions of overall variability in MA. Thus, similar to the results by Helmbold et al. [32], temporal discrimination was related to MA and this relation was dissociable from (non-temporal) frequency discrimination even at an early level of processing as indicated by MMN. Troche et al. [33] tentatively interpreted this finding as evidence for the notion that the relation between temporal information processing and MA is independent from attentional processes as MMN is commonly seen to reflect a pre-attentive process even when participants attended the stimuli.

More recently, Troche, Houlihan, Stelmack, and Rammsayer [38] examined the relation of MA to duration and frequency MMN amplitude when participants' attention was directed away from the stimulus tones [38]. In this study, neither duration nor frequency MMN amplitude was related to discrimination performance. Moreover, larger frequency but not duration MMN amplitudes went with higher MA. This latter finding suggests that attentional processes may play a crucial role for the relation between temporal information processing and MA. Further research should clarify the interplay between TRP, attention, and MA to elucidate whether (and to what extent) the relation between TRP and MA is mediated by attentional processes.

5   Temporal Resolution Power, General Discrimination Ability, and Mental Ability

There is good evidence for the notion that the relation between sensory discrimination ability and MA substantially increases when sensory discrimination is examined at the level of latent variables. For example, Spearman [3] and, more recently, Deary et al. [1] and Meyer et al. [2] reported an almost perfect relationship between latent variables referring to *MA* and *General Discrimination Ability* with the latter derived from performances on several non-temporal discrimination tasks. Helmbold et al. [32] as well as Troche et al. [33], however, dissociated the relations of MA to duration and frequency discrimination performance with only one task, respectively. Hence, these studies do not answer the question of whether the observed relation between temporal information processing and MA reflects a time-specific neural property as suggested by the TRP hypothesis or whether it should be attributed primarily to a less specific association between MA and discrimination ability in general. Troche and Rammsayer [15], therefore, derived a latent variable *TRP* from a battery of timing tasks (duration discrimination, temporal generalization, rhythm, and temporal-order judgment) and a latent variable *Non-Temporal Discrimination Ability* from a frequency, an intensity, and a brightness discrimination task. Again, speed- and reasoning-related facets of MA were determined. It was tested whether the prediction of MA by temporal and non-temporal discrimination abilities could be dissociated from each other (see left panel of Fig. 3). *TRP* predicted both, reasoning- and speed-related aspects of MA, while *Non-Temporal Discrimination Ability* was related to reasoning- but not (directly) to speed-related aspects of MA. This differential pattern of results suggests two dissociable processes underlying temporal and non-temporal discrimination ability. There was, however, an almost perfect correlation of $r = .94$ between temporal and non-temporal discrimination ability indicating virtual identity of the two latent variables. Indeed, a one-factor solution with a latent variable *General Discrimination Ability* derived from all seven temporal and non-temporal discrimination tasks explained the data better than the former model (see right panel of Fig. 3).

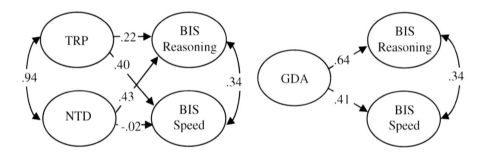

Fig. 3. The relations of TRP and non-temporal discrimination ability (NTD; left panel) as well as General Discrimination Ability (GDA; right panel) to reasoning- and speed-related aspects of MA as measured with the Berlin Intelligence Structure (BIS) test (adapted from [15])

This strong overlap of temporal and non-temporal discrimination may be explained by the high similarity of the discrimination tasks used to measure temporal and non-temporal discrimination performances. In future research, this explanation should be empirically tested by means of a multitrait-multimethod analysis controlling for the influence of variance due to the employed methods. Furthermore, future studies should also concentrate on the biological underpinnings of the relation between MA and temporal as well as non-temporal information processing. In a recent neuroimaging study using functional MRI techniques [39], MA, and timing accuracy were positively associated with prefrontal white matter volume (PWMV). PWMV reflects the extent of neuronal connections and represents a neurobiological basis for mental operations requiring neural synchrony in prefrontal neuronal networks. If future research could show that this functional relationship holds for temporal but not for non-temporal discrimination, this would provide converging evidence for distinct brain mechanisms involved in temporal but not in non-temporal discrimination ability.

6 Summary and Perspectives

In sum, the TRP hypothesis predicts that temporal acuity of the brain is a fundamental mechanism underlying MA. This assumption was confirmed repeatedly by the finding of highly reliable correlations between TRP and MA [4, 5, 13-15, 32, 40]. In line with the TRP hypothesis, it was shown that the association between MA and speed of information processing can be explained by the relation between MA and TRP [13]. Furthermore, TRP results in better coordinated mental operations as indicated by higher WM capacity which, in turn, leads to higher MA [14]. Nevertheless, there are open questions, which have to be addressed in future research. Can TRP be dissociated from general discrimination ability? Can TRP be increased experimentally as suggested recently by Jones, Allely, and Wearden [41] and how would such an increase affect the relation between TRP and MA? Psychophysiological measures such as alpha rhythm or event-related desynchronization, have been suggested to be related to temporal information processing [42,43] as well as to mental ability [44,45]. Can these methods help understand the relation between TRP and MA? Is it specifically the processing of temporal information, which accounts for the relation to MA? Or can the relation between TRP and MA be accounted for by rather general attentional processes required for both performances on timing tasks as well as on tasks assessing MA?

References

1. Deary, I.J., Bell, J., Bell, A.J., Campbell, M.L., Fazal, N.D.: Sensory discrimination and intelligence: Testing Spearman's other hypothesis. Am. J. Psychol. 117, 1–18 (2004)
2. Meyer, C.S., Hagmann von Arx, P., Lemola, S., Grob, A.: Correspondence between the general ability to discriminate sensory stimuli and general intelligence. J. Individ. Dif. 31, 46–56 (2010)
3. Spearman, C.: General intelligence objectively determined and measured. Am. J. Psychol. 15, 201–293 (1904)
4. Rammsayer, T.H., Brandler, S.: On the relationship between general fluid intelligence and psychophysical indicators of temporal resolution in the brain. J. Res. Pers. 36, 507–530 (2002)
5. Rammsayer, T.H., Brandler, S.: Performance on temporal information processing as an index of general intelligence. Intelligence 35, 123–139 (2007)
6. Creelman, C.D.: Human discrimination of auditory duration. J. Acoust. Soc. Am. 34, 582–593 (1962)
7. Gibbon, J.: Origins of scalar timing. Learn. Motiv. 22, 3–38 (1991)
8. Grondin, S.: From physical time to the first and second moments of psychological time. Psychol. Bull. 127, 22–44 (2001)
9. Surwillo, W.W.: Timing of behavior in senescence and the role of the central nervous system. In: Talland, G.A. (ed.) Human Aging and Behaviour, pp. 1–35. Academic Press, New York (1968)

10. Burle, B., Bonnet, M.: Further argument for the existence of a pacemaker in the human information processing system. Acta Psychol. 97, 129–143 (1997)
11. Burle, B., Bonnet, M.: What's an internal clock for? From temporal information processing to temporal processing of information. Behav. Process 45, 59–72 (1999)
12. Rammsayer, T.H., Brandler, S.: Aspects of temporal information processing: A dimensional analysis. Psychol. Res. 69, 115–123 (2004)
13. Helmbold, N., Troche, S., Rammsayer, T.: Processing of temporal and non-temporal information as predictors of psychometric intelligence: A structural-equation-modelling approach. J. Pers. 75, 985–1006 (2007)
14. Troche, S.J., Rammsayer, T.H.: The influence of temporal resolution power and working memory capacity on psychometric intelligence. Intelligence 37, 479–486 (2009)
15. Troche, S.J., Rammsayer, T.H.: Temporal and non-temporal sensory discrimination and their predictions of capacity- and speed-related aspects of psychometric intelligence. Pers. Indiv. Differ. 47, 52–57 (2009)
16. Jensen, A.R.: Reaction time and psychometric g. In: Eysenck, H.J. (ed.) A Model for Intelligence, pp. 93–132. Springer, New York (1982)
17. Jensen, A.R.: Clocking the mind: Mental chronometry and individual differences. Elsevier, Amsterdam (2006)
18. Eysenck, H.J.: Speed of information processing, reaction time, and the theory of intelligence. In: Vernon, P.A. (ed.) Speed of Information-Processing and Intelligence, pp. 21–67. Ablex, Norwood (1987)
19. Kranzler, J.H., Jensen, A.R.: Inspection time and intelligence: A meta-analysis. Intelligence 13, 329–347 (1989)
20. Hick, W.E.: On the rate of gain of information. Q. J. Exp. Psychol. 4, 11–26 (1952)
21. Sheppard, L.D., Vernon, P.A.: Intelligence and speed of information-processing: A review of 50 years of research. Pers. Indiv. Differ. 44, 535–551 (2008)
22. Jensen, A.R.: The g factor. Praeger Publishers, Westport (1998)
23. Kyllonen, P.C., Christal, R.E.: Reasoning ability is (little more than) working-memory capacity?! Intelligence 14, 389–433 (1990)
24. Miyake, A., Shah, P.: Models of working memory. Cambridge University Press, Cambridge (1999)
25. Baddeley, A.: Working memory. Oxford University Press, New York (1986)
26. Colom, R., Abad, F.J., Quiroga, Á., Shih, P.C., Flores-Mendoza, C.: Working memory and intelligence are highly related constructs, but why? Intelligence 36, 584–606 (2008)
27. Engle, R.W., Kane, M.J., Tuholski, S.W.: Individual differences in working memory capacity and what they tell us about controlled attention, general fluid intelligence, and functions of the prefrontal cortex. In: Miyake, A., Shah, P. (eds.) Models of Working Memory, pp. 102–134. Cambridge University Press, Cambridge (1999)
28. Jäger, A.O., Süß, H.M., Beauducel, A.: Berliner Intelligenzstruktur Test Form 4. Hogrefe, Göttingen (1997)
29. Raz, N., Willerman, L., Yama, M.: On sense and senses: Intelligence and auditory information processing. Pers. Indiv. Differ. 8, 201–210 (1987)
30. Acton, G.S., Schroeder, D.H.: Sensory discrimination as related to general intelligence. Intelligence 29, 263–271 (2001)
31. Stankov, L., Seizova-Cajić, T., Roberts, R.D.: Tactile and kinesthetic perceptual processes within the taxonomy of human cognitive abilities. Intelligence 29, 1–29 (2001)
32. Helmbold, N., Troche, S., Rammsayer, T.: Temporal information processing and pitch discrimination as predictors of general intelligence. Can. J. Exp. Psychol. 60, 294–306 (2006)

33. Troche, S.J., Houlihan, M.E., Stelmack, R.M., Rammsayer, T.H.: Mental ability, P300, and mismatch negativity: Analysis of frequency and duration discrimination. Intelligence 37, 365–373 (2009)
34. Kujala, T., Tervaniemi, M., Schröger, E.: The mismatch negativity in cognitive and clinical neuroscience: Theoretical and methodological considerations. Biol. Psychol. 74, 1–19 (2007)
35. Näätänen, R.: Attention and Brain Function. Erlbaum, London (1992)
36. Amenedo, E., Escera, C.: The accuracy of sound duration representation in the human brain determines the accuracy of behavioural perception. Eur. J. Neurosci. 12, 2570–2574 (2000)
37. Novitski, N., Tervaniemi, M., Huotilainen, M., Näätänen, R.: Frequency discrimination at different frequency levels as indexed by electrophysiological and behavioral measures. Cognitive Brain Res. 20, 26–36 (2004)
38. Troche, S.J., Houlihan, M.E., Stelmack, R.M., Rammsayer, T.H.: Mental ability and the discrimination of auditory frequency and duration change without focused attention: An analysis of mismatch negativity. Pers. Indiv. Differ. 49, 228–233 (2010)
39. Ullén, F., Forsman, L., Blom, O., Karabanov, A., Madison, G.: Intelligence and variability in a simple timing task share neural substrates in the prefrontal white matter. J. Neurosci. 28, 4238–4243 (2008)
40. Helmbold, N., Rammsayer, T.: Timing performance as a predictor of psychometric intelligence as measured by speed and power tests. J. Individ. Dif. 27, 20–37 (2006)
41. Jones, L.A., Allely, C.S., Wearden, J.H.: Clicktrains and the rate of information processing: Does "speeding up" subjective time make other psychological processes run faster? Q. J. Exp. Psychol. 64, 363–380 (2011)
42. Treisman, M.: Temporal rhythms and cerebral rhythms. In: Gibbon, J., Allan, L. (eds.) Annals of the New York Academy of Sciences: Timing and Time Perception, pp. 542–565. New York Academy of Sciences, New York (1984)
43. Mohl, W., Pfurtscheller, G.: The role of the right parietal region in a movement time estimation task. Neuroreport. 2, 309–312 (1991)
44. Klimesch, W.: EEG alpha and theta oscillations reflect cognitive and memory performance: A review and analysis. Brain Res. Rev. 29, 169–195 (1999)
45. Neubauer, A.C., Freudenthaler, H.H., Pfurtscheller, G.: Intelligence and spatiotemporal patterns of event-related desynchronisation (ERD). Intelligence 20, 249–266 (1995)

The Embodiment of Time Estimation

Ramon D. Castillo[1,2], Guy Van Orden[1], and Heidi Kloos[1]

[1] Center for Cognition, Action and Perception (CAP); University of Cincinnati, OH, USA
{guy.van.orden,heidi.kloos}@uc.edu
castilrn@mail.uc.edu
http://www.uc.edu/cap/
[2] Facultad de Psicologia; Universidad de Talca, Talca, Chile
http://www.utalca.cl/

Abstract. In this essay, we explain time estimation on the basis of principles of self-organization. Timing behavior can be seen as an outcome of the coupling and coordination across physiological events, overt behavior, and task demands. Such coupling reveals itself in scaling relations known as fractal patterns. The self-organization hypothesis posits a coherent relation between frequency and amplitude of change, as a single coordinated unity, that possess fractal features. Empirical data lend support of this hypothesis, initiating a discussion on how fractal properties of time estimation can be altered by the interplay of voluntary and involuntary control of behavior.

Keywords: Time Estimation, Pink noise, Fractal Time, Self-Organized Criticality, Involuntary and Voluntary Control.

1 Introduction

Timing is a central feature of behavior, whether the behavior pertains to physiological events such as brain activity, heartbeat, or breathing; overt motor behavior such as walking or dancing; or cognitive behaviors such reading, speaking, interacting socially, or participating in a laboratory task. In all these examples, the body finds a proper rhythm with surprising ease to ensure adaptive functioning (cf. for social coordination) [1-3]. What makes it possible that the activities of the body are so precisely orchestrated over time?

The question of timing has traditionally motivated a search for internal clocks – rhythmic structures of some sort that could supply timing information to human physiology and behavior. This approach to the many different timing concerns of the mind and body proposes a hierarchy of clock times ranging from circadian time, one day to the next, to the rapidly changing millisecond timescales of speech, movement coordination, and brain activity. Each timescale has been thought to be represented by its own clock network of brain structures, distributed across the brain [4-5].

The hypothesis of internal clocks has some drawbacks however. For example the results of neuroimaging studies have failed to converge on a set of distinct timing networks that could correspond to the hierarchy of internal clocks. Instead, it appears as though the same brain networks are reused in a multitude of unrelated functions – rather than being dedicated in a modular fashion to timing functions (or to any other

A. Vatakis et al. (Eds.): Time and Time Perception 2010, LNAI 6789, pp. 196–206, 2011.

mental functions, for that matter). Consequently, Anderson [6] has called for alternative hypotheses to make sense of neural reuse, which appears to be the basis for all cognitive functions.

In this essay, we describe such an alternative – one that is based on the idea of self-organization. Self-organization of a system's behavior takes place without a central executive authority or isolated causal timing structures. Instead local interactions among the components of a system yield the global pattern of the system's behavior. Examples of such self-organization come from a variety of domains in human behavior, including motor coordination [7], decision making [8], and brain activation [9]. For example, evidence from EEG studies suggests that the brain self-organizes global patterns of activity on the fly — even coming up with different functional organizations to suite the requirements of specific contexts [7, 10-13]. Similarly, networks of motor neurons and inter-neurons that produce rhythmic timing functions, so-called central pattern generators, were found to self-organize into context-dependent structures [14-16]. Previously inhibitory connections are reused as excitatory connections, new neurons that were not part of the network previously can be incorporated, or separate networks become fused into a new central pattern generator with changed timing pattern [17]. The inherent flexibility of the network structure originates in temporary synergies among the elements of the network that assemble to meet the demands of the immediate context [18-20].

Our goal in this essay is to explain behavioral phenomena of time estimation on the basis of these principles of self-organization. In doing so, we look at one particular task, one in which the participant first listens to a metronome beat marking the passing of repeatedly identical time intervals. The task is then to reproduce the duration of the time interval between metronome beats, repeatedly, after the metronome is turned off. This is a classic time-estimation task (cf. [5]) that has been used in several variations. For example, sometimes the participant controls the pace of responding, pressing a response key as each estimated interval passes. And sometimes a prompt appears (marking the beginning of the interval) and the participant responds when the estimated interval passes, after which another prompt will appear, and so on. What do data obtained from these kinds of tasks reveal about the kinds of processes that could give rise to time estimation?

The phenomena that are revealed in time estimation data are generic patterns of local changes that emerge across successive time-estimation trials [8, 21-24]. Figure 1 illustrates how such patterns are visualized in a spectral plot (following the prescriptions for spectral analysis of Holden, [25]): The raw data (a series of successive time estimates; shown at the top right of the figure) are decomposed by a Fourier transformation into sine waves (illustrated by examples on the left side of the Fig. 1). Slow changes in the data series are simulated by the low-frequency sine waves and fast changes are simulated by high-frequency waves. Similarly, large changes are simulated by high-amplitude sine waves, and small changes are simulated by low-amplitude sine waves. The ordered pairs of frequency and power (amplitude squared) for each of the obtained sine waves are then plotted on log/log scales (shown at the bottom right of the Fig. 1). The remarkable phenomenon is that the paired amplitudes and frequencies of the simulated changes turn out to be proportional, aligning themselves together along a regression line, also known as scaling relation.

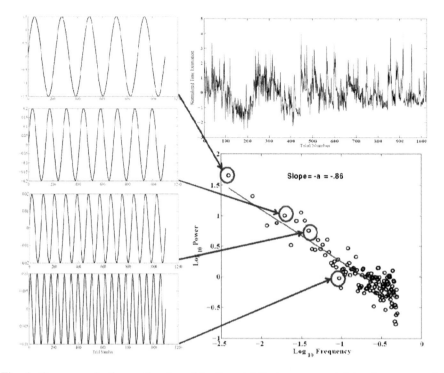

Fig. 1. One person's time estimation data (top right), decomposed into sign waves of a particular amplitude and frequency (examples of which are shown on the left). Each sign wave is plotted as a function of its amplitude (power) and frequency, in log-log coordinates, yielding a spectral plot (bottom right). The slope of the regression line reflects the scaling exponent α.

1.1 Fractal Variation in Time Estimation

Why does the lawful scaling relation between frequency and size of variation appear in time estimation? Some scientists entertain a hypothesis that the scaling relation is a universal feature of human performance [8, 23, 26-28]. If so, then it either is a spurious feature of behavior revealing little or nothing about the essential nature of human behavior. Or else, the scaling relation is a deeply rooted phenomenon that may reveal of the essential nature of human behavior. The latter possibility is assumed by proponents of a self-organization hypothesis, which views the universal scaling relation as a fractal pattern across time, a scaling relation that is sometimes called fractal time.

Fractal patterns are self-similar structures that exhibit the same statistical features at all scales of observation. They are simulated using iterative functions, such that the state of a system at one point in time serves as input to the state of the system at the next point in time. The function connecting one state to the next reflects the coupling among the component processes, which is accomplished in positive and negative feedback loops among the processes. This allows processes to cooperate as well as compete to determine the next state of the system.

The scaling relation illustrated in Fig. 1, aligning amplitude (power) and frequency of change, is a common identifier of fractal structure. Fractal structure suggests a coherence across scales, which in turn implies a coupling among the processes of the mind, brain, and body, across all the scales of the mind, brain, and body. Coupling allows continuous updating of each process by every other process, ensuring that each process informs the dynamics of every other process. Appropriately conceived, it provides a basis for the alignment of frequency and amplitude of change in the scaling relation [26, 28-30].

Applied to time estimation (as well as the observed timing of physiology and behavior), timing intervals of timing behavior can be seen as the outcomes of the coupling and coordination of the body. The self-organization of coordination itself is the paramount activity. Time estimation is simply a product of that activity, not the other way around. This view allows us to dispense with the anti-realist assumption that space and time constitute fundamental dimensions of human embodiment or phenomenology. Instead embodied time is a performance, physiological and behavioral events are primary, while their timing reflects the coordination across the sequential orders of events (cf., [31, 32]).

Of course, one could be skeptical of the self-organization hypothesis. The scaling relation might be an idiosyncratic feature of behavior; or it might be a simple aggregate of ordinary mechanisms that happen to change on different timescales. Alternatively, the scaling relation might be equated with one or more specific mechanisms, elicited by the particular task environment, in line with the conventional idea of distinct mental functions [33-36]. For example, the high-frequency range of the spectral plot might reflect a motor component, while the low-frequency range might reflect a conceivably cognitive timing-function underlying time estimates. Finally, the scaling relation could reflect a spectrum of distinct internal clock frequencies that accidentally align their amplitudes [37].

These contrasting viewpoints differ from our viewpoint in terms of their predictions about the coherence of the apparent scaling relation. They predict that the scaling relation comprises an independent process or is composed of independent processes. Thus the right kind of manipulation could possibly dissect a scaling relation into distinct components, with different frequencies and amplitudes of change. The self-organization hypothesis, on the other hand, predicts a coherent relation between frequency and amplitude of change, which means that it will change in unity, as a rigid line that changes in slope. Holden and collaborators tested this prediction by injecting random white noise into the experimental protocol of time estimation and manipulating its amplitude [38]. Findings show that the injected low-amplitude noise changed the slope of a spectral plot toward whiter noise, but without splitting the spectral plot along lines of frequency or amplitude. Similarly, the injected high-amplitude noise changed the slope toward whiter noise (much more than before), but again without splitting the spectral plot. In both cases, spectral slopes changed equivalently across the spectrum of amplitudes, as a coherent relation between frequency and amplitude (cf. [39-40]). These findings undermine the idea of causally independent processes within the scaling relation. Instead they suggest that timing behavior results from the coupling and coordination of all the components of body and mind [26, 41].

1.2 The Meaning of Spectral Slopes

So far we have ignored an important aspect of spectral plots: the slope of the regression line between the amplitude, S (f), and frequency of change, f. The negative slope of the regression line, indicated as $- \alpha$, is used to estimate a scaling exponent α, such that: S $(f) = 1/f \, \alpha = f - \alpha$. In the data set shown in Fig. 1, the obtained scaling exponent is $\alpha \approx$ 0.86, a value close to $\alpha = 1.0$. This value (and values near to $\alpha = 1.0$) is explicitly predicted by a core feature of the self-organization: self-organized criticality [28]. The value $\alpha = 1.0$ represents the ideal scaling relation of fractal time, predicted to appear near criticality [42, 43]. So-called critical states are tipping points at which complex systems spontaneously reorganize, consistent with the neural reuse hypothesis and observed spontaneous reorganization of the central nervous system [7]. Indeed, skilled motor performance will converge on the scaling relation of $\alpha = 1$ over extended or developmental time (e.g., for Fitts task performance: [44]; for walking: [45]).

Time estimation data often reveal near pristine examples of fractal time [26]. Likewise, time estimation performance appears to converge on the scaling relation α = 1 across development [46]. The task was identical to the generic time-estimation task: after the metronome was switched off, children between 4 and 12 years of age pressed a button repeatedly to indicate when the designated time interval had passed. Data were subjected to analyses like that portrayed in Fig. 1, yielding a reliable developmental trend. Younger children produced patterns more like overly random white noise, while older children and adults produced patterns more like fractal time with $\alpha = 1$. Younger children might lack capacities to sufficiently control the degrees of freedom afforded by the unusual task. With development, they might better coordinate their bodies with an idiosyncratic task, and they might better sustain the intentions that follow from experimental instructions.

Despite findings of fractal time, note that the scaling relation of $\alpha = 1$ is not equally present in every time estimation performance (or, for that matter, in other task performances that reveal scaling relations). Different task conditions can change the pattern of variation across time estimation data, usually to become more like a random pattern of white noise. For example, the fractal parameter of the scaling relation is close to zero when the metronome is left on during testing trials – but not when or when participants tap in a syncopated rhythm, between the beats of a metronome [47]. Similarly, the fractal parameter is close to zero when participants are provided with feedback on every time-estimation trial [48]. What does the change in spectral slope reveal about the system that gives rise to the observed performance?

Figure 2 shows idealized data patterns and spectral plots that define the range of scaling relations discovered using different tasks and task conditions. The range runs from random white noise with $\alpha = 0$ to brown noise with $\alpha = 2$ at least or higher. We argue that the range of scaling relations can often be understood as a trade-off between voluntary and involuntary control [49]. To explain, we discuss the nature of control in more detail below (see also [28, 50]).

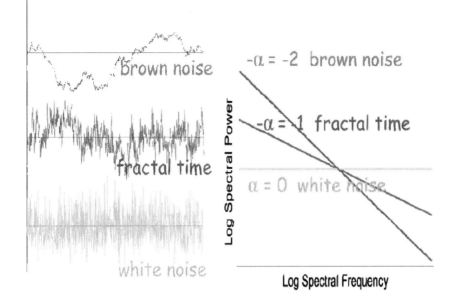

Fig. 2. Idealized data patterns of variation spanned by development, training, and manipulation of tasks and task demands (see text). Different task conditions change the pattern of variation across time estimation data to become more or less like a random pattern of white noise with α = 0 or the pattern of fractal time with α = 1 [28, 38]. Conditions of rigid or exaggerated control can change the variation in data to resemble brown noise with α = 2 (for a review [49]).

1.3 The Nature of Control

The starting point is our assumption that behavior is a self-organization of dynamical structures across all scales. The dynamical structures in the behaviors of organs, for example, combine in the coordination of organ systems, which in turn combine in the coordination of the behaving organism. One advantage of this view point is that the dynamics of the behavior of physiological systems – as well as the behavior of the entire organism – share common principles and the same theoretical language [51]. Control in all cases originates in sources of constraint that limit degrees of freedom (cf., [52]). Successful task performance therefore requires that a participant can exploit the controllable degrees of freedom that a task environment affords.

There are two broad sources of constraint that shape a particular task performance: involuntary control and voluntary control. Voluntary control pertains to a person's will, purpose, or intention; while involuntary control refers to all the other sources of control — including control in the task environment, embodied control, and an organism's capabilities and skills that concern successful task performance [53-54]. An increase in voluntary control relative to involuntary control is predicted to move the variation in performance data away from white noise and toward overly regular brown noise. And an increase in involuntary control relative to voluntary control is predicted to move variation in the direction of overly random white noise [50, 55]. Formula (1) reflects this relationship between voluntary and involuntary control as a ratio.

$$\text{Variation in Human Performance} : \frac{\text{Over Random}}{\text{Over Regular}} = \frac{\text{Involuntary Control}}{\text{Voluntary Control}}. \qquad (1)$$

More formally, voluntary and involuntary control can be reframed with respect to the timescales of observation. Voluntary control brings temporary constraints into and out of existence as task performance requires. These constraints tighten or loosen the coupling between task and participant in vigilance, poise, mental set, anticipation, and so on. Such waxing and waning sources of voluntary control unfold more slowly than the trial kinematics of measured behavior. That is, constraints due to voluntary control change more slowly than the trial performances that are controlled. These sources of constraints, changing more slowly than the pace of measurement, amplify slow frequency variation in performance to resemble brown noise. In other words, voluntary control exaggerates over regular, slower oscillations supplying higher amplitude, more slowly changing variation to the data. High-amplitude slow changes are the basis for change in the direction of brown noise with $\alpha = 2$ in the spectral portrait.

Involuntary control, on the other hand, concerns all other sources of constraints apart from voluntary control. Changes in the difficulty of a task or task demands, the knowledge or skill of a participant, or across the participant's development are all changes in involuntary control. Involuntary sources of constraint may affect all timescales of constraint. Sources of involuntary control that change on timescales faster than (or as fast as) the measurement will perturb performance unsystematically, changing the pattern of variation to resemble white noise. In contrast, sources of voluntary control that change on slower time scales than the time scale of the measurement will change the pattern of variation to resemble brown noise.

Taken together, these predictions give a good account of the observed changes in time estimation data. For instance, consider the baseline to be the fractal time obtained when participants listen to the metronome beat until the metronome is turned off, and then produce the remembered time interval. An increase in involuntary control can be enacted by leaving the metronome on, eliminating the need to remember the time interval, and ceding this source of control to the task metronome. Indeed, leaving the metronome on, as an enhanced source of involuntary control, yields the expected change in variation toward overly random white noise [47]. Anecdotally, we have also observed skilled drummers who cede control to their automatic skill set, producing white noise in the metronome-off condition.

Now taking the metronome-on condition as a baseline, an increase in voluntary control can be necessitated by another change in the task instructions. Instead of instructions to produce intervals in synch with the metronome, the participant is instructed to produce syncopated intervals that begin and end between the beats of the metronome. Compared to the in-synch condition, the more difficult syncopated intervals require a concentrated voluntary effort to sustain accurate performance. The enhanced voluntary control moves the pattern of time estimate variation back away from a resemblance to white noise and $\alpha = 0$ toward brown noise with $\alpha = 2$ [47].

Finally, consider the change in control that comes from the presence or absence of trial feedback. Feedback perturbs time estimation data, trial to trial, resulting in an unsystematic source of perturbations with respect to the behavioral measures of tapping. In contrast, feedback is a source of slow changes with respect to more rapidly changing brain activity. Slowly changing constraints on brain dynamics originate in the voluntary use of feedback to constrain and improve an upcoming performance. In other words, it is the relative timescales of the measurement that determines whether trial-to-trial feedback moves variation in data toward white noise or brown noise. Feedback in time estimation fits these predictions. When the measurement pertains to tapping, trial feedback is a source of involuntary control, which in turn perturbs the pattern of variation in the direction of white noise [48]. On the other hand, when the measurement pertains to rapidly changing brain dynamics, slow trial feedback moves the variation in measurements of brain dynamics in the direction of brown noise [56, 57].

2 Conclusions

Our goal was to address the issue of timing under the framework of self-organization. Under this framework, performance – in this case proper timing – does not require separate causal structures. No internal clock needs to be postulated to explain the intricate and apparently effortless timing performances that humans display. Self-organization postulates instead that higher-order structures arise from the interplay among a multitude of component processes that interact as a balance of competing and cooperating tendencies. Timing performance is a product of such an interaction.

Evidence for our claims comes from the persistent coherence between the ordered pairs of amplitude (power) and frequency of sine waves that simulate variation in performance. Whether the task involves tapping out a learned rhythm, or syncopated tapping between the beats of a metronome, spectral analyses reveal a characteristic pattern: Rather than arbitrary pairings of possible amplitudes and frequencies, systematic changes are apparent. A scaling relation changing in unity speaks to the interdependence of the component processes of the system. Whether a process changes on a faster or slower time scale, it is coordinated with other processes, which self-organize human performance in task specific and participant specific ways. Timing then is a result of such self-organization embodied in the interaction of processes at all the scales of the body and brain.

Acknowledgements. Preparation of this article was supported by grants to Guy Van Orden (NSF BCS #0642716; NSF BCS #0843133), Heidi Kloos (NSF DRL #723638; NICHD HD055324), and Guy Van Orden and Heidi Kloos (NSF DHB #0728743). Please send correspondence either to Guy Van Orden (guy.van.orden@uc.edu) or to Heidi Kloos (heidi.kloos@uc.edu).

References

1. Konvalinka, I., Xygalatas, D., Bulbulia, J., Schjodt, U., Jegindo, E.-M., Wallot, S., Van Orden, G., Roepstorff, A.: Synchronized arousal between performers and related spectators in a fire-walking ritual. Proc. Natl. Acad. Sci. USA 108(20), 8514–8519 (2001)
2. Richardson, M.J., Marsh, K.L., Isenhower, R., Goodman, J., Schmidt, R.C.: Rocking together: Dynamics of intentional and unintentional interpersonal coordination. Hum. Mov. Sci. 26, 867–891 (2007)
3. Shockley, K., Richardson, D.C., Dale, R.: Conversation and coordinative structures. Topics Cog. Sci. 1, 305–319 (2009)
4. Bhattacharjee, Y.: A Timely Debate About the Brain. Science 311(5761), 596–598 (2006)

5. Buhusi, C.V., Meck, W.H.: What makes us tick? Functional and neural mechanisms of interval timing. Nature Rev. Neurosci. 6, 755–765 (2005)
6. Anderson, M.L.: Neural reuse: A fundamental organizational principle of the brain. Behav. Brain Sci. 33, 245–313 (2010)
7. Kelso, J.A.S.: Dynamic patterns: The self-organization of brain and behavior. MIT Press, Cambridge (1995)
8. Gilden, D.L.: Cognitive emissions of 1/f noise. Psychol. Rev. 108(1), 33–56 (2001)
9. Bhattacharya, J.: Increase of universality in human brain during mental imagery from visual perception. PLoS One 4(1), e4121 (2009)
10. Bhattacharya, J., Petsche, H.: Universality in the brain while listening to music. Proc. Biol. Sci. 268(1484), 2423–2433 (2001)
11. Gong, P., Nikolaev, A., van Leeuwen, C.: Scale-invariant fluctuations of the dynamical synchronization in human brain electrical activity. Neurosci. Lett. 336, 33–36 (2003)
12. Linkenkaer-Hansen, K., Nikulin, V.V., Palva, J.M., Kaila, K., Ilmoniemi, R.J.: Stimulus-induced change in long-range temporal correlations and scaling behaviour of sensorimotor oscillations. Eur. J. Neurosci. 19(1), 203–211 (2004)
13. Stam, C.J., de Bruin, E.A.: Scale-Free Dynamics of Global Functional Connectivity in the Human Brain. Hum. Brain Mapp. 22, 97–109 (2004)
14. Harris-Warrick, R.M., Marder, E.: Modulation of neural networks for behavior. Annu. Rev. Neurosci. 14, 39–57 (1991)
15. Hooper, S.L.: Central pattern generators. Curr. Biol. 10(5), R176–R177 (2000)
16. Morton, D.W., Chiel, H.J.: Neural architectures for adaptive behavior. Trends Neurosci. 17, 413–420 (1994)
17. Nishikawa, K., Biewener, A.A., Aerts, P., Ahn, A.N., Chiel, H.J., Daley, M.A., Daniel, T.L., Full, R.J., Hale, M.E., Hedrick, T.L., Lappin, A.K., Nichols, T.R., Quinn, R.D., Satterlie, R.A., Szymik, B.: Neuromechanics: an integrative approach for understanding motor control. Integr. Comp. Biol. 47, 16–54 (2007)
18. Kugler, P.N., Turvey, M.T.: Information, natural law, and the self-assembly of rhythmic movement. Lawrence Erlbaum Associates, Inc., Hillsdale (1987)
19. Riley, M., Shockley, K., Van Orden, G.: Learning from the body about the mind. Topics Cogn. Sci. (in press)
20. Turvey, M.T.: Action and perception at the level of synergies. Hum. Mov. Sci. 26, 657–697 (2007)
21. Gilden, D.L.: Fluctuations in the time required for elementary decisions. Psychol. Sci. 8, 296–301 (1997)
22. Gilden, D.L.: Global model analysis of cognitive variability. Cogn. Sci. 33, 1441–1467 (2009)
23. Gilden, D.L., Thornton, T., Mallon, M.W.: 1/f noise in human cognition. Science 267, 1837–1839 (1995)
24. Thornton, T.L., Gilden, D.L.: Provenance of correlations in psychological data. Psychon. Bull. & Rev. 12(3), 409–441 (2005)
25. Holden, J.G.: Gauging the fractal dimension of response times from cognitive tasks. In: Riley, M.A., Van Orden, G.C. (eds.) Contemporary Nonlinear Methods for Behavioral Scientists, pp. 267–318 (2005),
    http://www.nsf.gov/sbe/bcs/pac/nmbs/nmbs.jsp
26. Kello, C.T., Van Orden, G.: Soft-assembly of sensorimotor function. Nonlinear Dynamics Psychol. Life Sci. 13(1), 57–78 (2009)
27. Riley, M.A., Turvey, M.T.: Variability and determinism in motor behavior. J. Motor Behav. 34, 99–125 (2002)

28. Van Orden, G., Holden, J.G., Turvey, M.T.: Self-organization of cognitive performance. J. Exp. Psychol (Gen.) 132, 331–350 (2003)
29. Holden, J.G., Van Orden, G., Turvey, M.T.: Dispersion of response times reveals cognitive dynamics. Psychol. Rev. 116, 318–342 (2009)
30. Van Orden, G., Kello, C.T., Holden, J.G.: Situated behavior and the place of measurement in psychological theory. Ecol. Psychol. 22, 24–43 (2010)
31. Gibson, J.J.: The Ecological Approach to Visual Perception. Houghton Mifflin, Boston (1979)
32. Turvey, M.T.: Affordances and prospective control: An outline of the ontology. Ecol. Psychol. 4(3), 173–187 (1992)
33. Delignières, D., Lemoine, L., Torre, K.: Time intervals production in tapping and oscillatory motion. Hum. Mov. Sci. 23, 87–103 (2004)
34. Delignières, D., Torre, K., Lemoine, L.: Fractal models for event-based and dynamical timers. Acta Psychol. (Amst) 127, 382–397 (2008)
35. Diniz, A., Wijnants, M.L., Torre, K., Barreiros, J., Crato, N., Bosman, A.M.T., Hasselman, F., Cox, R.F.A., Van Orden, G., Delignières, D.: Contemporary theories of 1/f noise in motor control. Hum. Mov. Sci. (in press)
36. Lemoine, L., Delignières, D.: Detrended Windowed (Lag One) Auto-correlation: A new method for distinguishing between event based and emergent timing. Q. J. Exp. Psychol. (Colchester) 62, 585–604 (2009)
37. Wagenmakers, E.-J., Farrell, S., Ratcliff, R.: Estimation and interpretation of 1/fα noise in human cognition. Psychon. Bull. Rev. 11, 579–615 (2004)
38. Holden, J.G., Choi, I., Amazeen, P.G., Van Orden, G.: Fractal 1/f Dynamics Suggest Entanglement of Measurement and Human Performance. J. Exp. Psychol. (Hum Percept.) 37(3), 935–948 (2011)
39. Brown, C., Liebovitch, L.: Fractal analysis. Sage, London (2010)
40. Kello, C.T., Brown, G.D.A., Ferrer-i-Cancho, R., Holden, J.G., Linkenkaer-Hansen, K., Rhodes, T., Van Orden, G.: Scaling laws in cognitive sciences. Trends Cogn. Sci. 14(5), 223–232 (2010)
41. Kello, C.T., Beltz, B.C., Holden, J.G., Van Orden, G.: The emergent coordination of cognitive function. J. Exp. Psychol. [Gen.] 136(4), 551–568 (2007)
42. Bak, P.: How Nature Works. In: The Science of Self-organized Criticality. University Press, Oxford (1997)
43. Jensen, H.J.: Organized Criticality. In: Emergent Complex Behavior in Physical and Biological Systems. Univiversity Press, Cambridge (1998)
44. Wijnants, M.L., Bosman, A.M.T., Hasselman, F., Cox, R.F.A., Van Orden, G.: 1/f scaling in movement time changes with practice in precision aiming. Nonlinear Dynamics Psychol. Life Sci. 13, 79–98 (2009)
45. Hausdorff, J.M., Zemany, L., Peng, C.-K., Goldberger, A.L.: Maturation of gait dynamics: Stride-to-stride variability and its temporal organization in children. J. Appl. Physiol. 86, 1040–1047 (1999)
46. Gresham, L.J., Kloos, H., Wallot, S., Van Orden, G.: Fractals in children's time estimation: Evidence for developing coordination. In: Proc. Annu. Cogn. Sci. Conf. (2011)
47. Chen, Y., Ding, M., Kelso, J.A.S.: Origins of timing errors in human sensorimotor coordination. J. Motor Behav. 33, 3–8 (2001)
48. Kuznetsov, N.A., Wallot, S.: Accuracy Feedback in Continuous Temporal Estimation: Changes in the fractal and multifractal spectra (submitted)
49. Van Orden, G., Kloos, H., Wallot, S.: Living in the Pink: Intentionality, Wellbeing, and Complexity. In: Hooker, C.A. (ed.) Philosophy of Complex Systems. Handbook of the Philosophy of Science, vol. 10. Elsevier, Amsterdam (2011)

50. Kloos, H., Van Orden, G.: Voluntary behavior in cognitive and motor tasks. Mind and Matter 8(1), 19–43 (2010)
51. West, B.J.: Where medicine went wrong. In: Rediscovering the Path to Complexity. World Scientific, London (2006)
52. Bernstein, N.A.: The co-ordination and regulation of movements. Pergamon Press, Oxford (1967)
53. Michaels, C.F., Carello, C.: Direct perception. Prentice-Hall, Englewood Cliffs (1981)
54. Wallot, S., Van Orden, G.: Grounding language in the anticipatory dynamics of the body. Ecol. Psychol. (in press)
55. Van Orden, G.: Voluntary peformance. Medicina 46, 581–594 (2010)
56. Buiatti, M., Papo, D., Baudonnière, P.-M., van Vreeswijk, C.: Feedback modulates the temporal scale-free dynamics of brain electrical activity in a hypothesis testing task. Neuroscience 146(3), 1400–1412 (2007)
57. van Rooij, M., Van Orden, G.: Its about space, its about time, neuroeconomics and the brain sublime. J. Econ. Perspect. (in press)

What Can Be Inferred from Multiple-task Psychophysical Studies about the Mechanisms for Temporal Processing?

Hugo Merchant, Ramón Bartolo, Juan Carlos Méndez, Oswaldo Pérez,
Wilbert Zarco, and Germán Mendoza

Instituto de Neurobiología, UNAM, Campus Juriquilla.
Boulevard Juriquilla No. 3001 Querétaro, Qro. 76230 México
hugomerchant@unam.mx, merch006@umn.edu

Abstract. We used different tools from experimental psychology to obtain a broad picture of the possible neural underpinnings of temporal processing in the range of milliseconds. The temporal variability of human subjects was measured in timing tasks that differed in terms of: explicit-implicit timing, perception-production, single-multiple intervals, and auditory-visual interval markers. The results showed a dissociation between implicit and explicit timing. Inside explicit timing, we found a complex interaction in the temporal variability between tasks. These findings do not support neither a unique nor a ubiquitous mechanism for explicit timing, but support the notion of a partially distributed timing mechanism, integrated by main core structures such as the cortico-thalamic-basal ganglia circuit, and areas that are selectively engaged depending on the specific behavioral requirement of a task. A learning-generalization study of motor timing also supports this hypothesis and suggests that neurons of the timing circuit should be tuned to interval durations.

Keywords: Interval perception and production, circle drawing, multi-dimensional statistics, learning and generalization.

1 Introduction

Time is among the most crucial magnitudes that living beings must quantify in order to survive. From microseconds to circadian rhythms, temporal information is used to guide behavior and specific brain mechanisms have been suggested for the time processing in different time scales covering twelve orders of magnitude. Even though there is not a time sensory organ, organisms are able to extract temporal information from stimuli of all sensory modalities, whether it is the interval between two notes in a symphony or the duration of an eclipse. In addition, during music execution and dancing human beings can generate complex sequences of time intervals with their movements. In some behaviors, an explicit representation of the interval to be timed is used as in tapping with a rhythm,

A. Vatakis et al. (Eds.): Time and Time Perception 2010, LNAI 6789, pp. 207–229, 2011.

while in others time processing is covertly present or implicit as during continuous drawing, where timing is an emergent property of the trajectory produced [1]. Also, time intervals can be produced or estimated just once or as many times as it is needed. Therefore, some of the key elements of temporal processing include the time scale being quantified, the modality of the stimulus, whether time is being measured for a movement or for a perceptual decision, whether the task involves single or multiple intervals, and the implicit or explicit nature of timing.

A central question among time researchers is whether a single neural mechanism is employed for the measurement of time across all kinds of behaviors or if, on the contrary, different areas and encoding strategies are employed by the brain depending on the behavioral context in which time is processed. These two opposing views regarding the mechanism of explicit timing are mainly used for the range of hundreds of milliseconds, a time scale that has been investigated in our laboratory. Although many behaviors that are essential for survival require the temporal processing in this range, the search for the brain mechanisms for time measurement in the scale of milliseconds has not been investigated until recently. In contrast, the psychophysics of temporal quantification started as early as the late XIX century (see [2]), and many timing tasks have been used to test the existence of one or multiple neural clocks. As a natural extension of the psychophysical experiments, a large amount of neuroimaging studies have been conducted recently to describe the brain circuits that are activated in a number of timing tasks.

The present chapter is divided in two sections. The first one is devoted to the comparison between the neuroimaging results and the predictions made by the psychophysical measurements performed in our laboratory regarding the functional organization of a dedicated timing mechanism. The last section focuses on the predictions generated by our study on learning and generalization of time intervals that states that the timing mechanism is multimodal and that at least a fraction of the neurons of the timing circuit should be tuned to different interval durations. The last prediction is supported by neural network simulations.

2   fMRI of Temporal Processing

Functional brain imaging studies have yielded useful information about the structures that participate in time measurement. Numerous perceptual or motor tasks using single or multiple time intervals in the hundreds of milliseconds range have consistently found that structures like the striatum of the basal ganglia and the supplementary motor areas are activated, regardless of the non-timing factors involved in the task, such as the modality of the stimuli used to define the intervals [3, 4, 5, 6, 7, 8, 9]. This has led some to conclude that the same structures are always recruited for temporal processing in this range and that different task features, such as the perceptual or motor nature of the task, or if single or multiple intervals are involved, do not significantly modify which brain regions are activated [10]. In this regard, it has been proposed that some interconnected structures, like the dorsal premotor and supplementary motor areas, the basal ganglia and the thalamus, which are essential for movement planning and execution, also form a timing circuit [11,12]. This is an appealing view, since time perception and production go hand by hand while interacting with the environment. Indeed, various perceptual studies, using auditory [3,6,8], visual [7,9,13,14] and tactile [10] stimuli have reported consistent activation of some or all of the structures of this hypothetical timing circuit. Importantly, humans are not the only primate species that has been investigated. A PET study by Onoe and collaborators [15] using macaque monkeys trained to discriminate between two visually defined time intervals found some of these areas, like the basal ganglia, to be activated. This is a relevant finding, because it implies that these animals can be good models for the neurophysiological study of timing.

However, these are not the only regions that have been reported to increase their activity while timing. A relevant example is the cerebellum, a structure known to have profuse connections with the neocortex. While a group of investigators have reported activation of medial cerebellar structures [6] during timing tasks, others have found activation in the lateral part of the hemispheres [13,16], and still others have not reported their activation at all [3]. The cerebellar activation is regarded by some investigators as an evidence for its involvement in timing but others propose that it may simply reflect its role in sensorimotor integration. A similar example is the dorsolateral prefrontal and the inferior parietal cortices. These structures have also been considered as candidates for a dedicated timing network, albeit more frequently in the seconds range [9]. Some research groups claim that the parietal and prefrontal cortices are activated because they are important nodes in the temporal processing network. Nevertheless, since these regions have important roles in attention and working memory, their activation may reflect that these cognitive processes are needed to solve the tasks. Additionally, some of these studies have also pointed out that a bias seems to exist towards the activation of right hemispheric structures [13], although results from other studies can be considered as a challenge to such view [17].

Fewer studies have focused on interval production rather than perception, but the majority has found again the supplementary motor area, the basal ganglia, the thalamus and the cerebellum to be involved [5,14,17]. In fact, Bueti and collaborators [14] directly investigated whether different regions were activated for perceptual or for motor timing. They found that in both conditions the basal ganglia and the cerebellum increased their signal, but a more complex network that included the supplementary motor areas and the inferior parietal cortex, was preferentially activated during production tasks. Finally, a recent meta-analysis using an activation likelihood estimation algorithm on the data of 20 fMRI studies showed that when maps of both motor and perceptual tasks in the sub-second range are displayed on a single template, the following overlapping areas were detected: SMA, middle frontal gyrus (BA 6), IPL (BA 40), IFG, right caudate and putamen, right insula and the posterior cerebellum [12].

Overall, these findings point out that no single brain structure can be considered as the sole responsible for time quantification. Furthermore, temporal estimation can be viewed as the result of the interaction of multiple cortical and subcortical areas. However, there are some regions that consistently appear to participate conforming the main core timing network that includes the supplementary motor area and the basal ganglia, while others are not that consistent, like the cerebellum, the dorsolateral prefrontal cortex, and the inferior parietal cortex. Other structures may also be recruited depending on particular task demands such as the primary sensory cortical areas. Nevertheless, the functional imaging literature does not support the notion that the representation of time could be ubiquitous, arising from the intrinsic dynamics of non-dedicated neural mechanisms, as suggested by modeling studies [18,19,20]. Thus, these results can begin to shed light on our main question. While there's no unique brain clock, some of its structures definitely seem to conform a partially distributed timing network devoted to the scale of hundreds of milliseconds.

3   Psychophysics of Temporal Processing Across Behavioral Contexts

We have addressed these issues in our laboratory by testing human volunteers on different perceptual and production timing tasks [21, 22]. In order to study the effects of factors other than timing on the performance variability of human subjects we designed four tasks that differed in their sensorimotor processing, the number of intervals, and the modality of the stimuli used to define the intervals (Fig. 1). Importantly, in all the tasks the subjects temporalized their behavior in the range of 350 to 1000 ms. Using these factors we could group the tasks as follows: If timing was required for the guidance of movements, they were classified as time-production tasks, whereas time-perception tasks were those in which perceived intervals had to be compared. Depending on the number of time intervals being produced or compared, they could be categorized as single or multiple-timing tasks. Finally, the stimuli used to cue the subjects could be either visual or auditory [21].

Two tasks could be considered as perceptual. In the time interval Discrimination Task (Dis), subjects were presented with five stimuli that created four isochronous base intervals which were immediately followed by a sixth stimulus that produced a comparison interval. This could be shorter or longer than the base and subjects had to tell which it was by pressing one of two keys on the computer keyboard. The Categorization Task (Cat) had two phases, training and execution. In the training phase, two single intervals were presented to the subjects, an extremely short one and an extremely long one. After 20 trials were performed in this fashion, subjects were presented with six intermediate intervals additionally to the trained ones and subjects were instructed to categorize them as short or long using the prototypes acquired during training (Fig. 1).

In the other two tasks, time intervals were produced with movements. The Multiple Tapping Task (MTap) consisted on producing multiple isochronous intervals by tapping on a button. The first intervals were produced in synchronization with stimuli, which were immediately eliminated after the completion of four intervals and the subjects had to produce four additional internally-timed

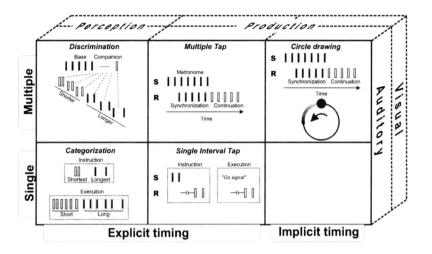

Fig. 1. Timing tasks. Five timing tasks, performed with auditory or visual interval markers, were used to evaluate the influence of four factors on timing performance: explicit vs. implicit, visual vs. auditory modality, single vs. multiple intervals, and perception vs. production of the intervals. Modified from [21, 22]

intervals. The second production task, named Single Tapping Task (STap) had also two phases, instruction and execution. In the instruction phase two stimuli were presented sequentially, creating an interval that the subject was required to reproduce by tapping twice in the push-button. After five instruction trials, subjects did ten trials in the execution phase, in which no interval was presented and only a go signal indicated the subject to produce the instructed interval (Fig. 1).

An important feature of this study is that all subjects performed all the tasks, which increased the ability to detect intra- and inter-task differences in the temporal and non-temporal components of the behavior (Fig. 1). The first crucial observation in this study was that in all tasks the temporal variance increased as a function of the interval, following the scalar property of interval timing [23]. However, as it can be seen in Fig. 2, this relation differed across tasks and modalities. Experimental psychologists have used different analytical strategies to decompose the total variability of task performance into temporal and non-temporal elements. Such methods include the Wing-Kristofferson model [24] and the Slope model [25]. According to the Slope model, variability can be decomposed into time-dependent and time-independent processes from a linear regression between the variability and the squared interval duration. The former correspond to the slope in the regression, since it is directly related with the scalar property of interval timing, and the latter to the intercept. The intercept can be associated with the inherent sensorimotor and memory components of a particular task, which are constant across all the processed interval durations [25]. We used this analysis to test the difference in time-dependent variability between the tasks and found that perceptual, visual and single interval

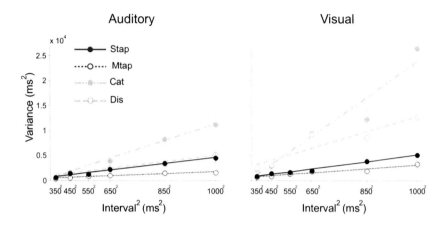

Fig. 2. Mean variances plotted as a function of the interval duration squared for the 4 different tasks in the auditory and visual conditions. Taken from [21].

tasks had significantly larger slopes than the production, auditory and multiple tasks (Fig. 2). These results have at least two interpretations: whether different mechanisms are being used for each task and modality or a common timing system is being modulated by the nature of the task.

We reasoned that if a common timing mechanism was being used to solve all the tasks, then a subject with small timing variability in one task would also have small variability in the other three behavioral paradigms [26]. Consequently, we performed a correlation analysis to compare the performance variability of each subject between pairs of tasks for all interval durations. Indeed, the results are graphically presented in Fig. 3 and show that subjects' performance showed a complex set of significant correlations between many tasks, with consistent correlations between the same task across modalities. These data cannot be interpreted as evidence for multiple timing mechanisms specific for each task context, nor as evidence for a common timing mechanism that functions equally every time a subject quantifies time. Hence, in concordance with the neuroimaging observations, we suggest the existence of a partially distributed timing mechanism, integrated by main core interconnected structures such as the cortico-thalamic-basal ganglia circuit, and areas that are selectively engaged depending on the specific behavioral requirement of a task. These task-dependent areas may interact with the main core timing system to produce the characteristic pattern of performance variability in a paradigm (Fig. 2) and the set of intertask correlations described in Fig. 3. Nevertheless, a precautionary note is in place here, since significant correlations could also be due to common individual cognitive strategies across many tasks.

In the tasks described above time was explicitly present. However, it has been shown that timing variability differs depending on the temporal goals of the task and whether time is guiding behavior directly or if it is an emergent property of the actions [1]. To tackle whether our explicit timing tasks differed from a task

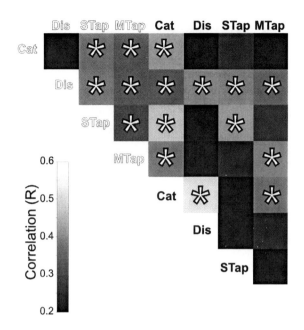

Fig. 3. Correlation matrix showing the Pearson R value in a grayscale (inset, bottom left) for all possible pairwise task comparisons. Asterisks indicate significant correlations (P < 0.05) between specific pairs of tasks. Open and closed fonts correspond to tasks with auditory and visual markers, respectively. Modified from [21].

where time processing is covertly present, we tested the same group of subjects on a Circle Drawing (CirD) task. This task has been regarded as an implicit-timing task, since the kinematic properties of continuous drawing can generate temporal behavior without engaging a neural explicit-timing clock [27]. By manipulating a joystick, subjects controlled the position of a cursor displayed in a monitor and were required to draw a circle following a path of 5 cm of diameter with it. Importantly, subjects were instructed to attempt to pass the cursor through a window in the path in coincidence with the presentation of isochronous auditory or visual stimuli. Once the subjects drew four circles, stimuli were extinguished and four additional circles had to be drawn at the same rate. Hence, the CirD task has the same structure of the MTT but instead of tapping, subjects continuously drew circles in a rhythmic fashion (Fig. 1).

With the subjects' performance variability we constructed a 9x9 dissimilarity matrix, which quantifies the distances in variability between all pairs of tasks [22]. This matrix was initially used for a hierarchical clustering analysis. This analysis accommodates the tasks in a representative spatial configuration known as dendrogram, which reflects how much of the variability in one task is related to the variability in the others. The clustering pattern we obtained is depicted in Fig. 4A and shows three important relationships between the tasks. First of all, the only implicit timing task we tested, circle drawing with both modalities, is

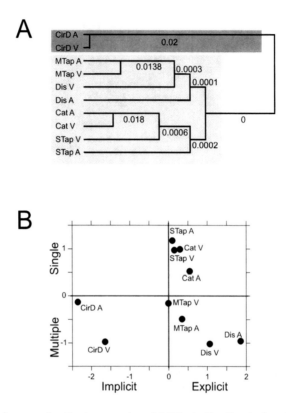

Fig. 4. A. Dendrogram for the temporal variability in the five tasks with both marker modalities, auditory (A) and visual (V). **B.** Two dimensional representation of the performance in the same tasks using multidimensional scaling analysis. Modified from [22].

isolated from the rest of the tasks that require explicit timing. Second, the two single interval tasks (STap and Cat), again with both modalities, are separated from the two multiple interval tasks by the next big branch. Finally, the same tasks with the different modalities are clustered together. The number on the top of the figure is the probability that each tree ramification was a random event. All the branches have a chance likelihood of $p < 0.05$.

Finally, we performed a multidimensional scaling analysis, a method that reduces the dimensionality of a data set, in our case the dissimilarity matrix, to create a two or three dimensional representation of the complex relation between the data. In this way we can obtain the most important underlying dimensions of our data set [22]. Fig. 4B presents our results, where it can be seen that the most important dimension, the abscissa, again separated the circle drawing task from the rest, whereas the second dimension, the ordinate, separated single from multiple interval tasks. Thus, explicit and implicit timing, as well as cyclic or multiple and single interval tasks generate clear differences in performance. The statistical significance of our results is less than 0.0087.

The results of these psychophysical comparisons suggest that the neural underpinnings of implicit timing is different from the dedicated mechanism for explicit timing. Indeed, the performance dissociation of explicit and implicit timing in repetitive tapping and drawing tasks has been meticulously documented using correlation [1, 27, 28] and slope [29] analyses. For example, the temporal consistency during a continuous circle drawing task (very similar to our circle drawing) is not correlated with the timing variability during multiple interval tapping, discrimination, or a task where circle drawing is intermittent [1, 27]. Therefore, it has been suggested that the neural mechanism for implicit timing depends of the motor and premotor areas that control the kinematic properties of continuous rhythmic movement behaviors, such as the circle drawing task, and is not quantifying the passage of time but controlling the velocity of the continuous movement [28]. The present results also showed an important segregation in the performance variability between single and multiple interval timing. This suggests that the activation of a cyclic pattern of behavior not only confers an advantage regarding temporal variability and accuracy in multiple interval tasks as reported before [21, 25, 30], but also may engage a distinctive neural substrate that can be discriminated from the single interval mechanisms using multivariate analytical approaches. Finally, the marker modality did not create superordinate dimensions in the resulting MDS axes. These results are at odds with studies showing that, in both perceptual and production tasks, visual stimuli produce more variable time estimates than auditory ones [21,31,32]. However, our present MDS results may reflect the fact that the explicit-implicit and number of timed intervals functional distinctions are more important than the task modality. In fact, the dendrograms obtained (Fig. 2), which showed a more comprehensive picture of the grouping between behavioral parameters, demonstrated the relevance of task modality.

Our results are in close agreement with those of the neuroimaging literature. They imply that the brain may use some common resources for explicit timing in the hundreds of milliseconds range, but that there are factors that can modify the processing of these intervals, probably by recruiting different structures depending on behavioral constrains. Future studies could measure the changes in the intensity of BOLD signal as a function of some of the mentioned non-temporal factors and the range of intervals that we used, and thus could help in the clarification of these issues. Indeed, multidimensional statistics could be used in order to test whether the structure of the multi-task temporal variability observed in our studies can be replicated using the changes in both the timing circuit configuration and the magnitude of the BOLD signal across brain areas. Needless to say that through neuroimaging and psychophysical studies we can only speculate about the cellular mechanisms behind time quantification. These mechanisms can be addressed with neurophysiological studies that have the spatial and temporal resolution needed to determine the neural codes behind time quantification. Some laboratories, including our own, are beginning to investigate this interesting problem in behaving non-human primates, that seem to be a promising animal model for this research area [33, 34, 35].

4   Contribution of Learning Studies to the Knowledge of Timing Systems

Learning experiments have been another useful tool, although indirect, for the study of different cognitive processes including temporal processing. The characterization of the properties of learning can provide important insights about the neural underpinnings of the behaviors being studied. The changes in behavior induced by training in a controlled context are informative per se, but if we also assess changes in non trained conditions, varying the behavioral context in a systematic way, we can get important additional information about the organization of the underlying neural systems.

Several studies have shown that timing can be improved by practice [36, 37, 38, 39, 40, 41]. In addition, most of these studies have also shown that these improvements can generalize to other timing behaviors. Thus, in this section we review the findings of timing learning-generalization literature including our recent experiment on the matter, which explored other information processing properties of the timing system engaged in the hundreds of milliseconds scale.

The rationale of the learning approach is the following. Let's imagine a network that processes the gray level of a visual stimulus, and that this network has to discriminate a specific gray level (50%-black) from a gradient ranging from 10% to 100%-black, producing a categorical output-signal every time that 50%-black is presented to the network (Fig. 5A). Then, let's assume that this network is able to perform this function from the beginning with a certain precision degree, giving an incorrect output in some trials. Next, we can train the network and produce an increase in its precision for the 50%-black stimulus, promoting a change in the network dynamics every time the output is incorrect while reinforcing correct responses. Finally, after training we can evaluate the precision for the discrimination not only for the 50%-black trained stimulus but also for the complete gray-gradient. This strategy allows to test whether the processing of other gray levels can also profit from the training, suggesting a functional overlap in how the network responds to the trained and non-trained conditions. We would expect that the discrimination errors will decrease with training, producing an output discrimination function that will be more precise for the gray levels surrounding and including the 50%-black, compared with the initial behavior of the network (Fig. 5A). Thus, these effects give us an idea of how the network processes information around the trained parameter, as well as its processing limits. This strategy is followed frequently in the artificial neural network literature. In the specific case of timing, an improvement in time perception induced by training would generalize toward untrained conditions if the time information is processed by the same network. Thus, the amplitude of the generalization window will be determined by the processing capabilities of a dedicated timing network under different timing contexts, which is another psychophysical tool to address the problem of one or multiple clocks, discussed above.

One of the first timing studies that used this approach reported a gradual improvement in a temporal discrimination task across a series of practice sessions [36]. Human subjects were requested to discriminate a standard interval,

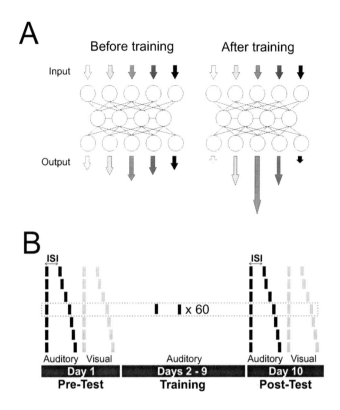

Fig. 5. A. Schematic representation of the learning generalization approach. A network that responds to the presentation of a gray-level stimulus, represented by the input arrows, with a probability of response represented by the size of the output arrow. **B.** Experimental design. The number of days is showed for each of three phases of the experiment (pre-test, training phase, and post-test). ISI - inter-stimuli interval. Modified from [44].

delimited by two tones of a given pitch, from comparison intervals in order to estimate the discrimination threshold. It was observed that the threshold gradually decreased with training, and that the total decrease of the threshold was statistically significant. Additionally, the subjects were tested in non trained conditions, in which the frequency of the tones or the duration of the standard interval were changed. Interestingly, it was observed that the learning effect was transferred to the discrimination of time intervals defined by stimuli with different pitch. However, there was no transfer of learning to standard intervals with different durations [36]. These results revealed that the temporal features are extracted from the auditory stimuli independently of the frequency, and suggest that a common timing network is recruited for time processing regardless of features of the auditory stimuli. On the other hand, the results also imply the existence of interval specific networks, since no learning transfer was observed between the durations of the trained and non-trained standard intervals. It has been suggested that the learning transfer depends on the improvement of temporal processing and not on more efficient memory or decision processes, at least for auditory interval discrimination [40].

In confirmation to the previous study, it has been observed that learning induces an improvement in the discrimination of intervals delimited by tactile stimuli, and that this learning generalizes: (1) across untrained skin locations on the trained hand, (2) to the corresponding untrained skin location in the contralateral hand, and (3) to a timing discrimination task of auditory stimuli [37]. The learning transfer in this study occurs again only in the trained duration [37]. In addition, it has also been observed that intensive learning in a time perception task can cause an improvement in a motor timing task that is restricted to the trained duration, suggesting that motor and perceptual timing share a common neural substrate, and that this substrate is duration-specific [39, 41]. The learning transfer from a perceptual to a motor task has been demonstrated with auditory [39] and tactile [41] interval markers, emphasizing the multimodal nature of the timing mechanism.

On the other hand, some studies suggest that early sensory areas play an important role on temporal processing. For example, it has been shown that learning to discriminate temporal modulation rates was accompanied not only by a specific learning transfer to a temporal interval discrimination (and not to a frequency discrimination task), but also by an increase in the amplitude of the early auditory evoked responses to trained stimuli [42]. This learning induced enhancement of early bilateral auditory evoked responses occurred in conjunction with an increase in the power of gamma oscillations in the inferior frontal cortex, suggesting that plasticity is not confined to auditory cortices and rather engages a distributed timing network [42]. Furthermore, a recent TMS study reported that the disruption of the auditory cortex impaired not only time discrimination of auditory stimuli but also impaired that of visual stimuli to the same degree. In contrast, TMS over the primary visual cortex impaired performance only in visual time discrimination. These asymmetric contributions of the auditory and visual cortices in time perception may be explained by a superiority of the auditory cortex in temporal processing [43]. Hence, these studies emphasize the role of sensory areas in time quantification, showing that auditory areas have a privileged status on temporal processing.

Overall, these studies support the idea of a common timing network that has access to multimodal information, with no topographical organization in the auditory (frequency based) or somatosensory (somatotopic organization) modalities, and that shares resources during time perception and time production. Therefore, this area of timing research also confirms our hypothesis of the existence of a partially distributed timing circuit, where the core network is affected by sensory areas in a context dependent fashion. In addition, these studies show a consistent duration specificity in the learning transfer of timing abilities, which suggest that timing neurons in the partially distributed timing circuit should be tuned to interval durations with relatively sharp tuning curves.

Regarding the latter point, the studies that have reported no learning generalization across interval durations have tested intervals with very different magnitudes (more than 50% of the trained interval), and, therefore, their sensitivity to measure learning transfer in the temporal domain has been low. Hence, one of the questions we had was whether the hypothetical groups of cells that are tuned to different interval durations show sharp or broad tuning curves, and whether the specificity of interval tuning depends on the magnitude of the processed interval. In order to study the learning of motor timing and the transfer of learning in the time domain, we designed an experiment in which several durations surrounding a standard interval (Fig. 5B) were used as targets in the Single Tapping Task (STap), described in the previous section (Fig. 1). Three groups of human subjects were submitted to extensive training (8 days) in one out of three standard Inter-Stimuli Intervals ([ISI] 450, 650 or 850 ms). The subjects completed 60 blocks of trials per day, and each block consisted of 5 instruction trials plus 15 execution trials (900 execution trials per day) using only the standard interval delimited by auditory stimuli [44]. With the purpose of evaluating the transfer of learning across intervals, the performance variability (standard deviation of the produced intervals) of a set of seven target ISI's was assessed using auditory and visual marker stimuli independently, before and after training (Fig. 5B). Therefore, this design allowed us to evaluate the transfer of motor timing learning across different intervals and modalities [44].

The first finding in our study was that human subjects showed a learning process for motor timing (Fig. 6). Learning was manifested as a gradual reduction in performance variability across training sessions, describing a decaying function similar to those observed in perceptual timing tasks [36, 37, 40, 45]. In fact, we found a significant decrease in intertap variability during the execution phase of the STap across training days (ANOVA, $p < 0.01$). In addition, we studied the learning dynamics for each subject by fitting the following power function:

$$SD = bT^m \qquad (1)$$

where SD is the Standard Deviation of the produced intervals (dependent variable), T is the training day (independent variable), m is the time constant (slope) of the function, and b is the intercept, an estimate of the initial value of the curve. We found a significant difference in the intercept b but not in the slope of the power function across trained intervals. These results suggest that the initial value of the curve follows the scalar property of interval timing with a larger variability for larger interval magnitudes, a finding expected from the results reported above. In addition, our findings suggest that the learning dynamics is independent of the trained interval.

The next step was to characterize the transfer of learning in the temporal domain (transfer towards untrained intervals) and between sensory modalities. To this end, we constructed transfer curves where the difference in temporal variability before and after training (Pre-test - Post test) was plotted as a function of the interval magnitude. In addition, we performed one-sample t tests to determine whether the variability reduction was significantly different from

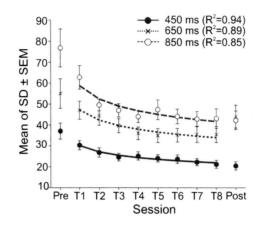

Fig. 6. Learning curves for motor timing. SD (mean ± SEM) of the produced intervals plotted as a function of the training day (T1-T8). Filled circles, crosses, and open circles are data for 450ms, 650ms, and 850ms, respectively. Lines are predicted curves from the fitting to a power function. Modified from [44].

zero for each interval. A clear transfer of learning was observed within the time domain for the three different trained intervals (Fig. 7). However, the generalization pattern (e.g. the intensity of transfer across intervals or modalities) was different for different trained intervals, as follows. For the trained interval of 450ms, we observed a strong generalization of learning only for intervals close to 450ms, whereas for the trained interval of 850ms we found a large learning transfer across a wide range of interval durations. The generalization pattern for the trained interval of 650ms showed intermediate values in terms of magnitude and interval spread; however, the transfer was less organized that the previous two intervals, with contiguous intervals showing inconsistent effects (Fig. 7). Interestingly, the transfer pattern was cross-modal across the three trained intervals. Although subjects were trained using only auditory stimuli, significant improvements were observed for the visual modality.

We performed Gaussian function fittings to the generalization patterns in Fig. 7. High coefficients of determination (R^2) were observed for the transfer curves of 450ms and 850ms, as it would be expected for an organized, gradually decreasing transfer of learning. In contrast, for the 650ms standard a low R^2 was found, in concordance the scattered pattern revealed by the t tests. More importantly, we found that the amplitude of the Gaussians (at the half height) showed a linear increase with the duration of the standard interval, following the scalar property of timing. Finally, the peak of the curves (the mean) was not centered on the trained interval, showing a bias between modalities. Indeed, the bias in the transfer functions might be related to the fact that auditory stimuli tend to be judged longer than visual stimuli [31,46]. Overall, these findings give indirect support for the presence of two important properties of the brain network involved in time quantification during the execution of the STT. First, at least a

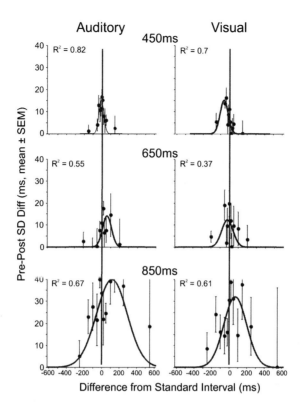

Fig. 7. Transfer curves. Mean (± SEM) difference in performance (Pre-training SD - post-training SD) is plotted as a function of the difference of the target interval with respect to the trained standard. Gaussian fittings were applied to the data and the coefficient of determination (R^2) is showed for each fitting. Taken from [44].

group of neurons in the timing circuit may be tuned to interval durations. The tuning curves of such neurons probably show an increase in tuning dispersion as a function of the preferred interval. This increase in tuning specificity could be one of the neural correlates of the scalar properties of interval timing [47]. Furthermore, our results give additional support for the existence of a multimodal timing circuit that shows a bias towards auditory stimuli (see also Figures 2 and 4). The asymmetrical effects of auditory and visual stimuli on temporal processing are probably due to the privileged access of auditory information [42, 43, 48] to the core timing network. During intensive learning, however, it is possible that not only the auditory areas but also part or the entire main core timing structures are subjected to plastic changes that increased their information processing [42]. Hence, the complete generalization from the auditory to the visual condition observed in our data could be the result of plastic changes in the main core explicit timing network.

The inconsistent transfer of learning for the 650ms standard is very peculiar and should give us a hint about the organization of the duration-specific or tuned neuronal populations. Previous studies have shown that the preferred (unpaced) tapping rate of humans has a bimodal distribution, with peaks around 270ms and 450ms [49, 50]. In addition, a language timing study showed that the distribution of pauses between phrases or paragraphs has also a bimodal distribution with peaks around 400ms and 1200ms, and where the intervals between 600ms and 750ms are the less frequent [51]. Hence, the interval of 650ms could be a duration that is not processed in a common fashion. Based on this evidence we can speculate that the properties of the timing network are shaped by the occurrence of the intervals present in our everyday life, so that the neurons that are tuned to interval durations show a distribution of preferred intervals that reflects the most common processed durations. Thus, we predict that the number of cells with preferred intervals around 650ms should be smaller than the cells with preferred intervals around 450ms and 850ms. An additional thought is that the sculpting of the preferred interval distribution by the environmental temporal patterns should be limited by the innate properties of the timing mechanism, in such a way that our abilities to quantify time across behavioral contexts should depend on the interaction between these two phenomena.

5   Interval Tuning Properties of an Artificial Neural Network

Previous neural network studies have suggested that neural circuits with dynamical changes in their excitatory-inhibitory interactions are able to process temporal information [18, 19, 52]. Consequently, in order to test some of the tuning properties of timing cells predicted by the previous learning and generalization study, we simulated a recurrent neural network. This neural network model was constructed using integrate-and-fire (I&F) units that are simple models of the electrical behavior of a single neuron. The I&F units are characterized by their passive integration in the subthreshold voltage range and the generation of stereotypic spikes above threshold [53]. In addition, we modeled three different time dependent properties of the postsynaptic integration: the paired-pulse facilitation of monosynaptic excitatory postsynaptic potentials (EPSPs), paired-pulse depression of fast inhibitory postsynaptic potentials (IPSPs), and the slow IPSPs produced by the activation of GABAb receptors (Fig. 8A). This network included 400 excitatory units and 100 inhibitory units, with a 20% of random recurrent connectivity and has a similar structure of the network reported by Buonomano in 2000 [18] (Fig. 8B). We used as input stimuli the same intervals included in the generalization experiment in humans: 450, 650, and 850 ms. In fact, two short bursts of activity separated by these durations were used to simulate the input intervals. In addition, we used a layer of perceptron units with backpropagation learning as the reading output of the network. The perceptron layer was connected to the excitatory neurons of the recurrent network and included 3 perceptron units, each associated with the discrimination of our tested intervals (450, 650 and 850 ms; Fig. 8B).

It is important to clarify that this neural network was designed to understand some basic principles of interval tuning in the hundreds of milliseconds range

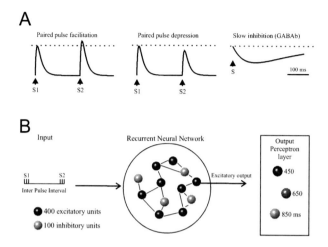

Fig. 8. A. Simulated pair-pulse facilitation of excitatory postsynaptic potential and pair-pulse depression of inhibitory postsynaptic potential in response to pairs of stimuli using a transmitter release probability $\tau_\alpha \frac{dP_\alpha}{dt} = P_\alpha - P_0$, and slow inhibition simulated with a double exponential $\frac{d^2 I}{dt^2} + (\tau_r + \tau_d) \frac{dI}{dt} + (\tau_r \tau_d) I = \sum_j \sum_{ispike} w_{i,j} \delta (t_i - t)$. **B.** The recurrent neural network is composed of 400 excitatory and 100 inhibitory I&F neurons, with a 20% random connectivity. A layer of perceptron units with backpropagation learning was used as a reading output. We have 3 perceptrons corresponding to intervals 450, 650 and 850ms, which received inputs from the excitatory neurons of the recurrent network.

and how these tuning mechanisms could explain the patterns of generalization observed in our experiments. Hence, we are assuming that tuning is an important element used by the main core timing network to encode explicit temporal information. We are not addressing the multimodal or context-independency of interval tuning with these simulations. In fact, we are currently implementing a more sophisticated neural network in order to test how the main core timing areas can generate the scalar property of interval timing and how the specific areas that are engaged depending on the behavioral constrains can produce, in conjunction with the core areas, the patterns of temporal variability observed in the multitask and the learning-generalization studies. Seminal modeling work has suggested that an ubiquitous [19,54] or a centralized timing mechanism, like the Striatal Beat Frequency (SBF) model [55], can explain a range of temporal behaviors.

Interestingly, we found that the recurrent network was able to show interval tuning, characterized by selective neural responses to pairs of input stimuli separated by a particular duration (see the inset of the left panel of Fig. 9A). The tuning specificity depends on the weights of the set of inhibitory and excitatory inputs, as well as the time dependent properties that these inputs produce on the tuned cells. Changing systematically the weights of the excitatory connections with paired-pulse facilitation, as well as the weights of the GABAb connections

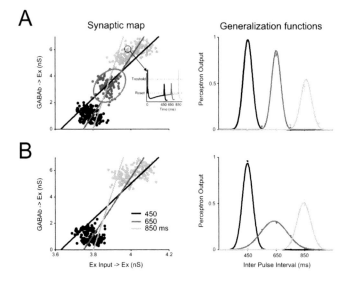

Fig. 9. A. *Left panel*: Synaptic map of the efficacy of GABAb connections (ordinate) and excitatory connections (abscissa) to excitatory neurons in response to pairs of input pulses separated by 450 (black dots), 650 (dark gray dots), or 850 (light gray dots) ms. Thus, depending of the strength of synaptic weights the excitatory neurons respond selectively to inter pulse intervals. The inset panel shows an excitatory neuron that responds selectively to 850ms due to the specific combination of input weights. Lines show the threshold for the interval specific response to the second input pulse stimulus. Black line: 450ms, dark gray line: 650ms, and light gray line: 850ms. *Right panel*: Probability of correct classification by perceptron units to inter pulse interval ranging from 350 to 950 ms. **B.** The same than A but with a synaptic map configuration that does not include the weights for the 650ms selective responses.

to the excitatory cells of the network, we were able to determine a synaptic space where different interval specificities were produced (Fig. 9A, left panel). For example, when both the excitatory and the GABAb inputs weights are high, the circuit produces tuned responses to the 850ms interval. In contrast, when the excitatory weight is moderate, and the facilitation of the excitatory input over-weights the GABAb low input, the circuit shows a selective activation for the 450ms interval (Fig. 9A, left panel).

Initially, we tested the generalization pattern of the recurrent network using a homogenous distribution of weights in the synaptic map (Fig. 9A, left panel). The generalization function for each trained interval was obtained once the perceptron layer was trained to discriminate that interval, and the network was tested to a wide range of intervals without allowing for further learning. Indeed, the right panel of Fig. 9A shows the probability of correct classification by the perceptron units to interval durations ranging from 350 to 950 ms after the network was trained to the 450, 650 and 850 ms intervals independently. It is evident that the width of the generalization curve increased as a function of the duration of the trained interval, following the same organizations observed in the learning and generalization study in human subjects. Therefore, these results suggest that interval tuning can be generated in the timing network through a combination of inhibitory and excitatory weights that show different time dependent properties, such as paired-pulse facilitation of EPSPs, paired-pulse depression of fast IPSPs, and slow IPSPs.

The learning transfer of the interval specificities in the recurrent network showed similar properties observed in the generalization study of motor learning in the STap task. However, an important difference in our network simulations was that the 650ms trained interval showed a strong and systematic generalization across neighbor intervals. In contrast, human subjects showed an inconsistent transfer pattern for interval surrounding the trained 650ms interval. The final question, then, was what is the configuration of weights in the synaptic map that could produce generalization functions in the recurrent network that follow more closely the results obtained in the human subjects study. After testing different synaptic map configurations, we found that a synaptic map with two discrete distributions of weights, one in the lower left quadrant of the map (around the 450ms selective weight area), and another in the upper right quadrant (around the 850ms selective weight area; see the left panel of Fig. 9B), produced generalization functions that were closer to the human timing performance. In fact, the generalization functions depicted in the right panel of Fig. 9B show that the learning transfer for the interval of 650ms was smaller than the 450 and 850 ms trained intervals. Therefore, these findings suggest that the deficient learning transfer for the 650ms in human subjects could be due to a decrease in the frequency of the synaptic weights that lead to the interval specificity to this duration. The decrease in the frequency of specific synaptic weight combinations could be imposed by the occurrence of the intervals processed in our daily life behaviors, as discussed in the previous section.

Overall, our simulation experiments showed that a recurrent network that includes synaptic time dependent properties can produce interval selective responses with a pattern of generalization that was similar to the one observed in the psychometric study in human subjects, with an increase in the width of the generalization function as a function of the duration of the trained interval and a dip in the transfer height for the 650ms interval. The latter effect can be produced by a synaptic map that shows a strong bias towards the synaptic weights associated with the tuning of the 450 and 850 ms intervals.

6   Concluding Remarks

Learning and generalization studies, including our own, provide evidence for the existence of a dedicated general timing mechanism that has access to multimodal information and is engaged in the perception and production of time intervals. Furthermore, our multiple-task psychophysical studies suggest that these behavioral parameters, together with the number of processed intervals, can influence in a specific fashion the performance of the timing mechanism. These latter observations have refined our hypothesis, suggesting that time quantification in the hundreds of milliseconds depends on a partially distributed circuit of interconnected brain areas. In addition, our learning and generalization study gave support to the notion that at least a fraction of the neurons of the time processing neural circuit should be tuned to different interval durations, and that the width of their tuning curves may increase as a function of their preferred intervals. Artificial neural network simulations demonstrated that interval tuning can be produced in a simple recurrent network that includes different time dependent synaptic properties. Indeed, preliminary neurophysiological studies performed in our laboratory on behaving monkeys, have shown that a portion of neurons in the supplementary motor cortex are tuned to interval durations during the execution of different timing tasks.

Acknowledgements. We thank Luis Prado and Raul Paulín for their technical assistance. Supported by CONACYT: 053944, PAPIIT: IN206508.

References

1. Zelaznik, H.N., Spencer, R.M.C., Ivry, R.B.: Dissociation of Explicit and Implicit Timing in Repetitive Tapping and Drawing Movements. J. Exp. Psychol: Human Percept Perform 28, 575–588 (2002)
2. Boring, E.G.: Sensation and perception in the history of experimental psychology. Appleton-Century-Crofts, New York (1942)
3. Nenadic, I., Gaser, C., Volz, H.P., Rammsayer, T., Hager, F., Sauer, H.: Processing of temporal information and the basal ganglia: new evidence from fMRI. Exp. Brain Res. 148, 238–246 (2003)
4. Coull, J.T., Vidal, F., Nazarian, B., Macar, F.: Functional Anatomy of the Attentional Modulation of Time Estimation. Science 303, 1506–1508 (2004)
5. Rao, S.M., Harrington, D.L., Haaland, K.Y., Bobholz, J.A., Cox, R.W., Binder, J.R.: Distributed Neural Systems Underlying the Timing of Movements. J. Neurosci. 17, 5528–5535 (1997)
6. Rao, S.M., Mayer, A.R., Harrington, D.L.: The evolution of brain activation during temporal processing. Nat. Neurosci. 4, 317–323 (2001)
7. Ferrandez, A.M., Hugueville, L., Lehericy, S., Poline, J.B., Marsault, C., Pouthas, V.: Basal ganglia and supplementary motor area subtend duration perception: an fMRI study. Neuroimage 19, 1532–1544 (2003)
8. Harrington, D.L., Boyd, L.A., Mayer, A.R., Sheltraw, D.M., Lee, R.R., Mingxiong, H., Rao, S.M.: Neural representation of interval encoding and decision making. Cogn. Brain Res. 21, 193–205 (2004)
9. Lewis, P., Miall, C.: Distinct systems for automatic and cognitively controlled time measurement: evidence from neuroimaging. Curr. Opin. Neurobiol. 13, 250–255 (2003)
10. Macar, F., Lejeune, H., Bonnet, M., Ferrara, A., Pouthas, V., Vidal, F., Maquet, P.: Activation of the supplementary motor area and of attentional networks during temporal processing. Exp. Brain Res. 142, 475–485 (2002)
11. Schubotz, R.I., Friederici, A.D., von Cramon, D.Y.: Time Perception and Motor Timing: A Common Cortical and Subcortical Basis Revealed by fMRI. Neuroimage 11, 1–12 (2000)

12. Wiener, M., Turkeltaub, P., Coslett, H.H.: The image of time: A voxel-wise meta-analysis. Neuroimage 49, 1728–1740 (2010)
13. Smith, A., Taylor, E., Lidzba, K., Rubia, K.: A right hemispheric frontocerebellar network for time discrimination of several hundreds of milliseconds. Neuroimage 20, 344–350 (2003)
14. Bueti, D., Walsh, V., Frith, C., Rees, G.: Different Brain Circuits Underlie Motor and Perceptual Representations of Temporal Intervals. J. Cogn. Neurosci. 20, 204–214 (2008)
15. Onoe, H., Komori, M., Onoe, K., Takechi, H., Tsukada, H., Watanabe, Y.: Cortical Networks Recruited for Time Perception: A Monkey Positron Emission Tomography (PET) Study. Neuroimage 13, 37–45 (2001)
16. Ivry, R.B., Keele, S.W., Diener, H.C.: Dissociation of the lateral and medial cerebellum in movement timing and movement execution. Exp. Brain Res. 73, 167–180 (1988)
17. Rubia, K., Overmeyer, S., Taylor, E., Brammer, M., Williams, S., Simmons, A., Andrew, C., Bullmore, E.: Prefrontal involvement in "temporal bridging" and timing movement. Neuropsychologia 36, 1283–1293 (1998)
18. Buonomano, D.V.: Decoding temporal information: A model based on short-term synaptic plasticity. J. Neurosci. 20, 1129–1141 (2000)
19. Karmarkar, U.R., Buonomano, D.V.: Timing in the absence of clocks: encoding time in neural network states. Neuron 53, 427–438 (2007)
20. Ivry, R.B., Schlerf, J.E.: Dedicated and intrinsic models of time perception. Trends Cogn. Sci. 12, 273–280 (2008)
21. Merchant, H., Zarco, W., Prado, L.: Do We Have a Common Mechanism for Measuring Time in the Hundreds of Millisecond Range? Evidence From Multiple-Interval Timing Tasks. J. Neurophysiol. 99, 939–949 (2008)
22. Merchant, H., Zarco, W., Bartolo, R., Prado, L.: The Context of Temporal Processing Is Represented in the Multidemensional Relationships between Timing Tasks. PLoS One 3, e3169 (2008)
23. Gibbon, J., Malapani, C., Dale, C.L., Gallistel, C.R.: Toward a neurobiology of temporal cognition: advances and challenges. Curr. Opin. Neurobiol. 7, 170–184 (1997)
24. Wing, A.M., Kristofferson, A.B.: Response delays and the timing of discrete motor responses. Percept. Psychophys. 14, 5–12 (1973)
25. Ivry, R.B., Hazeltine, R.E.: Perception and production of temporal intervals across a range of durations: evidence of a common timing mechanism. J. Exp. Psychol. Hum. Percept. Perform. 21, 3–18 (1995)
26. Keele, S., Nicoletti, R., Ivry, R., Pokorny, R.: Do perception and motor production share common timing mechanisms? A correlational analysis. Acta Psychol. 60, 173–191 (1985)
27. Robertson, S.D., Zelaznik, H.N., Lantero, D.A., Bojczyk, K.G., Spencer, R.M., Doffin, J.G., Schneidt, T.: Correlations for timing consistency among tapping and drawing tasks: evidence against a single timing process for motor control. J. Exp. Psychol. Hum. Percept. Perform. 25, 1316–1330 (1999)
28. Zelaznik, H.N., Spencer, R.M., Ivry, R.B., Baria, A., Bloom, M., Dolansky, L., Justice, S., Patterson, K., Whetter, E.: Timing variability in circle drawing and tapping: probing the relationship between event and emergent timing. J. Mot. Behav. 3, 395–403 (2005)

29. Spencer, R.M., Zelaznik, H.N.: Weber (slope) analyses of timing variability in tapping and drawing tasks. J. Mot. Behav. 35, 371–381 (2003)
30. Grondin, S.: Discriminating time intervals presented in sequences marked by visual signals. Percep. Psychophys. 63, 1214–1228 (2001)
31. Wearden, J.H., Edwards, H., Fakhri, M., Percival, A.: Why "sounds are judged longer than lights": application of a model of the internal clock in humans. Q. J. Exp. Psychol. 51B, 97–120 (1998)
32. Repp, B.H., Penel, A.: Auditory dominance in temporal processing: New evidence from synchronization with simultaneous visual and auditory sequences. J. Exp. Psychol. Hum. Perfor. 28, 1085–1099 (2002)
33. Leon, M.I., Shadlen, M.N.: Representation of time by neurons in the posterior parietal cortex of the macaque. Neuron 38, 317–327 (2003)
34. Mita, A., Mushiake, H., Shima, K., Matsuzaka, Y., Tanji, J.: Interval time coding by neurons in the presupplementary and supplementary motor areas. Nat. Neurosci. 12, 502–507 (2009)
35. Zarco, W., Merchant, H., Prado, L., Mendez, J.C.: Subsecond timing in primates: comparison of interval production between human subjects and Rhesus monkeys. J. Neurophysiol. 102, 3191–3202 (2009)
36. Wright, B.A., Buonomano, D.V., Mahncke, H.W., Merzenich, M.M.: Learning and generalization of auditory temporal-interval discrimination in humans. J. Neurosci. 17, 3956–3963 (1997)
37. Nagarajan, S.S., Blake, D.T., Wright, B.A., Byl, N., Merzenich, M.: Practice related improvements in somatosensory interval discrimination are temporally specific but generalize across skin location, hemisphere, and modality. J. Neurosci. 18, 1559–1570 (1998)
38. Westheimer, G.: Discrimination of short time intervals by the human observer. Exp. Brain. Res. 129, 121–126 (1999)
39. Meegan, D.V., Aslin, R.N., Jacobs, R.A.: Motor timing learned without motor training. Nat. Neurosci. 3, 860–862 (2000)
40. Karmarkar, U.R., Buonomano, D.V.: Temporal specificity of perceptual learning in an auditory discrimination task. Learn. Mem. 10, 141–147 (2003)
41. Planetta, P., Servos, P.: Somatosensory temporal discrimination learning generalizes to motor interval production. Brain Res. 1233, 51–57 (2008)
42. Wassenhove, V., Nagarajan, S.S.: Auditory Cortical Plasticity in Learning to Discriminate Modulation Rate. J. Neurosci. 27, 2663–2672 (2007)
43. Kanai, R., Lloyd, H., Bueti, D., Walsh, V.: Modality-independent role of the primary auditory cortex in time estimation. Exp. Brain. Res. 209, 465–471 (2011)
44. Bartolo, R., Merchant, H.: Learning and generalization of time production in humans: rules of transfer across modalities and interval durations. Exp. Brain Res. 197, 91–100 (2009)
45. Kristofferson, A.B.: A quantal step function in duration discrimination. Percept. Psychophys. 27, 300–306 (1980)
46. Grondin, S.: From physical time to the first and second moments of psychological time. Psychol. Bull. 127, 22–44 (2001)
47. Ivry, R.: The representation of temporal information in perception and motor control. Curr. Opin. Neurobiol. 6, 851–857 (1996)
48. Gamache, P.L., Grondin, S.: Sensory-specific clock components and memory mechanisms: investigation with parallel timing. Eur. J. Neurosci. 31, 1908–1914 (2010)
49. Collyer, C.E., Broadbent, H.A., Church, R.M.: Categorical time production: evidence for discrete timing in motor control. Percept. Psychophys. 51, 134–144 (1992)

50. Collyer, C.E., Broadbent, H.A., Church, R.M.: Preferred rates of repetitive tapping and categorical time production. Percept. Psychophys. 55, 443–453 (1994)
51. Fant, G., Kruckenberg, A.: On the quantal nature of speech timing. In: Proceedings of ICSLP 1996, Philadelphia, pp. 2044–2047 (1996)
52. Durstewitz, D.: Self-organizing neural integrator predicts interval times through climbing activity. J. Neurosci. 23, 5342–5353 (2003)
53. Dayan, P., Abbott, L.F.: Theoretical Neuroscience. In: Computational and Mathematical Modeling of Neural Systems, p. 460. MIT Press, Cambridge Mass (2001)
54. Buonomano, D.V., Laje, R.: Population clocks: motor timing with neural dynamics. Trends Cogn. Sci. 14, 520–527 (2010)
55. Matell, M.S., Meck, W.H.: Cortico-striatal circuits and interval timing: coincidence detection of oscillatory processes. Cogn. Brain Res. 21, 139–170 (2004)

Quality Space Model of Temporal Perception

Michał Klincewicz*

Graduate Center, City University of New York, Philosophy and Cognitive Science
365 5th Avenue, New York, NY 10016-4309, USA
michal.klincewicz@gmail.com

Abstract. Quality Space Theory is a holistic model of qualitative states. On this view, individual mental qualities are defined by their locations in a space of relations, which reflects a similar space of relations among perceptible properties. This paper offers an extension of Quality Space Theory to temporal perception. Unconscious segmentation of events, the involvement of early sensory areas, and asymmetries of dominance in multi-modal perception of time are presented as evidence for the view.

Keywords: temporal perception, quality space theory, event segmentation, multi-modal perception.

1 Mental Qualities

The dominant view in philosophy is that mental states represent by instantiating various representational properties. The nature of these properties remains controversial. Nonetheless, it is widely noted that intentional states, such as thoughts, have intentional content, which can be captured in a clause that follows a mental verb and "that." For example, the sentence "Pam thinks that ripe strawberries are red" captures the content of Pam's thought, which is {ripe strawberries are red}. If Pam chooses to express that thought verbally by saying "strawberries are red," her utterance will reflect that thought's intentional content.

The situation is different with qualitative states, such as sensations. The sentence "Pam sees red" ostensibly fails to capture the red quality of Pam's visual sensation of red. Pam's verbal utterance "I see red" expresses her judgment that she is seeing red, but does not express the qualitative character of her red experience. Consequently, the qualitative character of sensations might seem to be ineffable. And contrasted with the relative ease with which we appear to be able to verbally express the content of thoughts, this might lead one to think that qualitative character is mysterious and perhaps even beyond scientific description.

---

* I'm indebted to Valtteri Arstila and especially David Rooonthal for input on ideas contained herein. I would also like to thank an anonymous reviewer of the present volume for many insightful and challenging comments. Any mistakes are entirely my own.

A. Vatakis et al. (Eds.): Time and Time Perception 2010, LNAI 6789, pp. 230–245, 2011.

The seeming mysteriousness of qualitative character is the result of an assumption about a close connection between mental qualities and conscious experience. We know about mental red, it seems, only from conscious experiences of red things. Consequently, it might appear that qualitative character is present only in consciousness.

This assumption carries over to all qualities of experience, including the temporal ones. The qualitative character of, for example, the passing of time is something that is often thought to be manifest only in consciousness. In fact, there is a tradition in philosophy of making an explanation of the temporal aspect of consciousness central to a theory of consciousness itself [1–3].

But the assumption that mental qualities and consciousness are connected in this way is questionable. And there are alternative theories of mental qualities that do not come saddled with the assumption about their connection to conscious experience. According to some alternative views, we can describe and individuate mental qualities independently of how they appear in conscious experience.

One class of such theories relies on perceptual role. Proponents of this approach focus on the discriminations that an organism makes in its interactions with the environment. On perceptual role views, the states of the organism that enable it to make discriminations instantiate mental qualities, so we can define mental qualities in terms of the discriminations that they make possible.

The states that enable an organism to discriminate must reflect, in some way, the perceptible properties in the environment, such as surface reflectance or chemical composition. But these states do not themselves instantiate the perceptible properties–the properties that allows an organism to discriminate the electromagnetic spectrum are properties of the organism, not of the electromagnetic spectrum. However, the organisms states must be such as to enable the discriminations, and reflect the discriminable differences between the perceptible properties.

There are several versions of the perceptual role approach. Some focus on the causal and informational relationships between perceptible properties and mental qualities [4]. But, for various reasons, the causal and informational approach is unappealing as an account of qualitative character manifest in conscious experience. It is especially problematic for conscious sensations of time [5].

There are also other approaches, which defend the special role of consciousness in identifying mental qualities, by making a case for the distinction between access and phenomenal consciousness [6]. There also other views, such as naive realism or representationalism. But since this is a paper about a particular view of temporal mental qualities, and not a survey, I will not expand on these.

Instead, for the purposes of this paper, I will simply assume the perceptual role strategy is most promising and its best version is Quality Space Theory (QST), also known as Homomorphism Theory [7, 8]. QST is the view that the states of the organism that enable it to make discriminations between stimuli are related to each other in ways that parallel the ways that perceptible properties are related. QST is a holistic theory of mental qualities, in that it defines them as members of families of other similarly related properties.

According to QST, the relationships between the perceptible properties are paralleled in the relationships between states of the organism that allow it to make discriminations among them. Given this, QST takes advantage of the similarities and differences between perceptible properties, such as red being more similar to orange than to blue, or C-sharp being closer to D than to A-flat. These similarities and differences are reflected, according to QST, in the relations between mental red and mental orange, and mental C-sharp, D, and A-flat.

Similarities and differences naturally form distance metrics, which in turn define spaces. Perhaps the most famous of these is the three-dimensional space of the color spectrum, which represents all similarity and difference relations that hold between individual hues and saturations [9]. According to QST, the discriminations an organism can make among visually perceptible properties defines a similar space of relations [8].

So when Pam sees a ripe strawberry, she is in a qualitative state that bears a set of relations to other states of the same kind. Because these relations reflect the relations that a particular visible property bears to a family of properties in the same family, Pam's state enables her to discern and respond differentially to the ripeness of the strawberry. The mental quality of Pam's state reflects those relations in the relevant way.

According to QST, it is an entirely different question why Pam's conscious experience appears to her to have the qualitative character that it does. Mental red is, according to QST, a property relevantly located within a space of similar properties, all of which play a role in visual perception. Qualitative redness of Pam's conscious experience is explanatorily idle as far as her visual discriminations are concerned.

Given this, QST does not need to appeal to the qualitative character manifest in conscious experience to describe individual mental qualities. According to QST, as with other perceptual role accounts, discriminations are enough. This avoids mysterianism, and lends the account to empirical confirmation.

However, the limited sketch of QST I've given here does not yet yield an explanation of more complex mental qualities, such as shape, location, timing, and duration. The theory has been extended to account for mental qualities relevant to perception of space, and I direct the interested reader to the relevant literature [8, 10, 11]. This paper offers an extension of QST to temporal mental qualities, such as duration and timing.

There are several existing hypothesis about the neurbiological underpinnings of temporal perception. Among them are various inner clock models, which posit a dedicated time mechanism, often in the cerebellum and the basal ganglia [12–18]. Alternatives to the dedicated models posit distributed mechanisms that keep track of energy levels in neuron populations or patterns of neural activation [19–21].

It is important to note that the extension of QST to temporal perception that is presented in the last section of this paper is not meant to be in competition with those or any other neurobiological hypotheses. The model on offer here is stated at the psychological level of description, not at the neurobiological level. Nonetheless, in the final analysis QST and/or its extension to temporal perception could turn out to be incompatible with some or all of the abovementioned neurobiological hypotheses.

Hence, before the temporal quality space model is stated I will outline some of the constraints on a philosophical theory of mental time set by the significant amount of psychophysical and neuroimagining research into the mechanisms of time perception. A philosophical theory of mental time should, of course, be compatible with these results, but it should also aim to illuminate how they hang together. The temporal quality space model does both of these things and this is a distinct advantage of the model.

2   Constraints

2.1   Temporal Boundary Detection and Filling-in Durations

This section offers evidence for two constraints on a successful philosophical theory of mental time from a selected number of avenues of research into temporal perception. The two constraints are: (1) the theory should predict that temporal mental qualities can be instantiated unconsciously; (2) the theory should predict that each sensory modality has its own proprietary temporal qualities. Both are predictions of the extension to QST I will offer in the last section.

We know that the mechanisms responsible for processing the timing of stimuli have a consistent sampling rate. For humans, this rate is approximately 30 milliseconds and holds for all modalities [22]. Distinct stimuli have to be separated by at least 30 milliseconds to be perceived as successive. Otherwise they appear simultaneous.

There is also evidence that there is a second timing mechanism that operates with a 3 second sampling window, which is independent of the one operating at 30 milliseconds. Evidence for this second mechanism comes from ambiguous stimuli such as the necker cube, which alternate their perceptual interpretation approximately every 3 seconds [23]. Similarly, sequences of phonemes such as CU-BA-CU alternate between the CUBA interpretation and BACU interpretation approximately every 3 seconds [24]. The 3 second sampling rate can be found in a number of other studies of perception in all modalities, which all suggest that every 3 seconds "the brain asks: 'what is new?' " in the perceptual input [22].

The relatively constant sampling rates at 30 milliseconds and at 3 seconds suggest that the perceptual system breaks the input stream into units and tracks changes between them. When a relevant difference is detected, the sensory system either marks the onset of a completely new stimulus or marks the onset of a change in an existing stimulus. When no difference is detected between successive units, the system treats the stimulus as extended in time, that is, as having an extended duration.

There are at least two levels at which the machinery of temporal perception can be analyzed, and these sampling rates probably reflect the operation of different functional levels of the perceptual hierarchy. On this hierarchical model, the sensory system first provides a temporal frame and then passes it onto the next level in the processing hierarchy, which is responsible for generating temporal perceptual content [25, 26]. The generation of content could be done by an inner clock or one of the other neurobiological mechanisms I mentioned in the first section or by some other process.

A critical issue for supporting constraint (1) is whether the perceptual system can detect change, and thereby mark the onset or offset of a stimulus, unconsciously. In other words, can the brain ask "what is new?" without us being aware of it? Below I outline some of what I take to be the most suggestive evidence that it can, even though some of the evidence is indirect and my discussion of it speculative.

The first piece of evidence comes from event segmentation in the visual system. In one fMRI study, participants were asked to watch several uncut movies of everyday activities such as making a bed [27]. Each movie was shown three times. During the first presentation of the movie, participants were asked to simply pay attention. In the next two presentations of the movie, participants were asked to segment the movies into events that were meaningful to them and to press a button to mark the beginning of one event and the end of another.

In the second viewing, participants were asked to segment in a coarse-grained way. In the third viewing, they were asked to segment finely. fMRI recordings taken during these two active trials were then compared with fMRI recordings taken during the initial passive viewing. The prediction here was that the differences between recordings would uncover the mechanism of active event segmentation.

The fMRI recordings taken during active segmentation showed significant activation in areas V5 (MT) FEF, and V1. Furthermore, when time-locked to the active segmentation times, the imagining data obtained from the passive viewing showed similar activation. The same visual areas were active in all three viewings, even though in one of them the observer was not consciously tracking onset and offset of events.

This result suggests that the brain tracks temporal event structure in virtue of a visual mechanism, which is sensitive to the timing of the onset and offset of a stimulus. V5 (MT) activations during the passive viewing indicate that temporal boundaries are sensed even when the observer is not aware doing so [28]. Segmentation of events involves the detection of temporal boundaries of a stimulus. Such boundaries are treated by the sensory system as markers of onset and offset.

My interpretation of these results in context of the hierarchical model of temporal perception is that V1 and V5 (MT) are the earliest level of temporal processing and set up the temporal frame. The frame set up by this mechanism is then passed on to higher levels of the perceptual processing hierarchy, where event structure is explicitly represented. Importantly for the present discussion, event structure is represented without the perceiver being aware of it. If this interpretation is correct, the just mentioned study informs us about some of the neural mechanisms involved in processing the onset and offset of visual events and supports the view that the mechanism that does this can operate without us being aware of it any way.

But, of course, temporal perception does not limit itself to the detection of onset and offset of stimuli. The other important dimension of temporal perception is duration, which does not always correspond to the boundaries set by onset and offset. There is some indirect evidence, however, that duration can be perceived unconsciously as well.

Stimuli are perceived to have duration when they are perceived as unchanged, that is, when no offset is detected. So when no offset is detected two distinct stimuli presented close to each other and in succession can appear to be fused into one moving stimulus. This illusory effect is sometimes referred to as apparent motion.

Several fMRI studies of apparent motion show that area V1 is active both when the two stimuli are not fused, and when they are, as during apparent motion. However, area V5 (MT) is more active during apparent motion [29, 30]. This suggests that V5 (MT) is involved in the filling-in between the temporal boundaries set by the pair of distinct stimuli. Its important to note that these are the same visual areas implicated in the abovementioned fMRI study of event segmentation.

But a mere activation pattern does not tell us what role V5 (MT) has in that filling-in. To explore the role that V5 (MT) plays in the effect, V5 (MT) activation would have to not only be correlated with the effect, but also shown to be its cause. This was the aim of another fMRI based study, which used activation patterns in apparent motion effects to model connections between V1 and V5 (MT) [31].

The prediction in that study was that activity in the neural connections between V5 (MT) and V1 could be correlated with the filling-in of individual parts of an illusory curve created in V1 by apparent motion. As predicted, the model that best fit the data had no lateral connections in V1, but lots of feedback from V5 (MT). The authors conclude that V5 (MT) has causes the filling-in of the path of the illusory stimulus.

Supporting the view that V5 (MT) is involved in filling-in between temporal boundaries, repetitive TMS to V5 (MT) reduces the apparent motion effect [32]. And without the filling-in between onset and offset, a single stimulus with an extended duration is perceived as two distinct stimuli with shorter durations. This suggests that visual detection of duration is impaired without V5 (MT).

On the interpretation I have proposed above in connection with event segmentation, V1 and V5 (MT) are involved in setting up the temporal frame needed for further processing at the level of content. I have speculated that V5 (MT) is involved in the filling-in that is relevant to discriminations of duration. Together, this suggests that the early visual system and V5 (MT) in particular, is involved in processing timing as well as the duration of stimuli.

But can all of this happen unconsciously? There is strong independent evidence that V5 (MT) can operate without the involvement of awareness. And if that is so, we should suppose that whatever role V5 (MT) has in temporal perception, at whatever level of the processing hierarchy, can occur unconsciously.

The strongest evidence for this claim, it seems to me, comes from blindsighters, who typically have focal damage to V1 and are not aware of having visual sensations in some portion of their visual field. Blindsighters tend to perform significantly above chance in visual discrimination tasks that involve the part of the visual field in which they report having no visual sensations [33]. And in particular, they do well in tasks that involve rapid motion detection [34, 35].

Motion illusions are particularly telling here. In normal perceivers, a square visual stimulus followed by a rectangular visual stimulus presented next to the square stimulus results in a motion aftereffect in which the rectangle appears to be drawn away from the location of the square. This effect is usually referred to as the line motion illusion.

When this stimulus is presented in the blindsighted participant's (G.Y.) blind visual field, they are significantly above chance in telling the direction of apparent motion [36]. G.Y. is susceptible to the motion aftereffect of the line motion illusion, even though they report having no relevant conscious visual sensations. This shows that motion processing carried out by V5 (MT) can occur without awareness. That is already enough to give some credence to the hypothesis that the mechanisms of temporal perception function without awareness.

Together with the evidence about unconscious segmentation, we have reason to think that both timing and duration can be discriminated unconsciously. A philosophical theory of sensation of time should be compatible with this claim. And this is my case for constraint (1), which states that mental qualities can be instantiated unconsciously.

Furthermore, the studies mentioned above also give us some idea of how the visual system processes time. The mechanisms responsible for the sensation of timing depend on the detection of temporal boundaries. The early visual area V1 is critical to this process. Visual mechanisms responsible for the sensation of duration depend on filling-in between the temporal boundaries detected by V1. I have speculated that the early visual area V5 (MT) is critical to that process.

Other modalities have neural structures that are functionally analogous to V1 [37–39]. Hence it is likely that each sensory modality has distinct mechanisms for temporal boundary detection and filling-in. Given this, the abovementioned constraints about unconscious processing of time and involvement of early sensory areas can probably be generalized to other modalities, but that is further speculation that is beyond the scope of this paper.

Temporal processing in early sensory areas suggests that each sensory modality can process time independently of the others. And if a stronger case can be made for this view, it can support constraint (2), which is that each sensory modality has its own proprietary temporal qualities. In the next section I give some more evidence that I take to support constraint (2).

2.2 Cross-Modal Effects and Time

The first problem a multi-sensory system faces lies in the physical differences between the stimuli and the sensory organs that detect them. Light travels faster than sound, for example, and requires more neural processing. And the sense of touch depends on the transmission of signal from variously spaced nerve endings; a signal that starts in the foot has a larger distance to travel than a signal that starts in the neck.

Given all these differences, the perceptual system faces a substantive computational challenge in syncing up information from different modalities. Especially pressing here is the challenge of representing the timing of the stimulus accurately relative to other stimuli. Multi-sensory integration of temporal information has been studied extensively, but little is yet known about the mechanisms that underlie it [40].

What seems clear, however, is that the brain compensates for cross-modal differences by treating some signals as originating in a single source. Presumably, this is carried out by a modality-neutral mechanism, which takes information from distinct modalities and integrates them into a final temporal percept. This modality-neutral mechanism matches input streams from different modalities and syncs them up in an appropriate way.

But positing such a mechanism goes only so far. The perceptual system does not seem to treat input from different modalities in the same way. And various effects support the view that at the later stages of the perceptual processing hierarchy, where timing and duration are represented, different sensory modalities represent time differently.

In one study concerned with multi-modal perception, participants were presented with a sound and a light with up to a 200 millisecond delay between them [41]. The distance between the origin of the stimulus and the perceiver varied from 1 to 32 meters. And the stimuli themselves also varied in intensity.

The participants were asked to press one of two buttons to indicate whether the sound or the light occurred first. Analysis of the reaction times recorded with these button presses shows that simultaneous audio-visual pairs are perceived as being simultaneous despite differences in the time it takes the signal to get from its source to the sense organ. This effect is simultaneity constancy.

As with other types of perceptual constancy, simultaneity constancy allows us to perceive things as constant across variations in incoming signal. Color constancy, for example, allows us to perceive a green wall as being the same color, even though what we actually see is a large number of different shades of green. Simultaneity constancy allows us to perceive signals that arrive at our sensory organs at different times, and which are processed at different rates, as occurring at the same time.

In color constancy, there is a point when the shade differences are too pronounced to go unnoticed. This can happen when the wall is illuminated by a spotlight, for example, or dimmed by a shadow. Similarly, two simultaneously occurring stimuli will be perceived as non-simultaneous if the two signals reach the perceiver at too great a temporal distance apart [42].

Simultaneity constancy also encompasses touch. In one study, participants were first presented with visual and tactile stimuli and then asked to respond as quickly as possible by pressing a button [43]. Their reaction times to visual stimuli were constant, but reactions to tactile stimuli were slower the further away the stimulus was from the brain. The obtained results allowed the experimenters to create a function that could then be used to predict the temporal window in which differently located visual and tactile stimuli are perceived as simultaneous.

In the second experiment of that study, the participants were presented with pairs of variously offset (0-200 milliseconds) visual-visual and visual-tactile stimuli located on different parts of their body. For example, a light on the foot and a tap on the hand. The participants were then asked to press one of two buttons to indicate which of the two stimuli came first. The results were then compared with the data collected in the first experiment.

The participants' reaction times to visual-visual pairs presented at different body parts resulted in same reaction times and the same point of simultaneity, as those predicted in the first experiment. Tactile-tactile pairs presented at different body parts resulted in a different pattern of reaction times depending on the distance that the signal has to travel to the brain via the nervous system, also as predicted by experiment one. However, the point at which two tactile stimuli were perceived as simultaneous was slightly different than the point of simultaneity predicted by the function obtained from the first experiment.

The reaction times to pairs of visual-tactile stimuli presented at different body parts did not differ from the prediction in the first experiment at all. But, importantly, pairs of visual-tactile stimuli presented to the same body part did not match the predictions of the same experiment. Visual-tactile pairs presented in the same location were treated as if they were one event, ignoring the differences in the signals. This result indicates that the mechanism coordinating visual and tactile timing compensates for processing time differences across those modalities to maintain simultaneity constancy.

In the third experiment the participants were exposed to a 5 minute series of visual-auditory stimuli pairs with a 250 millisecond interval between them. As a consequence of this exposure, the participants reaction times changed in such a way as to move the point of subjective simultaneity by 40 milliseconds. So a sound needed to be presented 40 milliseconds earlier than the light to achieve the same point of subjective simultaneity that was obtained in the first experiment.

After this training, the participants were also shown visual-tactile stimulus pairs. And, strikingly, there was no shift in their subjective judgments of simultaneity for visual-tactile pairs. So the adaptation effect from a stream of visual-auditory pairs affected simultaneity judgments for consequent visual-auditory pairs, but not for visual/tactile pairs.

The asymmetry of this effect suggests that the mechanism responsible for simultanelty constancy effect between audition and vision is distinct from the mechanism that handles simultaneity constancy between touch and vision. Given this, the third experiment of this study together with other similar studies of simultaneity constancy supports the view that timing is processed differently across modalities [44, 45].

Of course, it is possible that modality-specific adaptation effects concern processes that are earlier than any part of the processing hierarchy relevant to perceived simultaneity. They could be the result of a process in LGN, for example, which presumably precedes the level of perceptions[1]. This alternate interpretation of the abovementioned effects calls in question their value as support for constraint (2).

However, there are independent avenues of research that allow us to speculate that the LGN has a more substative role in perception, and is not merely a relay station for the signal coming from the retina. This is suggested by the complex circuitry of the LGN [46, 47], and also by the increased bilateral connections between the LGN and V5 (MT) in blindsighted patient G.Y. [48]. In addition, there is also some evidence that the LGN can be affected top-down by selective attention [49].

Nonetheless, I recognize that this as a point at which a reader could resist my interpretation of the evidence and defer to future research in settling the issue. But even though the significance of these adaptation effects is not uncontroversial, and more work needs to be done, they at least motivate constraint (2). But all of this is a little bit besides the point, given the perceptual role strategy I assumed in the beginning of this paper.

On to the perceptual role strategy, mental qualities are individuated by the discriminations that an organism can make and their role in the organism's overall mental economy. The asymmetry in the aforementioned adaptation effects is a systematic difference in a perceiver's ability to discriminate, and as such are relevant to individuating mental qualities. Visual, auditory, and tactile discriminations. And this is true whatever the nature of the underlying neurobiological machinery–LGN included.

And there is another avenue of research that supports the claim that each sensory modality processes and represents temporal information differently. Auditory information about timing usually affects how timing is processed in vision, but visual information about timing does not equally affect how timing is processed by audition. One striking example of this is the temporal ventriloquism effect in which an auditory stimulus changes the perceived timing of a visual stimulus, moving its perceived timing closer to the timing of the auditory stimulus [50, 51].

In general, audition usually dominates vision when it comes to timing, even though this is not always the case. However, this dominance is so pronounced, that it can even result in completely illusory stimuli. For example, when a flash is accompanied by more than one beep, the flash is perceived to occur twice [52]. If all sensory mechanisms processed timing in the same way, there would be no such asymmetry–all timing information would be treated the same and have equal importance in determining timing.

---

[1] I am grateful to an anonymous reviewer of this volume for pointing out this possibility.

In the case of multi-modal perception of duration the direction of dominance is different. Visual information can, to some extent, affect auditory perception of duration, but auditory information does not affect visual perception of duration to the same extent.

In one study of multi-modal perception of duration, participants were presented with a stream of steady (not looming) stimuli interrupted by a looming stimulus (disk increasing in size or upward frequency-modulated sweep) in the same modality [53]. The reports of the participants indicate a subjective dilation of the duration of the looming stimulus, that is, the looming stimulus is consistently judged to be longer than it is. And when a series of looming stimuli is interrupted by a steady stimulus, the steady stimulus is judged to be of shorter duration than it is. This holds for visual and visual-auditory stimuli equally.

But if a series of looming visual or visual-auditory stimuli is interrupted by a steady auditory stimulus, no subjective time dilation occurs for the auditory stimulus. So while looming auditory streams affect visual stimuli, looming visual and visual-auditory streams do not affect auditory stimuli. This indicates that duration distortions do not transfer from vision to audition. Similar asymmetry occurs when the presented series is composed of steady visual stimuli paired with steady auditory stimuli [54]. The duration judgments of an odd-ball looming auditory stimulus presented after such a series are typically accurate. This indicates that visual information blocks the auditory dilation effect that would occur if the steady stream were composed of only auditory stimuli.

Finally, when steady visual stimuli are paired with looming auditory stimuli in a stream, the subjective duration of the oddball steady auditory-visual stimulus is not compressed. Again, no dilation occurs because of the influence of information about duration of the event coming in from vision. The asymmetry demonstrates the dominance of vision over audition in perception of duration.

On its own, asymmetrical dominance across modalities does not show that each modality has its own proprietary time mechanism, even if it would hold in all cases, which it does not. The abovementioned effects could be explained on a model on which timing information is processed by the same mechanism, but with different emphasis given to different modalities[2]. But that does not affect the relevance of dominance effects in supporting constraint (2).

Regardless of which computational model turns out to be correct–multiple mechanisms or a single mechanism–there are pronounced differences in temporal perception at the level of content. And this is where the dominance affects are important in constraining a theory of temporal mental qualities. The architecture of the mechanisms that process temporal information before we get to the top level of the processing hierarchy does not matter much in this case.

What matters in the dominance effects and also in the adaptation effects I mentioned above is that information about timing and duration is systematically not processed in the same way across different modalities. Auditory representations of timing do not have the same perceptual role as visual representations of timing or tactile representations of timing. And, on the perceptual role account I

---

[2] I am grateful to an anomymous reviewer of this volume for stressing this point.

take for granted in this paper, such a difference matters to individuating mental qualities and categorizing them into modality-specific families.

3   Temporal Mental Qualities

In the previous section I presented several avenues of research that I take to support two constraints on a philosophical theory of temporal mental qualities. Constraint (1) is that temporal mental qualities can occur unconsciously. Constraint (2) is that that each sensory modality has its own proprietary temporal qualities.

The evidence I presented is empirical, and therefore open to a number of challenges. Hence the case I made for these two constraints is speculative, and independent of whatever merits QST or its extension to temporal perception might otherwise have. In this section, I offer a model of temporal mental qualities that I take to be compatible with (1) and (2), as well as provide a unifying theoretical framework in which temporal perception can be better understood

Similarly to the way that spatial boundaries of basic perceptible properties allow organisms to discriminate shapes, temporal boundaries of such properties allow them to discriminate the timing of an event. And the similarities and differences between these individual temporal boundaries can define a space of relations within which each perceptible timing property is located.

Unlike other spaces of perceptible properties, such as the visible colors, timing properties are related to each other along a single axis. Temporal boundaries of a stimulus can be related to each other only by two relations: before and after. Two simultaneously occurring boundaries bear the same set of before and after relations to other boundaries, and can be distinguished from each other only along other, non-temporal dimensions, such as hue or location.

On this view, timing properties are nothing but the temporal boundaries of other more basic perceptible properties. So an organisms ability to make timing discriminations depends on its ability to discriminate between more basic properties. This comports with constraint (2), according to which each sensory modality has its own set of temporal mental qualities.

For example, the onset of a red stimulus on a white background at t=1 occurs after t=0 and before t=3 and is further from t=6 than from t=4. The offset of the same red stimulus at t=5 occurs at a point at which it is replaced by the background white in the same location. Just as on a number line, where every number bears either a 'before' or 'after' relation to every other number on the line, the timing (onset or offset) of a particular perceptible property is related to all of the others by one of these two relations.

Just as with other perceptible properties, any perceptible timing property has a corresponding mental quality. And mental timing qualities play a perceptual role in the organisms mental economy, which allow it to make timing discriminations. This is because the similarities and differences that define the one-dimensional space of timing properties are reflected in the temporal discriminations that an organism can make.

For example, a mental quality that is relevant to the organism discerning the onset of a stimulus at t=1, will be closer in the corresponding temporal mental quality space to mental t=0 than to mental t=3, and further from mental t=6 than from mental t=4. In this way, any single timing quality will be similar and different to other timing qualities in ways that parallel the similarities and differences between the perceptible timing properties.

Paralleling the structure of the space of relations that define perceptible timing properties, the mental temporal quality space is one-dimensional. The temporal quality space has the structure of a number line, which naturally incorporates 'before' and 'after' relations, that hold between the timing of perceptible events. The mapping between the one dimensional temporal quality space and the one dimensional structure of time enables the organism to make the relevant timing discriminations.

Of course, in addition to sensing the timing of a stimulus, an organism can also sense it as enduring for a period of time. But we do not need to add a new dimension to the one-dimensional temporal quality space to accommodate duration. Duration is reflected in the relations that hold between individual timings.

When a red stimulus is onset at t=1 and offset at t=3, two visual timing qualities are involved, one for each of the temporal boundaries of the event. And the two mental timing qualities that correspond to t=1 and t=3 constitute the temporal mental boundaries of the occurrence of the more basic mental qualities. Together, these boundaries define the duration of the red stimulus.

Consequently, the two timing qualities can also represent the duration of the red stimulus, just as subtracting the value of t=1 from t=3 is sufficient to represent real time duration of the event (as 2 seconds, for example). Consequently, the relations between mental timings can also define other relations, such as 'longer than' and 'shorter than,' which are the relations that hold between durations. Mental duration defined by t=1 and t=3 is shorter than the mental duration defined by t=4 and t=7.

The one-dimensional temporal quality space is sufficient to enable an organism to represent and respond differentially to both timing and duration; there is no need for an extra dimension or quality space for duration. Nonetheless, discriminations of duration are possible only when the temporal mental qualities are available and the temporal distance between them is discerned as being filled-in with sufficiently similar mental qualities.

When the basic qualities change, that will usually mark a new temporal boundary. And when no change is detected, no new timing quality will be instantiated. Consequently, the duration of a stimulus (or background) will be discerned to be longer. But nothing over the mental qualities relevant to timing are necessary in this process–durations, and possibly other, more complex temporal qualities are built up out of them and their relations.

On the temporal quality space model I offered above, timing qualities define the boundaries of duration qualities. And similarly to the way that the boundaries of colors define shape, temporal mental qualities corresponding to perceived timing define the temporal boundaries between occurrences of more basic qualities such as color. The similarities and differences that an organism can discriminate between temporal properties of objects reflect the similarities and differences between corresponding temporal qualities.

The resulting similarity metric reflects the temporal properties that an organism can discriminate and how many discriminations it can make between temporal properties. This metric in turn defines a temporal quality space for a particular modality. And, reflecting the one-dimensional nature of perceptible time, all of the modality-specific temporal quality spaces are themselves one-dimensional.

On this view, time discrimination depends on an ability to discriminate more basic mental qualities such as color and sound. This makes the temporal quality space model compatible with constraint (2). Each modality has its own quality space of temporal mental qualities that is independent of similar quality spaces in other modalities.

Nothing in the temporal quality space model violates constraint (1), either. Temporal mental qualities are defined by their perceptual role, not by the temporal qualitative character of conscious experience. Given this, mental qualities are themselves independent of conscious experience, and can be instantiated without us being aware of it in any way.

This QST model of temporal perception also implies that temporal judgments do not have to coincide with temporal perception. A subjective duration judgment might indicate a duration of 1 second, say, while performance on an objectively measured duration discrimination task might indicate that the perceptual system represents a duration of 1.5 seconds. On the view offered here, an account of the temporal aspect of conscious experience relevant to subjective judgments demands a theory that is distinct from a theory of temporal perception.

References

1. Kant, I.: Critique of Pure Reason. St. Martins Press, New York (1965/1781)
2. Husserl, E.: On the Phenomenology of the Consciousness of Internal Time (1893-1917). Kluwer, Dordrecht (1990/1928)
3. Bergson, H.: Time and Free Will: An Essay on the Immediate Data of Consciousness. Dover, Mineola NY (2001/1913)
4. Dretske, F.: Experience as Representation. Philosophical Issues 13(1), 67–82 (2003)
5. Dennett, D.C., Kinsbourne, M.: Time and the Observer: The Where and When of Consciousness in the Brain. Behavioral and Brain Sciences 15, 183–201 (1992)
6. Block, N.: Consciousness and Cognitive Access. Proceedings of the Aristotelian Society 108 (1pt3), 289–317 (2008)
7. Sellars, W.: Empiricism and the Philosophy of Mind. Harvard University Press, Cambridge MA (1997/1956)
8. Rosenthal, D.M.: Consciousness and Mind. Oxford University Press, USA (2005)
9. Broadbent, A.D.: A Critical Review of the Development of the CIE1931 RGB Color-matching Functions. Color Research and Application 29(4), 267–272 (2004)
10. Meehan, D.B.: Qualitative Character and Sensory Representation. Consciousness and Cognition 11(4), 630–641 (2002)

11. Meehan, D.B.: The Qualitative Character of Spatial Perception. Doctoral Thesis, City University of New York (2007)
12. Rammsayer, T., Ulrich, R.: Counting Models of Temporal Discrimination. Psychonomic Bulletin and Review 8(2), 270–277 (2001)
13. Ivry, R.B.: The Representation of Temporal Information in Perception and Motor Control. Current Opinion in Neuropbiology 6(6), 851–857 (1996)
14. Miall, R.C.: The Storage of Time IntervalsUsing Oscillating Neurons. Neural Computation 1(3), 359–371 (1989)
15. Wearden, J.H., Edwards, R., Fakhri, M., Percival, A.: Why 'sounds are judged longer than lights': Application of a Model of the Internal Clock in Humans. Quarterly Journal of Experimental Psychology 51B, 97–120 (1998)
16. Creelman, D.C.: Human Discrimination of Auditory Duration. The Journal of the Acoustical Society of America 34(5), 582–593 (1962)
17. Treisman, M., Faulkner, A., Naish, P.L.N., Brogan, D.: The Internal Clock: Evidence for a Temporal Oscillator Underlying Time Perception with Some Estimates of its Characteristic Frequency. Perception 19(6), 705–743 (1990)
18. Gibbon, J.: Scalar Expectancy Theory and Weber's Law in Animal Timing. Psychological Review 84, 279–325 (1977)
19. Mauk, M.D., Buonomano, D.V.: The Neural Basis of Temporal Processing. Annual Review of Neuroscience 27, 307–340 (2004)
20. Karmarkar, U.R., Buonomano, D.V.: Timing in the Absence of Clocks: Encoding Time in Neural Network States. Neuron 53(3), 427–438 (2007)
21. Pariyadath, V., Eagleman, D.M.: The Effect of Predictability on Subjective Duration. PLoS One 2(11), e1264 (2007)
22. Pöppel, E.: A Hierarchical Model of Temporal Perception. Trends in Cognitive Sciences 1(2), 56–61 (1997)
23. von Steinbüchel, N., Wittmann, M., Pöppel, E.: Timing in Perceptual and Motor Tasks after Disturbances of the Brain. Advances in Psychology 115, 281–304 (1996)
24. Pöppel, E.: Lost in Time: A Historical Frame, Elementary Processing Units and the 3-Second Window. Acta Neurobiologiae Experimentalis 64(3), 295–302 (2004)
25. Pöppel, E.: Temporal Mechanisms in Perception. International Review of Neurobiology 37, 185–202 (1994)
26. Pöppel, E.: Taxonomy of the Subjective: an Evolutionary Perspective. In: Brown, J.W. (ed.) Neuropsychology of Visual Perecption, pp. 219–232. Lawrence Erlbaum Associates, Hillsdale NJ (1989)
27. Zacks, J.M., Braver, T.S., Sheridan, M.A., Donaldson, D.I., Snyder, A.Z., Ollinger, J.M., Buchner, R.L., Raichle, M.E.: Human Brain Activity Time-locked to Perceptual Event Boundaries. Nature Neuroscience 4(6), 651–655 (2001)
28. Tong, F.: Brain at Work: Play by Play. Nature 4(6), 560–562 (2001)
29. Muckli, L., Kriegeskorte, N., Lanfermann, H., Zanella, F.E., Singer, W., Goebel, R.: Apparent Motion: Event-Related Functional Magnetic Resonance Imaging of Perceptual Switches and States. Journal of Neuroscience, 1–5 (2002)
30. Muckli, L., Kohler, A., Kriegeskorte, N., Singer, W.: Primary Visual Cortex Activity Along the Apparent-Motion Trace Reflects Illusory Perception. PLoS Biology 3(8), 1501–1510 (2005)
31. Sterzer, P., Haynes, J., Reesa, G.: Primary Visual Cortex Activation on the Path of Apparent Motion is Mediated by Feedback from hMT+/V5. NeuroImage 32(3), 1308–1316 (2006)
32. Matsuyoshi, D., Hirose, N., Mima, T., Fukuyama, H., Osaka, H.: Repetitive Transcranial Magnetic Stimulation of Human Mt+ Reduces Apparent Motion Perception. Neuroscience Letters 429(2-3), 131–135 (2007)

33. Rees, G.: The Anatomy of Blindsight. Brain 131(6), 1414–1415 (2008)
34. Azzopardi, P., Cowey, A.: Motion Discrimination in Cortically Blind Patients. Brain 124(1), 30–46 (2001)
35. Goebel, R., Muckli, L., Zanella, F.E., Singer, W., Stoerig, P.: Sustained Extrastriate Cortical Activation without Visual Awareness Revealed by fMRI Studies of Hemianopic Patients. Vision Research 41(10-11), 1459–1474 (2001)
36. Azzopardi, P., Hock, H.S.: Illusory Motion Perception in Blindsight. Proceedings of the National Academy of Sciences 108(2), 876–881 (2011)
37. Pantev, C., Bertrand, O., Eulitz, C., Verkindt, C., Hampson, S., Schuierer, G., Elbert, T.: Specific Tonotopic Organizations of Different Areas of the Human Auditory Cortex Revealed by Simultaneous Magnetic and Electric Recordings. Electroencephalography and Clinical Neurophysiology 94(1), 26–40 (1995)
38. Penfield, W., Rasmussen, T.: The Cerebral Cortex of Man: A Clinical Study of Localization of Function. Macmillan, New York (1950)
39. Verhagen, J.V.: The Neurocognitive Bases of Human Multimodal Food Perception: Consciousness. Brain Research Reviews 53, 271–286 (2007)
40. Vroomen, J., Keetels, M.: Perception of Intersensory Synchrony: A Tutorial Review. Attention, Perception, and Psychophysics 72(4), 871–884 (2010)
41. Kopinska, A., Harris, L.R.: Simultaneity Constancy. Perception 33(9), 1049–1060 (2004)
42. Dixon, N.F., Spitz, L.: The Detection of Auditory Visual Desychrony. Perception 9(6), 719–721 (1980)
43. Harrar, V., Harris, L.R.: Simultaneity Constancy: Detecting Events with Touch and Sound. Experimental Brain Research 166(3), 465–473 (2005)
44. Harrar, V., Harris, L.R.: The Effect of Exposure to Asynchronous Audio, Visual, and Tactile Stimulus Combinations on the Perception of Simultaneity. Experimental Brain Research 186(4), 517–524 (2008)
45. Hanson, J.V.M., Heron, J., Whitaker, D.: Recalibration of Perceived Time Across Sensory Modalities. Experimental Brain Research 185(2), 347–352 (2008)
46. Sherman, S.M., Guillery, R.W.: Exploring the Thalamus. Academic Press, San Diego (2001)
47. Sherman, S.M., Guillery, R.W.: The Role of the Thalamus in the Flow of Information to the Cortex. Philosophical Transactions of the Royal Society London B 357, 1695–1708 (2002)
48. Bridge, H., Thomas, O., Jbabdi, S., Cowey, A.: Changes in Connectivity after Visual Cortical Brain Damage Underlie Altered Visual Function. Brain 131, 1433–1444 (2008)
49. O'Connor, D.H., Fukui, M.M., Pinsk, M.A., Kastner, S.: Attention Modulates Responses in the Human Lateral Geniculate Nucleus. Nature Neuroscience 5, 1203–1209 (2002)
50. Fendrich, R., Corballis, P.M.: The Temporal Cross-Capture of Audition and Vision. Perception and Psychophysics 63(4), 719–725 (2001)
51. Bertelson, P., Aschersleben, G.: Temporal Ventriloquism: Crossmodal Interaction on the Time Dimension. 1. Evidence from Auditory-Visual Temporal Order Judgment. International Journal of Psychophysiology 50(1-2), 147–155 (2003)
52. Shams, L.Y., Kamitani, Y., Shimojo, S.: Illusions: What You See is What you Hear. Nature 408(6814), 788 (2000)
53. Van Wassenhove, V., Buonomano, D., Shimojo, S., Shams, L.: Distortions of Subjective Time Perception Within and Across Senses. PLoS One 3(1), 1–13 (2008)
54. New, J.J., Scholl, B.J.: Subjective Time Dilation: Spatially Local, Object-based, or a Global Visual Experience? Journal of Vision 9(2), 1–11 (2009)

On Clocks, Models and Metaphors
Understanding the Klepsydra Model

Jiří Wackermann

Dept. of Empirical and Analytical Psychophysics,
Institute for Frontier Areas of Psychology and Mental Health,
D-79098 Freiburg i. Br., Germany
jw@igpp.de

Abstract. In the present paper, the rôle of metaphors and models in scientific theories is discussed, with particular focus on the klepsydraic model of internal time representation and on the 'internal clock model'. The conceptual background and the basic principles of the klepsydraic model are explained, and its non-computational character is emphasized.

1   Models and Theory Building

> The images which we may form of things are not determined without ambiguity [...]. Various images of the same objects are possible, and these images may differ in various respects.
>
> — H. Hertz [1]

Models are, briefly speaking, things or systems sharing some features with other things or systems, namely, those being modeled. The use of models is ubiquitous in arts and technology: models serve as aids to study important properties of things of interest, which are inaccessible, unobservable or even not-yet-existing, by examining other things, which are accessible, tangible, easy to fabricate, grasp, visualize, and to experiment with. But there is an important distinction between models and 'model systems'. The former are objects of thought, subject to reasoning; the latter are material objects, subject to experimentation. In life sciences, easily obtainable and manipulable organs or organisms have been used as model systems, e. g. *Aplysia* neuronal fibres or *Limulus* eye in neurophysiology, *Drosophila* in genetics. However, the pragmatic utility of such 'model systems' alone does not guarantee their theoretic utility as working models.

Of interest is here the use of models in science, their relation to scientific *theories* and, particularly, their rôle in developing and formulating theories. This rôle is often obscured by the diversity of meanings of the terms 'model' and 'theory', these words being used differently in different disciplines, and in different philosophical traditions. In this essay we adhere to the functional view of theory [2], and interpret models from that point of view. Models in science are mental objects displaying structural or functional similarities with the real objects of study. Examining their properties, we discover relations which shall

A. Vatakis et al. (Eds.): Time and Time Perception 2010, LNAI 6789, pp. 246–257, 2011.

enter theories of the modeled reality. Models as such are not theories, they are only heuristic aids in the process of theory building; and they are not hypotheses about the 'true nature' of things.[1]

This view was clearly articulated by the physicist H. Hertz in the Preface to his *Principles of Mechanics* [1]. Hertz understood our conceptions of physical reality as 'images' (*Bilder*) or 'pictures',[2] constructed so that "we develop by means of them, as by means of models, the consequences in the external world." Models are to be evaluated in terms of their *correctness* (logical admissibility), *distinctness* and *appropriateness*, not their verity: "two permissible and correct images of the same external objects" may exist, which "differ in respect of appropriateness." The sole criterion of choice is the utility of the model: "one image may be more suitable for one purpose, another for another."

A special class of models are *mechanical* models, typical for the 'Victorian physics' of the late 19th century, and valued for their visual character and intuitive grasp (*Anschaulichkeit*) of their functioning. In W. Thomson's words: "If I can make a mechanical model, I understand it. As long as I cannot make a mechanical model all the way through I cannot understand" [3, quote in p. 71f]. — However, P. Duhem attributed the progress of "mechanical theories [...] to a lapse in the faculty of abstracting, that is, to a victory of imagination over reason" [3, p. 73]. — This may sound strange to a modern reader, who is conditioned to take a 'mechanism' for an explanation; nonetheless, the criticism is well justified. The proper goal of a theory is to reproduce the structure of the phenomenal field under study, to express *formal* relations in a system of equations, not to depict auxiliary, fictitious entities. Commenting on Maxwell's electromagnetic theory, R. Feynman observed that the early form of theory makes use of "imaginary wheels and idlers [...] but when you get rid of all the idlers and things in space the thing is OK" [4, p. 57].

A good example of a successful model in the history of science is the Rutherford–Bohr model of the internal structure of the atom: electrons circling around the massive nucleus as planets around the sun. This model not only provided a visual picture of spatial distribution of the sub-atomic constituents, suggested by revsome experimental facts, but it also served as a basis for further developments, e. g. for explanation of emission and absorption spectra [5]. And yet, it was a *temporary* success, to be superseded by a more sophisticated wave-mechanical concept of the sub-atomic structure. Thus a good model may initiate a theoretical development which finally demolishes the original picture.

In modeling, we substitute a thing for another thing. Now, in *metaphor* we substitute a name for another name; and indeed there is no sharp demarca-

---

[1] Models are never directly confronted with observational facts; they only provide a basis for construction of theories to be tested empirically. Models play a similar rôle in theory development as financial advisors in our practical lives: if, following their suggestions, we succeed, they expect appreciation; if we fail, they deny any responsibility.

[2] Translated as 'images' in the English edition of Hertz' work, although 'picture' might be a better translation. However, none of these two English words fully expresses the constructive character of 'Bild' (from German verb 'bilden', cf. English 'build'.)

tion line between models and metaphors.[3] Models may develop from vague metaphors; or a suggestive metaphor may mimic the 'explanatory power' of a model. Comparing time with the majestic flow of a grand river is nothing but a poetic metaphor; comparing the subjective 'flow of time' with the passage of a fluid through a tube *may be* a point of departure for a working model. It is only the productive potential of the model image what really matters.

2   Internal Clock: Model or Metaphor?

A person who is able to wake up at a specified time, not using an alarm-clock, is popularly said to "have a clock in her head"[6]. The orientation ability of migrating birds' in long-distance flights is reminiscent of a navigator's using astronomical observations plus a portable clock as a time reference to determine his actual location; we may say that the birds behave *as if* they had an 'internal clock'[7]. In both cases, the use of the term 'clock' is merely metaphorical; it does not imply that the sleeper or the migrant bird really reads an internal clock and 'knows the time' all the time.

We—human beings—are acting with respect to time, and make judgments of time, referring to the common 'objective time' indicated by clocks. The plain fact that we need an external clock reference suggests that we have 'no clock in us'. Or, if we extend the notion of a clock and attribute our acting in time and judgments of time to a 'clock in us', then it must be a rather poor clock; as R. Descartes aptly observed: "On voit qu'un horologe, qui n'est composé que de roues et de ressorts, peut compter les heures, et mesurer le temps, plus justement que nous avec toute notre prudence." [8][4] Still, a bad clock is a clock; the study of its mechanics should reveal why its data so often and so grossly deviate from those given by other, 'good' clocks. This has been the leading motive of the search for an 'internal clock', dominating research in timing behavior and time experience[5] for more than half a century.

The 'internal clock model' (ICM) is considered the most influential model in the timing research so far. Its original idea, going back to Treisman [9],[6] is based on a four-fold structure: pacemaker–counter–memory store–comparator. The pacemaker–counter couple is the core of the model: the pacemaker generates

---

[3] This, of course, is a minimal characteristic, not a full account of metaphor and its functioning. A good metaphor is more than a bare metonymy; and a good model is more than just a metaphor.

[4] "One can see that a clock, which is composed only of wheels and springs, can count hours and measure time more precisely than we, with all acuity we are able of."

[5] For simplicity, we will use the term 'timing' as a cover term for behavior *in* and experience *of* time, including the traditional research field of 'time perception'.

[6] We should note that other authors, e. g. Creelman [10], advanced similar ideas independently of or before him. A number of authors considering periodic physiological processes as a possible basis for timing could be named here, whether they postulated a 'counter' or not. Historical reviews usually halt at Hoagland's seminal paper [11], but the very idea can be traced back to the beginning of the 20th century.

regular series of 'pulses', while the counter holds the sum of pulses across a given time interval; its state thus serves as an internal representation of the interval duration. Variations of response in different timing tasks (production, reproduction, verbal estimates, etc.) are explained by variations of pacemaker frequency, which is modulated by a hypothetical state variable, "specific arousal."

Conceptual proximity to the animal behavior research-based 'scalar expectation theory' (SET) [12] certainly helped the ICM to gain popularity. A marker of this alliance was the parallel appearance of Treisman's study [13] and Church's analytical discussion of the 'properties' of the internal clock [14] in one influential volume [15]. While the physiologist and behaviorist paradigms quite easily met at the ICM concept, the reception from cognitive psychology was less straightforward. Early cognitivists vigorously refuted the idea of an endogenous oscillatory 'clock' process and emphasized exogenous factors and information-processing aspects [16,17]. Block's discussion of 'internal clock models' (*sic!*) in [18] was still utterly critical. And yet, the 'attentional-gate' model [19] essentially reproduces the original ICM structure, with its components re-labeled in a cognitivist fashion, and with some psychological accessories added.

In spite of its proclaimed success, the ICM has never been unanimously accepted. Alternative models have been proposed and various points of criticism raised (cf. Sect. 4). Here we wish to prepend some general observations:

(i) Firstly, there is an essential ambiguity concerning the aim of the modeling. Treisman's four-fold structure was proposed as *a* model for *the* clock; while *the* (internal) clock serves as *a* model (or metaphor?) for observed timing behavior. This important distinction is hardly given any attention in the literature.

(ii) The pacemaker–counter principle, proposed by Galileo and utilized by Huygens in his pendulum clock [20], is now the base of most human-made timekeepers (for short, GH-clocks), whether the pacemaker is a swinging pendulum, a vibrating quartz crystal, or another oscillator. However, there is nothing special about time reference based on discrete 'ticks' or 'pulses', except for technological convenience. Counting is nothing but a special case of integration. A device based on integration of a continuous variable—e.g. a constant inflow water-clock—would serve the same purpose equally well.[7]

(iii) It is true that (*a*) in humans and animals, kinds of behavior are observed which can be simulated by using and reading a private clock, and (*b*) modern human-made clocks are usually GH-clocks. But it does *not* follow from *a* & *b* that an organism *must* have a built-in ('internal') GH-clock to display a timing ability. Such a conclusion would be a plain *non sequitur*, or rather a cascade of them.

(iv) Periodicity *per se* does not 'make' time. For practical reasons, much attention has been given in physical chronometry to the properties of the clock's oscillator, especially to the conditions of *isochrony* (equity of generated periods). However, a pacemaker alone is not the clock; another, essentially *time asymmetric* subsystem is needed to generate a measure of time—be it a counter, a simple integrator, or a more complex structure (see Sect. 3).

---

[7] In fact, Galileo's early measurements of time intervals in his physical investigations were based on this principle [21].

Consequently, it was proposed to reserve "the term 'pacemaker' for the source of the temporal reference frequency, and the term 'internal clock' for the complete set of mechanisms" [13] (i. e., all four essential components). But this is exactly where a difficulty begins: what is the "complete set"? Where are the boundaries of the clock system as a whole?

These ambiguities lead to divergent use of the term 'clock' in different threads of literature. Some authors criticized "internal-clock models [for] an oversimplified view of the complex set of processes that underlie psychological time" [18], or claimed that "behavior on all timing tasks results from more than just properties of an internal clock" [22]. Other authors identified the 'clock' with the pacemaker–counter core of the ICM, and argued for models of timing "without a clock" [23], or in a rather curious wording, "in absence of clocks" [24]. Moreover, some authors use the word 'clock' synonymously for *any* time-keeping mechanism, or for a time representation ability in general. This conceptual confusion then culminates in statements of frustration: "We know the human brain contains some kind of clock, but determining its neural underpinnings and teasing apart its components have proven difficult." [25] But, if we cannot say anything positively about some-thing, how can we say we *know* that there is such a thing?

The value of the ICM for a theory of timing thus appears questionable: less than a model, rather a vague metaphor merging physical/technological principles with abstract psychological constructs. Its alleged success, or its astonishing persistence, seems to be partly due to its lack of specificity, partly to its 'technomorphic' appeal. Or should we say with Duhem, yet another "victory of imagination"?

3   Klepsydra Model, Its Working and Its Merits

The 'dual klepsydra model' (DKM) [26,27,28] was designed to model data from duration reproduction experiments with human subjects in the supra-second domain. The supra-second region is relatively neglected in the contemporary research, and under-represented in the literature, but it is the domain where subjective experience of duration fully develops [29]. Of interest is the functional dependence, $r = f(s)$, of the reproduced duration r on the presented duration s.

The most striking phenomenon, seen almost universally in the reproduction data, is the progressive under-reproduction, that is, shortening of the response r with respect to the presented duration s. 'Progressive' here says that not only $r/s < 1$, but the ratio r/s itself is a decreasing function of s, so that the response function f is not linear but displays a negative curvature. This phenomenon, corresponding to the "perspectival contraction" of elapsed times, described already by E. Mach [30], and later known as the "subjective shortening in memory" [31], presents a challenge for all models of duration reproduction [32].

The klepsydra model is, similarly to the ICM, an integration model. The points of difference are that (i) the duration representation is built *continuously* in time, by (ii) integration of an ongoing 'flow', while the integrator's state is (iii) decremented at a speed of which is a function of its state ('lossy' integration). The

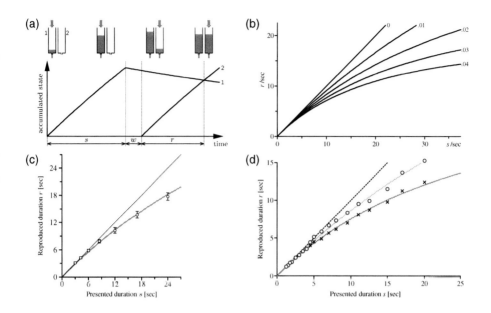

Fig. 1. (a) Dual klepsydra model of duration reproduction [27]. (b) Klepsydraic reproduction functions (KRF) with $w = 0$, $\eta = 1$, and κ varied in the range 0 to 0.04 s^{-1}. (c) Reproduction data (group average across 12 subjects) + KRF fit, $\kappa = 0.013$ s^{-1} [33]. (d) Reproduction data + KRF fits for two populations, native Swedish (o, $\kappa = 0.016$ s^{-1}) and Afro-Swedish ($\times$, $\kappa = 0.032$ s^{-1}), based on Eisler's data [34].

integrator thus acts as an inflow–outflow unit (IOU) accumulating some physical quantity as, for example, volume of water in a leaky bucket.[8] Assuming a linear loss function, the IOU is described by an ordinary differential equation,

$$\frac{\mathrm{d}y}{\mathrm{d}t} = i - \kappa\, y \,, \tag{1}$$

where y is the momentary state, i is the inflow, and κ is the 'loss coefficient'.

In a model of the duration reproduction task, two IOUs are allocated for representation of the first and second interval, and equality of their states translates into subjective experience of the two durations (Fig. 1a). Mathematical analysis easily yields an expression for r as a function of s,

$$r = \kappa^{-1} \ln\left(1 + \eta\left(1 - \mathrm{e}^{-\kappa s}\right) \mathrm{e}^{-\kappa w}\right) \,, \tag{2}$$

where w is the inter-stimulus interval, κ is the loss coefficient as in (1), and $\eta = i_1/i_2$ is the ratio of inflows into the 1st and 2nd IOU. Eq. (2) is known as the

---

[8] Hence the name of the model, derived from Greek *klepsydra* = water-clock [20]. The physical nature of the model does not matter: it could be quantity of heat in a warmed-up tea-pot, or electrical charge on a capacitor with a shunt resistor. In fact, the latter systems better fit the linear eq. (1) than a hydrodynamic model.

'klepsydraic reproduction function' (KRF) [28]. For a fixed experimental constant w and model parameters κ, η, the KRF is an increasing, upper bound function of s, showing a negative curvature (Fig. 1b) depending on κ. In the limiting case $\kappa \to 0$, the response function becomes linear, $r = \eta\, s$.

It has been shown [28,33,35,36] that the KRF fits duration reproduction data with excellent accuracy (cf. Figs. 1c,d). The DKM can be applied also to duration discrimination data, where the "subjective shortening" is indicated by a shift of the point of subjective equality (PSE) [37,38,39]. Estimates of κ obtained by both methods are usually in the range from 1 to $3 \times 10^{-2}\,\mathrm{s}^{-1}$. The characteristic half-decay times $(\ln 2)/\kappa$ of the putative lossy integrators are thus in the range from ~ 20 s to one minute. These results show that reproduction/discrimination data in the supra-second domain (especially for $s > 3$ s) can be quantitatively modeled by a lossy integration and comparison-based mechanism. For contrast, the ICM can explain the shortening or PSE-shift effects only by variations of pulse rates,[9] while the DKM predicts these effects naturally, *all things* (flows and loss rates) *being constant.*

Economy of data representation is not the only argument in favour of the DKM. The model also allows, and in fact suggests, separation of endogenous and exogenous effects. For example [40], discrimination of visually marked intervals exhibits an effect of stimulus brightness onto perceived duration, explicable in terms of inflow ratios (η), which is superimposed on the above-mentioned PSE-shift effect (due to $\kappa > 0$).

4   Modeling and Realism

Obviously, the components of the DKM (as of other physical models) are not 'real things' but merely useful fictions, illustrating the model's working and motivating its analysis. After all, what matters is the mathematical content of the resulting theory; paraphrasing Feynman's quote in Sect. 1, we can say "when we get rid of the leaky buckets and heated tea-pots, the thing is OK."

This is a bifurcation point where the working philosophies of (psycho)physicists and (neuro)biologists diverge. The physicist willingly throws away auxiliary constructions and imaginary things, but the biologist wishes to replace them, in the final theory, with 'real things': *what* and *where* in the organism, in the brain, in the neural cell correspond to this or that element of the model? Now, how is this intent to reconcile with Hertz' pragmatism, according to which models are just convenient 'images' of reality, not the real thing itself?

For some researchers this is not an issue at all. The 'representation economy' conception of theory is easily accepted by behavioral scientists. For example, Staddon and Higa [41] asserted that "behavioral theories [...] are valid to the extent that they describe behavioral data accurately and economically," and

---

[9] Either the pacemaker's fundamental frequency ('specific arousal' hypothesis) or the effective pulse rate must change (cognitivist 'attentional gate' hypothesis). In either case, a time-dependent, frequency modulating mechanism is needed to account for the non-linear character of the effects: an additional complication.

argued that "the notion of 'biological plausibility' is a slippery one."[10] May be; but 'slippery' does not imply 'meaningless', and the subtle issue of biological realism is not settled with a slippy comment. A few remarks are in order.

Firstly, the pacemaker–counter principle, a basis of the GH-clock, is biologically *unnatural*. The ubiquity of physiological periodicities is not an argument for a pacemaker; exactly the opposite is true. Heart contractions, respiration cycles, or alpha-waves in the EEG are no 'chunks of time', no 'paces' of a pacemaker; they are phenomena occurring periodically *in* time. As explained in Sect. 2, periodicity *per se* does not 'make' time; the seductive formula 'time-keeping is based on periodicity' is a mental short-cut. Time-keeping requires temporal asymmetry of states [33], which is realized in the *counter*: a system capable of irreversible transitions between discrete, linearly ordered states. However, the representation of a continuous magnitude by a counted quantity needs stability with respect to external perturbations and sufficient resolution; that's why much technological sophistication is necessary. Counters and shift-registers are good for building arithmetic machines, but they are not found in living bodies. Briefly, counter is an utterly *non-physiological* principle.

If, in the DKM, we supersede pulse trains and counters by 'flows' and 'leaky accumulators', it is not because we 'know' that these things are real, those others not—it is to build-up the model functionality on principles natural to the system under study: collective structures, mass action, continuous state changes. The 'flows' in the model system must not be imagined as energy conduction or substance transmission in space; it is an abstract concept. Any change of an intensive magnitude in time may be called 'flow', or inversely, the 'accumulated' magnitude is understood as integral of the flow over a time interval.

In modeling, we construct images of nature out of things and processes found in nature: physics matters. Suggesting that dissipative processes "may provide metaphors or models more adequate to biological reality than mechanical models" [28], we were referring to this realism of underlying functional principles. A few years ago we proposed to consider ensembles of excitable cells [42] as possible realization for the 'accumulators', where excitatory input corresponds to the 'inflow', and spontaneous de-excitation to the 'outflow' (dissipative component). It is a task for computational neurophysics to test such 'semi-realistic' models. Recent critiques of the ICM [43,44,45,24], based on the last decade's progress of knowledge in brain physiology, also emphasize network-distributed action as opposed to a centralized pacemaker–counter structure. FMRI-derived data on cumulative activity in localized cortical areas during time perception tasks [46,47] seem to support the accumulator model. Also, a recently reported relation between the loss-rate parameter κ and activity of serotonergic brain subsystems [39] suggests a link between the DKM and 'real' neurophysiology. It is thus conceivable that the abstract flows and states will find a neurobiological interpretation. However, these questions are beyond limits of our psychophysical modeling approach, and will have to be decided on other grounds.

---

[10] This decided position, however, did not prevent the authors from referring to (then recent) magnetoencephalographic data as a support for their memory trace model.

5   Timing without Numbers

> We really notice immediately only the identity or non-indentity of two times.
>
> — E. Mach [30]

In the modern technological culture, our understanding of time is shaped by omnipresence of external clocks, implementing the notion of 'arithmetized time'. Speaking about time, we usually refer explicitly or implicitly to numerical equivalents of temporal extensions, i. e. durations in conventional time units. The ICM transposes the arithmetics of time into the organism: internal representation is still modeled by a numerical quantity, derived from the pacemaker frequency.

In the DKM the internal states representing perceived durations are scaleless magnitudes, not numerical quantities. Therefore, the states of the integrators cannot be subtracted or submitted to other arithmetic operations; they can be only compared in terms of 'less-than', 'greater-than', or 'indifferent' relations. The DKM operates on a *pre-metric* principle. This is sufficient to model tasks such as reproduction or discrimination of time intervals. The DKM was not designed to account for data from interval production or numerical estimation experiments. In this sense, the DKM is not a universal model—but none of the models known to us is really universal. The pacemaker–counter coupling, is not a full model, either: an extensive circuitry surrounding the core subsystem is required to make it a working model for a given experimental task, e. g. interval production.[11]

In our view, the limitation of the DKM to pre-metric operations is not a deficiency; rather, it reflects the fundamental character of reproduction as a *scale-producing* operation. This notion has been formalized in the 'klepsydraic clock' (KC), a device generating a time-scale by iterated DKM-reproduction of an initial interval [33]. This does not mean that subjects in reproduction or discrimination experiments 'read' their internal KCs; they operate directly on the DKM principle. The KC is only a theoretical construct to study mathematical properties of DKM-based time-scales.

As said above, physics matters. Nature in its workings is mathematical, yet non-computational. It is only us, observers and interpreters of nature, who need measurements and computations as instruments for encoding and decoding the universal nexus of natural phenomena. Swinging pendula, falling stones and orbiting planets do not have to watch 'internal clocks' and to calculate their motions.[12] Natural processes happen as they happen; not obeying universal time as a supreme instance, rather defining time by their own course. Applying this principle to timing behavior of a living organism: in an elementary action such as interval reproduction, the organism 'knows' the time-to-act without knowing what-time-it-is and acting so, it *creates* a time-scale.

---

[11] In Treisman's ICM a "verbal selective mechanism" [9] was assumed to determine a reference value against which the momentary state of the counter is compared.

[12] Interestingly, the 'internal clock' metaphor entered popularizing accounts of physics, too. This is probably harmless; no intelligent reader will take literally metaphors such as "internal clocks" of elementary particles [48, p. xii].

6   Concluding Remarks

> We have just used a metaphor and now the metaphor
> tyrannizes us. While in the language of the metaphor,
> I am unable to move outside of the metaphor.
> — L. Wittgenstein [49]

The search for an internal clock—which was once ironically named "the holy grail of timing research" [25]—is really reminiscent of a relentless quest driven by a myth (or a dogma). Until present days, the search has produced a large literature, reporting and interpreting data, redrawing the picture of the object of search, or questioning its very existence. From a plainly sociological view of science—"science is when research is being done and published"—the idea of 'internal clock' has been undoubtedly successful. From a soberly epistemological perspective the success appears to be rather problematic. The expression 'internal clock' provides an image, a metaphor, a convenient *façon de parler* to circumscribe some observed phenomena. But the image is misleading since the very beginning, as it suggests an instance in the organism 'knowing' and 'telling' time, and thus controlling time-oriented behavior or time cognition. All attempts to convert the metaphor into a working model inherit this difficulty. To break the spell of this truly tyrannizing metaphor, we should abandon the idea of being driven by an 'internal clock', and adopt a notion of living beings creating time by their own actions.

Acknowledgements. The author wishes to thank Marc Wittmann and two anonymous reviewers for helpful comments on an earlier version of the present paper.

References

1. Hertz, H.: The Principles of Mechanics. Dover, New York (1956)
2. Wackermann, J.: Rationality, Universality, and Individuality in a Functional Conception of Theory. Int. J. Psychophysiol. 62, 411–426 (2006)
3. Duhem, P.: The Aim and Structure of Physical Theory. Princeton University Press, Princeton (1954)
4. Feynman, R.P.: The Character of Physical Law. Penguin, Harmondsworth (1992)
5. von Laue, M.: History of Physics. Academic Press, New York (1950)
6. Clauser, G.: Die Kopfuhr. Das automatische Erwachen. Enke, Stuttgart (1954)
7. Matthews, G.V.T.: Bird Navigation. Cambridge University Press, New York (1955)
8. Descartes, R.: Discours de la méthode. Meiner, Hamburg (1997)
9. Treisman, M.: Temporal Discrimination and the Indifference Interval: Implications for a Model of the "Internal Clock". Psychol. Monogr. 77(576), 1–31 (1963)
10. Creelman, C.D.: Human Discrimination of Auditory Duration. J. Acoust. Soc. Am. 34, 582–593 (1962)
11. Hoagland, H.: The Physiological Control of Judgments of Duration: Evidence for a Chemical Clock. J. Gen. Psychol. 9, 267–287 (1933)
12. Gibbon, J., Church, R.M., Meck, W.H.: Scalar Timing in Memory. In: [15], pp. 52–77

13. Treisman, M.: Temporal Rhythms and Cerebral Rhythms. In [15], pp. 542–565
14. Church, R. M.: Properties of the Internal Clock. In: [15], pp. 566–582
15. Gibbon, J., Allan, L. (eds.): Timing and Time Perception. Annals of the New York Academy of Sciences, New York, vol. 423 (1984)
16. Ornstein, R.E.: On the Experience of Time. Penguin, Harmondsworth (1969)
17. Michon, J.A.: Processing of Temporal Information and the Cognitive Theory of Time Experience. In: Fraser, J.T., Haber, F.C., Müller, G.H. (eds.) The Study of Time, pp. 242–258. Springer, Berlin (1972)
18. Block, R.A.: Models of Psychological Time. In: Block, R.A. (ed.) Cognitive Models of Psychological Time, pp. 1–35. Lawrence Erlbaum, Hillsdale (1990)
19. Zakay, D., Block, R.A.: Temporal cognition. Curr. Dir. Psychol. Sci. 6, 12–16 (1997)
20. Whitrow, G.J.: Time in History. Oxford University Press, Oxford (1988)
21. Galilei, G.: Dialogues Concerning Two New Sciences. MacMillan, New York (1914)
22. Wearden, J.: H.: Applying the Scalar Timing Model to Human Time Psychology: Progress and Challenges. In: Helfrich, H. (ed.) Time and Mind II: Information-processing Perspectives, Hogrefe & Huber, Göttingen, pp. 21–39 (2003)
23. Zeiler, M.D.: Time Without Clocks. J. Exp. Anal. Behav. 71, 288–291 (1999)
24. Karmarkar, U.R., Buonomano, D.V.: Timing in the Absence of Clocks: Encoding Time in Neural Network States. Neuron 53, 427–438 (2007)
25. Lewis, P.A., Walsh, V.: Time Perception: Components of the Brain's Clock. Curr. Biol. 15, R389–R391 (2005)
26. Wackermann, J., Ehm, W., Späti, J.: The 'Klepsydra Model' of Internal Time Representation. In: Berglund, B., Borg, E. (eds.) Fechner Day 2003, pp. 331–336. Intl. Society for Psychophysics, Stockholm (2003)
27. Wackermann, J.: From Neural Mechanics to the Measure of Subjective Time: The Klepsydra Model. In: Oliveira, A., et al. (eds.) Fechner Day 2004, pp. 164–169. Intl. Society for Psychophysics, Coimbra (2004)
28. Wackermann, J., Ehm, W.: The Dual Klepsydra Model of Internal Time Representation and Time Reproduction. J. Theor. Biol. 239, 482–493 (2006)
29. Wackermann, J.: Inner and Outer Horizons of Time Experience. Span. J. Psychol. 10, 20–32 (2007)
30. Mach, E.: The Analysis of Sensations. Dover, New York (1959)
31. Wearden, J.H., Ferrara, A.: Subjective Shortening in Human's Memory for Stimulus Duration. Q. J. Exp. Psychol. 46B, 163–186 (1993)
32. Wackermann, J., Späti, J., Ehm, W.: Individual Response Characteristics in Time Reproduction and Time Production Tasks. In: Monahan, J.S., Sheffert, S.M., Townsend, J.T. (eds.) Fechner Day 2005, pp. 359–364. Intl. Society for Psychophysics, Traverse City (2005)
33. Wackermann, J.: Measure of Time: A Meeting Point of Psychophysics and Fundamental Physics. Mind & Matter 6(1), 9–50 (2008)
34. Eisler, A.D.: The Human Sense of Time: Biological, Cognitive and Cultural Considerations. In: Buccheri, R., et al. (eds.) The Nature of Time: Geometry, Physics and Perception, pp. 5–18. Kluwer, Dordrecht (2003)
35. Wackermann, J., Wittmann, M., Hasler, F., Vollenweider, F.X.: Effects of Varied Doses of Psilocybin on Time Interval Reproduction in Human Subjects. Neurosci. Lett. 435, 51–55 (2008)
36. Wittmann, M., Simmons, A.N., Flagan, T., Lane, S.D., Wackermann, J., Paulus, M.P.: Neural Substrates of Time Perception and Impulsivity. Brain Res. 1406, 43–58 (2011)
37. Wackermann, J., Späti, J.: Asymmetry of the Discrimination Function for Temporal Durations in Human Subjects. Acta Neurobiol. Exp. 66, 245–254 (2006)

38. Wackermann, J., Ehm, W.: Dual Klepsydra Model of Duration Discrimination. In: Mori, S., Miyaoka, T., Wong, W. (eds.) Fechner Day 2007, pp. 515–520. Intl. Society for Psychophysics, Tokyo (2007)

39. Sysoeva, O.V., Tonevitsky, A.G., Wackermann, J.: Genetic Determinants of Time Perception Mediated by the Serotonergic System. PLoS One 5(9), e12650 (2010)

40. Wackermann, J., Meyer-Blankenburg, N.: Differential Effect of Stimulus Brightness in Visual Duration Discrimination. In: Elliott, M.,, A., et al. (eds.) Fechner Day 2009, pp. 459–464. Intl. Society for Psychophysics, Galway (2009)

41. Staddon, J.E.R., Higa, J.J.: Time and Memory: Towards a Pacemaker-Free Theory of Interval Timing. J. Exp. Anal. Behav. 71, 215–251 (1999)

42. Wackermann, J.: Experience of Time Passage: Phenomenology, Psychophysics, and Biophysical Modelling. In: Buccheri, R., et al. (eds.) Time, Quantum and the Subjective, pp. 189–208. World Scientific, Singapore (2005)

43. Mauk, M.D., Buonomano, D.V.: The Neural Basis of Temporal Processing. Annu. Rev. Neurosci. 27, 307–340 (2004)

44. Buhusi, C.T., Meck, W.H.: What Makes Us Tick? Functional and Neural Mechanisms of Interval Timing. Nature Rev. Neurosci. 6, 755–765 (2005)

45. Burr, D., Morrone, C.: Time Perception: Space–Time in the Brain. Curr. Biol. 16, R171–R173 (2006)

46. Wittmann, M.: The Inner Experience of Time. Phil. Trans. R. Soc. B 364, 1955–1967 (2009)

47. Wittmann, M., Simmons, A.N., Aron, J., Paulus, M.P.: Accumulation of Neural Activity in the Posterior Insula Encodes the Passage of Time. Neuropsychologia 48, 3110–3120 (2010)

48. Greene, B.: Introduction. In: Einstein, A. The Meaning of Relativity, Princeton University Press, Princeton (2005)

49. Wittgenstein, L.: Philosophical Remarks. Blackwell, Oxford (1975)

Time Reference in Fluent Aphasia: Evidence from Serbian

Vanja Kljajevic[1] and Roelien Bastiaanse[2]

[1] Instituto Gerontológico Matia, San Sebastian, Spain
[2] University of Groningen, Groningen, Netherlands
vanja.kljajevic@gmail.com

Abstract. Cognitive representation of time, in particular time reference (TR) through verb forms, and its reflection in abnormal language have been extensively studied in nonfluent aphasia across languages. In contrast, there is currently little evidence on patterns of TR deficits in fluent aphasia. The present study investigates production and comprehension of TR through verb forms in four fluent aphasic speakers of Serbian, a Slavic language with rich verb morphology. While the data indicate a deficit similar to the one found in nonfluent aphasic speakers, a detailed error analysis reveals that the underlying deficit must be different. Whereas agrammatic speakers predominantly substituted past verb forms with present verb forms, the Serbian fluent aphasic speakers exhibited a pattern in which within-the-same-time-frame errors dominated production of non-past reference, while out-of-time-frame errors dominated production of reference to the past. Thus, the data indicate impairment in these speakers' reference to the past.

Keywords: Time reference, Verbs, Past-nonpast, Fluent aphasia, Within time frame errors, Serbian.

1 Introduction

Aphasia is a language disorder typically caused by a stroke, traumatic brain injury or tumor. Aphasic speakers exhibit different patterns of language deficit, which mostly depend on the size and location of brain lesion. While there are numerous classifications of aphasias, all aphasic types can be roughly divided into non-fluent (such as Broca's aphasia, transcortical motor or global aphasia) and fluent aphasias (e.g., Wernicke's aphasia, anomic and transcortical sensory aphasia). Most of the evidence on verb production and comprehension in aphasia comes from research on nonfluent aphasia, although fluent aphasic speakers too demonstrate verb deficits. Impairment in the production of verb forms is one of the defining features of agrammatic Broca's aphasia [1-4], which is characterized by relatively spared comprehension and non-fluent, effortful, and impoverished speech, from which so-called small words, such as auxiliaries (e.g., *is, will*) are omitted. However, verb is a very complex category and it is not clear at the moment, which of its aspects are impaired in Broca's speakers. More specifically, in addition to carrying lexical meanings and sound structures, verbs also have argument and thematic structures,

A. Vatakis et al. (Eds.): Time and Time Perception 2010, LNAI 6789, pp. 258–274, 2011.

which determine the number and type of arguments (e.g., agent: *The girl* kissed the boy, patient: *The boy* was kissed by the girl, source: She received an invitation *from the dean*, etc.). Verbs carry inflection (e.g., *-ed* in *kissed*) for tense (e.g., past vs. present), agreement (e.g., singular vs. plural), and aspect (e.g., habitual vs. progressive), which specifies intra- and inter-sentential relationships. In structurally different languages the verb production deficit in agrammatism may vary [5]. Still, growing cross-linguistic evidence indicates that the common features of the verb deficit in agrammatic aphasic speakers are paucity of verbs in spontaneous speech, omission of auxiliaries, and omission or substitution of inflectional affixes [4,6-15].

It has been shown that paucity of verbs in speech production of agrammatic speakers is not due to a deficit in lexical retrieval of words belonging to the grammatical category of verb. Bastiaanse and Jonkers [16] showed that there is no correlation between the diversity of lexical verbs in spontaneous speech and action naming performance. Shapiro and Caramazza [17] and Shapiro, Shelton, and Caramazza [18] have shown that two patients with lesions implicating the left inferior frontal lobe, and with deficits in producing nouns (JR) and verbs (RC), had poor results when "using words of the impaired category in morphological transformation tasks" [19, p.202], even when the transformations involved pseudo-words (e.g., *these are wugs*; *this person wugs*) [17]. This finding indicates a disruption of the computational processes implicated in morphological transformations of grammatical categories rather than impairment of words as sets of stored features [19]. Furthermore, research on verb inflection has shown that not all grammatical morphemes are impaired to the same degree. For example, *-ing* in *He is walking* is better preserved in comparison to *– ed* in *He walked* in English agrammatic speakers [13]. Evidence on impaired tense and spared agreement marking inflections has been reported for agrammatic speakers of Arabic [14], German [10], Hebrew [8,20], Spanish [21], and other languages. Such findings have motivated several influential accounts of the verb production deficit in agrammatic aphasia that emphasize its syntactic nature.

For example, Hagiwara [7], and Friedmann and Grodzinsky [8], proposed that chances for verbal inflection to be impaired depend on its position in the syntactic tree: the higher the position to which the verb needs to move in order to check its syntactic features, the more vulnerable the inflections. The assumption here is that the verb cannot move over an impaired node. Thus, the dissociation in production of tense and agreement inflections can be explained in terms of their respective positions in the syntactic tree: the Tense (T) node is higher up than the agreement node (Agr), and thus inaccessible to agrammatic speakers. While this explanation accounts for the Hebrew data [8], it cannot capture the relevant data from other, structurally different languages, in which the order of functional categories differs from the one found in Hebrew, such as Moroccan Arabic [14], Greek [22] or German [10]. It also does not capture the recent findings on the impairment of agreement in agrammatic speakers [12,15].

In addition, more recent developments of linguistic theory do not assume that T and Agr are hosted by separate nodes [23]. The new approach allows tense to be construed as an interpretable feature of the syntactic category T. Furthermore, agreement is not construed as a functional category in this approach, but as an operation—*Agree*, that regulates structural relationships between the features of the clausal subject and verb. Relying on this approach, Wenzlaff and Clahsen [10-11], have proposed that, unlike other finiteness features that are well preserved in agrammatism, T is underspecified for tense and, hence, prone to impairment. As a possible explanation, they point to the anaphoric nature of tense, that is, its extrasentential reference, but a principled explanation along these lines is still lacking. However, what is interesting about their account is the idea that it is not the position of T in the syntactic tree that causes the verb deficit in agrammatism, but rather its features related to time reference.

Further research on verb deficit in agrammatism has shown that some interesting findings from Dutch and Turkish cannot be explained in terms of the discussed accounts. Data from Dutch indicate that agrammatic speakers have more difficulty producing the past than present verb forms, regardless of whether the simple present or the present continuous forms are used [15]. The Turkish data show that agrammatic speakers have more difficulty producing the past tense than future tense [24]. Greek data [25] also show that reference to the past is difficult for agrammatic speakers and that perfect and perfective aspects are more difficult than imperfective aspect. These data indicate that reference to the past and not tense itself may underlie agrammatic speakers' difficulty in production of verb forms.

While evidence on verb deficit in nonfluent aphasia abounds, there is currently little insight into the patterns of verb impairment in fluent aphasia, which is characterized by fluent but meaningless speech combined with comprehension impairment. This gap in research is perhaps due to an early-observed double dissociation between verb and noun production in aphasia, manifested as better production of verbs than nouns in fluent, and better production of nouns than verbs in nonfluent aphasia. The dissociation indicates that different neural mechanisms are implicated in production of these two grammatical categories, further supporting the classical view that grammatical category is a major organizing principle of language in the brain. More specifically, such evidence is widely interpreted as indication that verb production is supported by the left frontal lobe, while production of nouns is associated with the left temporal lobe. However, neuroimaging evidence on the neural substrates of verbs and nouns is heterogeneous [26-30], with some indications that specific brain areas, such as Brodmann areas (BAs) 45 and 9, are implicated in encoding of grammatical properties of words, regardless of the word class. While the heterogeneity of neuroimaging evidence may reflect the fact that verb processing is not a monolithic task, Luzzatti et al. [30] found that lesions at three different areas in the left hemisphere are associated with verb deficit: the posterior temporo-parietal, the fronto-temporal perisylvian, and deep insula and basal ganglia lesions. Furthermore, growing evidence indicates that an aphasia syndrome can have different localizations [31].

In line with these findings is the cross-linguistic evidence obtained in a variety of tasks that indicate that fluent aphasic speakers, too, have difficulty with verbs. For instance, they produce fewer verbs in spontaneous speech than non-brain-damaged speakers [32-34] and exhibit problems with verb retrieval [16,35], finite verb inflection [36-37], access to argument structure and thematic representation of verbs [38]. It appears then that difficulty with verbs is present in aphasia regardless of whether the lesion causing the disorder is located in the anterior vs. posterior cortical areas, or whether it runs subcortically [30]. However, due to the more typical differences in lesion site between fluent (posterior) and nonfluent (anterior) aphasic speakers, and their overall distinct language behavior patterns (e.g., *agrammatism* in nonfluent vs. *paragrammatism* in fluent aphasia), different patterns of verb impairment may emerge in fluent aphasia.

The main goal of the present study was to investigate whether the patterns of verb deficit in fluent aphasia reflect a deficit in TR or in verb inflection. More specifically, we set out to investigate whether temporal aspects of information conveyed by a verb or verb morphology was impaired in fluent aphasia, and whether the possible impairment patterns differed from those reported for nonfluent aphasic speakers. We chose to study TR through comprehension and production of verb forms in fluent aphasic speakers of Serbian, not only because of rich verbal morphology in this language, but also because of an interesting interplay between its markings of external time (tense) and internal time (aspect). Furthermore, since fluent aphasic speakers may have difficulty with the verb's lexical, semantic, and grammatical information, or a more general monitoring or information integration problem [37], we looked for the verb deficit patterns in fluent aphasia considering which of these problems they would reflect.

2   Verb System in Serbian

Serbian is a South-Slavic language with a rich morphological system. For example, it has seven morphological cases (Nominative, Genitive, Dative, Accusative, Vocative, Instrumental, and Locative), three genders (masculine, feminine, and neuter), and two numbers (singular and plural). Its word order is relatively free, so in a sentence such as *Marko čita knjigu* "Mark is reading a book" any of 6 possible word orders, made by combination of subject, verb and object, is grammatically correct and acceptable. Temporal location of situations is expressed in this language by grammaticalized items, which are regulated by the tense system, and lexical items, such as temporal adverbials (e.g., *sada* "now", *sutra* "tomorrow") and lexically composite items (e.g., *pre zore* "*before the dawn*"). Serbian tense system differentiates between absolute and relative tenses, which differ with regard to whether the moment of speech (as in former) or some other temporal point (in latter) is the reference for encoding and temporal interpretation of a situation[1]. It consists of simple and compound tenses. Here we discuss only the verb forms that are relevant for the present study. They are: infinitive, the perfect tense, aorist, the present tense, and future I tense. The infinitive is a basic verb form and appears as a lemma in the Serbian dictionary (e.g., *voleti* "to love") [39]. The perfect tense refers to a past situation that was either completed or not completed before the moment of speech, while aorist expresses a completed past situation. The present tense is used for a situation that coincides with the time of speech. Future I tense refers to a situation that is located in time after the present moment. Examples of verb forms tested in the present study are given in Table 1.

As shown in Table 1, perfect tense is a compound tense, consisting of the clitic form (*sam, si, je, smo, ste, su*) of the suppletive present of the auxiliary *biti* "to be" (Table 2), which also carries information on person and number, and the active, so-called *l*-participle of the main verb (e.g., *napisao*), which carries information on gender and number. In other words, the auxiliary is inflected and finite, while the participle is inflected and non-finite. Future I tense appears in a simple (e.g., *Radiće*.

---

[1] Following Comrie [40-41], we use the term *situation* as a general term to refer to all: processes, events, states, etc.

"He will work.") and periphrastic form (*On će raditi*. "He will work."). The periphrastic form consists of the clitic of the auxiliary *hteti* "to want" in present tense (*ću, ćeš, će, ćemo, ćete, će*) (Table 2) and a main verb in infinitive. The order of the auxiliary clitic and the main verb in sentences containing compound tenses is regulated by a general rule prohibiting appearance of clitics in the sentence initial position. Typically, the auxiliary clitic appears in the second position, but other Aux-V orders in sentences with these two tenses also result in grammatically correct and acceptable sentences. Bošković [42] has presented convincing evidence against the fixed structure position for Serbian clitics, which runs against the traditional so-called second-position, purely structural accounts of clitic position in this language.

Table 1. Pisati (imperfective) "to write"/ napisati (perfective) "to finish writing"

	Perfect tense	Aorist	Present tense	Futur I tense
1.sg	(na)pisao/la sam	napisah	pišem	(na)pisaću/ ja ću (na)pisati
2.sg	(na)pisao/la/lo si	napisa	pišeš	(na)pisaćeš/ ti ćes (na)pisati
3.sg	(na)pisao/la/lo je	napisa	piše	(na)pisaće/ on/a/o će (na)pisati
1.pl.	(na)pisali/le smo	napisasmo	pišemo	(na)pisaćemo/ mi ćemo (na)pisati
2.pl.	(na)pisali/le/la ste	napisaste	pišete	(na)pisaćete/ vi ćete (na)pisati
3.pl	(na)pisali/le/la su	napisaše	pišu	(na)pisaće/ oni/e/a će (na)pisati

Table 2. Auxiliaries *biti* "to be"and *hteti* "to want": Present

	Biti		Hteti	
	Full form	Clitic	Full form	Clitic
1sg	jesam	sam	hoću	ću
2sg	jesi	si	hoćeš	ćeš
3sg	jeste	je	hoće	će
1pl	jesmo	smo	hoćemo	ćemo
2pl	jeste	ste	hoćete	ćete
3pl	jesu	su	hoće	će

Verb forms in Serbian express either the imperfective or perfective aspect, which is realized on the verb. The aspectual oppositions are typically formed by prefixation, in which case a perfective form is formed from the imperfective form (e.g., *pisati* "to write" → *na-pisati* "to write up") or by suffixation, in which case an imperfective form is formed from the perfective one (e.g., *kupiti* "to buy" → *kupo-va-ti*). Serbian imposes certain restrictions on the interplay between the tense and aspect. For example, present tense is typically associated with the imperfective aspect, allowing the perfective aspect only when referring to present situations that do not coincide with the moment of speech (as in gnomic expressions or when referring to a habitual situation). Similarly, aorist typically appears with the perfective aspect, although it is also possible to find the imperfective aspect in aorist (examples include gnomic expressions and reference to habitual situations in the past) [39]. As shown in Table 1, perfect tense, future I, and infinitive exhibit more flexibility in expressing aspectual viewpoints, typically allowing both the imperfective and perfective aspects.

3 Methods

3.1 Participants

Four anomic aphasic speakers with relatively good comprehension participated in this study. The aphasic participants underwent a neurological exam, computed tomography (CT) scanning, and assessment by speech pathologists. They all had had an ischemic stroke in the left hemisphere that was followed by aphasia. A1 had a temporo-parietal cortico-subcortical lesion. A2 had a lesion in the posterior part of the corona radiata, the putamen, and the postcentral gyrus. A3 had a lesion in the supramarginal gyrus affecting the white matter as well as a smaller insulo-opercular lesion that originated from the same stroke as the first lesion. Finally, A4 had a fronto-temporal lesion affecting the supraventricular area. The post-onset time varied from 4 months to 14 years. Participants' profiles are summarized in Table 3. There were four neurologically intact control participants, whose performance was at ceiling.

Table 3. Participants' profile

Patient	Age	Sex	Edu	Post-onset time	Type of stroke	Lesion site	Type of aphasi	Hand.	BDAE max=72
A1	58	F	12	9	Ischemi	LH	Fluent	Right	72
A2	71	F	12	7	Ischemi	LH	Fluent	Right	70.5
A3	64	F	16	4	Ischemi	LH	Fluent	Right	70.5
A4	60	M	16	14 years	Ischemi	LH	Fluent	Right	72

Edu. – years of education; Hand. – handedness.

3.2 Materials

The materials used in the present study have been specifically designed to assess TR through verb forms in aphasic speakers and titled *Test for Assessing Reference of Time* (TART) [43]. Here we used the Serbian version of TART [44].

The evaluative measures administered in the present study comprised two tests of word comprehension from the Boston Diagnostic Aphasia Evaluation (BDAE) [3]. The *Flood rescue* photograph that helped to elicit a wide range of verb forms in a study by Olness [45] was also used to elicit speech in this study.

The experimental stimuli testing *production* of TR through verb forms were presented within a sentence-completion paradigm (see Fig. 1). Here the participants were prompted to complete a sentence by producing the requested verb form and its object. There were also two pictures, depicting different situations, one of which was associated with the sentence to be completed. Above each picture a verb in infinitive form that accurately referred to the situation depicted on the picture was printed. The experimenter read aloud a sentence that referred to the first picture, and then she read aloud the second sentence up to the point where a verb form and object needed to be produced, pointing to the other picture. The participants were required to complete the sentence by producing the full predicate, that is a verb form and object, using the verb printed above the second picture. Crucially, the verb form that the participants were required to produce needed to match the verb form in the first sentence. There were 20 sentences testing each of the five verb forms—infinitive, the perfect tense, aorist, the present tense, and future I tense, giving a total of 100 sentences. We tested the form of perfect tense with the participle-aux order, because only that order allowed us to test the production of the full predicate. As for the future I tense, we tested the simple form. Examples of sentence stimuli for all tested verb forms in both experiments are given in Table 4. The sentences were randomized in Excel. The corresponding pictures were ordered to match the randomized order of the sentences. Pair of sentences with accompanying pictorial stimuli for experiments 1 and 2 are given in Figures 1 and 2 respectively. There were four trial sets of stimuli for practicing performance on this task.

For the test of *comprehension*, a sentence-picture matching paradigm was used, in which the participants were required to point to the picture that corresponded to the sentence that was read aloud by the experimenter (see Fig. 2). Crucially, the sentence meaning depended on the verb form in such a way that in order to successfully complete the task and pick the correct picture, the participants needed to correctly identify TR of the verb form used in the sentence and match it with the corresponding picture. In this experiment, there were always two pictures and one sentence. The two pictures depicted an action that required the same verb, but in a different time frame. Thus, in order to match the sentence with a correct picture, the participant had to comprehend TR in the sentence. For each time frame the most common verb form was given: past → perfect tense; present → present tense; future → future I tense. With 20 sentences testing each time frame, the comprehension test contained a total of 60 sentences. The sentences were randomized and each sentence was then matched with a pair of pictures. In addition, there were three trial sets of stimuli administered at the beginning of the test.

Table 4. The verb forms tested with the TART

Verb form	Serbian example	Example from English
Production		
Infinitive	Ovde čovek želi piti mleko.	Here the man wants to drink milk.
Perfect Tense	Juče žena peglala je šal.	Yesterday the woman ironed the scarf.
Aorist	Evo čovek oguli jabuku.	Here the man has peeled the apple.
Present	Sada žena oštri olovku.	Now the woman is sharpening the pencil.
Future I	Uskoro čovek poješće jabuku.	Soon the man will eat the apple.
Comprehension		
Perfect Tense	Žena je naslikala kvadrat.	The woman painted the square.
Present Tense	Žena oštri olovku.	The woman is sharpening the pencil.
Future I Tense	Čovek će pojesti jabuku.	The man will eat the apple.

gurati   vući

Fig. 1. An example of the Sentence Completion Task in TART. *Ovde čovek gura kolica.* "Here the man is pushing the cart." *Ovde čovek ... (vuče kolica)* "Here the man ... (is pulling the cart)."

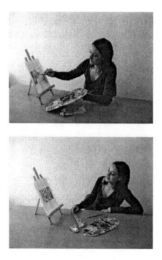

Fig. 2. An example of the Sentence-Picture Matching Task in TART. The target sentence is: *Žena je naslikala kvadrat.* "The woman painted the square."

3.3 Procedure

All participants were tested individually, in a quiet room, at the Center for Aphasia of the Institute for Psychophysiological Disorders and Speech Pathology "Cvetko Brajović" in Belgrade, Serbia. The testing was completed within a single session with each participant. During testing, only neutral feedback was provided. Self-corrections were allowed, and one sentence repetition on request. Time was not measured and the participants were encouraged to take a break if they felt tired. Including a short break between the tests, it took about 50-60 minutes to complete testing with each participant.

3.4 Scoring

In the production test, a response was counted as correct if it consisted of a correct verb form and object. Cases of paraphasias in which one verb stem was replaced by another, as in _sipa-ti_ "to pour" versus _pi-ti_ "to drink", were not counted as errors, provided the correct verb form was produced. Responses without the required auxiliary in perfect tense were counted as substitution errors, because when the auxiliary is left out from the perfect tense, what remains is another verb form—the _l_-participle. Production of the imperfective versus perfective aspect and thus the use of aspectual markers in the perfect tense, infinitive and future I tense were not grammatically relevant and responses including either the perfective or imperfective aspect in these three verb forms were counted as correct. However, since production of the perfective aspect and use of prefixes are crucial in aorist, leaving out the prefixes would be an omission. Responses substituting future I tense and infinitive with expressions containing the construction "_da_ + present" were counted as substitution errors. The infinitive constructions that were produced without the required modal verb _želeti_ "want" were counted as omission errors (see Table 4).

In the comprehension test, a response was counted as correct if the participant pointed to the picture that corresponded to the sentence that was read aloud.

4 Results

4.1 Evaluative Measures

The results of the BDAE tests are presented in Table 3 above, together with the aphasic participants' profile. These tests show that the patients' comprehension of words for actions, colors, and numbers, and words for objects, letters, and forms was relatively well preserved. Further, speech samples from telling a story reveal no statistically significant differences between verb production of aphasic and control participants. Details of speech sample from telling a story are summarized in Table 5, which shows _some_ differences in production of modal and auxiliary verbs as well in finite verbs token production, with a smaller number of such verbs produced by aphasic than control participants. Also, aphasic speakers produced more reference to present than controls. Nevertheless, these differences are not statistically significant. A plausible explanation of this finding is that aphasic speakers chose to produce only those verb forms that they were comfortable producing, such as present tense. However, the experimental production test, in which the participants were required to produce other verb forms, revealed a subtle pattern of deficit in aphasic speakers.

4.2 Production Results

4.2.1 General Overview

The individual scores of aphasic patients on the production task are given in Appendix A. In general, the only tense that the fluent aphasic speakers produced without a problem was the present tense (93.75%). They had difficulty with reference to the past regardless of tense; producing only 28.75% correct responses for perfect tense and 22.5% correct responses for aorist. In addition, their production scores on future I tense (37.5%) were almost as low as the reference to the past and, even more surprisingly, production of infinitive constructions was also rather low (42.5%). Fisher exact test revealed statistically significant differences between their production of present and perfect tense ($p < 0.0001$, two tailed), present and aorist ($p < 0.0001$, two tailed), present and infinitive ($p < 0.0001$, two tailed), as well as present and future ($p < 0.0001$, two tailed). There were no statistically significant differences in their production of perfect tense and aorist ($p = 0.4691$), perfect tense and future I tense ($p = 0.3136$), or future and infinitive ($p = 0.6285$). However, the difference between infinitive and aorist was significant ($p = 0.0110$), while the difference between perfect tense and infinitive ($p = 0.0984$) and between aorist and future I tense ($p = 0.0571$) was approaching significance. Thus, the data show that Serbian fluent aphasic speakers' production of present tense was superior to their production of other verb forms, indicating that the deictic center of the verb system plays an important role in the production of TR through verb forms. This finding is aligned with the previous evidence on relative stability of the present tense in aphasia.

Table 5. Speech sample from telling a story

Elicited speech	Fluent aphasic speakers		Non-brain-damaged speakers	
	Mean	Range	Mean	Range
Number of utterances	8.75	8-17	10.25	7-14
Utterance length	9.07	6.76-11.25	11.31	7.64-14.14
Finiteness index	0.95	0.90-1.00	0.97	0.88-1.00
Modals & Auxiliaries	9.5	2-14	12.5	10-15
Lexical verbs Type	11	9-12	12.75	8-15
Lexical verbs Token	17.25	11-23	16.5	14-20
Finite verbs Type	11.5	8-14	11.75	8-14
Finite verbs Token	19	15-24	21	18-23
Non-finite verbs Type	4.25	1-7	5	3-9
Non-finite verbs Token	4.75	1-8	6.75	4-12
Reference Past	3.25	0-6	4.75	2-9
Reference Present	12.75	3-22	10.5	7-13
Reference Future	1.75	0-2	2.5	1-3

4.2.2 Tense-Aspect Interaction

Since production of correct verb forms depends not only on tense, but also on aspect, we inspected the tense-aspect patterns in the Serbian production data. The most notable finding is that Serbian fluent aphasic speakers mainly used the imperfective aspect in all verb forms, regardless of grammatical and semantic constraints, producing 73% of imperfective and only 27% of perfective verb forms across all conditions. Greek data from nonfluent aphasia also show difficulty with the perfective aspect, in particular when it is combined with past tenses [25].

While using both perfective and imperfective aspects was appropriate in infinitive, perfect tense and future I tense, producing a correct form of aorist always required the perfective aspect. The correct form of aorist was produced only in 22.5% cases, whereas some perfective verb form was produced in 40% of cases when the target form was aorist. In contrast, producing a correct form of the present tense always required the imperfective aspect. While there were 93.75% correct responses, some of the incorrect responses that were produced instead of the present tense also had the imperfective aspectual view, which resulted in 98.75% of imperfective forms produced when the target form was the present tense. The data indicate a graded difficulty in production of TR through verb forms with regard to aspectual viewpoint: the imperfective forms are easier than the verb forms that allow both the perfective and imperfective aspects, which in turn are easier to produce than the verb forms that allow only the perfective aspect.

Thus, we can conclude that in Serbian fluent aphasic speakers reference to the present and imperfective aspect are relatively well preserved. In order to understand better the patterns of impairment, we conducted a detailed error analysis.

4.2.3 Production Results: Error Analysis

The most typical type of errors in the Serbian data was substitution of the target verb form with another verb form (84.54%). More specifically, the produced verb form was not either in the correct tense (as in producing the present tense instead of the perfect tense) or in the target form of a specific tense (as in producing the periphrastic instead of the simple form of future I tense). Omissions were found in 10.9% of all errors (e.g., leaving out modal verbs), while the rest of errors consisted of nonexistent forms, such as combination of an auxiliary clitic with the present tense, use of a double auxiliary without a main verb, or use of an auxiliary-main verb-auxiliary string.

4.2.3.1 Within time frame errors

An interesting pattern of substitution errors emerged from further analysis of the data. As shown in Figure 3, Serbian fluent aphasic speakers made two types of substitution errors: within time frame errors and out of time frame errors. In the first case, they made paradigmatic simplifications by choosing a verb form within the same time frame. For instance, producing the periphrastic (e.g., *će plesti* "will knit") instead of the simple form (*plešće*) of future I tense, which constitutes 62.5% of all the substitutions in production of that tense, is a *within time frame* error. Note that they both refer to the same time frame—future, but only one of them is the target verb form. Such errors, where a produced verb form falls within the correct time frame and yet it does not coincide with the target verb form, we call *within time frame errors*. On the other hand, substitutions of future I tense (e.g., *plešće*) with present tense (e.g., *plete* "he/she is knitting") (22.9%) and with the construction "*da* + present" (4.1%) do not refer to the future time frame, and so these are *out of time frame* errors. Thus, majority of errors in the production of future tense in Serbian aphasic speakers is specifically tied to the simple form of future I tense and not to the TR deficit.

Note also that there were 10 errors in the production of perfect tense caused by the fronting of the auxiliary (marked by an asterisk in Appendix A), instead of placing it after the participle, which was the target form. We considered this an error in production of the target verb form, although this is not an error in time reference. Thus, we reanalyzed the data counting the responses with the periphrastic form of future I tense and the aux-participle order in past tense as correct with regard to time reference, adding the remaining within time frame substitutions to the correct scores. In addition to confirming the previously established differences, the reanalysis has revealed three additional statistically significant differences: One of them is the difference between the perfect tense and future I tense (p < 0.0001, two tailed). The differences between aorist and future I tense, and between perfect tense and infinitive, which were approaching significance in the original analysis, appeared to be statistically significant when the within time frame substitutions were counted as correct in time reference and added to the correct responses (p < 0.0018, and p < 0.0008, two-tailed). The difference between perfect tense and aorist was not statistically significant (p = 0.4280, two-tailed). Thus, the reanalysis has shown that the production of future I tense and infinitive was better than the production of perfect tense and aorist, indicating difficulty with the reference to past.

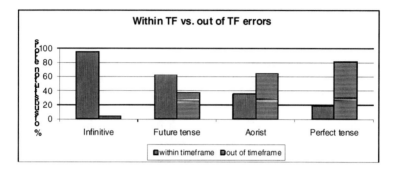

Fig. 3. Substitution errors

It appears then that the pattern of substitution errors in Serbian fluent aphasic speakers crucially depends on the past-nonpast distinction. More than 60% of the paradigmatic substitutions or within time frame errors were found in the nonpast verb forms, like future I tense and infinitive, while more than 60% of out of time frame substitutions, which indicate difficulty with time reference, were found in the past tenses, such as aorist and perfect tense. Thus, simplification via paradigmatic substitutions was a useful TR adaptive strategy in production of nonpast verb forms, but that was not the case when verb forms referred to the past. This finding indicates impaired reference to the past in Serbian fluent aphasic speakers.

4.2.4 Summary of the Production Results

The data show that Serbian fluent aphasic speakers produced present tense at ceiling. Their ability to produce verb forms referring to the future was also relatively spared, because they produced some form that correctly referred to the future in 87.5% of cases. Their difficulty consisted in producing the simple form of future I tense, which indicates a morphosyntactic problem rather than a problem with TR to future. Crucially, their ability to produce verb forms referring to the past was impaired, regardless of whether the target verb form was in perfect tense or aorist. Finally, their low scores on infinitive are somewhat surprising, given that infinitive is considered a basic verb form in Serbian. However, this may be due to the fact that Serbian, like some other Balkan languages, for example, Greek, Macedonian, and Bulgarian, is in the process of losing infinitive [39,46].

4.3 Comprehension Results

Serbian aphasic speakers exhibited better comprehension of the present (85%) and past (81.25%) than future TR (63.75%). The individual scores of aphasic patients on the comprehension task are given in Appendix B. The Fisher exact test revealed statistically significant differences between comprehension of past and future (p = 0.0208, two tailed), and present and future (p = 0.0035, two tailed), while comparing comprehension of reference to the past and present did not result in a statistically significant difference (p = 0.6735, two tailed). Interestingly, 3 out of 4 patients performed at chance level on the sentences with future I tense. Poor comprehension of this tense is addressed in Discussion.

5 Discussion

The main finding of our study is that Serbian fluent aphasic speakers have difficulty with reference to the past in speech *production*. This finding indicates that the verb production difficulty with past versus nonpast reference may be common to at least some fluent and nonfluent aphasic speakers. More specifically, despite their generally low scores in the production of all target verb forms other than the present tense, Serbian fluent aphasic speakers exhibited a pattern of substitution errors that upon a closer look revealed a strategy of within time frame production of verb form substitutions for the nonpast reference. Producing within time frame substitutions indicates that TR in these cases was preserved, and reflects a strategy of the impaired system to deal with the task demands. This error pattern is theoretically important, because it reveals how the general paragrammatic pattern of fluent aphasia works at the level of verb category, allowing us also to make inferences on the intact system.

Furthermore, the error pattern in Serbian fluent aphasic speakers indicates a breakdown in the conceptual-syntactic domain of the Levelt et al.'s model [47], and not in the access of (morpho-)phonological representation, which has been reported for another type of fluent aphasia in Greek [35]. In Serbian, verb lemmas have features for number, person, tense, aspect and mood. According to Levelt et al.'s model, values of these features partially depend on the conceptual representation. For instance, tense requires the speakers to check the temporal properties of the external time, aspect –properties of the internal time, and so on. In production of TR through verb forms, Serbian fluent aphasic speakers fail to correctly value features such as tense and aspect for further encoding. In addition, production of the tested verb forms requires an integration of the features carried by the auxiliary clitics (*je, će*) or modal verb (*želeti*) with those of the main verb. Recall that the auxiliaries *je* and *će* refer to the present, and yet the former is used to build the past tense and the latter to build the future I tense. Crucial to this integration is the precondition to *overlook* TR of the auxiliaries as well as the lack of it in the participle and infinitive, and to encode TR of a compound verb form as a single temporal meaning. More research needs to be done in order to better understand how these unique temporal meanings derive from the different temporal meanings of their constituents in compound tenses. Finally, the Serbian production data are aligned with the previous findings in reflecting the general tendency in aphasia to replace the marked forms with less marked forms or with unmarked forms [4]. For instance, we found the former in the Serbian aphasic speakers' substitutions of aorist with the perfect tense, and the latter in the substitutions of the perfective with the imperfective aspect.

The data further indicate that Serbian fluent aphasic speakers had access to the grammatical information relevant for *comprehension* of TR through verb forms, at least for the past and present time frame. These findings are compatible with the previous research on aphasic comprehension of complex syntax in this highly inflected language that reported strategic reliance on morphological information in Serbian/Croatian Broca's, anomic, and speakers with mixed aphasia [48-51] The comprehension data reveal only difficulty with the future TR. However, we tested only comprehension of the periphrastic form of future I tense, which makes it difficult to conclude whether the poor comprehension results reflect a more general impairment in future TR or a morphosyntactic deficit related to the tested form of future I tense.

In conclusion, the Serbian data presented in this paper deepen our understanding of TR and verb deficit in fluent aphasia. Our study shows that fluent aphasic speakers, like nonfluent aphasic speakers, have difficulty with production of *verb forms* that refer to past or future. However, they employ different adaptive strategies: while agrammatic patients tend to make simplifications by omission or substitutions with the present tense, the fluent aphasic speakers in our study employed a substitution strategy that allowed them to pick *correct time reference* through a *misselected verb form*. The strategy, however, was productive only for the nonpast reference, indicating that reference to the past is impaired in these speakers. Further research needs to address specifically which processes participate in inference and encoding of TR, and how the values of implicated features derive from the conceptual representation of time in aphasia, aiming to develop models that will be able to account for data from structurally different languages.

Acknowledgments. We wish to thank Dr. Dragan Čauševac at the Institute for psychophysiological disorders and speech pathology "Cvetko Brajovic", Belgrade, for his assistance in finding the aphasic participants for this study. We are especially grateful to the participants in our study. We would like to thank David Guise for his comments as well as to the audience of the 22nd annual CUNY conference on human sentence processing, held at the University of California Davis (March 26-28, 2009), for their comments on an earlier version of the production part of the study. Finally, we thank the editors and three anonymous reviewers for their excellent comments and suggestions on how to improve the paper.

References

1. Kertesz, A.: Aphasia and associated disorders. In: Kertesz, A. (ed.) Taxonomy, Localization, and Recovery. Grune & Stratton, New York (1979)
2. Darley, F.L.: Aphasia. W.B. Saunders Company, Philadelphia (1982)
3. Goodglass, H., Kaplan, E.: Assessment of aphasia and related disorders, 2nd edn. Lea and Febiger, Philadelphia (1983)

4. Menn, L., Obler, L.K.: Cross-language data and theories of agrammatism. In: Menn, L., Obler, L.K. (eds.) Agrammatic aphasia: A Cross-language Narrative Sourcebook, pp. 1369–1389. John Benjamins Publishing Co., Amsterdam (1990)

5. Paradis, M.: The need for awareness of aphasia symptoms in different languages. Journal of Neurolinguistics 14, 85–91 (2001)

6. Miceli, G., Silveri, C.M., Villa, G., Caramazza, A.: On the basis for the agrammatic's difficulty in producing main verbs. Cortex 20, 207–220 (1984)

7. Hagiwara, H.: The breakdown of functional categories and the economy of derivation. Brain and Language 50, 92–116 (1995)

8. Friedmann, N., Grodzinsky, Y.: Tense and agreement in agrammatic production: pruning the syntactic tree. Brain and Language 56, 397–425 (1997)

9. Bastiaanse, R., Thompson, C.K.: Verb and auxiliary movement in agrammatic Broca's aphasia. Brain and Language 84, 286–305 (2003)

10. Wenzlaff, M., Clahsen, H.: Tense and agreement in German agrammatism. Brain and Language 89, 57–68 (2004)

11. Wenzlaff, M., Clahsen, H.: Finiteness and verb-second in German agrammatism. Brain and Language 92, 33–44 (2005)

12. Burchert, F., Swoboda-Moll, M., De Bleser, R.: Tense and agreement dissociations in German agrammatic speakers: Underspecification versus hierarchy. Brain and Language 94, 188–199 (2005)

13. Druks, J., Caroll, E.: The crucial role of tense for verb production. Brain and Language 94, 1–18 (2005)

14. Diouny, S.: Tense/agreement in Moroccan Arabic: The Tree-Pruning Hypothesis. SKY Journal of Linguistics 20, 141–169 (2007)

15. Bastiaanse, R.: Production of verbs in base position by Dutch agrammatic speakers: Inflection versus finiteness. Journal of Neurolinguistics 21, 104–119 (2008)

16. Bastiaanse, R., Jonkers, R.: Verb retrieval in action naming and spontaneous speech in agrammatic and anomic aphasia. Aphasiology 12, 951–969 (1998)

17. Shapiro, K., Caramazza, A.: Grammatical processing of nouns and verbs in left frontal cortex? Neuropsychologia 41, 1189–1198 (2003a)

18. Shapiro, K., Shelton, J., Caramazza, A.: Grammatical class in lexical production and morphological processing: evidence from a case of fluent aphasia. Cognitive Neuropsychology 17, 665–682 (2000)

19. Shapiro, K., Caramazza, A.: The representation of grammatical categories in the brain. Trends in Cognitive Sciences 7, 201–206 (2003b)

20. Friedmann, N.: Moving Verbs in Agrammatic Production. In: Bastiaanse, R., Grodzinsky, Y. (eds.) Grammatical Disorders in Aphasia: A Neurolinguistic Perspective, pp. 152–170. Whurr, London (2000)

21. Benedet, M., Christiansen, J., Goodglass, H.: A cross-linguistic study of grammatical morphology in Spanish and English speaking agrammatic patients. Cortex 34, 309–336 (1998)

22. Stavrakaki, S., Kouvava, S.: Functional categories in agrammatism: Evidence from Greek. Brain and Language 89, 129–141 (2003)

23. Chomsky, N.: Minimalist Inquiries: The Framework. In: Martin, R., Michaels, D., Uriagereka, J. (eds.) Step by step: Essays on Minimalist Syntax, pp. 89–155. MIT Press, Cambridge (2000)

24. Yarbay Duman, T., Bastiaanse, R.: Time reference through inflection in Turkish agrammatic aphasia. Brain and Language 108, 30–39 (2009)

25. Nanousi, V., Masterson, J., Druks, J., Atkinson, M.: Interpretable vs. uninterpretable features: Evidence from six Greek-speaking agrammatic patients. Journal of Neurolinguistics 19, 209–238 (2006)
26. Perani, D., Cappa, S.F., Schnur, T., Tettamanti, M., Collina, S., Rosa, M.M., Fazio, F.: The neural correlates of verb and noun processing. A PET Study. Brain 122, 2337–2344 (1999)
27. Tyler, L.K., Russell, R., Fadili, J., Moss, H.E.: The neural representation of nouns and verbs: PET study. Brain 124, 1619–1634 (2001)
28. Shapiro, K.A., Moo, L.R., Carmazza, A.: Cortical signatures of noun and verb production. PNAS 103, 1644–1649 (2006)
29. Arévalo, A., Perani, D., Cappa, S.F., Butler, A., Bates, E., Dronkers, N.: Action and object processing in aphasia: From nouns and verbs to the effect of manipulability. Brain and Language 100, 79–94 (2007)
30. Luzzatti, C., Aggujaro, S., Crepaldi, D.: Verb-Noun Double Dissociation in Aphasia: Theoretical and Neuroanatomical Foundations. Cortex 42, 875–883 (2006)
31. Ardila, A.: A Proposed Reinterpretation and Reclassification of Aphasic Syndromes. Aphasiology 24, 363–394 (2010)
32. Bastiaanse, R., Edwards, S., Kiss, K.: Fluent aphasia in three languages: Aspects of spontaneous speech. Aphasiology 10, 561–575 (1996)
33. Edwards, S.: Grammar and fluent aphasia. In: Fava, E. (ed.) Clinical Linguistic Theory and Applications in Speech Pathology and Therapy, pp. 249–266. John Benjamins, Amsterdam/ Philadelphia (2002)
34. Kim, M., Leach, T.: Verb retrieval in fluent aphasia in two elicitation contexts. In: Clinical Aphasiology Conference, Park City, UT (May 2004)
35. Kambanaros, M.: The trouble with nouns and verbs in Greek fluent aphasia. Journal of Communication Disorders 44, 1–19 (2008)
36. Varlakosta, S., Valeonti, N., Kakavoulia, M., Lazaridou, M., Economou, A., Protopapas, A.: The breakdown of functional categories in Greek aphasia: Evidence from agreement, tense, and aspect. Aphasiology 20, 723–743 (2006)
37. Bastiaanse, R.: The retrieval and inflection of verbs in the spontaneous speech of fluent aphasic speakers. Journal of Neurolinguistics 24, 163–172 (2011)
38. Russo, K.D., Peach, P., Shapiro, L.S.: Verb preference effects in the sentence comprehension of fluent aphasic individuals. Aphasiology 12, 537–545 (1998)
39. Piper, P.: Srpski jezik. In: Piper, P. (ed.) Južnoslovenski jezici: gramatičke strukture i funkcije, pp. 381–552. Beogradska knjiga, Beograd (2009)
40. Comrie, B.: Aspect. An Introduction to the Study of Verbal Aspect and Related Problems. Cambridge University Press, Cambridge (1976)
41. Comrie, B.: Tense. Cambridge University Press, Cambridge (1985)
42. Bošković, Ž.: Participle movement and second position cliticization in Serbo-Croatian. Lingua 96, 245–266 (1995)
43. Bastiaanse, R., Jonkers, R., Thompson, C.K.: Test for Assessing Reference of Time (TART). University of Groningen, Groningen (2008)
44. Kljajevic, V., Bastiaanse, R.: Test for Assessing Reference of Time (TART): Serbian/ Croatian version. University of Groningen, Groningen (2008)
45. Olness, G.S.: Genre, verb, and coherence in picture-elicited discourse of adults with aphasia. Aphasiology 20, 175–187 (2006)
46. Tanasić, S.: Verb Syntax. In: Ivić, M. (ed.) Sintaksa savremenog srpskog jezika (Syntax of the Contemporary Serbian Language). Matica srpska, Belgrade (2005)

47. Levelt, W.M., Roelofs, A., Meyer, A.S.: A theory of lexical access in speech production. Behavioral and Brain Sciences 22, 1–75 (1999)
48. Smith, S.D., Mimica, I.: Agrammatism in a case-inflected language: Comprehension of agent-object relations. Brain and Language 21, 274–290 (1984)
49. Smith, S.D., Bates, E.: Accessibility of case and gender contrasts for agent-object assignment in Broca's aphasics and fluent anomics. Brain and Language 30, 8–32 (1987)
50. Lukatela, K., Crain, S., Shankweiler, D.: Sensitivity to inflectional morphology in agrammatism: Investigation of a highly inflected language. Brain and Language 33, 1–15 (1988)
51. Kljajevic, V., Murasugi, K.: The role of morphology in the comprehension of wh-dependencies in Croatian aphasic speakers. Aphasiology 24, 1354–1376 (2010)

Logical and Experiential Time in Narratives

Stavroula Samartzi, Smaragda Kazi, and Miltiadis Koustoumbardis

Department of Psychology, Panteion University, 136,
Syngrou Avenue, 17671, Athens, Greece
{roulasa,smakazi}@otenet.gr

Abstract. In cognitive psychological research, time includes two main subcategories: experiential (temporal experiences) and logical (temporal reasoning). Our research focuses on estimations of experiential and logical time in narrative text reading in relation to emotion. In Study One, participants read an emotionally positive and a negative text and the actual and estimated duration of the reading activity were compared. Results showed that the duration of reading the unpleasant text was overestimated as compared to the pleasant one. In Study Two, participants of Study One were asked to read another positive or negative text, but this time they were asked to estimate the duration of the described events in the text (logical time). Results showed that, although participants again garnered emotion information from text, this did not affect their estimations of the narrative events' duration, thus revealing that time and emotion are differently intertwined in the case of narrative text reading.

Keywords: Time estimation; Narrative text reading; Emotion.

1   Introduction

Psychological time is a complex concept that includes at least two fundamental subcategories: experiential and logical [1]. *Experiential time* refers to our experience of the order of events and their duration. *Logical time* involves the understanding of logical relations among the order of events and their duration. Relevant research draws special attention to human capacity to estimate short [2-4] or long event duration [5], either in real-life situations or in media-based presentations [6-7].

   Historically, one of the first approaches in this field relate to the internal clock models. The basic concept of these models is associated with the arousal of the organism and it has its origin in behavioral and animal psychology. In this context, Treisman [8], proposed a model, where a pacemaker produces a regular series of pulses, although the pulse rate increases as an organism's specific arousal level increases. A successor to Treisman's model was the Scalar Expectancy Theory (SET) of Gibbon and colleagues [9], who suggested that a pacemaker generates short-duration pulses at a fixed rate and when a signal (event) is presented, a switch directs these pulses to working memory.

   The estimation of event duration is considered to be influenced by various factors. Among them, emotion is a principal one: "time flies while you're having fun" whereas "bad things last for ever" [10]. Thus, the *subjective* time, that is our personal experience of duration can contract or expand in relation to *objective* time, that is,

A. Vatakis et al. (Eds.): Time and Time Perception 2010, LNAI 6789, pp. 275–289, 2011.

time measured by a clock [11-12], and the term *subjectivisation* is used to refer to this interfering role of the emotional content of information (either positive or negative) in time estimation of events [7].

An event is defined as a "segment of time at a given location that is conceived by an observer to have a beginning and an end" [13]. Given this, all types of events, real-life and narrative (prose-based events, that is, events described in narrative texts and screen-based events) [14-16] can be considered as analogue to each other, at least as far as the following are concerned:

(a) The *Temporal organization*: The event's specific temporal segmentation, organization and structure [13,17-18].

(b) The individual's *previous knowledge and representations*: Explanation of past and anticipation of future events [13,17,19-20]. In the case of text-narrative comprehension, representations, and inferences contribute to the construction of models specific to the situation, termed as *situation models* [21-23]. According to Zwaan and his colleagues [21-22], readers construct multidimensional representations of situations with *time* being one of them.

(c) The *Emotionality*: Various types of emotions elicited by narrative events, as well as by real-life events [23-24]. For example, in narratives (texts and films), affective responses such as surprise, curiosity, and suspense are produced by certain discourse structures and manipulations, or when the reader is identified with the hero [6,17,20,25].

As noted already, emotionality affects real-life events' duration estimations. Additionally, research on screen-based narratives (i.e., films) has shown that duration estimates depend on temporal segmentation of the scenes and their emotional valence, such as suspense [6,25]. So far, temporal information in text has not been adequately studied [22], nor has its relation to its emotional content. Relevant literature is limited to the description of temporal and emotional components in the construction of mental representations, without detecting the type of relation that connects them [21,26-36]. In a recent study, Samartzi and Kazi [7] have suggested that the emotional valence imparted through narrative texts does not affect temporal estimations.

The aim of the present research is to study the two subcategories of time (experiential and logical) in narrative texts, as a function of emotionality and to investigate if the mentioned divergence between objective and subjective time also appears in the case of reading about events in a text. This can be informative in two aspects: first, in clarifying the conditions under which the subjectivity of time emerges, and second, in clarifying the special aspects of reading texts as cognitive activity.

2 Study One: Duration Estimation of Reading a Narrative

The first study concerns the experiential time in reading texts. Specifically, this study examined whether the estimation of long duration events, such as reading texts, depends on the emotional tone (positive-pleasant/negative-unpleasant) of the text. Our hypothesis is that the emotional state of the reader, triggered by the tone of the texts, affects the duration estimation of the reading activity resulting in time subjectivisation, invariable to the presentation order of the texts. In our research, tone refers to the genre of the texts.

In order to enhance the ecological validity of our study, and given our interest in the activation of complex cognitive functions, such as representing and understanding the content of a text, we engaged participants in long duration events, i.e., in reading narratives. Our approach differs from other studies that examine more basic cognitive functions, such as the perception of emotional stimuli (i.e., pictures, photographs, or words [37-39]), arousal, or other neurocognitive mechanisms that underlie the effects of emotion on timing and time perception [40-42].

In accordance to the methodology of recent studies, that also use media-based event presentations, we engaged participants in reading activities lasting about 12 minutes, a length that seems to be a critical temporal interval on duration estimation (compared to longer intervals) [43].

2.1 Methods

2.1.1 Participants
This research involved sixty adults (50 females and 10 males), first-year University students in the Department of Psychology, aged 18 to 21.

2.1.2 Material
We selected two texts from the Modern Greek literature (*The Great Hagiography* by M. Karagatsis, published in 1951, and *Airing dirty linen ... in public* by Z. Chatzifotiou, published in 1973), consisting of almost the same number of paragraphs (54 and 55, respectively) and words (2537 and 2534, respectively). The first story presents the life of a lonely and withdrawn person, enclave in a hostile social environment. The second story describes the childhood of a naughty boy and the troubles he causes to his family.

A pilot study, with 20 participants, showed that the mean reading time was about 12 minutes (12.30 for the first story and 12.00 for the second one) and that the two texts differed significantly in terms of the emotions they triggered. The first text significantly evoked negative emotions (i.e., burden, sadness, and pessimism), thus, this text is the emotionally *negative* one of Study One. The second one significantly evoked positive emotions (i.e., pleasure, joy, and optimism), thus, this text is the emotionally *positive* one of the Study.

Apart from the texts, participants were also presented with a 15-items self-reported Emotionality Inventory, consisting of three subscales: the Positive Emotions (pleasure, joy, optimism, relaxation, and lightsome), the Negative (burden, sadness, anxiety, unpleasantly, and pessimism), and the Flat (monotony, indifference, neutrally, apathy, and vapidly). Emotions appeared in random order. Participants were asked to state on a seven-point Likert-type scale (with 1- corresponding to 'not at all' and 7- to 'absolutely') the degree to which each emotion was evoked.

2.1.3 Procedure
Participants were randomly placed in two groups, with 30 participants in each. They were tested individually and they were asked to read both texts but in reverse order (Negative-Positive text group and Positive-Negative one). After signing an informed-consent form, each participant was asked to read carefully the first text (positive or negative, depending on the experimental condition), and to notify when s/he had

finished reading it. The exact duration of the reading activity (minutes and seconds) was recorded by the experimenter. After participants' notification, the experimenter was saying: "When you started reading, the time was .... (stating the exact time that the participant had started reading). What time do you think it is now?", thus eliciting the participants' estimation for the duration of the reading activity. All of the participants reported duration to the nearest minute (e.g., they would say: Now it is 10:16). None of the participants stated an actual duration (e.g., by checking the time on his/her watch or cell phone), although it was pre-decided that in such a case participant's data would be excluded from the study. Participants then completed the self-reported emotionality inventory. The procedure was done in exactly the same way for the second text.

2.2 Results

First, the composite scores for the Positive, Negative, and Flat subscale of the Emotionality Inventory were computed (Cronbach's alpha: .816, .870, and .833, respectively[1]). At this point, it must be noted that, although participants were, by no means, instructed to prospectively estimate the duration of their second reading activity, after having read the first text (either emotionally negative or emotionally positive, depending on the group they were assigned to), they were probably familiarized with the experimental procedure. Thus, they were probably prepared to estimate, again retrospectively according to the experimental instructions the duration of their following reading activity. For this reason, a comparison across experimental conditions, concerning the effect of the order of presentation of the two texts (positive-negative vs. negative-positive) was judged as essential. This possible carry-over effect was statistically tested and, as will be shown below, was found non-significant.

To specify the possible influence of texts on emotionality and in order to check whether there was a carry-over effect across experimental conditions, a 2 (the two experimental conditions) x 2 (the two texts: positive and negative) x 3 (emotionality: positive, negative, and flat) multivariate analysis of variance was run. Specifically, the main effect of emotionality, $F_{(2, 57)}=5.509$, $p<.01$, $\eta^2=.16$; and the text x emotionality interaction, $F_{(2, 57)}=30.994$, $p<.001$, $\eta^2=.52$; were significant, whereas the main effect of text was not significant, $F_{(1, 58)}=1.856$, $p=.178$. Results, also, showed that the experimental condition (reading first the positive text followed by the negative one and vice versa) did not influence participants' responses, $F_{(1, 58)}=.280$, $p=.599$, or showed any significant interactions: experimental condition x text, $F_{(1, 58)}=.435$, $p=.512$; experimental condition x emotionality, $F_{(2, 57)}=2.234$, $p=.116$.

These results are illustrated in Fig. 1. The interaction between text and emotionality revealed that the negative text elicited stronger negative emotions, the positive text elicited stronger positive emotions, and the two texts were not differentiated as far as the flat emotions were concerned.

---

[1] Participants completed the Emotionality Inventory twice, once after reading the positive text and once after reading the negative text. Half of the participants were encountered first with the positive text, while the rest were encountered first with the negative one. Reliability scores were computed on the data from participants' first completion of this Inventory, irrespectively of whether it was after reading the positive or the negative text.

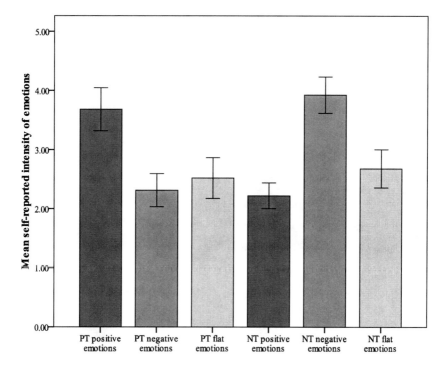

Fig. 1. Emotionality as a function of reading positive (PT) and negative (NT) texts. Bars represent standard error of the mean.

To specify whether the estimated duration of reading, in comparison to its actual duration, varied across the two types of text, first, the following transformation was applied to the raw data: (estimated duration – actual duration)/actual duration. The calculation of this index, termed as *mean relative time estimation*, ensured that the differences between actual and estimated durations of reading would be comparable across texts. It is noted that, in this index, values around zero show that the actual and estimated duration of reading converge, negative values show that the reading activity was estimated as enduring shorter than it actually did, and positive values show the opposite, that the reading activity was estimated as enduring longer than it actually did. Then, a 2 (the two experimental conditions) x 2 (two texts: positive and negative) multivariate analysis of variance was run. Specifically, the main effect of text, $F_{(1, 58)}=15.041$, p<.001, $\eta^2=.21$, was significant. These results are illustrated in Fig. 2. Results, also, showed that the experimental condition (reading first the positive text followed by the negative one and vice versa) did not influence participants' duration estimations, $F_{(1, 58)}=.157$, p=.693, or showed significant interaction: experimental condition x text, $F_{(1, 58)}=.385$, p=.538. Overall, results showed that participants were fairly accurate when estimating the duration of reading the positive text. The same does not apply for the negative text: here the estimated duration of its' reading clearly surpassed the actual one.

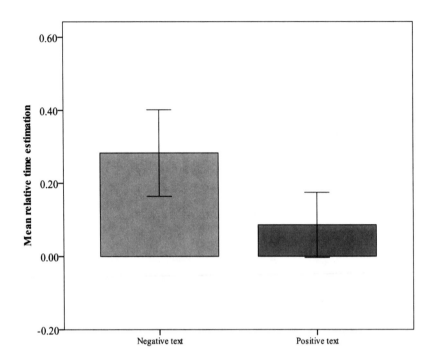

Fig. 2. Mean relative time estimation as a function of reading texts. Bars represent the standard error of the mean.

2.3 Discussion

Our results showed that reading an emotional text, indeed, produces specific emotions. We need to stress out, at this point, that our main interest in this research was not placed on the exact parameters (i.e., the prosody or the specific semantic characteristics) or the procedures (i.e., the memory reactivation) that produce or affect emotionality after reading a text. Our interest mainly focuses on time estimation, and, specifically, on the effect of emotionally-positive and emotionally-negative texts on it. Tagging the texts as emotionally negative or positive resulted from the participants' answers on the self-reported emotionality inventory.

We remind that in our text, we presented participants with three emotional subscales: the Positive Emotions, the Negative, and the Flat. The finding that the flat emotions were not statistically differentiated across texts strengthens our interpretation of the results. The non-significant differentiation of the flat emotions means that both texts were equally interesting to the participants. We note that the mean score for the flat emotions after reading the positive text is 2.523, and the mean score for the flat emotions after reading the negative text is 2.683. In case there was a statistical difference in the flat emotions across texts, that would be problematic, since it would mean that one of the two texts was found as more interesting or as more boring compared to the other. Moreover, this result shows that the positive and the negative emotions were significantly differentiated across texts. That is, participants experienced significantly stronger positive emotions after reading the positive text, and significantly stronger negative emotions after reading the negative text, revealing that the two texts were sufficiently differentiated in terms of emotion. Still, neither the positive nor the negative emotions co-varied with emotional flatness or indifference, as the non-significant effect revealed. The above-mentioned observed self-reported differentiation across texts permits to test our hypothesis, that is, the effect of emotionality on time estimation.

As this study has shown, readers cannot always accurately estimate the duration of their reading activity. Participants' estimations are affected by their emotional states. These results fully supported the hypothesis of this Study, showing that reading emotionally-valent narratives convey emotions that affect the estimation of the activity. When the text conveys pleasant emotions, reader's experiential time is rather accurate, whereas when it conveys unpleasant ones, experiential time expands, as in similar cases where time-subjectivity applies [11-12].

Does this emotionality effect apply to the processing of text information? In other words, is the duration estimation of described events also affected by the emotional tone of the texts? Or, alternatively, is time in narratives [7,21-22] a logical representation constructed by the reader, even in the absence of temporal markers in a text and independently of the emotional valence of the text and the degree of identification of the reader with the heroes? These questions are addressed in Study Two.

3   Study Two: Duration Estimation of Described Events in Text Narrative

This study examines narrative time. In contrast to the time of a reading activity, which resides at the experiential level and suggests subjectivity, we propose that narrative time is a logical construction that resides at the representational level. Since the temporal organization of events, along with the activation of previous knowledge and representations, consist in principles that apply on all types of events [13,17-19], first, we hypothesize that readers are able to construct a logical-narrative time, even in the absence of temporal markers. Second, we hypothesize that, as a logical construction, the narrative time is not subjected to distortion and is not amenable to readers' emotionality [7]. Thus, we expect that the emotional state of the reader, as induced by the tone of the text and the degree of identification, do not affect the duration estimation of the described events.

In this study, we have chosen to engage the participants of Study One for a very specific reason: We were interested in seeing whether the same readers, who were misled in the estimation of the duration of their own reading activity (experiential time) as a function of the emotional tone of a text, would be also misled in the estimation of the duration of the described events (narrative time), again as a function of the emotional tone of the texts.

3.1   Methods

3.1.1   Participants
Fifty-five adults from the sample of Study One were recruited for this study (46 females and 9 males). Participants were randomly placed in two groups (Negative

Text=29, and Positive Text=26 participants, respectively). Each group received a different text (negative or positive).

3.1.2 Material

In this study we used the material constructed by Samartzi and Kazi [7]. The authors, based on a "Harry Potter" text (from "Harry Potter and the Goblet of Fire") describing the adventures of a group of children taking a walk in a forest and eliciting negative emotions, constructed another text that elicited positive emotions by replacing words and phrases. In the *negative* text, the protagonists had to cope with enemies, whereas, in the *positive* text they were dealing with friends. Samartzi and Kazi [7] have shown, using a self-reported inventory, that these two texts were clearly differentiated as far as their emotional valence was concerned.

These two texts were of equal length (ten paragraphs, about 510 words), and they did not convey any explicit temporal information. One may object that all narratives are heavily marked by overt and covert temporal categories, such as tense, grammatical and lexical aspect and the isomorphic relation between the order of appearance of predicates and the order of appearance of events/states. Still, in the construction of the negative and the positive text [7], it was taken care that all covert temporal categories were exactly the same, as the authors kept exactly the same structure across texts, i.e., the description of the events was linear and no flash back or any information about the past or the future was presented in the text. The absence of temporal markers was ensured by the absence or deletion of any explicit or overt temporal linguistic element/information (e.g., temporal adverbs etc.) in the texts.

In the present study, two inventories were administered. The first one was the same self-reported Emotionality Inventory of Study One. The second one was a self-reported inventory aiming to measure participants' degree of identification with the heroes of the texts. Participants were asked to state on a 7-point Likert-type scale (with 1- corresponding to 'not at all' and 7- to 'absolutely') the degree to which they 1. Were identified with the heroes, 2. Got carried away, 3. Empathized with the heroes, 4. Felt as if they were in the shoes of the heroes, and 5. Lived the adventure as if they were present.

3.1.3 Procedure

Each participant was individually tested and s/he was presented with one of the texts, with the instruction to read it carefully and notify the experimenter when they s/he was done reading it. As in the previous study, the experimenter recorded the exact duration of the reading activity (minutes and seconds). Immediately after participant's notification, the experimenter handed her/him a page on which the following question was typed:

"The adventure began at 10:00:00. What time do you think it was when the adventure ended?". This way, we had provided all participants with a stable and shared temporal marker, as a reference point, after reading the texts. The participants were prompted to state the duration of the described event in hours, minutes and seconds. Finally, the two self-reported inventories (the identification and the emotionality one) were administered.

3.2 Results

As previously, the composite scores for the Emotionality Inventory subscales and the Identification scale were computed (Cronbach's alpha: .752, .876, .938, and .931 for the Negative, Positive, Flat subscale, and Identification scale, respectively). In order to test the emotional valence of the texts and the level of participants' identification after reading the different types of text, a 2 (the two texts: positive and negative) x 4 (the four emotional states: positive, negative, flat emotions, and level of identification) multivariate analysis of variance was run. The main effect of text, $F_{(4, 50)}=2.804$, p<.05, $\eta^2=.18$, was significant. Results of the Univariate Analyses indicated that the two texts were differentiated as far as the negative emotions they elicited, $F_{(1, 53)}=5.527$, p<.05, $\eta^2=.09$, and the degree of identification, $F_{(1, 53)}=5.694$, p<.05, $\eta^2=.09$ were concerned, but they were not significantly differentiated as far as the positive, $F_{(1, 53)}=1.223$, p=.274, and the flat, $F_{(1, 53)}=1.284$, p=.262, emotions were concerned. These results are illustrated in Fig. 3. As it can be seen, although the negative text elicited stronger negative feeling and higher degree of identification, both texts seem to have induced rather strong positive emotions, even in the negative text condition.

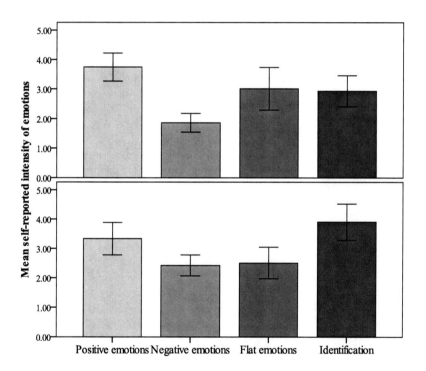

Fig. 3. Emotionality and Identification as a function of reading Harry Potter texts Bars are standard error of the mean. Upper panel refers to the Positive text and lower panel refers to the Negative text.

As far as duration is concerned, results of Univariate Analysis of Variance showed that the actual duration of reading the texts did not vary across conditions, $F_{(1, 53)}=.298$, p=.587 (Mean: 2.473, Std.Dev=.634, minimum=1 minute, maximum=4 minutes). Also, the estimated duration of the events described in the negative and the positive text, $F_{(1, 53)}=.059$, p=.809, did not differ. It is noted that none of the participants had any difficulty or hesitated in estimating the duration of the described events, but these estimations ranged considerably across participants (Mean: 24.87, Std.Dev=27.168, minimum=2 minutes, maximum=150 minutes).

In order to check whether the actual duration of reading and the degree of identification with the heroes influence the estimation of the described events, these variables were entered in the Analysis as covariates. None of these covariates altered the results or was shown to be statistically significant: When entering the actual duration of reading as a covariate, $F_{(1, 52)}=.072$, p=.789 for the duration of the described events as a function of the negative and the positive text, and $F_{(1, 52)}=.146$, p=.704 for the covariate. Entering the level of identification as a covariate, $F_{(1, 52)}=.001$, p=.977 for the duration of the described events as a function of the negative and the positive text, and $F_{(1, 52)}=.418$, p=.521 for the covariate.

3.3 Discussion

Readers construct narrative time even in the absence of temporal markers and estimation of the duration of described events is not affected by readers' emotionality. As presented earlier, these estimations of described events ranged considerably across participants. The absence of time reference in the texts probably explains the large distribution of internal representations of adventure's duration. Still, our main interest in this study focused on the difference in the range of these representations as a function of texts' emotional tone, which appeared as non-significant.

The finding that the negative text also triggered positive emotions can be probably attributed to participants' familiarity with the particular text. Reading a Harry Potter text is probably a pleasant activity per se. Still, we strongly believe that the emphasis is worth-placing on the findings that the two Harry Potter texts were significantly differentiated as far as (a) the negative emotions, and (b) as far as the degree of identification were concerned.

In other words, time-subjectivisation as an effect of emotionality does not seem to apply at described events. These results fully support our hypotheses and suggest that narrative time is a logical construction [7]. The finding becomes more interesting considering the fact that the same participants were previously (see Study One) misled in the estimations of their own reading activity, as an effect of the text's emotional tone.

4 General Discussion

The aim of the present research was to study the experiential and the logical time in narrative texts as a function of emotionality, and to investigate whether the divergence between objective and subjective time observed for real-life and screen-based events, also applies in the case of reading about events in a text. This study focuses on the estimation of time as a result of the representation of emotional information concerning events in a narrative text. As such, it differentiates from other studies on time perception, where the main concern is the estimation of time as a result of the perception of emotional stimuli (e.g., pictures, photographs, and words) [40-42], and the presentation of the stimuli and participants' reactions are measured in seconds. Although this area of research is very interesting, its methodology does not apply in our research or the one reported by Samartzi and Kazi [7]. There are two reasons why presentations of simple stimuli were not suitable for our research:

(a) Whereas events (both narrative and real-life) are temporally organized, this is not the case for stimuli. In this research we were primarily interested in whether this temporal organization of events reflects or is affected by emotionality. Additionally, as mentioned above, in our research area, where the examined events resemble real-life events, it is not uncommon to present events that endure longer (for example, see a recent study by Tobin, Bisson, & Grondin [43], where the events to be estimated endured from 12 to 58 minutes).

(b) We were also interested in the deep-level-processing (i.e., text understanding and representation). It is not certain, up to date, how emotionality emerges and when its effect disappears during deep-level-processing. Keeping in mind, though, that Angrilli et al. [37] have shown that the effect of perceiving emotional stimuli on time estimation disappears at stimulus durations longer than 4 s, we gathered participants' time estimation of the activity within the first seconds after the end of the activity.

One might wonder why, to date, the extented literature on time in texts refers to the temporal and emotional components in the construction of mental representations, without investigating the type of relation that connects them [21,26-36]. Recently, it has been reported that the emotional tone imparted through narrative texts has no effect on temporal estimations [7]. However, the question concerning the interrelations among time, emotion and reading has not yet been adequately answered. That is, it is unclear whether the emotionality effect on time estimation observed in previous research [6,10,25] with real-life or screen-based events apply in the case of reading. In order to answer the above question, we implemented two complementary experiments (see Table 1).

Table 1. Summary of the experimental designs and results in Study One and Study Two

Studies	Materials' emotional tone	Difference in the elicited emotional tone	Difference in the estimated duration
Study One (N=60)	Negative/positive - tone literature texts	Sig	Of the reading event: Sig [pos < neg]
Study Two (N=55, part of the sample of Study One)	Negative/positive -tone Harry Potter texts	Sig for the negative emotions	Of the narrative event: Ns

In both studies, we presented, to the same participants, texts of the same structure (narratives), the instruction to participants were replicated in exactly the same way across experimental conditions, and even the questions that elicited the estimations about duration were posed in exactly the same way. The dimensions that we manipulated were the emotional tone (positive vs. negative) of the texts and the elicited duration estimations (experiential in the first study and logical in the second one).

Taken together, the results of the two experiments reported in the present study demonstrate that, in reading narratives, at least two parameters of time can be identified, that is, experiential and logical [1], both simultaneously present but each differentially affected by the texts' emotional tone. Experiential time, which refers to the reading activity per se, is closely connected to and influenced by the emotionality conveyed by the text. Participants were misled in the estimations of their reading activity as an effect of the text's emotional tone (Study One). On the other hand, logical-narrative time seems to be independent of the text's emotional tone and the readers' degree of identification (Study Two). This finding becomes more interesting considering the fact that the same participants had previously (see Study One) reported incorrect time estimations of their own reading activity, as a function of the text's emotional tone. One might wonder whether the temporal evaluation of experiential duration in Study One affected participants' evaluation of narrative duration in Study Two. Since the findings of Study Two replicate the findings by Samartzi and Kazi [7] -where, again, it was shown that the construction of the narrative time is not affected by the emotional tone of the texts- we have reasons to believe that a carry-over effect across Studies is not likely.

It seems that reading texts fails to convey an experiential dimension in the informational content. Despite the facts that (a) readers garner emotion information from text, and (b) they were differentially identified with the hero of the unpleasant text, these did not affect their estimation of the narrative time. In other words, time-subjectivisation as an effect of emotionality and identification does not seem to apply at described events. Readers seem to be aware of the distance separating their own experienced feelings from those of the heroes of the story. Just as for Samartzi and Kazi [7], in the second experiment we failed to find any reliable effect of emotionality on logical time. Overall, these studies demonstrate that while emotionality can influence our temporal experience, it does not necessarily have any such effect on our temporal reasoning.

One possible interpretation for the findings outlined here relies on the role and the levels of representation during the process of text reading and understanding. It might be argued that, in contrast to the estimation of the experiential time that resides at a first-order-representation (the reader represents, on a time line, the duration of the event, with him/herself being the agent), the estimation of the logical-narrative time resides at a higher-order-representation (the reader re-represents the events that are represented on a time line in the text). The construction of such a representation requires the activation and implementation of reasoning procedures deriving from the text's temporal information [33-35]. In the case of reading texts that do not contain temporal information (such as the texts used in this study), the reader still constructs a re-representation of the narrative-logical time, as clearly demonstrated by our results. The content of this re-representation is rather unpredictable and arbitrary, as shown by the range of participants' estimations. The above approach is consistent with a) the principal quality of temporal organization of real-life and narrative events [13,17-18], and b) the contribution of previous knowledge and representation to the construction of situation models specific to the situation [21-23].

There are certain limitations in our studies. First, in both studies, participants were presented only with a negative and a positive text of considerable length (about 2600 words), and not with a neutral one. Presenting a neutral text as a control text is an interesting idea, and, from this point of view, our studies may be considered as exploratory experiments. Nevertheless, selection of an appropriate neutral text is very challenging, for the following reasons: (a) A neutral narrative text of a comparable length, which will be neither pleasant nor unpleasant, will be, potentially, boring. (b) On the other hand, if the text is neutral but not of a narrative structure (i.e., a technical guide), it could be emotionally neutral but not appealing to the reader, thus experienced again as boring in content, and, additionally, not comparable to the positive and negative narrative. The second limitation concerns the measurement of emotionality. In our studies, emotional intensity was gathered solely through self-reports.

Despite its limitations, the present studies helped clarifying the conditions under which the subjectivity of time emerges and the special aspects of reading texts as cognitive activity. Future research can focus on other, interesting aspects of temporal representation in reading text narratives, for example, by using neutral and control texts, and also by using several different texts (i.e., shorter ones) for the same experimental conditions. Since arousal is a critical emotional dimension for brief stimulus, it would be interesting to investigate whether it will remain a critical dimension for complex, long-duration emotional activities. Thus, gathering neuropsychological measures (e.g., arousal), along with self-reports, would be very informative. Another interesting issue for future research would be the extension of the prospective/retrospective paradigm, applied in recent studies [43], in the case of reading narratives. For example, it would be interesting to examine the interrelation among pleasant/unpleasant texts, short/long temporal duration and prospective/retrospective timing. Finally, an interesting topic would be the comparison of the same variables in writing. Given that reading and writing share some fundamental cognitive and linguistic processes, it is interesting to see how the above issues apply to writing narratives texts.

References

1. Siegler, R.S.: Children's thinking. Prentice-Hall, Englewood Cliffs (1991)
2. Vatakis, A., Spence, C.: Evaluating the influence of the 'unity assumption' on the temporal perception of realistic audiovisual stimuli. Acta Psychologica 127, 12–23 (2008)
3. Vatakis, A., Spence, C.: Investigating the effects of inversion on configural processing using an audiovisual temporal order judgment task. Perceprion 37, 143–160 (2008)
4. Rammsayer, T., Troche, S.: Sex differences in the processing of temporal information in the sub-second range. Personality and Individual Differences 49, 923–927 (2010)
5. Verduyn, P., Delvaux, E., Van Coillie, H., Tuerlinckx, F., Van Mechelen, I.: Predicting the duration of emotional experience: Two experience sampling studies. Emotion 9, 83–91 (2009)

6. de Wied, M., Tan, E.S.H., Frijda, N.H.: Duration experience under conditions of suspense in films. In: Macar, F., Pouthas, V., Friedman, W.J. (eds.) Time, Action and Cognition: Towards Bridging the Gap, pp. 325–336. Kluwer Academic Publishers, Dordrecht (1992)
7. Samartzi, S., Kazi, S.: The role of the emotional context on the estimation of the duration of events: The case of text understanding. Time and Society (submitted)
8. Treisman, M.: Temporal discrimination and the indifference interval: Implications for a model of the "internal clock". American Psychological Association, Washington, DC (1963)
9. Gibbon, J., Church, R.M., Meck, W.H.: Scalar timing in memory. In: Gibbon, J., Allan, L.G. (eds.) Timing and Time Perception, pp. 52–77. New York Academy of Sciences, New York (1984)
10. Calaprice, A.: The quotable Einstein. Princeton University Press, Princeton (1996)
11. Angrilli, A., Cherubini, P., Pavese, A., Manfredini, S.: The influence of affective factors on time perception. Perception & Psychophysics 59, 972–982 (1997)
12. Gil, S., Niedenthal, P., Droit-Volet, S.: Anger and time perception in children. Emotion 7, 219–225 (2007)
13. Zacks, J.M., Tversky, B.: Event structure in perception and conception. Psychological Bulletin 127, 3–21 (2001)
14. Zacks, J.M., Speer, N.K., Reynolds, J.R.: Segmentation in reading and film comprehension. Journal of Experimental Psychology: General 138, 307–327 (2009)
15. Gordon, R., Gerrig, R.J., Franklin, N.: Qualitative characteristics of memories for real, imagined and media-based events. Discourse Processes 46, 70–91 (2009)
16. Magliano, J.P., Miller, J., Zwaan, R.A.: Indexing space and time in film understanding. Applied Cognitive Psychology 15, 533–545 (2001)
17. Brewer, W.F., Lichtenstein, E.H.: Event schemas, story schemas and story grammars. In: Long, P., Baddeley, A. (eds.) Attention and Performance IX, pp. 363–379. Lawrence Erlbaum Associates, Hillsdle (1981)
18. Lichtenstein, E.H., Brewer, W.F.: Memory for goal-directed events. Cognitive Psychology 12, 412–445 (1980)
19. Rapp, D.N., Gerrig, R.J.: Predictions for narrative outcomes: The impact of story contexts and reader preferences. Journal of Memory and Language 54, 54–67 (2006)
20. Brewer, W.F., Lichtenstein, E.H.: Stories are to entertain: a structural-affect theory of stories. Journal of Pragmatics 6, 473–486 (1982)
21. Zwaan, R.A., Langston, M.C., Graesser, A.C.: The construction of situation models in narrative comprehension: An event-indexing model. Psychological Science 6, 292–297 (1995)
22. Zwaan, R.A., Radvansky, G.A.: Situation models in language comprehension and memory. Psychological Bulletin 123, 162–185 (1998)
23. Komeda, H., Kusumi, T.: The effect of a protagonist's emotional shift on situation model construction. Memory and Cognition 34, 1548–1556 (2006)
24. Habermas, T., Diel, V.: The emotional impact of loss narratives: Event severity and narrative perspectives. Emotion 10, 312–323 (2010)
25. Newtson, D., Enquist, G.: The perceptual organization of ongoing behavior. Journal of Experimental and Social Psychology 12, 436–450 (1976)
26. Bower, G.H.: Mood and Memory. American Psychologist 36, 129–148 (1981)
27. Blanc, N., Brouillet, D..: Comprendre un texte: l'évaluation des processus cognitifs. Éditions in Press, Paris (2005)
28. Egidi, G., Gerrig, R.J.: How valence affects language processing: Negativity bias and mood congruence in narrative comprehension. Memory & Cognition 37, 547–555 (2009)

29. Gygax, P., Garnham, A., Oakhill, J.: Emotion in text comprehension: Do readers infer specific emotions? Cognition and Emotion 17, 413–428 (2003)
30. Kinstch, W., van Dijk, T.A.: Towards a model of text comprehension and production. Psychological Review 85, 363–394 (1978)
31. Mandler, J.M.: On the comprehension of temporal order. Language and Cognitive Processes 1, 309–320 (1986)
32. Ohtsuka, K., Brewer, W.F.: Discourse organization in the comprehension of temporal order narrative texts. Discourse Processes 15, 317–336 (1992)
33. Rinck, M., Hahnel, A., Becker, G.: Using temporal information to construct, update and retrieve situation models of narratives. Journal of Experimental Psychology: Learning, Memory and Cognition 27, 67–80 (2001)
34. Zwaan, R.A.: Processing narrative time shifts. Journal of Experimental Psychology: Learning, Memory and Cognition 22, 1196–1207 (1996)
35. Rapp, D.N., Taylor, H.: Interactive dimensions in the construction of mental representations for text. Journal of Experimental Psychology: Learning, Memory and Cognition 30, 988–1001 (2004)
36. Samartzi, S.: Time: From experience to mental representations through the comprehension of texts. Psychology 14, 217–230 (2007)
37. Angrilli, A., Cherubini, P., Pavese, A., Manfredini, S.: The influence of affective factors on time perception. Perception & Psychophysics 59, 972–982 (1997)
38. Bar-Haim, Y., Kerem, A., Lamy, D., Zakay, D.: When time slows down: The influence of threat on time perception in anxiety. Cognition & Emotion 24, 255–263 (2010)
39. Tipples, J.: Time flies when we read taboo words. Psychonomic Bulletin & Review 17, 563–568 (2010)
40. Droit-Volet, S., Meck, H.W.: How emotions colour our perception of time. Trends in Cognitive Sciences 11(12), 504–513 (2007)
41. Droit-Volet, S., Gil, S.: The time-emotion paradox. Philosophical Transactions of the Royal Society of London. Series B, Biological Sciences 364, 1943–1953 (2009)
42. Gil, S., Rousset, S., Droit-Volet, S.: How liked and disliked foods affect time perception. Emotion 9, 457–463 (2009)
43. Tobin, S., Bisson, N., Grondin, S.: An Ecological Approach to Prospective and Retrospective Timing of Long Durations: A Study Involving Gamers. PLoS ONE 5, e9271 (2010), doi:10.1371/journal.pone.0009271

Author Index